FOR THIS LAND

FOR
THIS LAND

WRITINGS ON RELIGION IN AMERICA

VINE DELORIA, JR.

EDITED AND WITH AN INTRODUCTION BY
JAMES TREAT

Routledge
New York and London

Published in 1999 by
Routledge
29 West 35th Street
New York, NY 10001

Published in Great Britain by
Routledge
11 New Fetter Lane
London EC4P 4EE

Cover photograph: Within the famous racetrack that encompasses the Black Hills of South Dakota, in a small prairie clearing, is a sacred place where generations of people have come to seek counsel with higher powers. Not all sacred places are large and overpowering, like Bear Butte or Bear Lodge, since silence is valued above all things when ceremonies are performed.

Cover photography by Vine Deloria, Jr.

Printed in the United States of America on acid-free paper.

Library of Congress Cataloging-in-Publication Data

Deloria, Vine.
    For this land : writings on religion in America / Vine Deloria, Jr. : edited by James Treat.
        p.   cm.
    Includes bibliographical references and index.
    ISBN 0-415-92114-7 (hardcover : alk. paper). — ISBN 0-415-92115-5
(pbk. : alk. paper)
        1. Indians of North America—Religion.   2. United States—Religion.
    3. Freedom of religion—United States.   I. Treat, James.   II. Title.
    E98.R3D43   1998
    199'.7—dc21   98-15500
                                                                            CIP

While America has produced great businessmen and scientists, it has been unable to produce one great philosopher or theologian.

—The Red Man in the New World Drama

Religion cannot be kept within the bounds of sermons and scriptures. It is a force in and of itself and it calls for the integration of lands and peoples in harmonious unity. The lands wait for those who can discern their rhythms. The peculiar genius of each continent, each river valley, the rugged mountains, the placid lakes—all call for relief from the constant burden of exploitation.

Who will find peace with the lands? The future of humankind lies waiting for those who will come to understand their lives and take up their responsibilities to all living things. Who will listen to the trees, the animals and birds, the voices of the places of the land? As the long-forgotten peoples of the respective continents rise and begin to reclaim their ancient heritage, they will discover the meaning of the lands of their ancestors. That is when the invaders of the North American continent will discover that for this land, God is red.

—God Is Red

CONTENTS

INTRODUCTION

AN AMERICAN CRITIQUE
OF RELIGION

On September 9, 1974, the weekly news magazine *Time* reported that a survey of religious leaders and scholars had produced a list of eleven "shapers and shakers of the Christian faith," including Vine Deloria, Jr.[1] It remains one of the most unusual honors Deloria has received in his long and distinguished career as activist, author, and educator. Interchurch Features, a New York-based consortium of Christian periodicals published in the United States and Canada, sponsored the poll; they asked survey participants to identify the most promising religious figures in the modern world, the "Theological Superstars of the Future." Named to the list along with Deloria were five Roman Catholics and five Protestants, including theologians Hans Küng and Jürgen Moltmann and evangelist Billy Graham.[2] *Time* identified Deloria only as a "Sioux Indian Lawyer" who "says flatly that he is no longer a Christian at all," though he offered evidence that his sense of humor had not wavered when, in another context, he described his religious affiliation as "Seven Day Absentist."[3]

Why would influential representatives of North America's Christian establishment choose such an iconoclast—and an apostate one at that—for their roster of religious luminaries? Writing in *The Christian Century*, one of the periodicals that sponsored the Interchurch Features survey, columnist Martin Marty suggested that some degree of liberal tokenism was involved in the process; the list also included one Latin American, one African, and one woman, three demographic strongholds of modern

---

1. "Shapers and Shakers," *Time* 104 (September 9, 1974): 66.
2. Others named to the list were Brazilian Archbishop Helder Câmara, Jesuit philosopher Bernard Lonergan, sociologist Andrew Greeley, feminist theologian Rosemary Radford Ruether, Christian ethicist James Gustafson, Rhodesian Methodist Bishop Abel Muzorewa, and Pentecostal leader David du Plessis.
3. "Deloria, Vine (Victor), Jr.," *Contemporary Authors*, vols. 53–56, edited by Clare D. Kinsman (Detroit, MI: Gale Research Company, 1975), 146.

Christianity that are still underrepresented in ecclesiastical leadership and theological scholarship.[4] American Indians have always occupied a special place in the colonial psychology of European immigrants, though many Indians have been less than enthusiastic about their involvement with those immigrants' religious communities. As a seminary graduate and one of the most prominent Indian leaders since the mid-sixties, Deloria likely seemed an obvious and convenient choice. Even more important, however, were his critical writings on the contemporary American predicament, which had not gone unnoticed in the nation's pulpits and pews. Five books published in as many years, including his provocatively titled works *Custer Died for Your Sins* (1969) and *God Is Red* (1973), aimed to disrupt the self-serving laziness of any tokenistic gestures. Apparently anticipating the objections of their more conservative readers, the Interchurch Features editors justified Deloria's inclusion on the list by pointing out that he "offers North Americans a stirring call for society's repentance and reform."[5]

If Deloria's selection as a "Theological Superstar of the Future" seemed an appropriate recognition at the time, it was not a particularly good predictor of his subsequent impact as a "shaper and shaker of the Christian faith." All of his fellow luminaries went on to distinguish themselves as religious leaders and scholars and today are among the most influential figures in their particular corners of the Christian world. Yet Deloria has never been listed in *Who's Who in Religion* (through four editions, 1975–92) or among the 550 individuals included in the *Dictionary of American Religious Biography*. The *Encyclopedia of the American Religious Experience* and *The Encyclopedia of American Religious History* also contain no reference to Deloria or his writings.[6] Mircea Eliade's definitive, sixteen-volume *Encyclopedia of Religion* includes only two brief mentions of Deloria's work: a quote from his introduction to the 1979 edition of *Black Elk Speaks*, and a bibliographic reference to *God Is Red*.[7] And although many American Indian leaders and American Indian

4. Martin E. Marty, "M.E.M.O.: Billy Et Al," *Christian Century* 91 (September 4, 1974): 831.

5. James A. Taylor, "Giants of Our Faith," *U.S. Catholic* 39, no. 12 (December 1974): 22.

6. *Who's Who in Religion*, 4th ed., 1992–93 (Wilmette, IL: Marquis Who's Who, 1992); Henry Warner Bowden, *Dictionary of American Religious Biography*, 2nd. ed. (Westport, CT: Greenwood Press, 1993); Charles H. Lippy and Peter W. Williams, eds., *Encyclopedia of the American Religious Experience: Studies of Traditions and Movements*, 3 vols. (New York, NY: Charles Scribner's Sons, 1988); Edward L. Queen II, Stephen R. Prothero, and Gardiner H. Shattuck, Jr., eds., *The Encyclopedia of American Religious History*, 2 vols. (New York, NY: Facts on File, 1996).

7. Joseph Epes Brown, "Black Elk," in *The Encyclopedia of Religion*, vol. 2, edited by Mircea Eliade (New York, NY: Macmillan Publishing Company, 1987), 234; Åke

studies scholars regard Deloria to be one of the most influential Indian figures of the twentieth century, he is best known today for his contributions in political and legal affairs, not for his critical insights on religious matters.[8] How should we account for this turn of events? Was Deloria a theological superstar or only a meteor, a charismatic streak of light in the religious firmament?

Like several of his fellow luminaries, Deloria's intellectual energies have been divided between religious affairs and other pressing concerns for much of his professional career. His continuing involvement in the persistent political struggles facing American Indians has precluded the kinds of theological contributions made by prolific European scholars such as Küng and Moltmann. And unlike all of the other ten superstars, Deloria has dissented from the Western religious mainstream by maintaining a non-Christian stance, not relying on any Christian institutions for bureaucratic legitimation. His writings have elicited very little critical response from scholars of religion, perhaps because his ideas are simply too far outside the bounds of prevailing academic sentiment, which is still burdened by an unfortunate intellectual parochialism. Only a few scholars of religion have responded in print to the criticisms and proposals contained in *God Is Red* and Deloria's other early writings.[9] Many have been put off by his polemical style or his incisive approach to contemporary conflicts.[10]

Hultkrantz, "North American Religions: Mythic Themes," in *The Encyclopedia of Religion*, vol. 10, 535.

8. For example, see: Roger Dunsmore, "Vine Deloria, Jr.," in *Dictionary of Native American Literature*, edited by Andrew Wiget (New York, NY: Garland Publishing, 1994), 411–15; "Vine Deloria, Jr.," in *The Native North American Almanac*, edited by Duane Champagne (Detroit, MI: Gale Research, 1994), 1043–44; Clifford M. Lytle, Jr., "Vine Deloria, Jr.," in *Leaders from the 1960s: A Biographical Sourcebook of American Activism*, edited by David DeLeon (Westport, CT: Greenwood Press, 1994), 72–78; Karen P. Zimmerman, "Vine Deloria, Jr.," in *Notable Native Americans*, edited by Sharon Malinowski (New York, NY: Gale Research, 1995), 118–21.

Deloria did appear in *Who's Who in America* (Chicago, IL: Marquis Who's Who) for two decades beginning with the 1972 edition, but was dropped for the 1992 edition, perhaps to commemorate the five-hundredth anniversary of the beginning of the church-sanctioned colonization of his homeland.

9. For example, see: James M. Wall, "Indian Theology and the White Man's Law," *Christian Century* 90 (September 19, 1973): 907–8; Carl Starkloff, S.J., "God Is Red: A Review Article," *Review for Religious* 33, no. 2 (1974): 353–64; Benjamin A. Reist, *Theology in Red, White, and Black* (Philadelphia, PA: Westminster, 1975); P. Joseph Cahill, "Vine Deloria: An Essay in Comparison of Christianity and Amerindian Religions," *Journal of the American Academy of Religion* 45 (June 1977): 419–46; Charles H. Long, "Freedom, Otherness and Religion: Theologies Opaque," *Chicago Theological Seminary Register* 73, no. 1 (Winter 1983): 13–24.

10. For example, see: Robert A. Coughenour, review of *God Is Red*, by Vine Deloria, Jr., *Christian Scholar's Review* 5 (1976): 381–82; Thomas A. Cloyd, review of *God Is Red*,

The essays collected in this volume demonstrate that despite the demands of his political involvements, and despite a lack of critical response to his religious publications, Deloria has not stopped thinking and writing about religion. In dozens of occasional pieces published during the last three decades, he has offered substantive and persistent contributions to understanding the complexity of religion in America. Some of his provocative essays have been written for scholarly journals or religious periodicals, while others have suggested perceptive interpretations of contemporary religious affairs aimed at a more general audience. Many readers assume that Deloria has offered a definitive statement of his views on religion in *God Is Red*, but this supposition overlooks a wide-ranging body of work articulating insightful perspectives on controversial religious issues. These occasional writings document an abiding concern for the religious dimensions and implications of human existence. Deloria's intellectual sensibilities developed out of his family background and organizational commitments; these essays are best understood in the context of his personal and professional experiences, which have framed his discursive intentions.

AN AMERICAN LIFE

Vine Deloria, Jr., was born in Martin, South Dakota, on March 26, 1933; he entered the world at the edge of the Pine Ridge Reservation and on the brink of a new era in Indian affairs. He seemed destined for a life spent straddling other kinds of frontiers as well, as the first child of a prominent Dakota Episcopal missionary priest and his Anglo-American

---

by Vine Deloria, Jr., *Religion in Life* 43 (Summer 1974): 246–47; Edward Witten, review of *Custer Died for Your Sins*, by Vine Deloria, Jr., *Commonweal* 91 (February 6, 1970): 515–16.

Still others simply may have been uninterested in engaging "a Native American perspective" on religious matters, as Deloria's writings are often framed when included in topical anthologies or thematic journal issues. For example, see: "A Native American Perspective on Liberation," *Occasional Bulletin of Missionary Research* 1, no. 3 (July 1977): 15–17; "A Native American Perspective on Liberation Theology," in *Is Liberation Theology for North America? The Response of First World Churches*, edited by Sergio Torres and others (New York, NY: Theology in the Americas, 1978), 12–20; "Christianity and Indigenous Religion: Friends or Enemies? A Native American Perspective," in *Creation and Culture: The Challenge of Indigenous Spirituality and Culture to Western Creation Thought*, edited by David G. Burke (New York, NY: Lutheran World Ministries, 1987), 31–43; "Vision and Community: A Native-American Voice," in *Yearning to Breathe Free: Liberation Theologies in the United States*, edited by Mar Peter-Raoul, Linda Rennie Forcey, and Robert Frederick Hunter, Jr. (Maryknoll, NY: Orbis Books, 1990), 71–79.

wife. Deloria inherited a number of important dispositions from his fore-bears, including an appreciation for disciplined education, a commitment to community life, a healthy suspicion toward colonial institutions, a preference for reformist activism, a sense of religious purpose, and the articulate voice of a prophet. These and other personal qualities have made him an effective advocate in a variety of contexts, sustaining a family tradition of leadership.

The family name Deloria is an anglicized form of the name of Phillippe des Lauriers, a French fur trader who settled in a Yankton community and married the daughter of a Yankton headman.[11] Their grandson Françoise (whose Christian name the Yanktons transformed into Saswe) had a visionary experience at the age of eighteen that paradoxically granted him powers as a medicine man, accurately predicted he would kill four Sioux men, and committed his descendants to serve as mediators with the dominant society. He went on to become a respected healer and leader of the White Swan community on the Yankton

---

11. Biographical information included in this sketch of Deloria's family history has been drawn from personal correspondence with the author and from the following sources: Sarah Emilia Olden, *The People of Tipi Sapa* (Milwaukee, WI: Morehouse Publishing Company, 1918); Ella C. Deloria, *Speaking of Indians* (New York, NY: Friendship Press, 1944), reprinted with introductory notes by Agnes Picotte and Paul N. Pavich (Vermillion, SD: Dakota Press, University of South Dakota, 1979); Vine Deloria [Sr.], "An Interview with Vine Deloria, a Santee Sioux Indian," interview by Marilyn Creel, June 23, 1968, typed transcription, New York Times Oral History Program, University of South Dakota, American Indian Oral History Research Project, Part I, No. 112 (Vermillion, SD: Institute of Indian Studies, 1975); Vine V. Deloria, Sr., "The Standing Rock Reservation: A Personal Reminiscence," in *American Indian II*, edited by John R. Milton (Vermillion, SD: Dakota Press, University of South Dakota, 1971), 169–95; Marion E. Gridley, *Contemporary American Indian Leaders* (New York, NY: Dodd, Mead and Company, 1972); Virginia Driving Hawk Sneve, *That They May Have Life: The Episcopal Church in South Dakota, 1859-1976* (New York, NY: Seabury Press, 1977); Joseph H. Cash and Herbert T. Hoover, eds., *To Be an Indian: An Oral History* (New York, NY: Holt, Rinehart and Winston, 1971); Vine V. Deloria, Sr., "The Establishment of Christianity among the Sioux," in *Sioux Indian Religion: Tradition and Innovation*, edited by Raymond J. DeMallie and Douglas R. Parks (Norman, OK: University of Oklahoma, 1987), 91–111; Leonard Rufus Bruguier, "A Legacy in Sioux Leadership: The Deloria Family," in *South Dakota Leaders: From Pierre Chouteau, Jr., to Oscar Howe*, edited by Herbert T. Hoover and Larry J. Zimmerman (Vermillion, SD: University of South Dakota Press, 1989), 367–81; Mary Beth Lamb, "Taming the Wild Heart into Disillusionment: Four Generations of Lakotas on American Christianity," unpublished manuscript, November 11, 1991; Herbert T. Hoover, "Vine Deloria, Jr., in American Historiography," in *Indians and Anthropologists: Vine Deloria, Jr., and the Critique of Anthropology*, edited by Thomas Biolsi and Larry J. Zimmerman (Tucson, AZ: University of Arizona Press, 1997), 27–34; Philip Deloria, "'I Am of the Body': Thoughts on My Grandfather, Culture, and Sports," *South Atlantic Quarterly* 95, no. 2 (Spring 1996): 321–38.

Reservation, where he settled in 1858. Saswe welcomed Presbyterian and Episcopal missionaries when they arrived, sending some of his children to day schools and having all of his children and grandchildren baptized. He attended church regularly himself but was not allowed to make any formal affiliation because he was married to three Sioux women. After one wife died and another returned to her home reservation, Saswe finally received Christian baptism in 1871, and disturbing visitations by his four victims ceased.

Saswe and his first wife Siha Sapewin, who was from the Standing Rock Reservation, had their first son in 1854. Saswe favored him and symbolically bequeathed to him his spiritual powers by giving him the name Tipi Sapa (Black Lodge), which had appeared as an important element in his original vision. Tipi Sapa assisted Saswe in his work as a medicine man and was his father's apparent successor as leader of the White Swan community. But at the age of sixteen he decided—with his father's encouragement—to pursue an academic education and to fulfill his religious vocation by becoming an Episcopal priest, in hopes of helping his people adjust to the changing circumstances of reservation life. He was baptized Philip Joseph Deloria on Christmas day and left home soon thereafter to attend an Episcopal mission school in Nebraska and, later, a military academy in Minnesota. Committed to religious leadership but dismayed by denominational competition among Congregational, Episcopal, Presbyterian, and Roman Catholic missionaries, Philip was one of three young Dakota leaders who in 1873 founded Wojo Okolakiciye (The Planting Society), an organization promoting ecumenical fellowship that later became known as the Brotherhood of Christian Unity. After completing his education, he served as a lay reader and was ordained as deacon in 1883 and as priest in 1892, then appointed to supervise all Episcopal mission work on the Standing Rock Reservation. He held this position until his retirement in 1925, by which time he had secured a national reputation as one of the most devoted and respected priests in the history of Episcopal missions to Indians. His cultural reminiscences were collected in a 1918 book titled *The People of Tipi Sapa*, and he is one of only three Americans included in the ninety-eight "Saints of the Ages" carved behind the altar of the National Cathedral in Washington, D.C.

Philip married Mary Sully Bordeaux and together they raised a family of six children as adopted members of the Hunkpapas living at Standing Rock. Their only son Vine Victor, whose Dakota name was Ohiya (Champion), was born in 1901. Mary died when Vine was fifteen and he was sent to a military academy in Nebraska to complete his secondary education. He excelled on the playing field, attending college in New York on an athletic scholarship and envisioning a career as a professional athlete, but instead agreed to follow his ailing father's footsteps into the Christian ministry. In 1931 Vine graduated from an Episcopal seminary in New York City and was assigned to All Saints Mission and other parishes on the Pine Ridge Reservation. He served there for seventeen years, then spent three years at the Sisseton Mission in eastern South Dakota and three years at an Anglo parish in Iowa. In 1954 he was appointed to the National Council of the Episcopal Church as Assistant Secretary for Indian Missions, the first Indian to serve as a denominational executive. He later recalled his time on national staff as the most frustrating experience of his career. Church leaders were unwilling to take his ideas and suggestions seriously, and he left after four years and returned to another Anglo parish in Iowa. He was soon appointed to be archdeacon of the Indian parishes in South Dakota and occupied that post until his retirement in 1968. Vine admitted to growing more critical of the institutional church in his later years, and the seeds of his eldest son's radicalism are evident in the fierce cultural pride and acute sense of justice Vine occasionally allowed to surface.

Vine and his wife Barbara had their first child in 1933 and bound him to his forebears by naming him Vine Victor Deloria, Jr.[12] The junior Deloria attended off-reservation schools in Martin and occasionally traveled to tribal dances, held openly once again after the passage of the Indian Reorganization Act in 1934. He once described a visit to the site of the 1890 Wounded Knee massacre as the most memorable event of his early childhood, and his father often pointed out survivors still living on the reservation. As a child he also participated in the rich communal and ceremonial life that has long characterized the Sioux Episcopal Church, which reaches its fullest expression in the annual Niobrara Convocation, now in its 126th year. Deloria left home in 1949 and finished his high school diploma during two years at the Kent School, a private college-preparatory school in Connecticut. He spent the next five years explor-

---

12. Biographical information included in this sketch of Deloria's childhood and education has been drawn from personal correspondence with the author and from the following sources: Vine Deloria, Jr., *Custer Died for Your Sins: An Indian Manifesto* (New York, NY: Macmillan, 1969); Vine Deloria, Jr., "This Country Was a Lot Better Off When the Indians Were Running It," *The New York Times Magazine*, March 8, 1970, reprinted in *Red Power: The American Indians' Fight for Freedom*, edited by Alvin M. Josephy, Jr. (New York, NY: McGraw-Hill, 1971), 235–47; Vine Deloria, Jr., "It Is a Good Day to Die," *Katallagete* 4, nos. 2–3 (Fall–Winter 1972): 62–65; Vine Deloria, Jr., "Colorado Requiem: On the Ravages of Rootlessness," *Colorado Quote* 1, no. 1 (September 1978): 18–21; Lytle, "Vine Deloria, Jr."; Owanah Anderson, *400 Years: Anglican/Episcopal Mission among American Indians* (Cincinnati, OH: Forward Movement Publications, 1997).

ing technology, first spending his University of Colorado freshman tuition money on a used car, later studying geology for two years at the Colorado School of Mines, and eventually enlisting in the Marine Corps Reserve where he was certified in telephone repair. In 1956 he enrolled at Iowa State University, where he completed a bachelor's degree in general science and met his future wife, Barbara Jeanne Nystrom.

They were married in the summer of 1958 and a year later moved to Illinois so Deloria could attend a Lutheran seminary in Rock Island. He had considered pursuing the ministry in his younger days but had also watched his father struggle with the denominational bureaucracy in more recent years. Instead of training for a Christian vocation, Deloria spent the next four years studying theology and philosophy by day and earning a living as a welder by night. He later wrote that "seminary, in spite of its avowed goals and tangible struggle with good intentions, provided an incredible variety of food for thought but a glaring lack of solutions or patterns of conceivable action which might be useful in facing a world in which the factors affecting human life change daily."[13] In 1963 he received a graduate degree in theology and accepted a staff position with the United Scholarship Service, a church-supported educational philanthropy based in Denver, Colorado.

AN AMERICAN REFORMER

Deloria directed a new program that placed Indian students in elite private schools on the East Coast, a position he had been offered on the basis of his own successful experience at the Kent School.[14] He insisted that students qualify for the program on the basis of academic credentials and quickly found scholarships for some thirty young people. But the denominational leaders who were funding the program wanted a

---

13. Deloria, "It Is a Good Day to Die," 63.

14. Biographical information included in this sketch of Deloria's professional career has been drawn from personal correspondence with the author and from the following sources: Stan Steiner, *The New Indians* (New York, NY: Dell Publishing, 1968); Deloria, *Custer Died for Your Sins*; Deloria, "This Country Was a Lot Better Off When the Indians Were Running It"; Deloria, "It Is a Good Day to Die"; Deloria, "Colorado Requiem: On the Ravages of Rootlessness"; Vine Deloria, Jr., "Perceptions and Maturity: Reflections on Feyerabend's Point of View," in *Versuchungen Aufsätze zur Philosophie Paul Feyerabends* (Frankfurt am Main, Germany: Shurkamp Verlag, 1980), reprinted in *Beyond Reason: Essays on the Philosophy of Paul Feyerabend*, edited by Gonzalo Munévar (Dordrecht, The Netherlands: Kluwer Academic Publishers, 1991), 389–401; Lytle, "Vine Deloria, Jr."; Vine Deloria, Jr., "Alcatraz, Activism, and Accommodation," *American Indian Culture and Research Journal* 18, no. 4 (1994): 25–32; Hoover, "Vine Deloria, Jr., in American Historiography"; Anderson, *400 Years*.

more paternalistic approach that would coddle Indians as token minorities, and they accused Deloria of elitism for his emphasis on excellence and hard work. In 1964 he drove to Sheridan, Wyoming, to promote his program at the annual convention of the National Congress of American Indians (NCAI). The preeminent intertribal organization was conflicted, deeply indebted, and dwindling in membership, and Deloria was soon chosen to be its new executive director. Until then a relatively anonymous young administrator known primarily in church circles, he was soon to become one of the most prominent national leaders in Indian affairs. Stan Steiner's landmark book *The New Indians*, a journalistic report on the growing Red Power movement published only four years later, quotes or refers to Deloria more often than any other single individual.

Resigning from his position with the United Scholarship Service, Deloria devoted considerable energy to reviving the NCAI as a political force. "I learned more about life in the NCAI in three years than I had in the previous thirty," he later recalled; during his tenure he experienced both the frustrations of tribal politics and the persistence of white liberal paternalism.[15] He began to see the importance of building a national power base through grassroots organizing at the local level, and he also came to appreciate the need for trained Indian lawyers who could defend tribal sovereignty and treaty rights within the American legal system. By the fall of 1967, Deloria was convinced that the rising popularity of certain outspoken traditionalists signaled the beginning of a revolutionary era in Indian affairs. He stepped down as the leader of the NCAI and enrolled in law school at the University of Colorado, setting an example many other young Indian activists soon followed, in much the same way that N. Scott Momaday's Pulitzer Prize-winning novel *House Made of Dawn* (1968) would come to inspire a generation of Indian writers.[16] Deloria continued working with the NCAI as a consultant, and during this period he also served on the boards of several national organizations, including the Citizens' Crusade Against Poverty, the Board of Inquiry into Hunger and Malnutrition in the USA, and the National Office for the Rights of the Indigent.

Deloria's administrative responsibilities with the NCAI included a quarterly newsletter, the *Sentinel*, which provided a forum for what would be his first published writings. In regular editorial columns, he turned out short pieces of social and political commentary laced with

---

15. Deloria, "This Country Was a Lot Better Off When the Indians Were Running It," 242.

16. N. Scott Momaday, *House Made of Dawn* (New York, NY: Harper and Row, 1968).

tribal nationalism and a sarcastic sense of humor, and he was not reluctant to poke fun at other Indian organizations as well (see Appendix 2). These commentaries tapped into a renewed sense of vitality and purpose developing in Indian country and were occasionally reprinted in tribal and denominational periodicals. Deloria also found himself speaking out against popular discourse perpetuating racial stereotypes, such as a whiskey advertisement invoking firewater and old squaws. One of his earliest unpublished essays, "The Missionary in a Cultural Trap," was an elaborate parody written in response to a 1965 article by a Jesuit missionary (see Appendix 1). He also remained involved in a few denominational activities during this period, and in 1968 Deloria was elected to the Executive Council of the Episcopal Church. He chaired the denomination's Ad-Hoc Committee on Indian Work and used this platform to propose sweeping changes in the institutional bureaucracy, circulating a document titled "More Real Involvement" in which he called for a series of reforms that would facilitate self-determination among Indian churches.

Despite the demands of law school classes, various organizational commitments, several trips to Alcatraz Island, and a growing family, Deloria also found time to write two books. *Custer Died for Your Sins: An Indian Manifesto* was published in 1969 and *We Talk, You Listen: New Tribes, New Turf* followed a year later. Both books were informed by his recent experiences with religious and political organizations, critiquing the "unrealities" of American society with a militant edge that caught many readers by surprise, and both also received national literary awards. He originally used the memorable title of his first book as a satirical slogan at a 1966 event in Washington; the phrase was immediately picked up by the National Council of Churches and also spread throughout Indian country within weeks. *Custer Died for Your Sins* was a remarkable feat of energy, breadth, insight, wit, and timing, securing Deloria's reputation as a leading commentator on Indian affairs. It remains his best-selling book and has been translated into Spanish, Swedish, and French. He had several motives and as many audiences in mind while writing the book, foremost among them the Christian missionaries still disrupting tribal communities. "Above all," he concluded in an autobiographical afterword, "I am hopeful that the churches will give up this passionate desire to steal sheep from each other's folds and get down to the business of helping Indian people. If, as they claim, Christianity is for all people, why not let Indian people worship God after their own concep-

---

17. Deloria, *Custer Died for Your Sins*, 269.

tions of Him?"[17] *We Talk, You Listen* continues in this line of thought by moving to a more theoretical exploration of tribalism in its modern manifestations. The book closes by examining the collective existential crisis confronting the mainline denominations, concluding that "the real issue to be faced today" in America is about religion.[18]

Deloria was awarded a law degree in 1970 and for the next eight years earned a living from a variety of lectureships, administrative positions, consultancies, legal cases, and publishing contracts. He taught in the College of Ethnic Studies at Western Washington University for a year and a half and at UCLA's American Indian Studies Center for four quarters, and later held brief visiting appointments at the Pacific School of Religion, the New School of Religion, and Colorado College. He founded the Institute for the Development of Indian Law in 1971 (with the support of four denominational Indian caucuses), assisted several tribes on political conflicts, and participated in the Wounded Knee trials as both defense attorney and expert witness. He also worked with various national organizations promoting social reform, including Christian groups such as the National Council of Churches, the American Lutheran Church, the United Presbyterian Church, and the Committee of Southern Churchmen.

Deloria's major writings during this period reflect his broad range of concerns and involvements. In 1971 he edited two books aimed at documenting Indian political history and reformulating the contemporary legal status of tribal nations in the United States. *The Red Man in the New World Drama* was originally published forty years earlier, written by Jennings C. Wise in the tradition of the historical grand narrative. Deloria took the trouble to revise, update, and republish Wise's work because it interprets the colonization of the Americas as "part of a world drama of conflicting religions," and Deloria considered this book an "opening wedge" in the effort to "shake people out of their traditional way of looking at the world."[19] *Of Utmost Good Faith* is an anthology of congressional acts, judicial rulings, and other legal documents that have circumscribed the rights of tribal people in American society. Unlike other popular anthologies that commemorate the Indian past in tragic terms, Deloria's forthright editorial bias here advances an optimistic outlook toward the future. Having outlined the historical basis for contemporary political

---

18. Vine Deloria, Jr., *We Talk, You Listen: New Tribes, New Turf* (New York, NY: Macmillan, 1970), 206.

19. Vine Deloria, Jr., ed., *The Red Man in the New World Drama: A Politico-Legal Study with a Pageantry of American Indian History*, by Jennings C. Wise (New York, NY: Macmillan, 1971), ix–xi.

and legal disputes in these two volumes, he proposed a systematic refor-
mulation of tribal sovereignty in *Behind the Trail of Broken Treaties: An
Indian Declaration of Independence*, published in 1974. This collaborative
study grew out of the protest activism leading up to the Wounded Knee
confrontation; it argues that Congress should address Indian claims by
reopening the treaty-making process. Deloria explored these questions
again three years later in *Indians of the Pacific Northwest*, a case study in
tribal political and legal history on a regional scale.

Deloria summarized his ideas for a Christian audience in *The Indian
Affair*. Published by a National Council of Churches press in 1974, the
same year Interchurch Features named him a theological superstar, this
short book on contemporary issues is more moderate in tone than many
of his other writings on Christianity, in part because it emphasizes pragmatic considerations. His intentions were clearly more theoretical a year
earlier in *God Is Red*, his most influential publication after *Custer Died for
Your Sins* and the book that brought him special notoriety among church
people. *God Is Red* addresses the profound spiritual malaise in American
society by deconstructing the Western religious worldview, which many
have read as an attack on diverse Christian communities. Dismayed by
the early response to his book, Deloria told a group of church leaders that
"a substantial number of reviewers seem to think that I'm mad at
Christianity or that I'm appalled by Christian excesses a hundred years
ago, and therefore wrote the book in an attempt to get even. And that's
not it at all." He was more concerned about the institutional churches'
"credibility gap," a symptom of "religious breakdown" and the "spiritual
desperation" it has generated in the contemporary situation. The questions he really wanted to raise were: "What are religions? How do they
originate? And what can you anticipate [experiencing] in an ongoing
religious life?"[20] He concludes in *God Is Red* that religion "is a force in and
of itself" that "calls for the integration of lands and peoples in harmonious unity."[21]

In 1975 *Christianity and Crisis* published a perceptive interview with
Deloria by contributing editor James R. McGraw, who posed his own
response to the book in the form of a question: "Would it be fair to say reconciliation is what Christians must be about, not reconciling souls to
Christ but reconciling themselves to the land?" Deloria assented, hoping

---

20. Vine Deloria, Jr., "Why I Wrote *God Is Red*," audiotape recording of address at the
biennial meeting of the National Fellowship of Indian Workers, Estes Park, CO, July
1974 (Tempe, AZ: Cook Christian Training School, 1974).

21. Vine Deloria, Jr., *God Is Red: A Native View of Religion*, 2nd ed. (Golden, CO:
North American Press, 1992), 292.

for "an emergence of white theology which would be derived not from the European tradition but from an American tradition," a sense of identity "steeped in American history. . . . I don't think we've confronted the American experience in any profound way at all. So nobody understands who we are or where we're going. And that's white *and* Indian."[22] Deloria examined these questions more closely in his second major philosophical work, *The Metaphysics of Modern Existence*, published in 1979. Again eschewing public expectation that he write only as Indian informant, he surveyed Western philosophy and its social implications, identifying various trends that indicate a new vision of reality—one more compatible with tribal worldviews—may be emerging in American culture. In this book he "tried to develop the thesis that real knowledge of reality must be primarily a matter of perception and a careful handling of the process of deriving concepts of knowledge from those perceptions," but few critics perceived the usefulness of Deloria's generalist approach.[23]

In 1978 Deloria accepted a tenured appointment as professor of law and political science at the University of Arizona, where he developed a master's degree program as chair of American Indian studies. His decision to move into a full-time academic position did not mean an end to his extensive involvement in organizational activism, though he did develop a more rigorous focus in his research and writing over the next decade. During the eighties he published several books and numerous articles on tribal political and legal history, most notably two volumes coauthored with colleague Clifford Lytle, *American Indians, American Justice* (1983) and *The Nations Within: The Past and Future of American Indian Sovereignty* (1984). Lytle later characterized Deloria's approach to social change as both energetic and inconspicuous: "He has been connected with most of the major movements in Indian politics" since the sixties but has "adopted a style of action that seeks to minimize public presence," since fame often undermines effectiveness. "But it is a rare issue that does not have his footprints somewhere in the background."[24] *Custer Died for Your Sins* was reprinted in 1988 with a new preface, in which Deloria marveled at the changes two decades had wrought in Indian country. He reminded his readers that "the Indian task of keeping an informed public available to assist the tribes in their efforts to survive is never ending," and he asserted that "the central message of this book,

---

22. Vine Deloria, Jr., "God Is Also Red: An Interview with Vine Deloria Jr.," interview by James R. McGraw, *Christianity and Crisis* 35 (September 15, 1975): 206.

23. Vine Deloria, Jr., *The Metaphysics of Modern Existence* (San Francisco, CA: Harper and Row, 1979), 217.

24. Lytle, "Vine Deloria, Jr.," 76.

that Indians are alive, have certain dreams of their own, and are being overrun by the ignorance and the mistaken, misdirected efforts of those who would help them, can never be repeated too often."[25]

Deloria left Arizona for the University of Colorado in 1990, accepting an appointment as professor of American Indian studies and history with adjunct appointments in law, political science, and religious studies. These varied departmental affiliations reflect the range of his interests and scholarly contributions and are also a measure of his stature as a respected leader in Indian affairs. The move was a homecoming of sorts, recalling childhood visits to Denver's cathedral with his father, several adventurous years as a college student, his first professional position out of seminary, the publication of his first two books while in law school, and intense organizational activism throughout the seventies.

During the nineties Deloria has continued to provide leadership for a variety of local, regional, and national organizations, addressing specifically Indian issues but also working with groups such as the Friends of the Denver Public Library, the Institute of the North American West, and the Disabilities Rights Education and Defense Fund. He also has been the recipient of many awards and honors, including several citations for lifetime achievement. He demonstrated his expertise in yet another field by writing a number of articles on education for *Winds of Change* magazine, the quarterly periodical of the American Indian Science and Engineering Society, which published eight of these essays in 1991 as a collection titled *Indian Education in America*. He also cooperated with that organization in sponsoring a series of conferences on traditional tribal knowledge about astronomy, animal and plant life, and creation and migration accounts.

Deloria marked the Columbus Quincentenary in 1992 by publishing a second edition of his classic work *God Is Red*. Now subtitled *A Native View of Religion,* as if to make his theoretical intentions more explicit, it is the only one of his seventeen books he has revised for republication. The second edition underscores the impending "ecological meltdown" by raising "additional questions about our species and our ultimate fate." Convinced that relentless exploitation of nature will soon produce an "earthly wasteland," Deloria asserted that "clearly the struggle is between a religious view of life and the secularization that science and industry have brought."[26] These concerns and long-standing doubts about the integrity of Western science led him to the subject of his latest book, *Red Earth,*

---

25. Deloria, *Custer Died for Your Sins*, xiii.
26. Deloria, *God Is Red: A Native View of Religion*, 2–3.

White Lies: Native Americans and the Myth of Scientific Fact, published in 1995. Framing the philosophy and methodology of Western science as a type of religious theory and practice, he argued that the institutionalization of science has led it to take on the form and function of religion in an increasingly secularized society. This has allowed scientists to "act like priests and defer to doctrine and dogma when determining what truths would be admitted, how they would be phrased, and how scientists themselves would be protected from the questions of the mass of people whose lives were becoming increasingly dependent on them."[27]

Deloria's lifelong contributions to religious affairs and in the field of religious studies were recognized by the scholarly community in 1996, when he was invited to deliver one of three plenary addresses at the annual meeting of the American Academy of Religion. He applied his legendary sense of humor to the task and his address, titled "Origins: Physical Reality and Religious Belief," was one of the most entertaining conference presentations in recent memory. The message he brought, however, was of a very serious nature. He prefaced his comments by saying that he had worked most of the year trying to build a "centered intellectual structure" somewhere between religion and science, an epistemology that will allow us to interpret those anomalous human experiences neither approach can account for. But over the course of the year, he "kept getting dragged in backwards" to work on various legal conflicts involving issues of religious freedom. He went on to remind his audience that the analytical categories used in the study of religion are largely derived from Christianity, then described the ways in which these intellectual biases enter into legal proceedings. Calling on religion scholars to apply their expertise to these struggles, he asked them to get involved and help "straighten out religion":

> To what degree do we do violence to non-Western religious traditions when we try and force them into pre-existing categories? When are we going to free ourselves up and just look at these things?
>
> I have been in ceremonies. I have talked to spirits. I'm an educated man, I have three degrees . . . I'm no damn fool. And I go through experiences like that and I have to find a way to integrate those kinds of experiences with what I already know and believe. And I can't deny those experiences. They're as real to me as anything in the world.
>
> I think a lot of the material we have on American Indians is real material. And if we give it credence, then we expand the area in which we can

---

27. Vine Deloria, Jr., *Red Earth, White Lies: Native Americans and the Myth of Scientific Fact* (New York, NY: Scribner, 1995), 17.

examine religious phenomena. I don't believe that people having spiritual experiences are necessarily deluded. . . . People have experiences. They may misinterpret what an experience means. But the experience, as related in a narrative straightaway, is a valid experience. We should gather more data into the study of religion.[28]

AN AMERICAN CRITIQUE OF RELIGION

During the early days of his public career, Deloria was dubbed "the Rousseau of the new Indians" and "the red man's Ralph Nader"; three decades later he is widely respected as one of the most important living Indian figures, a quiet leader with the familiar yet enigmatic face of a tribal elder.[29] The foregoing intellectual biography has briefly highlighted his lifelong involvement in religious affairs and his abiding interest in exploring the religious dimensions and implications of human existence. Deloria's family background, educational experiences, professional accomplishments, and published writings evince a certain consistency in a life marked by pragmatic eclecticism. His many books and articles have engaged a remarkable range of disciplines—history, anthropology, politics, law, theology, philosophy, science, education, and literary criticism—and together demonstrate his broad vision of intellectual activism. He is an impassioned advocate when addressing specific issues, but there is always something more to his polemic than can be expressed in a political slogan; writing as a religious intellectual, he is quick to see the wider ramifications behind immediate dilemmas. Deloria is the consummate American generalist, with religion serving as the overarching motif that unifies his varied writings.

Some critics have attempted to systematize these diverse texts into a theoretical or ideological unity, a project Deloria wants to debunk.[30] There are, however, a number of recurring features in his books and articles that suggest a consistent approach to written discourse. He is an interdisciplinary scholar who relies on painstaking documentary research to ground his arguments. His historical accounts are synthetic interpretations in the tradition of the grand narrative, although he is motivated by a holistic vision of human experience rather than a craving

---

28. Vine Deloria, Jr., "Origins: Physical Reality and Religious Belief," audiotape recording of plenary address at the annual meeting of the American Academy of Religion, New Orleans, LA, November 23, 1996.

29. Steiner, *The New Indians*, 26; Douglas N. Mount, "Authors and Editors," *Publishers' Weekly* 196, no. 22 (December 1, 1969): 7; Lytle, "Vine Deloria, Jr.," 77.

30. See Vine Deloria, Jr., "But It Was All Ad Hoc: Comment on Gulliksen's Paper," *European Review of Native American Studies* 7, no. 1 (1993): 7–8.

for intellectual hegemony. He has frequently collaborated with other scholars as co-author, editor, or contributor, though always as a popular writer speaking to the general public and not just to others in the academy. It is also worth noting that Deloria hasn't engaged in conventional ethnographic scholarship; the seemingly essentialist arguments in *God Is Red* and elsewhere implicate social theories, not ethnic identities.

At the heart of his distinctly American critique of religion is the land itself, the physical place called "America" by many of its current inhabitants. *God Is Red* ends with a prophetic challenge to "the invaders of the North American continent," whom Deloria predicts will soon discover that "for this land, God is red."[31] The American earth functions as the source of human existence and the norm of religious insight in this place. It is not merely the premise for some ambiguous notion of sacred geography or a socially constructed devotion to landscape; it is the stuff of reality itself. As a stalwart defender of the rights of humans and their earthmates, Deloria is *for this land*—grounded, particular, engaged—and whatever he proposes in the way of a theoretical system is rooted in a physical, not ideological, space. His writings on religion in America give voice to this intellectual passion by calling into question our conventional religious institutions, commitments, worldviews, freedoms, and experiences.

The essays that follow originally appeared in various religious periodicals and other publications during the last three decades, though not all of Deloria's occasional writings on religion could be included here.[32]

---

31. Deloria, *God Is Red*, 301.

32. Other essays by Deloria on religious themes include: "The New Exodus," *Civil Rights Digest* 4 (Spring 1971): 38–44; "Indian Affairs 1973: Hebrews 13:8," *North American Review* 258, no. 4 (Winter 1973): 108–12; "Myth and the Origin of Religion," *Pensée* 4, no. 4 (Fall 1974): 45–50; "Why the U.S. Never Fought the Indians," *The Christian Century* 93 (January 7–14, 1976): 9–12; "The Fascination of Heresy," *Katallagete* 6, no. 4 (Spring 1977): 47–50; "The Confusion of History," *Historical Magazine of the Protestant Episcopal Church* 46 (September 1977): 349–53; "A Native American Perspective on Liberation Theology"; "Catastrophism and Planetary History," *Kronos* 3, no. 4 (Summer 1978): 45–51; "Kinship with the World," *Journal of Current Social Issues* 15, no. 3 (Fall 1978): 19–21; "Perceptions and Maturity: Reflections on Feyerabend's Point of View"; "Circling the Same Old Rock," in *Marxism and Native Americans*, edited by Ward Churchill (Boston, MA: South End Press, 1983), 113–36; "The Traditional Western Answers Offer No Solution to Me," in *Stories of Survival: Conversations with Native North Americans*, edited by Remmelt Hummelen and Kathleen Hummelen (New York, NY: Friendship Press, 1985), 13–15; "Indians and Other Americans: The Cultural Chasm," *Church and Society* 75, no. 3 (January/ February 1985): 10–19; "Law and Theology III: Theme," *Church and Society* 79 (September/October 1988): 8–13; "Trouble in High Places: Erosion of American Indian Rights to Religious Freedom in the United States," in *The State of Native America: Genocide, Colonization, and Resistance*, edited by M. Annette Jaimes (Boston, MA: South End Press, 1992), 267–90; "Indians, Archaeologists, and the Future,"

They have been arranged in five thematic sections, ordered in a loosely chronological fashion to reflect the development of his thought over time. Interpretive headnotes at the beginning of each section introduce the essays and suggest how these unifying themes reflect his discursive practices. "My intent is to plant seeds of ideas and raise doubts about what we believe," Deloria wrote in a recent forum of public intellectuals. "Many of our beliefs are inherited, not opinions that we have thought through." Asked to identify "the greatest urgencies facing writers and critics" today, he responded:

> We are actually in the midst of a "Dark Age" of intellectual activity. The Darwinian-Freudian-Marxist synthesis that has dominated the century has long since come apart but Americans refuse to admit it. We have a duty to move beyond it—ethical demands of personal integrity require it—but I see almost no one willing to undertake such a task or even nibble at the edges of the current synthesis to begin a critique. All this hesitancy while the hard sciences are returning study after study that contradicts this synthesis.[33]

This volume of Deloria's collected writings on religion in America concludes with a retrospective afterword that appears here for the first time. "Why," he asks, "do we do what we do, why do we believe what we believe, and why do our practices seem to fall so short of what is possible for us?"[34]

J. T.

American Antiquity 57, no. 4 (1992): 595–98; "Spiritual Management: Prospects for Restoration on Tribal Lands," *Restoration and Management Notes* 10, no. 1 (Summer 1992): 48–50; "Frank Waters: Prophet and Explorer," in *Frank Waters: Man and Mystic*, edited by Vine Deloria, Jr. (Athens, OH: Swallow Press/Ohio University Press, 1993), 166–73; "If You Think About It, You Will See That It Is True," *Noetic Sciences Review* no. 27 (Fall 1993): 62–71.

33. Vine Deloria, Jr., "Thinking in Public: A Forum," *American Literary History* 10, no. 1 (1998): 25.

34. The research for this collection began in 1988 as part of a master's thesis project and has been updated periodically, in collaboration with Deloria, since 1994. I am grateful to Vine and his wife Barbara for their enthusiasm and generosity in bringing this work to completion. My research would not have been possible without the services of reference librarians at the Graduate Theological Union, the University of California at Santa Cruz, the University of New Mexico, and the Denver Public Library, and Cynthia Chavez and David Mahooty provided helpful last-minute research assistance. I have enjoyed working with Bill Germano at Routledge and appreciate his spirited interest in this manuscript. I was fortunate to spend the 1996–97 academic year as a research associate affiliated with the Center for Cultural Studies at the University of California at Santa Cruz, where I worked on this project while waiting for Rita Keresztesi. We originally met just in time for her to help me celebrate the publication of an earlier book, and now I celebrate the fact that we will be spending a lot more time together in the future. I couldn't have done it without you, sweetie.

WHITE CHURCH,
RED POWER

Deloria's recent book *Red Earth, White Lies* places tribal tradition and Western science in conversation around the question of planetary history. Framing scientific narratives as secular manifestations of religious beliefs and practices, he wants to disrupt the epistemological authority of scientific orthodoxy while simultaneously recovering the historical knowledge contained in tribal mythic narratives. This juxtaposition of colonial ideologies and indigenous realities has been a familiar weapon in Deloria's discursive arsenal and is evident in his earliest writings. The essays in this first section explore the complex relationship between Christian denominations and tribal activists, between institutions and movements, between the static center and the dynamic margins. The dialectic of rationality and experience is always evident in social relations; here we find Deloria examining this process at the conflicted intersections of religion and racial politics in America.

"Missionaries and the Religious Vacuum" is excerpted from *Custer Died for Your Sins* and constitutes his first published critique of institutional Christianity, though it picks up on themes he explored four years earlier in his widely circulated parody "The Missionary in a Cultural Trap" (see Appendix 1). Deloria's assessment of the missionary enterprise and its aftermath highlights the symbiotic relationship between cross-cultural proselytism and land dispossession in colonial contexts. Institutionalizing religious colonialism in tribal communities has produced the state of mutual dependency that still exists wherever there are mission churches on reservation lands, and declining congregations are justifiably threatened by the renewal of homeland traditions.

In the next two essays, Deloria surveys the highly publicized occupations and protests that made "Red Power" widely known, if not generally understood. "The Theological Dimension of the Indian Protest Movement" was originally published as a cover story (accompanied by an interview with Deloria) in *The Christian Century*, a liberal Protestant weekly news magazine. "Religion and Revolution Among American Indians" appeared a few

19

months later in *Worldview,* a monthly publication of the Council on Religion and International Affairs, in a special issue examining U.S. culpability in several recent "regional" military conflicts. Both essays chronicle the rise of tribal political activism and explore "the relation of the present Indian movement to the problems, ideologies and energies of domestic America." The occupation of Alcatraz Island raised the question of land as a fundamental dilemma; activists were widely misunderstood because they pursued goals that are religious in origin. Christian churches have exacerbated this situation by overlooking the importance of both nature and culture in favor of an other-worldly individualism. Out of this "mass of contradictions," Deloria issues a call for reformed social relations and innovative tribal traditions, all grounded in a moral vision of human existence.

Deloria reflects on one of the key protest strategies of the sixties and seventies in "Non-Violence in American Society," which was the lead article for a thematic issue of *Katallagete—Be Reconciled,* the quarterly journal of the Committee of Southern Churchmen based in Nashville, Tennessee. Struggling to make sense of the movement in the wake of the Watergate scandal, he examines the assumptions about human nature that undergird both political citizenship and religious commitment. We are still searching for a minimum definition of human decency on which to base our pursuit of social justice. Quoting an organic metaphor used by the biblical prophet Jeremiah, Deloria emphasizes the creative power of redemptive suffering and concludes that "the non-violent response to conditions is perhaps the most explosive method of change available to the human species."

The last two essays in this section offer retrospective insights on the intersections of religion and racial politics. "The Churches and Cultural Change" is chapter five of *The Indian Affair.* This succinct assessment of Christian missions is more measured and balanced than the polemical criticisms of *Custer Died for Your Sins,* and Deloria concludes by emphasizing the vital role denominational churches can play as "a tangible expression of whatever sense of morality or integrity American society has left." Describing the situation since 1960 as "the 'ideological' period of church involvement with American Indians," he expands on this "decade of disaster" in his autobiographical account "GCSP: The Demons at Work." This essay was originally presented at a conference on Episcopal Church history and was subsequently published in the *Historical Magazine of the Protestant Episcopal Church* for a special issue assessing that denomination's recent outreach efforts. Here Deloria offers a detailed case study of how one mainline denomination responded to the power movements. Criticizing the self-serving excesses of church officials and activist leaders alike, he concludes that effective social change must be rooted in dependable, long-term relationships: "We badly need a consistent and comprehensive theology which relates human experiences of divinity in an intelligent context and speaks to human conditions that the secularization of the old Christian worldview has created. We must understand our separate historical journeys and come to see ourselves as planetary peoples with responsibilities extending to all parts and beings of the universe. . . . We must come to see that real differences exist among the various groups that come into contact with ecclesiastical institutions and that these differences make it imperative that church programs are not conceived as a homogenous solution to be applied with force and intolerance to conditions and peoples." This autobiographical narrative also depicts Deloria's struggle as both insider and outsider to the institutional church as well as the activist movement, functioning alternately as advocate or critic depending on the situation and the audience, pushed and pulled from both directions, negotiating his own personal intersection of religion and racial politics.

J. T.

1

MISSIONARIES AND
THE RELIGIOUS VACUUM

One of the major problems of the Indian people is the missionary. It has been said of missionaries that when they arrived they had only the Book and we had the land; now we have the Book and they have the land. An old Indian once told me that when the missionaries arrived they fell on their knees and prayed. Then they got up, fell on the Indians, and preyed.

Columbus managed to combine religion and real estate in his proclamation of discovery, claiming the new world for Catholicism and Spain. Missionaries have been unable to distinguish between their religious mission and their hunger for land since that time.

The first concern of mission work was land on which to build churches, homes, storehouses, and other necessary religious monuments. Like the men from New England in *Hawaii* by Michener, missionaries on the North American continent came to preach and stayed to rule. Or at least prepared the way for others to conquer and exploit.

Sacrifices often matched mistakes. Missionaries did more to open up the West than any other group, but in doing so they increased the possibility of exploitation of the people they purported to save. Land acquisition and missionary work always went hand in hand in American history.

While the thrust of Christian missions was to save the individual Indian, its result was to shatter Indian societies and destroy the cohesiveness of the Indian communities. Tribes that resisted the overtures of the missionaries seemed to survive. Tribes that converted were never heard of again. Where Christianity failed, and insofar as it failed, Indians were able to withstand the cultural deluge that threatened to engulf them.

The conflict between the Indian and white religions was classic. Each religion expressed the outlook and understanding of its respective group. Religious ideas of the two groups never confronted each other directly. The conflict was one of rites and techniques. Christianity destroyed many Indian religious practices by offering a much easier and more practical religion. It was something one could immediately understand, not a paving of the way for what ultimately confronted one.

The credal rhetoric of Christianity filled the vacuum it had created by its redefinition of religion as a commodity to be controlled. Although prohibited for several generations, Indian beliefs have always retained the capacity to return from their exile because they have always related to the Indian's deepest concern. . . .

Missionaries approached the Indian tribes in an effort to bring them into western European religious life. Their primary message sought to invalidate the totality of Indian life and replace it with Christian values. Because Christian reality had been broken into credal definitions, all the missionaries could present to the Indians were words and phrases that had a magical connotation.

Missionaries looked at the feats of the medicine men and proclaimed them to be works of the devil. They overlooked the fact that the medicine men were able to do marvelous things. Above all, they overlooked the fact that what the Indian medicine men did *worked.*

Most activity centered on teaching and preaching. The thrust was to get the Indians to memorize the Large Catechism, the Small Catechism, the Apostles Creed, the Nicene Creed, the Ten Commandments, and other magic rites and formulas dear to Christianity. Salvation became a matter of regurgitation of creeds. In a very real sense, then, Christianity replaced living religions with magic.

And the white man had much magic. Blessed with the gun, the printing press, the iron kettle, and whiskey, it was obvious to many Indians that the white man's god took pretty good care of his people. Since there were no distinctions made between religion and life's other activities by the Indian people, the natural tendency was to adopt the white religion of recitation and forego the rigors of fasting, sacrifice, and prayer.

Missionary activity became an earthly parallel of what Christians thought was happening in heaven. Like the rich burghers of Europe, whom God bribed with earthly treasures, missionaries bribed their way into Indian societies. Once established, they began the laborious task of imprinting two thousand years of sterile dogmas on the unstructured Indian psyche. . . .

The determination of white churches to keep Indian congregations in a mission status is their greatest sin. But it is more a sin against themselves than it is against Indian people. For the national churches do not realize how obsolete their conceptions have become and they continue to tread the same path they walked centuries ago.

The epitome of this blithe ignorance is the work of the Presbyterian Church among the Shinnecocks on Long Island. At a missionary conference two years ago, a Presbyterian minister, in charge of the Indian work for his denomination, described his church's work among this tribe. Then he asked for questions.

I asked him how long the Presbyterians intended to conduct mission activities among a tribe that had lived as Christians for over three hundred and fifty years. His answer to my question was representative of Christian attitudes toward Indian people today: "Until the job is done."

Christianity, which had laid the ancient world prostrate in less than three hundred years and conquered the mighty Roman Empire, has not been able in the same time period to subdue one hundred Indians huddled on Long Island. Needless to say, my faith was shaken to the core by this statement.

The impotence and irrelevancy of the Christian message has meant a return to traditional religion by Indian people. Tribal religions are making a strong comeback on most reservations. Only in the past few years have the Oglala Sioux and Rosebud Sioux revived their ancient Sioux Sun Dance. And this revival is not simply a reenactment for tourists. The dance is done in the most reverent manner and with the old custom of piercing the dancers' breasts.

Pathetically, the response of the white missionaries has been to set up tipis and attempt to compete with the Indian religion by holding Masses and communions during the celebration. Nervously they try to convince the Indians that the Sun Dance and the Holy Communion are really the same thing and that Christianity is therefore "relevant" to the Indian people.

In the Great Lakes area the old Medicine Lodge religion has been making inroads with the Chippewas and Winnebagos. Two years ago at an annual conference of the Wisconsin tribes, a panel of Indians discussed native religions. Eagerly the younger conference participants listened to the old men talk. They left that conference with the conviction that Indian religion was for Indian people and Christian religion was for whites.

The Native American Church, famed for its use of the peyote button in its sacramental worship life, has doubled its membership in the last few years. It appears to be the religion of the future among the Indian people. At first a southwestern-based religion, it has spread since the last world war into a great number of northern tribes. Eventually it will replace Christianity among the Indian people.

When I was growing up on the Pine Ridge reservation before and during World War II, the Native American Church was something far away and officially "bad." Few adherents to this faith could be found among the two large Sioux reservations in southern South Dakota. Today a reasonable estimate would be that some 40 percent of the people are members of the Native American Church there.

Indian people have always been confused at the public stance of the Christian churches. The churches preached peace for years yet have always endorsed the wars in which the nation has been engaged. While the missionaries have never spoken about this obvious inconsistency, Indian people have been curious about it for some time. So the element of Indian people who believe deeply in pacifism has looked to other places for a religion of peace.

From the Hopi reservation has come a prophet of peace named Thomas Banyacya. He stands within the old Hopi religion and preaches to all Indians of their need to return to a life of peace and purity before the world ends. In 1967 Banyacya and some members of the Iroquois tribes traveled throughout the nation visiting the different reservations, bringing a message based on the prophecies of the Hopi and Iroquois. In June of 1968 Banyacya, "Mad Bear" Anderson, a Tuscarora prophet, and many of the traditional leaders of different tribes had two National Aboriginal conventions in Oklahoma and New York to discuss prophecies of their religion.

Banyacya's message, and its ultimate influence, appears to me to be the most significant movement in religion in Indian Affairs today. Banyacya is very spiritual and highly traditional. He stands solidly within Hopi legend which looks at world history as a catastrophic series of events all of which the Hopi have been saved from. In the late fifties a Hopi delegation went to the United Nations to deliver a message of peace, as Hopi prophecies had required them to do. Legends said that should the Hopi delegation be refused entrance—as they were—the series of events foretelling the end of the world would begin. Banyacya's message to other Indian people is to orient them as to the number of prophecies now fulfilled. . . .

The dilemma of Christian missions today is great. National churches have committed two great mistakes, the solution of which depends upon their foresight and ability to reconcile themselves to what they have been preaching to Indian people for years.

The different denominations have, over the years, invested an enormous amount of money in mission buildings and property. In the closing years of the last century, churches could receive a piece of tribal land simply by promising to conduct certain operations such as a school, hospital, or mission station. Consequently many of them applied for and received a great deal of tribal land.

Now they are caught with property which is suitable only for religious use and with a declining religious following. What use has a church building other than as a church? National churches have continued to pour thousands of dollars annually into their mission programs simply to keep up the value of their investments. They must soon be prepared either to take a devastating paper loss as their congregations vanish or give the properties to the Indian people for their own use. Either solution is distasteful to the materialistic instincts of the churches.

Added to the question of property is the obvious racial discrimination of the denominations against the Indian people, which is becoming apparent to the reservation people. Try as they might, the churches cannot admit that an Indian minister speaking in his native tongue to his own people is more efficient and more effective than a highly trained white missionary talking nonsense.

The major denominations are adamant in their determination to exclude Indian people from the ministry. A number of devices, which skirt "official" pronouncements of concern for an indigenous ministry, are used to bar Indian candidates.

One church refuses to admit Indians to the ministry because it is afraid that someday an Indian priest or clergyman may want to serve in a white parish. Indian ministers would not, by definition, be able to serve in a white parish. Therefore, the reasoning goes, they are not suitable for work among Indian congregations either. While they are welcome, I have been told, they don't seem to be able to qualify.

Other churches are frightened that when the sacred doctrines are translated into the native tongue, the subtle nuances created by theologians of the Reformation will lose some of their distinctions. A perfect example of this attitude happened at an orientation session for new missionaries which I attended in 1963.

A Navajo interpreter was asked to demonstrate how the missionary's sermon was translated into Navajo. So the white missionary gave a few homilies and the interpreter spoke a few words of Navajo. The trainees cooed with satisfaction that meaning could actually be transferred into a barbaric tongue like Navajo.

One missionary was skeptical, however, and asked if there were specific words in Navajo that were comparable to English words. He was afraid, he said, that the wrong messages might be transmitted. So he asked what the Navajo word for "faith" was. Quickly the Navajo replied with the desired word.

"Yes," the missionary commented, "that's all very nice. Now what does that word mean?"

"Faith," said the Navajo smiling.

Nevertheless, many denominations are skeptical about letting Indians enter the ministry because of the possibility that doctrine may become impure. So they continue to send white missionaries for posts in Indian country to ensure that the proper theological distinctions be drawn.

With the necessity of keeping large missions open and by refusing to bring Indian people into the ministry, churches have had great difficulty in filling their mission posts. The glory of intrepid pioneering is now gone, and the glory seekers as well as the devoted have long since written off Indian country as the place for service and advancement. Staff positions go unfilled for months and often the first white who comes wandering in across the desert is hired to operate the mission stations.

Some churches have an incredible turnover each spring and try all summer to fill their posts. Eventually they find some white who is a former basketball coach, a retired editor, an interested layman, or an ex-schoolteacher and promptly hand over the mission lock, stock, and barrel without further inquiry. The fact that the new appointee is white is sufficient to cover any theological or professional shortcomings.

Thus the quality of mission workers is at an all-time low. Most are not interested in their work and regard it as a job rather than a calling. Generally they have great contempt for the Indian people they are supposed to be helping.

But probably worse, much mission work is done by white clergymen who are not capable enough to run white parishes. In most cases, the Indian field is their last stop before leaving the ministry altogether. They are hauled from pillar to post by frantic church officials desperately trying to shore up the sagging fortunes of their mission fields. A great deal of money is spent covering up disasters created by these white misfits. When they cause too much controversy in one place they are transferred to another and turned loose again. More money is spent on them than on recruitment and training of Indian people for church work.

Pay is not high in mission work for either white or Indian workers. But it is universally higher for whites than it is for Indians. In the past there was some justification for a pay difference. Many Indian workers were only part-time workers and had another source of income. Gradually, however, Indian clergymen were assigned to remote areas and received less compensation.

Often the pay scale is based primarily upon whether a man is white or Indian. Indians receive less pay, even with seminary training. And Indians are still assigned to the remote areas with the poorest housing and least facilities. Go out to any mission field today and examine the placement of church workers and clergymen. You will discover that white workers have the best assignments, the best houses, the best fringe benefits, and receive the most consideration for advancement from their superiors.

No other field of endeavor in America today has as much blatant racial discrimination as does the field of Christian missions to the American Indian people. It is a marvel that so many Indian people still want to do work for the churches.

Documentation of discrimination and favoritism would be fairly easy were it not for the fantastic ability of the churches to cover their tracks. Instead of forcing resignations from the ministry, church officials transfer incompetents from station to station in order to protect the good name of the church. Thus some tribes are visited with a problem missionary who should have been sent on his way years ago but who has managed to hang on to his ministerial status by periodic transfer and the lack of moral courage by church officials to take action. . . .

The best thing that the national denominations could do to ensure the revitalization of Christian missions among Indian people would be to assist in the creation of a national Indian Christian Church. Such a church would incorporate all existing missions and programs into one national church to be wholly in the hands of Indian people.

Such a church would include all ordained Indian clergymen now serving as church workers in the Indian field. The actual form of the ministry would not be determined by obsolete theological distinctions preserved from the middle ages, but would rather incorporate the most feasible role that religion can now play in the expanding reservation societies.

Each denomination that has been putting funds into Indian work would contribute toward the total budget of the new church. Existing buildings and church structures would be evaluated by the new Indian church and the tribal council of the reservation on which the property is located. Congregations of the various denominations would be consolidated and reservation-wide boards of laymen would direct activities on each reservation.

With the religious function integrated into the ongoing life of the tribe, the Indian church would be able to achieve self-support in a short time as the role of religion clarified itself to the reservation communities.

Religious competition, which fractures present tribal life, would disappear and the movement toward ancient religions might not be so crucial.

Such a proposal is too comprehensive for most denominations to accept at the present time. The primary fear of turning over the sacred white religion to a group of pagans would probably outrage most denominations, too few of whom realize how ridiculous denominational competition really is.

The best example I can mention of denominational competition existed at Farmington, New Mexico, a couple of years ago. The situation has probably changed since 1965. But that year there were twenty-six different churches serving an estimated Navajo population of 250. That's less than ten Indians per denomination! Assuming each church had a choir of eight, the congregations must have totaled one or two people per Sunday. Which does not indicate a field ready for harvest.

I estimated that the total mission budget for the Farmington area that year was in excess of $250,000. Christianity, not tourism, was Farmington's most profitable industry in 1965.

Churches face literal dissolution on the reservations unless they radically change their method of operation. Younger Indians are finding in Indian nationalism and tribal religions sufficient meaning to continue their drift away from the established churches. Even though many churches had chaplaincies in the government boarding schools, the young are not accepting missionary overtures like their fathers and mothers did.

As Indian nationalism continues to rise, bumper stickers like "God is Red" will take on new meanings. Originally put out at the height of Altizer's "God is Dead" theological pronouncements, the slogan characterizes the trend in Indian religion today.

Many Indians believe that the Indian gods will return when the Indian people throw out the white man's religion and return to the ways of their fathers. Whether or not this thinking is realistic is not the question. Rather the question is one of response and responsibility of the missionaries today. Will they continue to be a burden or not?

Can the white man's religion make one final effort to be real, or must it too vanish like its predecessors from the old world? I personally would like to see Indians return to their old religions wherever possible. For me at least, Christianity has been a sham to cover over the white man's shortcomings. Yet I spent four years in a seminary finding out for myself where Christianity had fallen short.

I believe that an Indian version of Christianity could do much for our society. But there is little chance for such a melding of cards. Everyone in the religious sphere wants his trump to play on the last trick. In the meantime, Banyacya, Mad Bear Anderson, and others are silently changing the game from pinochle to one where all fifty-two cards are wild. They may, if the breaks fall their way, introduce religion to this continent once again.

(1969)

2

THE THEOLOGICAL DIMENSION
OF THE INDIAN
PROTEST MOVEMENT

Church groups in America have been severely buffeted in recent years because of their support of social causes. Their participation in the civil rights movement of the sixties was important in itself and proved sustaining when the outlook was bleak. Indeed, it was perhaps the church's involvement in concerns of this kind that provided a bridge across the contrarieties of the sixties so that the entire decade turned out to be one that fostered a concentrated drive for improvement and reform and the inculcation of a deeper sense of justice in the American people.

Part of the ideology which sustained this drive grew out of the Christian teaching of the brotherhood of man. Translated into the politics of integration under law, this concept swept the American psyche clean of the cobwebs of two centuries. But the shift from the ideological defense of integration to the launching of power movements by the racial minorities caught many people unawares. Hence there developed a furious backlash against church involvement in social issues. For the power movements stressed the group rather than individuals, and church people by and large could not apprehend within the Christian context the need for group identity felt by the various distinct minorities in the American mass.

On their part, the power movements themselves failed to develop a proper ideology. In North America, when the group or community becomes all important (as it has in recent years), Western notions of democratic leavening are somewhat beside the point. What is needed is a truly native ideology—that is, the tribal ideology of the American Indian.

Attaching themselves to the power movements when these were at their zenith, the Indians were welcomed into the mythological coalition that was to bring about the revolutionary changes which the civil rights movement had failed to engender. The possibilities of protest on a group basis were first discerned in the Poor People's March of 1968. This of course represented a negative value in that all its participants lacked economic power. Solving the problem of poverty would have required a more or less immediate redistribution of wealth, and the political and economic changes such a program would have involved posed a threat to white America. But though its results were meager, the Poor People's March did suggest that the group could wield positive power. Hence Indians were accepted by non-Indians primarily because they were seen as adding leverage in the pursuit of power.

It was in the following year, 1969, that Indians emerged in the media. The capture of Alcatraz provided a symbolic center for the Indian protest, but the message of Alcatraz failed utterly. Basically, Alcatraz raised the question of land, first in the political and property sense of ownership and second in the larger sense of the relationship of land to communities and, ultimately, to religious understanding. The result of Alcatraz was hardly comforting to Indians. They never received title to the island. White society simply evaded the whole problem by harking back to the days of Sitting Bull and Chief Joseph. People were damn sorry about the depredations of the past, but they could not recognize the depredations of the present because they could not go beyond the first step of the land question. The Christian religion had little to say concerning land and nature: it was an otherworldly religion which boasted that it was in the world but not of it. Failing to understand the Indians' relationship to the land, non-Indians saw Alcatraz as nothing more than a symbolic defiance of the federal government—in which nearly everyone had lost faith anyway. Thus they responded to the Indian protest by allowing Indians to have their day in the media sun. Oceans of pitying tears flowed down, but no waters of righteousness. The mood of white society seemed to be one of sadistic fairness: we have hurt them; now we must let them hurt us.

No wonder that Indian activists went wild. Between 1969 and early 1972, they took over piece after piece of federal surplus property, declaring that they had rights to it under the 1868 Sioux treaty. Invariably, charges of disturbing the peace and inciting to riot were lodged against them, though eventually they were able to negotiate amnesty on these. Their movement was at once exciting and boring. Would they one of these days uncover a piece of property that the federal government might give them? Yet watching another group of Indians on the evening news claiming another abandoned federal lighthouse grew wearying. In their own minds, the Indians' escalation of their demands and the increasing violence of their protest recalled the days of Indian glory. To the white society, the protest was novel because of its intensity.

The turning point came in 1972, when one of the Indian activists happened to read the 1868 Sioux treaty. There was the text in black and white. It said nothing about returning Alcatraz or the lighthouse in Milwaukee, but it did promise that the United States would protect the tribal form of government. To many Indians, this meant that the reservation governments which had been created in 1934 as quasi-modern corporations were contrary to Indian tradition. In the light of this discovery the activists began to talk with the old men of the tribes, and from them learned a new understanding of life. Hitherto they had believed that Indian identity depended on establishing a preferential pecking order in relationships with federal bureaucrats. Now, taught by the elders, many activists concluded that their own salvation and their people's lay in a return to the old ways, the old religion and the old political structure. Meanwhile, the failure of the reservation governments to minister to the needs of their people had induced a mood of frustration which, by the fall of 1972, turned into desperation. So when the organizers of the Trail of Broken Treaties arrived to recruit followers for the march on Washington, many Indians broke with the traditional rule of silence and joined the protest.

The ensuing occupation and destruction of the Bureau of Indian Affairs headquarters in Washington was completely misinterpreted by Indians and non-Indians alike. Many Indians saw it as a way of paying the white society in its own coin. They were entitled to doing a little demolition, they felt. But Washington officials—particularly those closest to the seats of power—said the destruction was the work of hoodlum urban Indians who were angry over the federal government's recently announced decision to refuse aid to off-reservation Indians. The fact is that this decision was taken in defiance of the Snyder Act of 1920.

The most important result of the Trail of Broken Treaties was the twenty-point program its participants drew up. Listing the Indians' grievances and suggestions for remedying them, this document was perhaps the most detailed ever presented to the U.S. government by an Indian group. Its proposals—insofar as they touched on the nature of the federal relationship—were designed to return Indian communities step by step to the status they had held in the 1870s. One point dealt with the institution of a new land policy reflecting the basic theology that the older tribal men had preserved. Federal officials could not fathom a program based on the assumption that tribal religious ideas were valid. Apparently they refused to consider the nature of the proposed changes and the fact that these would place additional responsibilities on the Indians. In January, after a Task Force had allegedly reviewed them, the twenty points were rejected by the federal government.

The people who had traveled the Trail of Broken Treaties felt betrayed. Many of them vowed to go on protesting. Toward the end of February a series of events on the Pine Ridge Sioux Reservation produced the Wounded Knee occupation. A grasping tribal chairman who used his tribal police as a personal bully squad, a force of federal marshals bewildered by not knowing which group of Indians would be shooting at them the next day, a White House staff that both welcomed Wounded Knee as a distraction from the then developing Watergate scandal and deplored it as further evidence of the bankruptcy of the Nixon domestic policies—all combined to make the seventy-two-day occupation one of the more entertaining incidents of the winter television season.

Fundamentally, the Wounded Knee issue was a moral one involving the Fort Laramie Treaty of 1868, which forbids the taking of any Sioux land without the approval of three-fourths of the adult males of the tribe concerned. In effect the Indians were asking the United States why it refused to live up to its own laws. A hard question which allowed no quibbling. When it signed the treaty, the United States surely anticipated that whites would want the Black Hills some day. Therefore it could not pretend that events had now created a situation so desperate as to require overriding the promises made in the treaty. To have given an adequate answer at Wounded Knee, the federal government would have had to admit that it is and always has been made up of pathological liars. But by definition whites and Christians, the civilized peoples of the world, do not lie.

Who knows whither the Indian movement is going? As we de-escalate from Wounded Knee and face the prospect of political trials, the religious dimensions of Indian protest become plain. On the one hand the Indian theology demands that the sacred places of the earth be discerned and communities of whole human beings be allowed to live on them. On the other hand the Indian protesters are intent on demonstrating that the white man's religion and his government are hollow, without honor and without substance. Experienced Indians regard this desire to show up the bankruptcy of the whites' values as suicidal. Of course practically every Indian is convinced that the white man is corrupt at the core, but many Indians reject attempts to demonstrate as much because—and they point to Vietnam and to the massacres of the 1800s—they believe that the white man will kill his opposition rather than win it over by example or reasoning. There was Ghost Dancing at Wounded Knee in 1890 and also in 1973, but in neither case did it stop the marshals' bullets.

A nation that has long conceived of political protest and social movement in theological terms must come to a new religious understanding of man in his community before it undertakes any more actions. For where such understanding is lacking, appeals to man's kinder and higher instincts are useless. The dilemma of the Indian today is: How call upon a more universal sense of justice than the world can presently sustain or fulfill?

(1973)

3

RELIGION AND REVOLUTION AMONG AMERICAN INDIANS

In the last year and a half the familiar stereotype of the faithful Indian companion silently marching alongside the white hero à la Tonto has been rudely shaken. First a group of Sioux Indians invaded a sleepy Nebraska town where one of their kinsmen had been brutally murdered and demanded justice. Then there was the occupation of the Bureau of Indian Affairs headquarters during the week of the 1972 national elections and the almost total destruction of that building. Tempers had hardly cooled by the end of 1972 when the same group of Indian activists invaded Custer, South Dakota, burned a stall-like Chamber of Commerce building and scared the settlers who had moved into the Black Hills, winding up their confrontation with the destruction of several bars in Rapid City, South Dakota.

Following the Custer confrontation American Indian movement leader Dennis Banks addressed the South Dakota legislature and pledged a new era of race relations in the state. Hardly a week had passed before Banks and three hundred other Indians seized the hamlet of Wounded Knee, South Dakota, a community on the Pine Ridge Indian Reservation and the scene of the brutal massacre of Sioux Indians by the United States Cavalry in 1890. Banks, Russell Means, Carter Camp and other Indian activists, reinforced by traditional leaders of the Oglala Sioux, held the little community for seventy-two days against the U.S. federal marshals, the marauding white vigilantes who prowled the reservation after dark and the tribal police, aptly called the "goon squad" by the harassed reservation residents.

If Indians have not been successful they have at least been energetic. Wounded Knee was already a familiar site to the many who had read Dee

Brown's *Bury My Heart at Wounded Knee,* but it achieved international status as Indian activists appeared nightly on the evening news and correspondents from around the world swarmed to South Dakota to record the most recent of America's Indian wars. The problem with all the attention focused on the series of incidents provoked by the new wave of Indian activists was that very few people understood just what all the fuss was about.

To be sure, the United States had broken the Indian treaties. But also in 1972 the United States moved toward abandoning Formosa after basing much of its post–World War II foreign policy on the defense of Nationalist China, so the breaking of treaties was hardly viewed as a mortal sin by the American people. Others attributed the troubles to demon poverty. Ever since Lyndon Johnson declared his desire to create a Great Society in 1964 it was commonly acknowledged that, of minority groups in poverty, Indians were at the very bottom, because the Pueblos of New Mexico still lived in dirt houses and the tribes of the Pacific Northwest still hunted and fished for food.

The most popular interpretation of the Indian outbreak, however, came from the New Left, which saw the future as a series of revolutions by the oppressed, and since they were suffering most from what the Nixon Administration termed benign neglect, it was a fulfillment of New Left doctrine when war-painted Indians on ponies appeared on television from the confines of Wounded Knee, South Dakota. Clearly, the revolution was just around the corner.

With the characteristic enthusiasm and penchant for cameo roles in symbolic demonstrations, the personalities of the "movement" of the sixties pilgrimaged to South Dakota to pledge their solidarity with the Indian protestors. A righteous Marlon Brando sent an Indian girl to spurn his Academy Award and announce to the outraged audience, which had made millions from cowboy-and-Indian movies, that Brando had not only disclaimed their morality but that he himself, that very night, was winging his way eastward to aid the besieged defenders of Wounded Knee.

They were all there. Ralph Abernathy arrived pledging to use his influence with Richard Nixon to bring the incident to a happy ending. Mark Lane showed up hoping for another Attica, and Bill Kunstler arrived offering his considerable skills as a trial lawyer to the leaders of the occupation. The National Council of Churches formed a human wall of noncombatant participants around Wounded Knee in an effort to prevent the federal forces from invading the little town. Successful in their initial effort, they promptly went on an undisguised ego trip as conciliators of the first rank and became useless in further discussions.

Unfortunately, Jane Fonda was busy delivering a child and so could not attend the festivities, but since her Oscar was already in hand, there was no apparent crisis in which her involvement was required.

Had it been simply a misunderstanding by the sympathetic liberal white community, the events of Wounded Knee might have been comprehensible, but the Indian participants had no better grasp of the situation than did their New Left allies or right-wing foes. While the White House was busy trying to trace a connection between the American Indian movement and the Communist conspiracy, Indians of various tribes alternately applauded and booed the Indians on both sides of the occupation. Richard Wilson, the Neanderthal chairman of the Oglala Sioux tribe, whose excesses had largely created the desperation of the Oglalas that led to the confrontation, demanded that federal forces leave the reservation so that he could lead a thousand of his followers to Wounded Knee and kill everyone.

Now that we are somewhat distanced from the sorry melodrama of Wounded Knee, we can better examine the nature of the Indian protests which have increased both in frequency and in violence over half a decade. What is the relation of the present Indian movement to the problems, ideologies and energies of domestic America? We cannot understand the Indian protest when it is clothed in the symbols of yesteryear and interpreted through the rhetoric of post-Vietnam America. The further question asks about the connection between the Indian movement and most Indians.

Despite the protestations of some Indian activists and despite the enthusiastic attempts of young whites to smuggle ammunition into Wounded Knee as a demonstration of their solidarity with the Indians, the connection between the Indian movement and the ideology of the New Left is utterly superficial. People who accept the Third World ideology or the various Marxist interpretations of social and class struggle find the real ideology behind the Indian protest incredible and outrageous. Rather than seeking a new social order or a new system of economic distribution and management, Indians are seeking no less than the restoration of the continent and the destruction, if necessary, of the white invaders who have stolen and raped their lands. As fantastic as such an aim may sound, it has deep roots in Indian consciousness.

The goal emerges from a variety of sources, mostly from religious legends and from prophecies that have been newly interpreted to fit today's situation. The first national exposition of these doctrines probably came from two sources, Wallace "Mad Bear" Anderson of the Tuscaroras, who, more than a decade ago, proclaimed Iroquois predictions of the coming and eventual demise of the white man, and from Clifton Hill, the Creek preacher, whose parabolic sermons have been rephrased in terms of impending moral and physical apocalypse. Such predictions of the end may or may not be authentic to tribal religions. They introduce the whole concept of time as a religious dimension. It was the absence of this dimension that distinguished the Indian version of the "chosen people" motif from the biblical version. The Indian religions worked in nature, the biblical in history. The concentration on land enabled the Indian to relate to his environment but prevented him from recognizing the historical forces which man had created and which were changing the environment. The predictions, with their sense of history, could not help but change the Indian perception of reality.

The eschatological visions of the contemporary Indian movement are not without precedent. The famous Ghost Dance of the last decade of the 1800's was based upon eschatology, but its theme was the moral worth of the Indian as opposed to the white. The movement of today asserts the cultural superiority of Indian traditions over those of Anglo-Saxon peoples. That inherent superiority will, it is alleged, become historically manifest. Whether this emerging worldview is sufficient to build a lasting movement or to reestablish tribal community is presently being tested; the evidence to date is not encouraging.

The widespread Indian failure to comprehend the experiences of the immediate past is matched by the inability of whites to relate to the modern Indian. Indians compare the best of past Indian cultural values with the worst behavior of contemporary whites; whites look at the most profound and sacrificial efforts of contemporary Indians and find them wanting because they, the whites, can only relate to the Indians of the past they come to know through movies and television. Confrontation on the level of ideas becomes impossible, and misunderstandings abound. Indians have won a temporary victory with the media recognition of their problems. The price of that victory for all of us was the missed opportunity to understand the nature of the deep gulf separating Indian and non-Indian.

The field of literature is strewn with such missed opportunities. Chief Red Fox, at best a cruel hoax on the Oglala Sioux, has sold more books than the five leading Indian authors now writing on modern problems combined. T. C. McLuhan's scissors-and-paste creation of *Touch the Earth* sold more copies and received more attention than Hyemeyohsts Storm's *Seven Arrows*. Both books deal with the religious dimensions of land and creation, Storm's book being an effort to translate Indian beliefs into a poetic form of teaching and McLuhan's book being a collection of sayings of famous Indian chiefs.

*

In all the contemporary discussions the least understood fact is that tribal governments are split between "treaty Indians" and "Indian Reorganization Act Indians." The traditional, or treaty, Indians draw the line of resistance at the last treaties signed by the tribe with the United States. They demand that the federal and tribal governments settle the argument over the legality of the treaty before embarking on any other development plans. If the treaty is considered to have been broken, as with the 1868 Treaty of the Sioux and Arapaho, the traditionals insist that no other acts of the United States can be binding on the tribe until the matter of the broken treaty is resolved.

"IRA Indians" feel that the past is past, although the various treaties and agreements remain as points of reference in dealing with the federal government. They accept the limitations placed upon them by the Indian Reorganization Act of 1934, but demand that they receive formal recognition from the United States as the legal successors to the aboriginal tribes. Their point is a strong one from a purely legal viewpoint. The IRA in effect created semiautonomous federal corporations out of the reservation population, thus defying the traditional political organization of the various tribes. The IRA "tribal governments" are no doubt successors to the old tribal communities in a legal sense, but culturally, religiously, historically they are aberrations of the old ways.

This distinction between traditional and IRA Indian carries over into economics with devastating effect. The traditionalists desire the old communal forms of economic life, which in most cases were built around the clan, band or extended family. Such a communal economy focuses on its own survival quite apart from the forces surrounding the tribal community. The IRA Indian views economic development as a goal in and of itself, clearly distinct from communal considerations.

As a result, under the IRA, tribal councils have leased tribal lands for strip-mining, introduced sweatshop factories into the reservations and developed housing programs based upon white suburban housing patterns. The failure rate of the new methods is incredible. Housing projects stand virtually empty because the people do not like suburban cluster-type housing. Factories and hour-wage projects are plagued with absenteeism and a high rate of employee turnover. Projects need continual and massive federal subsidies to keep going, and even then they eventually fail because they are so alien to the deeply felt needs of the Indian community.

Education is also a shambles. Federal expenditures skyrocket while the educational level of the Indian community remains almost the same generation after generation. Scholarships find their way to mixed-blood families that live off the reservations and have sufficient political clout to get the attention of the Bureau of Indian Affairs. Full-blood reservation people get little attention and fewer educational opportunities. In large part this is because they do not view education as a means of individual salvation and thus rebel against the conformity and depersonalization of the educational system. In most cases they learn only the code words necessary for getting the white man's world to leave them in peace and let them learn on their own what they feel is important.

On the federal policy level the conflict appears in the perennial question of whether to terminate the federal relationship with tribes in order to establish more individual equality, or to allow the tribes full self-government and thus invite a return to traditional forms. The federal position is curious. The present Administration denies it has any responsibility for individual Indians; its relationship is with the tribes. Yet it builds its policy upon an individualistic ideology which sees integration as the salvation of Indians. While insisting that treaties are a tribal question, the present Administration fails to comprehend the nature of the tribal concern. In August, 1973, a new Civil Rights unit was established in the Justice Department to deal with the civil rights questions of *individual* Indians. This after a year of violent protests demanding the enforcement of treaty—*tribal*—rights.

Within this mass of contradictions the present Indian movement has emerged; from such confusion the future is not easy to discern. Whichever way the Indian movement goes, it is bound to confuse both allies and enemies. The New Left, for example, still cherishes the vision of oppressed mankind rising in solidarity against the structures of oppression. From the universalistic viewpoint of Third World ideology the Indian drive to reassert the primacy of tribal identity and to reclaim ancestral land appears as an intolerable perversion of radical doctrine.

Those Indians who have assimilated are similarly put off by aspects of the Indian movement. They have "made it" in the white man's world, no small achievement, and they cannot allow the movement to go beyond what the American political center considers proper. They oppose the ideology and the violence of confrontations such as Wounded Knee; they are unable to distinguish between the ultimate philosophical base of resistance from the accompanying destruction of property. In this too they are good Middle Americans.

And, of course, tribal existence is anathema to the federal officials. They recognize a vague and ill-defined responsibility for Indian communities and justify their involvement on the basis of the federal government's having always had programs of assistance to Indian communities and there being no good political reason not to continue to have such programs. But little effort is made to understand Indians, tribal communities or even the nature of the government's legal responsibilities toward Indians.

The traditionalists also have problems in finding their way to a better future. A transformation of values is needed to bring tribal governments into line with the real conditions under which Indians live. This means traditionalists will have to recognize the historical nature of their beliefs. Customs and beliefs were shaped by particular times and places. The revelations received by the tribes in "olden days" shaped the religious forms and served the needs of distinct communities of another time. Even if the sacred medicine which called the buffalo to the tribe still worked today, there are no buffalo. Religious forms must, in order to be meaningful, relate to a dramatically changed community in a dramatically changed environment.

I believe that, when the traditionalists realize that the basis of Indian tribal religions is not preserving social forms and ceremonies but creating new forms and ceremonies to confront new situations, they will have an extremely promising future. Many tribal religious traditions have their roots in the distant past, but took on their present forms little more than a century before the coming of the white man. The religious traditions of many tribes have been transformed in very recent times through revelations encountered in new environments. Such is the genius of Indian religion.

Unlike many other religious traditions, tribal religions do not depend upon the teachings of a messiah, savior or central religious teacher. They have not been authoritatively set "once and for always." Truth is in the ever changing experiences of the community. For the traditional Indian to fail to appreciate this aspect of his own heritage is the saddest of heresies. It means the Indian has unwittingly fallen into the trap of Western religion, which seeks to freeze history in an unchanging and authoritative past.

I have tried, then, to trace some of the elements in the confusing ways Indians are thinking about themselves and being thought about by others. I have made clear, I trust, that little confidence should be placed in a federal government riddled through with contradictory approaches to "the Indian problem." Nor do the fantasies of the New Left help in anticipating the future—although, unfortunately, the American Indian Movement has tended to imitate the New Left, with the predictable result of a backlash among Indians of all viewpoints. The shape of the Indian future cannot be imported, either from Washington or from other struggles for social change.

Probably within the coming year there will be another major event—a violent confrontation, a struggle with Washington over treaty rights or whatever—that will seize attention throughout Indian country. Ideologies are so much up for grabs right now that any *Indian* faction that is able to interpret that event in a way that brings sense out of the present confusion may well determine how Indian people will view themselves for decades to come.

The gut question has to do with the meaning of the tribe. Should it continue to be a quasi-political entity? Or it could become primarily an economic structure. Or it could become, once again, a religious community. The future, perhaps the immediate future, will tell.

(1974)

4

NON-VIOLENCE IN AMERICAN SOCIETY

The world has grown much older and smaller, it seems, since the days when, summoned to a new frontier which could be subdued by sincerity and purity of heart, we began a process of non-violent social change. In the intervening decade and a half we have seen the world revolve many times, heard prophecies of doom and reassurances of the normality of our existence, and participated in the martydom of many prophets of non-violence. After a decade of social and political effort to make the American ideology applicable to all people, we stand dumbfounded while the greatest political criminal in American history retires from the scene, pardoned and with pension and sympathetic groupies in hand.

The bitterness of reflection these days dwells not on what was accomplished but on what could have been accomplished had men been reasonable, just, or even consistent with themselves. But the purpose of disillusion is to force us to clarify what and who we are and to enable us to examine, in the light of our goals and beliefs, those forces that changed our lives and manner, in which both incident and coincidence forever altered our lives.

One cannot satisfactorily date the beginnings of our modern social movement, for there are many events waiting as candidates for historical immortality, and in choosing which incident proved to be the spark that caused people to become dissatisfied with the conditions around them, we preclude examination of what it was, in the final analysis, that we were trying to do. Perhaps a better way to review the meaning of our adult lives, for that is what we are discussing, whether we are fifty years old or half that age, is to examine the basis upon which we expected changes to come about. If there was any single motivating strategy in the last decade and a half that had meaning, it was the commitment to seek change through non-violent protests, which carried symbolic and practical goals into the arena of history.

It is too easy to examine non-violence as a technique without recognizing that most significant practitioners of non-violence now lie in their graves, sacrificial victims of a process that demonstrated high ethical and social commitment in a world devoted to survival at any cost. We should not be concerned initially with the sacrificial victims, even though they form an indelible part of our world and describe for us the extent of commitment that non-violence requires. The task should be rather to question why we thought that non-violence was a viable option for any type of change that would certainly prove disruptive of existing conditions and institutions.

Non-violence, it seems to me, is a way of life that depends upon a number of factors that are generally assumed but rarely, if ever, exist in significant quantities in any society. It must certainly—for adherents of the Christian religion and peoples of some of the other traditions—stem from the religious worldview taught in religious institutions and promulgated in political theory as a justification for the concept of citizenship and its corresponding sets of responsibilities. Both citizenship and religious commitment seem to be based upon a number of propositions, two of which we must certainly confront in an examination of the place of non-violence in social existence.

One proposition that must be present when discussing non-violence would seem to be that societies and religions are built at least partially on the supposition that no significant number of people will be stirred from their inertia to accomplish anything. They will not think. They will not question. And, most important, they will not object to whatever happens until it directly affects the manner in which they view their own personal survival.

This inertia works constructively and destructively. A small group of dedicated people, enlivened with a vision of something better and more profound, can sway the inertial mass by introducing, symbolically and through non-violent refusal to go along, a new understanding of what it is that everyone thinks they believe. The genius of the early demonstrations of the civil rights movement was that the battle had already been decided in the courts. The symbolic question of integration that was raised was almost always "why *shouldn't* we integrate?" "Why shouldn't blacks have the same rights as whites?" The inertial mass had democracy, law, and ethics already defined for it in the courts, and the problem was one of bringing the message into tangible situations where it could be understood. Suffering, as a means for defining in concrete terms the abstractions of citizenship and morality, was a powerful and proper weapon.

The commitment to non-violence, however, was soon twisted in its symbolic impact because the medium of television consumed symbolic events much quicker than people consumed them. The technique of illustrating injustice and oppression via demonstrations began to back-fire as soon as the message of the demonstrations became complex. By the time of the Poor People's March, the issues were so profound and so much more complicated than the simplicity of integration that the iner-tial social mass could no longer understand the complexity of tangential issues which the leaders of social change could clearly see. Television became a demon creating instant leadership and raising issues of emo-tional intensity which had no structural place in the process of defining the meaning of human existence.

At this point in the process, the second basic proposition of non-vio-lence emerged. Non-violence assumed that there was a basic minimum level of decency present in any society. This proposition was expressed in many ways, but never articulated directly so that people for and against social change could adopt it as a basic boundary of the meaning of human existence. Non-violence had to be based upon the idea that sac-rifice and suffering were redemptive, because there was a minimum def-inition of the meaning of a human being which all people accepted and below which no person would dare to go.

The destructive nature of the inertial mass was thus able to assert itself, for as the situation became confused, the demagogic politician arose, who reassured the mass of the basic decency of human existence as defined by the old rules which the demagogue promised to reinstitute. By appealing to the fears and confusion of the inertial mass, the situation was reversed by proponents of the *status quo* and exploited for purely selfish and egotistical reasons. As we have seen from the Watergate rev-elations, there was no minimum sense of decency present in the admin-istration past, and there may be very little existing in the present administration.

Non-violence, therefore, was a partial answer to the question of social change because it described partially and optimistically the best that was possible in human experience. Yet the use of non-violence assumed the existence of a benevolent god who presided over a benign universe and whose actions were largely incomprehensible yet always produced a sat-isfactory conclusion. Like the pre-established harmony of the philoso-phers, social conditions were supposed to resolve themselves because the goal was right, people were sincere, and the principles on which change was predicated were consistent.

The mysticism of both the Christian religion and the American political system was examined minutely by the technique of non-violence and found wanting, because deep down there really was no basic definition of decency when confronting the reality of masses of people living together. Even the proponents of citizenship who believed deeply and not rhetorically in the American values, counseled people that it didn't matter how one voted, just as long as one did vote. Again the mystical assumption that beneath the tensions of social existence either the unseen hand of god or the wisdom of the people would automatically work to set things right.

Reliance on the unseen and unsuspected intervention of the minimum definition of decency seems to be a function of the prophetic role in Western religions. Jesus, in the New Testament, relates that the people who acclaimed him decried the fact that their fathers had killed the prophets and vowed that had they been alive in the times of the prophets they would have recognized the prophetic message and responded properly. Jesus' insight was merely an echo of what has been experienced in the past and what the future would one day realize. The attitude exists today and few people, if one were to ask seriously, would not have chosen to support abolition of slavery had they been alive a century ago, or would not have stolen Indian lands in fraudulent treaties had they been given the chance to negotiate the agreements.

If we understand the boundaries within which non-violence can work, we can see that we have been somewhat askew in understanding the nature of human existence. Neither our religious teachings nor our political institutions have been founded on firm foundations. We have traditionally skirted the question of evil in the world by observing, first, the needless suffering of people and jumping almost immediately to the question of how god can allow such things to happen. We have sought comfort before we have even understood the meaning of our problem. Instead of asking "why does evil exist?" we should have been asking, "why do men do evil things?"

The same principle comes into play with our political institutions. We have been taught to demand our rights, but there has been little emphasis on our responsibilities. The expectation has been that government exists to make us happy and to guarantee fulfillment of our personal whims whether by hook or crook, and the lower the profile the better. Political theory has demanded only that people assent to what does not

directly and immediately affect them, because the complexity of problems requires that we delegate decision-making and responsibility to our
chosen representatives. We dare not question what motivates our political leaders to do the things they do. Our only responsibility has been to
believe and to assume that somewhere a minimum definition of decency
and integrity exists because we have defined governments as the means
that individuals chose to order their social, political, economic and philosophical relationships.

The prophetic function of both religion and politics must stem less from
the romantic and more from the practical, if we are to understand where
we have been and why, upon reflection, we did not come the way we
intended to come. One can perhaps only remember Jeremiah's commission "to root out and pull down, and to destroy, and to throw down, *to
build, and to plant*" (Jer. 1:10) to recognize the naiveté with which people
in the domestic social movement approached non-violence as a
prophetic commission, for the commitment to change failed to describe
adequately or consistently the manner in which the world would again
become comprehensible politically or socially.

One could object that Martin Luther King's great speech at the
Reflecting Pond describing the new society that would be built on the
old, or the optimism of "Aquarius" and the Flower Children was sufficient
demonstration of a new order to attract a following and blunt the forces
of reaction. But again we assume in this objection that the minimum
definition of decency operates to pull people forward to a greater experience of their humanity. Spontaneity of visions can be inspirational,
but they do not provide the myriad of minutiae demanded by a society
in turmoil and change. Solutions in a social movement must come nearly
as fast or at least as profoundly as the events that disrupt the society.

We cannot conceive of non-violence today without remembering
the grandeur of former days when our motives were pure, our cause
just, and our movement charging with single-minded determination
toward a not-too-distant goal. As we recall former days, we should not
despair at our lost innocence or degrade our memories of times of crisis
and danger. Regardless of how far we appear to be from our original
goal, the fact remains that we have changed the world in an irreversible
manner, and in participating in what has been essentially an act of
creation, we have broadened the boundaries of a possible minimum
definition of decency which now needs to find the time to incarnate
itself and grow old, familiar, and wear thin until we can rediscover at an
even greater depth the absence of a commonly shared realization of our
humanity.

*

Non-violence seems to be an exhaustive and consuming avenue in which the conditions for creation can occur. As such it consumes lives either in a corresponding violence of reaction or in an enervating passage of time in which the passion of justice becomes the wisdom of perspective. It would do well for us, in these days of institutional paranoia and political perversion of our lives, to reflect on the nature of non-violence as the procreative act necessary to trigger forces beyond the comprehension of any expectations we might have had.

Social existence in a real sense is the continual testing, expansion, and retesting of possible definitions of the meaning of human existence. The non-violent response to conditions is perhaps the most explosive method of change available to the human species, for it instantaneously freezes the definitions which orient humans at the deepest level of identity crisis and it forces these definitions which have been covered over by vague and comfortable beliefs to come together for a testing of the integrity of the world. And when that integrity is found wanting, as it will always be, because of the nature of our existence in time, a creational process must certainly ensue which can be benign or evil, but which most certainly will come to pass.

The final question for any society, therefore, is not how much violence it can take, but how much non-violence it can take. American society quite probably can take no more non-violence at present. Its myths are facing a geometrically increasing rate of dissolution with the revelations that the most profound representatives of its former myths, the politicians, are far behind the ordinary citizen in discovering a minimum definition of a human being. The most profound disruption today would be the articulation of common-sense alternatives, common sense being the rarest of human characteristics.

The very logic of our institutions compels such disruption. Pardons, it would seem, must abound if the most profound criminal of all has already received his pardon. If success can only be achieved through trickery and deceit, then the only criteria for action can be inconsistency, and we already see this eloquently demonstrated in Congress and our other institutions, for even good trickery can be predicted and only the arbitrary can be seen as a rational principle of operation. The very chaos of our times would seem to indicate a change for the better, because we appear to be exhausting all possible rationales for our existence. The inevitable logics that locked our minds into predetermined patterns of behavior are giving way to the possibility of the freedom of exploration of the meaning of human existence.

It was perhaps this intuitive leap that Martin Luther King and others made when they described the civil rights results as being "free at last," for the connection is not immediately obvious to most of us. We come, then, to the original boundary of non-violence, the proposition that no significant number of people will depart from the generally anticipated patterns of behavior. In a society unwinding its rationale, there can be no deviations, merely a series of choices, but these choices will not be choices taught to us as the proper choices, they will simply be those paths of life that seem proper, attractive, and meaningful.

But finally, there is simply the profound sadness that comes to us when we hear old songs, recall half-forgotten incidents, or see the debris of places that once meant so much to so many people. Contrary to the American social doctrine, it is really good to be sad for a while. The final dimension of non-violence must certainly be in the comfort of the remembrance of having practiced it once in one's life and in allowing its mellowed wisdom to flow back in warmth, occasionally.

Debate over the validity of non-violence as a technique for social change must certainly and finally give way to one thing, among many that humans seem to share: expectations. Unless human beings have or are allowed to generate a certain number of expectations, they have no distinctions from the other life forms and probably do not do as well as the other life forms in fulfilling themselves. The demonstration of non-violence is the ultimate expression of expectation, because it opens the possibility of discovering that one is not alone—which is the only affirmation we have of our existence.

We have been and we will continue to be in a state of creation, generated a decade and a half ago. If we cannot see the waves of unexpected change sweeping over us as the direct result of the non-violence of the past and see that it is time to build and plant, then we have badly misunderstood the dimensions of our own existence. We will have mistakenly committed a final rejection of our own deepest beliefs in the efficacy of redemptive suffering which, once unleashed, energizes the universe and sweeps everything clean before it. We have no choice now but to follow the spirit where it leads.

There is, after all, no other way out.

(1974)

5

THE CHURCHES
AND CULTURAL CHANGE

Many accusations have been made in recent years about the role of the Christian churches in Indian Affairs. This role goes back to the earliest contacts between whites and Indians and one of the first and most continuous contributions of the churches has been in education. Many of the earliest colleges and schools of this country were originally set up for the education of Indian children. Such schools as Dartmouth, Harvard, and Oberlin were begun as Indian schools and gradually were transformed into private colleges.

The role of the churches in the education of Indians continued after the colonies broke with Great Britain and formed the United States. Many of the early treaties contained provisions giving the missionaries parcels of land in return for providing education. In the Ohio Valley and Great Lakes areas church groups received land for schools and by the 1830s much of the formal schooling of the eastern tribes was by missionaries.

One has to distinguish between the early missionary efforts and those of the later missionaries who came to the tribes in the West. In general the early missionaries were less inclined to become involved in the political affairs of the tribes and more concerned with providing good education and religious instruction. Many tribes favored specific denominations and often almost the whole tribe would become members. This was particularly true with the Five Civilized Tribes, who strongly favored the Baptists and Methodists. A native clergy existed quite early among the Choctaws, Cherokees, and Creeks, and the social customs were simply transformed from older Indian meanings to newer Christian forms of gathering.

In the early 1830s four Nez Percé arrived at St. Louis asking about a sacred book they had heard about. They were referring, of course, to the Bible, and their arrival happened to coincide with a desire of many Christians in the East that missionaries be sent to the distant tribes. Instead of the more intimate relationship that had grown up naturally between the tribes and the individual missionaries, the new missionary activity took on the aspect of cultural imperialism and religious activities took secondary place to the involvement of the churches in the great policy questions of Indian Affairs.

From 1830 to 1871 the churches played an important role in the development of government policy in the field of Indian Affairs. Church officials served on treaty commissions as official members, translators, and secretaries, and they often saw their role as helping subdue the Indians rather than impartially guaranteeing justice for the Indians. The result was great injustice to the tribes of the West, partly because the churches failed to carry out their promises in treaty negotiations.

One can easily compare the actions of the early missionaries with those of later years. The Rev. Samuel Worcester, a missionary to the Cherokees from the American Board of Commissioners for Foreign Missions, played a vital role in Cherokee history. After Sequoia invented the Cherokee alphabet, Worcester helped them get a printing press. Not only was the Bible printed in Cherokee, but also a newspaper, the *Cherokee Phoenix,* was printed on the press, indicating that Worcester considered his duties to encompass all of Cherokee life. Worcester and another missionary followed the Cherokee tribal laws and were thrown into prison by the Georgia state authorities for their loyalty to the Cherokee Nation. It was the Worcester case that finally justified the Cherokee position.

Contrasting the role of Samuel Worcester with that of other missionaries in later years, the difference is clear. Bishop Whipple, for example, and Bishop Hare, the Episcopal missionary leaders of Minnesota and South Dakota, were more concerned with the settlement of Minnesota and surrounding states than with the preservation of the Sioux and Chippewa tribes. They played a very influential role in having the reservations of their states allotted. Bishop Hare viewed the change of government policy as a great arena in which to test the validity of the Christian doctrines. Commenting on the General Allotment Act, he noted that "Time will show whether the world or the Church will be more on the alert to take advantage of the occasion" (of allotment).

It was, of course, no contest, since the churches did very little to ensure that the "world" did not take advantage of the Indians. During the allotment process many church missionary societies were on hand to get choice parcels of land for their activities. On the Sioux reservations, for example, the churches did not simply get land for churches and cemeteries, but they also received choice grazing lands and used the income from these lands to support their own ventures.

On the West Coast the most famous Protestant missionary was Marcus Whitman. He had been sent to the tribes of eastern Oregon and western Idaho to provide religious instruction and education to the people of that area. He proved to be so intractable in his attitude toward the Indians that eventually they rebelled against him and killed him. In view of his intolerable attitude toward all things Indian, it is a wonder that he was not dispatched earlier.

Perhaps the most brutal of the church missionary efforts was that conducted by the Catholic missionaries in New Mexico, Arizona, and California. They saw Indians as serfs to be placed upon the lands of their missions to do their bidding. These people were not above waging war against the small Indian tribes of their region in order to convert them or kill them. The radical attitude of intolerance found in the Catholic Inquisition carried over in their policies toward American Indians until very recent times. As late as 1966 a Catholic priest was intruding into the lives of the Pueblo Indians by degrading their ceremonies and demanding an absolute obedience to his dictates.

The accusation most frequently made against the churches concerns the role they played in the passage of the General Allotment Act by Congress. Many church bodies saw the policy as a means of civilizing the tribes and sent a constant stream of resolutions to Washington in support of the Allotment policy. The Presbyterians in particular seemed to regard the policy as the special instrument of Christian activities in the last quarter of the nineteenth century. It was their opinion that as long as the tribes held their lands in common the Indians would be able to continue the old ceremonies and maintain the traditional community life derived from the tribal religions. On the other hand, the division of tribal lands would split the clans and make it easier to convert them as individuals.

The era of the Allotment policy remains a mystery to people today because so little has been written about it. Defenders of church policy have claimed that the pressures for division of tribal lands was so strong among the non-religious peoples in American society that allotment actually saved some land for the Indians. Until more research is done, it will be difficult to judge whether the churches were correct in supporting allotment or not. Bishop Hare expressed an attitude supporting allotment, but the churches then refused to get involved in the problems created by allot-ment and allowed "the world" to triumph over the Indians by default.

The educational role of the churches continued to be an important one after the establishment of the reservations. Although the govern-ment advocated the creation of special boarding schools, it was very slow in building these schools and the only education available to the tribes for a long period was in church schools. These schools taught a combina-tion of American culture and Christianity which provided stability for the reservation communities. Many Indian community leaders during the 1920s and 1930s were trained in mission schools; without the church schooling it is doubtful whether many tribes could have maintained themselves as viable communities.

Resurgence of tribalism in the late 1920s and early 1930s stimulated the missionaries to oppose the Indian Reorganization Act and the Native American Church. Both the I.R.A. and the Native American Church offered opportunities for Indian communities to express themselves, but the missionaries did not see it that way. Many did not appreciate the value of the indigenous religious activity represented by the practices of the Native American Church and went to great lengths to discredit those who participated in the peyote rituals. The cry of religious freedom stirred Congress to write guarantees of religious freedom into the Indian Reorganization Act to ensure that the missionaries would leave the tradi-tional Indians alone.

An attitude of romance entered into missionary activities sometime during the twentieth century, transforming the missionaries as this atti-tude entrenched itself. Earlier missionaries, while playing policy-makers of Indian rights, had gradually become an important part of the lives of Indian communities. The stories of incredible hardships suffered by the missionaries in performing their duties were not exaggerations. More than one missionary drove his team of horses through a blizzard to min-ister to the sick and infirm and great distances were covered by these people who made themselves available to the reservation people when-ever they were needed.

In this century the missionary attitude seemed to change. A mission-ary would come for a few years, get a taste of the "white man's burden," and then move on. Missionaries became instant experts after a few weeks in the field and made no effort to understand the ancient tradi-tions of the people. Intolerance and impatience characterized this newer group and one of the first tangible indications of this new attitude was the refusal of the churches to recruit native clergy. From 1940 to 1960 many of the churches seemed to be deliberately avoiding the ordination of native clergy. Missionary work became a matter of expediency and not a mission at all.

The situation has changed somewhat since 1960 and has come to reflect what one can only call the "ideological" period of church involvement with American Indians. As the Civil Rights movement gained momentum church people began a subtle program to involve Indians in Civil Rights. Indians became, in their eyes, a sub-group of the black community; many lessons learned in working with American blacks were considered applicable to American Indians in spite of the cultural differences between the groups.

When the Civil Rights movement aborted and the "power movements" began, the churches abruptly switched their support to the more militant members of the Indian community. Much of the recent activism, both good and bad, was supported by church funds and given emphasis by church magazines and newsletters. Although not all of this support was bad, the attitudes which sparked such support were. Many high church officials were as intolerant of differences of opinion as their spiritual predecessors had been a century earlier in advocating allotment.

The situation is still badly out of balance. Many church officials, especially those at the national level, continue to deal almost exclusively with the activists and deliberately avoid contact with the other segments of the Indian community. As a result, church funds for Indian work go to support large demonstrations rather than to assist Indians and whites in solving complex problems. Some of the churches gave funds to the Alaska Natives to help them solve their land claims problem; this money was well spent. But when the Menominees sought financial support to overturn their termination legislation, few churches gave them support; instead they invested their funds in exotic and badly-conceived projects of little worth.

Among the churches working with Indians one group seems to stand out as more effective and more concerned than the others. That group is the Quakers. The American Friends Service Committee fought side by side with the Senecas to preserve their reservation at Salamanca, New York during the early 1960s. The battle was lost and Kinzua Dam was built by the Army Corps of Engineers, but no one can fault the Friends for their work on behalf of the Senecas. They did everything that a small group could have done.

In the Pacific Northwest the Friends have involved themselves in the fishing rights controversy. In 1967 they prepared a report, later issued as a paperback book by the University of Washington Press, entitled *Uncommon Controversy*. It is the best work to date on the nature and background of the fishing rights problem of the tribes of Washington, Oregon, and Idaho, even though it focuses only on three small tribes. Fishing rights in the Northwest is an ongoing problem charged with emotion but, with the exception of the Friends and Bishop Ivol Curtis of the Episcopal Church in Washington, few churches or church officials have supported the Indians.

One is always perplexed in attempting to evaluate the performance of the Christian churches in the field of Indian Affairs. National church bodies seem to be more concerned than the local or state church groups, but when policy is made by people two thousand miles away, mistakes are certain to be made. Such groups cannot be expected to be aware of all the developments taking place in remote parts of the nation. Yet church attention to Indian matters ebbs and flows. Not a single Christian church has a consistent policy concerning its role among American Indians. The Indian caucus has to do some tough lobbying at each church convention in order to save the programs for Indians. Every few years the policies of the churches shift, seeming to reflect the immediate concerns of the secular groups in American domestic politics, and Indians are expected to change with the new issues.

The commitment of the major denominations with Indian missions to develop a native clergy is, at best, weak. Over the last two decades one could only conclude that the churches will eventually give up all of their religious activities on the reservations. If this happens, the move may be viewed either as a final resolution of the Indian religious problem or as abandonment of the Indians by the churches. For better or for worse, the Christian churches *do* represent a tangible expression of whatever sense of morality or integrity American society has left. As such, the Indian people need some clearly defined relationship to the churches, since the issues of treaties and education that must be raised with the government are essentially moral and ethical and require the assistance of the churches.

Appreciation of the long history of church involvement with the tribes is desperately needed. Some major Protestant denominations have a record of worth going back for centuries. Yet, with every new reorganization of the national church staffs, this history is lost or deliberately neglected by the incoming staff members. Misunderstandings result from dealing with church people who do not appreciate their own past achievements in the field of Indian affairs. Too often the facts of social movement are allowed to determine the course of action and continuity is lost. As the power movements gained popularity and the demand for the employment of minority group members escalated, the reorganizations of church national bodies simply eliminated many experienced people with significant achievements and experience in Indian Affairs in favor of temporary and token people who spoke the current jargon of change. This type of thoughtless disruption of relationships must be discontinued if the churches are to preserve any relationship with Indian communities in the future.

(1974)

6

GCSP

The Demons At Work

In 1967 at the General Convention in Seattle the Episcopal Church authorized the creation of a "General Convention Special Program" designed to enable the church to meet the special needs of racial minorities and underprivileged peoples. By 1973 when the program was officially terminated the GCSP had alienated both majority and minority membership groups in the church. Contributions to the general program of the church had fallen precipitously. And the image of the Episcopal Church was badly tarnished. Many longtime members of the church had vowed never to return and the church has yet to recoup its former prestige.

The next generation of scholars may well examine the church archives and conclude that the GCSP was a heroic effort during a time of severe crisis in American society. Documents alone do not constitute an accurate historical appraisal and it will never be possible for future critics to transport themselves backwards into the tension-packed emotions which composed much of the activity of the program. But the increasing tensions of modern life and the deterioration of the quality of life which we are presently experiencing may lead many church members some day in the future to attempt to meet the needs of society by authorizing a similar program and thus it is imperative that some of us who participated in this program reflect on the nature of the beast and record our impressions for future scholars to heed.

I was a member of the Screening and Review Committee of the GCSP for several years (representing the American Indian community), I was a member of the Executive Council for nearly a year, and I had something of an insider's view to the deliberations of staff in their conception of the program and to the considerations of the Executive Council in meeting some of the crises generated by the program. I resigned in total disgust with the GCSP and the Executive Council in the fall of 1969 just after the Notre Dame convention. The pain involved in these decisions reflects more than intellectual disagreement since my family had been prominently involved in the mission of the Episcopal Church to the American Indian community since the 1870s.

The Episcopal Church slept peacefully in the post-war years assuming that the world had not fundamentally changed with the introduction of the United States in the role of dominant military power on the planet. During the 1950s the church was not in the forefront of the human rights movement. Indeed, some of the most prominent personalities who signed the letter to Martin Luther King asking him to cease demonstrations while he was in jail in Birmingham and chiding him for using the Christian religion for political purposes were Episcopal bishops. During the traumatic years of the middle 1950s when the Congress was aggressively violating Indian treaties the Episcopal church gave silent but powerful support to the policies of the Interior Department by refusing to support the efforts of American Indians to counter the destructive acts of the government. It was not until quite late in the 1950s that the church began to awaken to the problems then plaguing American society.

By the early sixties a few perceptive people in the church began to understand that radical changes were under way and some minor efforts to support reform movements were undertaken. Travel money was often supplied to activists in the different minority communities and small grants primarily designed to "enable" people to undertake new organizing efforts were made. On the whole these grants were extremely helpful since neither budgets nor organizations were large and the public had not yet accepted the thesis of reform which made larger activities imperative. As we entered the decade of disaster, the sixties, the Episcopal Church was seen by many people as friendly but somewhat aloof and represented a more mature tradition than most institutions on the American scene. Its entrance into the Civil Rights movement was one of the signals to many observers that the moral and ethical issues which Civil Rights symbolized were substantial and serious.

A constituency of social reformers emerged within the racial minorities which looked with increasing respect to the Episcopal Church. As an ally the church had much to offer; it was a friendly and sure hand, not a fatal embrace. Although far from a major commitment, the increasing trickle of aid given to minority groups left a gap between proclaimed values and practical commitment but served to preserve the independence of the organizations of the racial minorities both politically and financially. The Episcopal Church, like some of the other Protestant denominations, bought a little of the action. The religious institutions, however, represented a much greater influence, that of moral authority, when they participated in social movements. Secular authorities, perhaps remembering ecclesiastical participation in the abolition of slavery, were reluctant to test their powers against the churches in the civil rights area. Potential, rather than direct participation, seemed to pose the greater threat to those oppressing the blacks.

By the time of the March on Washington in 1963 the alliance between the major denominations and the Civil Rights movement had been firmly cemented. Personalities from all levels of church life emerged in the movement and the moral authority which the church possessed gave great impetus to the expanding concern for human rights. Some of the images etched in my mind during 1963 and 1964 are not flattering: sleek church bureaucrats rushing through airports with briefcases aflutter on their way to speak *for* Indians and blacks, personnel of "Church and Society" divisions purchasing new bib-overalls so they could participate in the final day of the Selma March and not look out of place, naive church officials explaining to Indians that they must not sing missionary hymns now but must adopt "We Shall Overcome" as their anthem. In retrospect, while these images seem hypocritical, they vividly chronicle an institution making up for lost time through the expenditure of vast sums of money and much personal energy and concern.

Some church leadership was creative and outstanding. In May 1964 under the leadership of the Episcopal Church, the American Indian community held a critical "National Conference on Indian Poverty," which coincided with the debates in the Senate on the Economic Opportunity Act. Recognizing that massive publicly had to be given to Indian poverty, Clifford Samuelson and Betty Rosenthal, then in charge of the Indian work, struggled and sweated and pulled together the most important single conference ever held dealing with Indian matters. Hubert Humphrey, then under consideration for the Vice Presidential spot on the Democratic ticket, spoke to the conference and pledged that Indians would not be forgotten. Indians were given a special designation in the Office of Economic Opportunity and in the years since the O.E.O. became law Indian tribes and communities benefitted to the tune of several billion dollars in program grants. Proper leverage, made possible by church involvement, meant significant results in the early sixties.

In 1966 when Black Power suddenly emerged, the media assumed the role of interpreter of national moral issues. Using graphic illustrations, many times staged beforehand, and searching for emotionally-laden images which would convey a belated sense of outrage, the media soon dominated the articulation of issues and it became more important for minority spokesmen to be seen than heard. Media domination with the subsequent reliance on increasing emotional shock value and the decrease of analytical articulation of strategy seemed to catch church officials off guard. One incident led to another and the propensity for violence seemed to increase geometrically. By mid-1967 there were probably more "staged" demonstrations than spontaneous outbursts and the emphasis became less the enforcement of rights and more the accusations of guilt. "Symbolic" demonstrations to communicate poverty and oppression replaced calculated protests designed to open specific fields of opportunity to the politically oppressed.

Perhaps the highlight of this era was the journey of James Foreman through the various church headquarters in New York City in May 1969. The bureaucrats at Episcopal Church headquarters at 815 programmed Foreman's visit and had several practice runs to ensure that they could entertain this symbolic event and escape unscathed with no one accidentally hurt or police running riot in the building. Foreman called for reparations of $500 million to be paid to the black community. The American Indian Movement, with new black berets on their heads, were not to be outdone. Later that year Dennis Banks attended a meeting of the National Council of Churches and demanded $750 million for Indians. No one, apparently, could yet think it terms of the billions that were already being spent in the War on Poverty.

I dwell on the background of GCSP to remind us that times were quite different. No one had the key to social problems and the movement seemed destined to stride across a tranquillity of American psyches and emerge on the other side with a regenerated social conscience that would end racism, poverty, and oppression in our lifetime. Paranoia still existed among the more conservative church members who could not understand the radical changes then engulfing America. One bishop took me aside at a conference after I had said that young Indians admired SNCC and in ominous terms warned me that SNCC's zip code in Atlanta, Georgia, was the same as the Communist Party headquarters in that city. The significance of this relationship always escaped me. But the important thing about those frantic years in which GCSP was born is the uncontrolled emotions which ebbed and flowed and had no value system or set of goals in which they could incarnate themselves. There were, therefore, no good guidelines in 1967 by which any program of massive financial assistance could have been regulated and in this confusion the Episcopal Church authorized a major program with substantial financial commitment.

The actual implementation of the GCSP can only be characterized charitably as "unfortunate." In the milieu of "power" movements it was impossible for the Presiding Bishop not to choose a member of a minority group and Leon Modeste, then a rather obscure church bureaucrat with a minor function in social programs, was propelled directly upwards in the church organization to the second most prominent and powerful post in 815. Modeste had as allies in his new role several people brought in with John Hines as part of his entourage—Walker Taylor and Jack Woodard in particular. These three men seemed to have but one rule of thumb—trust no one who has been in the field before. Minor staff members who were recruited to serve under Modeste, Taylor and Woodard reflected this attitude, shared their suspicions of former staff members and, to ensure themselves a place in the direction of power flowing from the new program, acted to reinforce and cultivate this feeling of mistrust.

The paranoia that characterized the Nixon White House can be seen first in the GCSP. Future historians may wonder at the flurry of resignations and reassignments which followed in the wake of the initiation of the GCSP. They need only interview the now bitter former employees of church headquarters. Not only were major staff personalities edged, pushed, and shunted aside; their secretaries and minor staff people were also fired or forced to resign for fear that they would have some lingering loyalty to their former bosses. Within a very short time the church headquarters had no collective memory of what had gone before. A desperate seige mentality affected the entire building and an unarticulated fear of GCSP infected the working relationships of the church.

The original guidelines of GCSP called for representation of the poor although it was no secret that the program had been called forth by the activities of the black community alone. Indians and Chicanos and the unorganized white poor had as yet played no major role in American politics and were unrecognized as forces which had to be placated. Thus there was a resentment by black bureaucrats and their new white liberal allies against the participation of other minority groups in the programs of GCSP. I fully understood their anger. They had died in countless incidents in the South. We had done little or nothing of a spectacular nature to warrant the benefits which were now accruing to us. Extending the spectrum of eligibility across the board to oppressed groups may have been a politically feasible way of getting the General Convention Special Program funded, but it handicapped the programs severely—I would insist fatally—by depriving the black community of the one real tangible victory they had won in the church and insisting that they share it with groups who had stood by while they bled.

In the late fall of 1969 I circulated a petition among the Indians of Episcopal missions throughout the church which called for "More Real

Involvement" of the Episcopal Church in Indian Affairs. With the departure of Clifford Samuelson the Episcopal Church had literally vanished from its prominent role in Indian matters, which had been achieved only a half-decade before in the conference on Indian Poverty. The petition received favorable action in the form of a resolution by the Executive Council at the December meeting and we were given funds to call conferences across the nation to determine what regular church membership among Indians thought the church should be doing. Unfortunately this program was destroyed bureaucratically before it could be implemented.

MRI (More Real Involvement for Indians) both terrified and annoyed Modeste and Woodard and, one can only conclude, both confused and frightened the Presiding Bishop. The petition came from Indians inside the Episcopal Church but the interpretation given to the Executive Council resolution by Jack Woodard required us to choose three Indians from inside the church and three from outside the church as members of the Steering Committee. It was then that I discovered the real paranoia of the GCSP staff. Before we could submit a list of members or confer with the Presiding Bishop a list of outside Indians was presented to us and contained the names of Indians who had achieved some media exposure but had accomplished little of substance as Indian leaders. One person was a delightful woman whose only qualification for the committee was that she was the widow of a formerly prominent Indian.

It was apparent to all informed Indians who had supported the petition that the GCSP staff had simply telephoned activists all over the country seeking the most inflammatory personalities to recommend for service on the committee. I tried to convey the sense of frustration to the Presiding Bishop in a meeting but he only listened silently and thanked me for talking with him. Leaving his office that day I realized that he was a prisoner of militant rhetoric who could not distinguish either issues or personalities. He seemed to support the general interpretation given at 815 about the Indian petition—that it was a direct threat and insult to GCSP. After much argument I got the name of Hank Adams, then the most prominent and constructive of the Indian activists, leader of the Survival of American Indians fishing rights group, named to the committee in place of one of the original outsiders.

Hank Adams is a very quiet, unassuming person who does his homework brilliantly, is consistently a decade ahead of the rest of the field, and relies upon the spectacular only when everything else fails. He attended the first meeting of the Steering Committee dressed in slacks, a sweater and military raincoat, spoke quietly but firmly and humorously, and made several very incisive comments on the nature of the task before us. Hank was hardly out of the building before the staff began accusing me of

doublecrossing them in insisting on Adams' appointment. I learned that
Adams' credentials as a militant were zilch because "he didn't dress like a
militant." That is to say, Hank didn't have buckskin and sunglasses and a
vocal, brutal style of rhetoric. My reliability in the eyes of 815 went to
zero because of Hank and thereafter everything I said was promptly discredited by zealous GCSP staff who would spend hours telephoning other
Indians in an effort to get another opinion on a subject.

I dwell at length on the Adams incident because it illustrates one of
the major flaws in the operations of GCSP and led directly to its failure.
GCSP staff had no natural constituency in the minorities and adopted the
attitude that anyone then in power in the various national organizations
which represented racial minorities was part of the problem, not a useful
and experienced ally in a great crusade, I remember Tollie Caution, who
had headed the church's program for blacks during the 1950s, walking
quietly out of 815 one day shaking his head and muttering about a GCSP
staff member who arrogantly asked if he had been at Selma. "I was at
Selma when a black man couldn't spend the night in Selma," he sighed
sadly. And one of the greatest black Christian priests in the history of the
Episcopal church was tagged a "Tom" because he wasn't one of the
protest generation and no one in GCSP knew enough about the Episcopal
Church to recognize the great contributions this man had made in a previous generation when things were tough.

GCSP thus deliberately created its own constituency. Through the use
of extensive travel and the capability of making grants the GCSP staff
made contacts in all parts of the country and made certain that only people of similar mind and attitude shared in the benefits of the program.
Since they were continually seeking more and more spectacular spokesmen it was natural that the program would drift perilously close to supporting violent revolutionaries. Protests by local bishops and informed
churchmen in various dioceses were turned aside with hints that the
protest was generated by racial considerations. Since no one wished to be
tagged as a racist when he was simply demanding accountability,
protests declined and this lack of friction was cited as evidence that the
program was working.

Church leadership backed away from the GCSP because its posture
precluded rational discussion. Conservatives were generally outvoted in
Executive Council and there was no doubt that the Presiding Bishop
would throw his prestige and political weight into the fray if any serious
effort were made to change the direction of GCSP. But formal protests
were few and far between. Bishop Bayne was always available to listen to
complaints and approached many of the questions in a rational, sympathetic manner but his loyalty to the Presiding Bishop outweighed his

concern or taste for additional conflict. Thus GCSP marched down the road of no return echoing the sentiments of an editorial published in *The Christian Century* discussing the Foreman Manifesto:

> Further deep down we know that to attempt to pay up could spell the death of the corrupt American church. In such an event the Church might by a miracle of grace be raised anew; but we can no longer trust in miracles, sold out as we are to secularism, and we fear for the very survival of our religiously useful institutions.

The insanity continued for six years and during its closing years theological recitations of the necessity of destroying the church in order to save it were heard at 815—the very rhetoric and reasoning which military experts used to justify the destruction of Vietnamese villages.

GCSP faced a critical meeting at Notre Dame and several of the program grants were discussed. Some of the liberal proponents argued that the church should respond to the ailments of society and justified their votes on the need for total commitment. After the first session of the Executive Council I had a short discussion with the Presiding Bishop. I told him that I thought the church was reactionary in that it had no theology or philosophy for understanding the crisis then engulfing American society and had adopted the posture of reacting to crises, some of which were wholly artificial and induced by the availability of grants rather than oppressing social conditions. But he was firmly set in the direction of GCSP and refused to consider my arguments. Since it was impossible to continue to support either the GCSP or the now co-opted Indian program, I left Notre Dame and wrote a letter of resignation from the Executive Council the evening I returned home. I wanted to send a letter of sympathy to John Hines when he retired but thought it might be taken as a further sign of disagreement. But I was delighted when the program was discontinued—enough damage had been done.

Discussing the pain and trauma of the sixties today is not a pleasant task and analysis of that decade should move beyond the personalities involved. It was a disastrous decade when frenzy gripped American society and I doubt we shall see its like again for such extravaganzas deplete the communal reservoir of moral outrage and spiritual energy. More important, I think, is that the church does not attempt to follow the traditional path of Western civilization and cover up the mistakes of GCSP. As we move away from that era of church history the emotions of those years will recede and memories will recast old conflicts into minor disagreements. Fearful that the church might be hurt by an honest admission of error, future historians will vest the activities of the sixties with generous interpretations attributing to motives and attitudes a charitable content which never existed.

The elements which serve to create, support, and justify the style and substance of the GCSP years are, to my way of thinking, of such fundamental nature that they transcend the personalities who happened to inhabit 815 during those years. The most important missing ingredient was the lack of a consistent and relevant theology. The Episcopal Church had embraced the shades of Rudyard Kipling and the styles of imperialistic England for too long to make a sudden, sophisticated, and substantial move into America of the sixties. When it did move the Episcopal Church chose the most tangible but least sophisticated weapon in its institutional arsenal: Money. Unless the church moves substantially into the support of theological education of considerable content, it will probably remain vulnerable to the ebb and flow of popular social issues and become a pale version of a private foundation.

Even without a sound theological base the church might have done significantly better during the sixties had it paid any attention to its own history. Not only did the church have little knowledge of its past accomplishments, with the departure of career employees it lost all knowledge of the immediate organizational past and GCSP's attitude that present conditions were a direct result of past staff failures eliminated any appeals to the history of the church and to its considerable previous achievements. The conditions of poverty and racism emphasized in the sixties were the cumulative products of many institutional failures not the least of which was the federal failure to guarantee individual and group citizenship rights. Yet the attitude of GCSP seemed to assume that the Episcopal Church alone had committed social and racial sins and the demand for institutional self-sacrifice cast aside any moral leadership which the church might have exercised in favor of wholly political considerations. An absolutely critical task for the church today is to recapture some knowledge of its past and ensure that anyone serving in an administrative capacity is fully aware of the church's historical mission and experience. Future decisions must take into account this history and see themselves as part of a continuing tradition of service, not as a fire department rushing about with a bucket of water in the bowels of a volcano.

Without any theological or historical base the church could not have escaped many of the errors and personal tragedies of GCSP but there need not have been these personal hardships had there been a tradition of respect for minority groups. GCSP should have been designed specifically for the black community. They had earned special attention and they had long-standing responsible organizations fully capable of initiating the proper reforms. There was no need for the church to handicap the black constituency within the church in favor of carrying approval from militants outside the church. The failure to bring the black clergy into a dominant role in the philosophy and programming of GCSP indicates a distrust and perhaps hatred of blacks within the church that had not been overcome. GCSP staff treated the other minority groups in the same way they had been treated. The other minorities were conceived to be smaller variants of the black militancy movement and those who behaved like black militants received grants, those who failed to conform to outward symbolic dress and rhetoric were excluded. Obviously this problem is longstanding and as much a peculiarity of the American psyche as a mortal sin of the Episcopal Church.

The real victims of this era are the countless anonymous people who were led on to senseless acts of violence or protest with the assurance that the churches would be beside them. At one point in my continuing battle with GCSP staff, and in discussions with IFCO, the National Council of Churches version of GCSP, I argued that increasingly hostile protests should not be supported and that revolutionary rhetoric should not be encouraged because there were many individuals who would not be able to draw the boundaries which distinguish useful activity from senseless acts. In the last several years I have gotten a number of letters from inmates in prisons or families who have relatives in prison whose conviction originated in the activities of the sixties. Almost universally they relate a story of disbelief—they did not believe they would be punished because everyone was doing it.

I think of the many nameless young Indians who grabbed their Sears and Roebuck twenty-two-caliber rifles and marched to Wounded Knee thinking that it would be exciting and heroic but never dreaming that it would be real and that the federal officers would be shooting back. That tragedy was averted there and in other instances is testimony to the basic decency and common sense shown by many law enforcement officials in those perilous times. While many activists were killed by police in the sixties, the potential which that decade held for mass killing is still chilling to contemplate.

We live now in a new decade in which the thirst for roots has often manifested itself in a selfish concentration on pleasures of the moment. The faddish "Marin County complex"—I want it all, now, and more tomorrow, and twice as much the next day—fatally affects our ability to regroup and resolve our perennial social problems. The churches must begin to deal with this final, and perhaps terminal, secularization of Protestant theology's solitary individual standing before an angry god because no one believes that such a creature exists.

The lessons of GCSP are manifold but can be summarized in three major areas. We badly need a consistent and comprehensive theology which relates human experiences of divinity in an intelligent context and speaks to the human conditions that the secularization of the old Christian worldview has created. We must understand our separate historical journeys and come to see ourselves as planetary peoples with responsibilities extending to all parts and beings of the universe. For those remaining in the Episcopal Church such an understanding must include the specific ventures of that institution, its considerable successes and its occasional mistakes. We must come to see that real differences exist among the various groups that come into contact with the ecclesiastical institutions and that these differences make it imperative that church programs are not conceived as a homogenous solution to be applied with force and intolerance to conditions and peoples. If we can learn these lessons, GCSP will have been one of the most valuable experiences in the historical life of the church.

(1979)

LIBERATING THEOLOGY

Political struggles taking place throughout Africa, Asia, and the Americas during the sixties and seventies provided fertile ground for the growth of a radically new variety of Christian theological discourse, a diffuse movement of critical, contextual formulations commonly referred to as theologies of liberation. Among the earliest expressions of liberation theology were Black Theology in the United States and Latin American Liberation Theology, which emerged simultaneously but independently in the late sixties, the former among black Protestant theologians and ministers, the latter among European-trained Roman Catholic theologians and priests. Despite the obvious differences in their religious orientations and sociopolitical contexts, these and other liberation theologians have made surprisingly compatible methodological choices and thematic interpretations. Liberation theologies lay claim to being the intellectual expressions of Christian life on the underside of history; they are rooted in rigorous social and cultural analysis and a personal commitment to solidarity with the oppressed, and they advocate a radical reordering of human relations guided by prophetic religious critique.

Liberation has been one of the most popular and influential motifs in contemporary Christian theology, though liberation theology has also had its detractors. Deloria was one of the first Americans to mount a sustained critique of the liberation theology movement—and one of the very few to challenge it from the *left*—when he questioned the validity of its epistemological roots. Concluding that liberation theology is methodologically problematic because of its (initially) uncritical dependence on Western philosophical assumptions and modes of social analysis, he suggested that theology itself needs to be liberated, not just patched up with some revolutionary rhetoric and biblical texts on social justice. If we are serious about "the necessity of liberation," he argued, "we are talking about the destruction of the whole complex of Western theories of knowledge and the construction of a new and more comprehensive synthesis of human knowledge and experience." The reversal of agency implied in the shift from *liberation* theology to *liberating* theology illustrates Deloria's rigorous approach to intellectual debates that address power relations.

The first two essays in this section explore the relationship between religious and political ideologies in American society. "A Violated Covenant" was written for an American Indian issue of *Event,* a monthly magazine for men in the American Lutheran Church. Deloria locates the theological basis for political treaties in the notion of covenant, and for their wholesale violation in the theological tension between covenant and the idea of dominion over creation. Contemporary Indian problems "stem almost directly from Protestant theology and a misapplication of basic biblical ideas in the arena of political thought," and these problems will persist until Americans take seriously their own moral integrity as a nation. "An Open Letter to the Heads of the Christian Churches in America" inaugurated a monthly series of public statements from political, religious, and intellectual leaders published by *The Forum for Contemporary History.* The theological dilemma of colonialism produced the Doctrine of Discovery, just as the theological dilemma of nationalism later produced the Doctrine of Manifest Destiny; "in every era of man's existence religions have acted to give to political institutions the justification, incentive, and heart to exist." Deloria challenges American Christian leaders to adopt a more credible theory of history and to hold their political leaders accountable to a higher sense of justice and humanity.

The next two essays, which originally appeared in *Katallagete—Be Reconciled,* pick up on these themes. "It Is a Good Day to Die" was Deloria's contribution to a thematic issue on vocation and religious commitment. He approaches the topic by probing the limits of religion and law as social systems. He shares with liberation theologians the conviction that our theologies follow from the kinds of commitments we make, but he is more adventurous than most in exploring how far-reaching these commitments might be. This autobiographical reflection recounts the tension between ideology and experience that Deloria encountered in both seminary and law school. He finds this dilemma evident most clearly in the circular logic that characterizes the relationship between American religion and law, "each ultimately pointing to the other as the binding thesis of its existence." Deloria argues that we should begin by examining the actual practices of living communities, understanding vocation as the courage to challenge one's own community to pursue a higher sense of itself in the world. "Escaping from Bankruptcy: The Future of the Theological Task" was published several years later as part of a thematic issue on theological language and meaning. Reviewing more recent developments in legal scholarship, Deloria considers their implications for theology and metaphysics. "In both intellectual and emotional terms," he writes, "the problems of the human species are approaching an intersection in which religion and metaphysics are not simply possible but are an absolute necessity." He faults minority, feminist, liberationist, and secular theologians for occupying themselves with language games rather than wrestling with the radical social transformations already taking place around them. Anticipating the emergence of a new vision of planetary existence, Deloria foresees it coming from the inspired leaders of grassroots communities, not professional scholars at the top of the intellectual food chain.

The last two essays respond more directly to the rise of the liberation motif in Christian theology. "On Liberation" was written for the *Occasional Bulletin of Missionary Research,* published by the interdenominational Overseas Ministries Study Center, for a thematic issue titled "Shifting Concepts of Mission." This piece is one of Deloria's earliest critiques of liberation theology in North America and reflects his continuing interest in underlying assumptions. He points out that widespread awareness of the limits of human knowledge is fundamentally liberating, since conventional approaches to current problems cannot claim absolute authority and "we are free to seek a new synthesis that draws information from every culture." The concluding eight-point summary of his challenge to Western epistemology is one of the most concise expressions of his position in print. "Vision and Community" is a more recent contribution; it was originally published in *Yearning to Breathe Free,* an anthology of essays on liberation theologies in the United States. Deloria uses the liberation motif as a lens through which to examine four prominent segments of the American Indian community. Some readers will be surprised by his relatively favorable assessment of a group we might call missionary traditionalists, but Deloria's primary concern here lies in changing how the average American thinks about reality, a kind of reverse liberation. Does liberation theology have a comprehensive vision of the future or only an assortment of abstract ideas about progress? "Eventually," Deloria reiterates, "liberation theology must engage in a massive critique of itself and its historico-theological context and inheritance."

J. T.

7

A VIOLATED COVENANT

American Indians are in the situation they are in today because of a total inability of the non-Indian Christian world to understand itself. Educational, economic, social, and legal problems of Indian peoples stem almost directly from Protestant theology and a misapplication of basic biblical ideas in the arena of political thought. Until the non-Indian peoples understand themselves and the religion they profess to confess, the situation of the American Indians will grow continually worse. The time may yet come within our lifetime of a genocidal war against American Indians being waged by these same churchgoing Christians who are now obliterating Vietnam and other parts of southeast Asia.

With such a prospect in the offing is it any wonder that from a variety of sources within the American Indian community have come voices attempting to raise a number of issues? For many Indian people understand all too well the inability of the Christian peoples to realize their religion here on earth as a viable social force. Too many times Indian peoples have seen the humanity of Christianity give way to more abstract forms of oppression by people firmly convinced they are following God's will. And fanatically determined to carry out God's will as they are able to understand it, they have perpetuated massacres and theft unparalleled in the history of mankind.

The most drastic error of Protestant theology as applied to the American Indian peoples has been the total inability of the Christians to understand their own idea of "covenant." Initially, a covenant was a pact between the peoples of two nations whereby the integrity of each nation was pledged to uphold the agreement. A covenant did not give people the right to intrude on the other partner of the agreement. Indeed, it meant that the spiritual faith of the two peoples was pledged so that the agreement called for the best efforts of the two groups to fulfill the terms of agreement.

With the development of Christian theology after the death of Jesus the whole idea of the New Covenant permeated explanations of the meaning of the life and death of the founder of the religion. Declaring that everyone who accepted the teachings of Jesus, later Paul, and still later Luther, the various Christian denominations found in the idea of a New Covenant a community transcending time and space and bound together by a faith in the uniqueness of history as exemplified in the Christian story.

Where the New Covenant meant a New Community, a gathering of saints, a communion of the saved, to that degree the individuals composing the heavenly city were required to act positively in response to the message they proclaimed to the world and by which they were encouraged to judge the secular world. Thus Christians were told they had been freed from the judgments of the law and were freed to live in a state of near-grace. By transcending law and dwelling permanently within a covenantal relationship Christians bound themselves to living a life of creative existence, a life in which they were not judged solely by their transgressions of law but by the vision of life in its totality toward which they marched.

But there was no corresponding understanding by Christians taken as a corporate group that they had a duty to incarnate the covenantal life in their relationships with peoples different from themselves. Law quickly replaced covenant and Christianity bogged down to the conception of a God who laboriously recorded each and every transgression of individuals for use in the afterlife when He would exact vengeance. It was this lower conception of divinity and hence society that Christians believed in when the New World was discovered. And the early colonial governments reflected a scales-and-balances concept of both law and covenant in their dealings with each other and with their own settlers.

Combined with the perversion of covenant was a misapplication of the concept of Genesis to go forth and multiply and the placement of man as having dominion over all other species of the creation. According to the Genesis legend when man was given the right to name the animals, he was given dominion over them since by creating their names he had in effect participated in their creation also. As co-creator, one might have argued, man had a corresponding responsibility to care for the non-human elements of creation. In tending the Garden of Eden man had a corresponding responsibility to the earth itself to maintain its fruitfulness. All of this, particularly the edict of man's responsibility, was perverted by Christian theologians.

Early in the history of North American exploration the fundamental responsibilities of Genesis became interpreted as man's right, and basically the white man's right, to use whatever he wanted and however he wanted to use it. Thus slavery was justified as God's rightful contribution to the economic well-being of the Americans, God's chosen people. Wholesale destruction of the forests, the game, and the original peoples of the continent were justified as part of God's plan to subdue and dominate an untamed wilderness. Nowhere was there any sense of stewardship between diverse elements of the new Christian settlers, either collectively or individually, and the continent as they found it.

Within this context one can trace the tragic story of the American Indian peoples. The United States and the individual colonies signed treaties with the various tribes at which the faith and good will of the United States and its component states was pledged. Missionaries representing the respective denominations attended these treaty-signing sessions each assuring the tribal leaders that if the government of the United States did not uphold the treaty, his church and his God would guarantee them. Indeed, missionaries promised that God himself wanted the tribes to sign the treaties because of his foreordained plan to create cities, suburbs, and shopping centers on the North American continent.

Within the treaty context, then, total faith and good will of the two parties, the Indian tribe and the United States, were pledged. Treaties were the covenants of the new lands insofar as they affected the relationships of individuals of the two disparate treaty groups. But as soon as the treaties were signed, and often even before the signing was official, large groups of settlers following God's divine command to subjugate the earth went forth into the reserved Indian lands. The tribes were thus pushed further and further backwards into the interior. At no point was there an acknowledgement by the allegedly religious people of the new nation that once having pledged the faith and validity of their religion, there was a corresponding responsibility to uphold the treaty.

The settlement of the continent, therefore, was one in which people, claiming to be divinely inspired members of a New Covenant, refused for a moment to keep their covenantal commitments to people to whom they had given them. Article by article, treaty by treaty, the spiritual faith given by the white Christians was violated in favor of God's other commandment, also misinterpreted, to subjugate the earth. It is, therefore, ridiculous to view Indian tribes as a people who have not and probably cannot understand the requirements of either religion or civilization. Both religion and civilization require, for their fundamental integrity, the premise that one can be taken at his word for what that word spiritually represents. Instead history has shown a marvelous ability of the white Christian to quibble on the meanings of specific words contained in treaties and statutes, finding in tortured interpretations of those words the loophole required when one is breaking faith.

In a corresponding development, responsibility to the earth and its creatures has been studiously avoided. Instead exploitation for the sake of exploitation has been the rule. Property rights have taken precedent over any sense of affinity for living creatures and their rights. The buffalo were exterminated to provide grazing lands for cattle, and misuse of these grazing lands resulted in the creation of a Great Dust Bowl followed by farm programs in which land is kept unproductive in order to maintain a false economy for selected landowners while millions throughout the world starve.

The justification for taking Indian lands has always been: they are not doing anything with them. Underlying this complaint has been the idea that the earth itself can have no rest. It also must be exploited and used. There is no responsibility of man not to destroy the world. On the contrary the more the world can be changed, the theology has run, the more concrete poured, the more freeways, apartment buildings, slums, football stadiums, in short, the more confused edifices created, the better God is pleased. God, then, created the earth most ineptly. It was fortunate for God that man was available to recreate the world as it should be.

Now the chickens have come back to roost. The entire Vietnam fiasco revolves around the question of covenant. To what extent are we bound by our promise to protect the South Vietnam republic? And the answer has been that we are bound to the point where it becomes our duty, our God-given duty, to massacre defenseless old men, women, children, and babies—for their own good—and for our good, to defend them. When eighty-three percent of the citizens of this country, this Christian country, think that Lieutenant Calley did right in executing the people at My Lai, then one can see how far from the reality of what they proclaim the arriving Christians have come in four centuries.

Instead of creating the world in a better way than the deity, Christian peoples have only succeeded in creating a situation in which mankind may well extinguish itself within a generation unless pollution is controlled. And even that statement is not really correct. Unless the white Christians control pollution, all of mankind, Christian and non-Christian, may become extinct. This obvious fact, rather than theological fancies of the past, tells us of the relative truth of the Genesis legend. For if man was given the right to totally subjugate, then no harm would come to him. Such, according to our best scientific minds, is not and has not been the case.

Outside of a massive repentance and a society turned completely around there appears to be no solution to modern problems. Unless mankind takes its responsibilities to the world, and unless Christians take their responsibilities to non-Christians, as serious and critical calls to action, we really have no future. We will have created our own judgment day far in advance of any divine plans for the event.

In the field of human rights there must be a radical change in attitudes. If it has been stated that Indian treaties will be upheld, then it is the responsibility to uphold them. No amount of quibbling over phraseology can change that basic response. If all men are really created in God's image, there should be no question, at least among those alleging to be Christians, to carrying out those programs and projects that will most nearly approximate that condition. The continual bickering over legal sophistries with respect to treaty rights, integration, welfare, the aged, orphans, speaks of a society in which law and not covenant dominates. That society and its members who so loudly proclaim to be members of the covenant, the New Covenant, should either put up or shut up.

Most of us really know what is right. We rarely do it. But there is a corresponding responsibility on Christians today that faces no other group. For Christians have not only proclaimed that they are right, they have proclaimed that they *alone* are right and that everyone else is wrong. And then they have backed away from their responsibilities to uphold the right. When minority groups have tried to get them to respond in a manner that speaks of the spiritual commitment to the principles which they proclaim and not the legalistic footnotes behind which they have always hidden, then the Christians have fought back thinking that all efforts to make them live up to their responsibilities are subversive to the great society that they, allegedly with God's help, have created.

The case of the American Indian is clear and uncomplicated. American Indians suffer because the non-Indians have devised ways and means of not keeping their word. Non-Indians have violated their covenants with Indian tribes. Let them fulfill these treaties and covenants and *then* come talk to us about problems. For it is then that we will be able to discern which problems are really *our* problems and which are problems created by non-Indians for us.

(1971)

8

AN OPEN LETTER TO THE
HEADS OF THE CHRISTIAN
CHURCHES IN AMERICA

It may seem strange to be receiving a letter concerning political matters from an American Indian. But when you understand the nature of my request you will see that it is to you gentlemen alone that we must turn for an answer to our question.

Nearly five centuries ago the European nations, thrilled with the discovery of a large and unknown world to the west, embarked upon the systematic exploration and conquest of the newly discovered continents which have since come to be known as North and South America. These nations were initially spurred on by the thought of inexhaustible riches to be gained through commerce with the nations of the west. It was not long, however, before questions of a theological nature arose. Who were these newly discovered peoples? What rights did they possess? How were they to be treated?

A gradual consensus of the learned scholars of Christendom decided that the peoples inhabiting the western continents were to be treated with respect BUT, that the peoples of the Americas were to have lands and rights only with respect to those nations which claimed the exclusive rights to deal with them. A bargain was struck, therefore, among the Christian nations of western Europe, that whoever discovered lands inhabited by non-Christian peoples would have the exclusive right to "extinguish" such title as against any other Christian nation.

The pattern was thus set that while other nations of the world were to have their lands confirmed to them, the aboriginal peoples of the western hemisphere were to have title and right to their lands only at the pleasure of the Christian nations which chose to recognize those titles. Thinking themselves justified by the god they worshipped, the nations of Europe proceeded to subdue both the lands and peoples of the western continents. They came to regard their actions as the inevitable result of the foreordained plan of God for the future history of the world.

The initial struggle for the right to rule the eastern seacoast of North America involved England, France, Sweden, Holland. After several centuries of struggle England stood supreme upon the shores of the Atlantic. But this success was temporary. Almost immediately following the triumph of England over France the English colonists conducted a successful revolution against their mother country. The colonists established a government in which the major documents of state proclaimed the right of every man to choose his own religion, to pick his own vocation, to have rights to his own property, his home, his job, and his time to be determined by himself.

In those days we inhabited and owned the continent upon which you now live. We followed our own laws and the dictates of our consciences and traditions of our tribes. We were powerful in those days and could easily have snuffed out the tiny settlements along the coast. But we were told that red men and white men could live in peace in such a large country provided each respected the laws and customs of the other. We were content with this agreement.

In the years that followed, another doctrine arose from the minds of Christian men. This doctrine announced that America, the new country, had a "Manifest Destiny." It was God's will, we were told, indeed, the people of America were told, that Christian civilization should extend from coast to coast; from "sea to shining sea" as it were. Everything non-Christian and lacking the customs and attributes of Christian civilization was to be pushed from the inevitable path of progress.

In 1787, the Congress of the United States declared that the "utmost good faith" would be shown the Indian tribes of the continent. Congress disclaimed any treachery or deceit in its dealings with us and promised that only in just wars would our lands be taken from us. You gentlemen know, as well as we do, what the result has been. I need not labor the point of perfidy and injustice with you. Since it is a matter of historical fact it is sufficient that we recognize the past for what it has been and not dwell on it but rather find those answers which will ensure that mistakes of the past are not continuously repeated in the future.

It is for that reason that I have chosen to address you gentlemen as representatives of Christendom. I seek only your honest response and heartfelt consideration of my questions. It is not the documented and footnoted answers that you can use to justify your position that I seek to invoke, but the beginning of honest inquiry by yourselves into the nature of your situation. And that situation is that I believe that you have taught mankind to find its identity in a re-writing of history and not an affirmation of it. It is this tendency, more than any other, that now confronts American Indian people in their relations with the United States government. We are content to live under the laws of this country. But the United States government has learned to continually change those laws with respect to us by viewing its own history as it chooses to view it and not as it was. And I would be so bold as to suggest that the government learned to do this by following the lead of its religious community.

Early missionaries, for example, told us the story of Adam and Eve. They went on at great length with the stories of Jonah and the whale. They regaled us with accounts of the Resurrection, the Exodus, and the Tower of Babel. We recognized these stories as myths by which a people explain how they came to consciousness as a national community. When we tried to explain our myths the missionaries grew angry and accused us of believing superstitions.

You gentlemen and your predecessors told us that God has given man a command in the Garden of Eden that he should subdue the earth. Out of this command came the vast industrial machine of modern America. We replied that the Great Spirit gave certain lands to each tribe to use, that no one tribe could own the lands exclusively against any other, that the plants and animals, even the rivers, mountains and valleys, each had a right to its own existence because it was made for that existence by the Great Spirit.

At each point and in every aspect you refused to confront our ideas but chose instead to force your opinions, myths, and superstitions on us. You have never chosen to know us. You have only come to us to confront and conquer us. And it is this tendency to continually pervert the experiences of life that you have passed on to the federal government that has created our present difficulty. As years have passed and memories have dimmed we have been told that our treaties and agreements did not ever mean what they appear to mean. We are told that promises made upon the most solemn occasions were mere subterfuges to gain time or to pacify the tribes. We are told that obligations of the United States were necessary conveniences to the settling of the west—a mission ultimately deriving from the Divine command of Eden.

Wishing that something happened long ago does not change what did happen at that time. Believing in myths does not give them historical reality. Indeed, it shields one from ever knowing that reality or from learning from it. So it is with government, so it is with religion.

For nearly a century your own scholars have been pointing out that the best estimates of history are that no Garden of Eden existed, that the Tower of Babel was at best an effort to explain the multiplicity of languages and nations to be found on earth. More recently Biblical criticism has pointed out that Jesus in all probability did not rise from the dead in bodily form. He did not ascend to heaven by leaving the earth in a cloud. (Indeed, with escape velocity of the planet set at some 25,000 miles per hour, conceiving the cloud alone takes some imagination.)

All indications appear to be that while Christianity has certain religious forms that provide a satisfactory religious experience for a segment of mankind, it is hardly the final answer either to man's experience on earth or to his status in any life hereafter. Believing in the Divinity of Jesus does not alter the historical facts of his existence. A theory of history, no matter how broad, is not a historical explanation of the things that have happened if it cannot account for what has in fact happened.

At one time in man's history the explanations given by Christianity were sufficient to cover man's knowledge of his world. This is no longer true. The ruins of the past civilizations of the Orient and the western hemispheres alone suffice to reject the traditional Christian interpretation of history as the specific plan of a particular God to do a particular thing with a particular people. You gentlemen know this far better than I. But you continue to perpetuate the traditional interpretation of the world as it has been taught to you. You surely realize the inadequacy of the Christian interpretation of man's historical experience.

You do not lack faith in your religion. In many instances you have gone the extra mile to attempt to make amends for errors of the past. The only white men willing to help the Cherokee Nation in its conflict with Georgia were missionaries. The final and significant force brought to bear for Civil Rights of the black man was the effort made by Christians, most of them white Christians of western European background.

You lack credibility.

Not so much in what you do. You lack credibility in what you say. And so long as you feel no need to present a credible and comprehensible understanding of man's history the governments of the societies in which you live will see no need to have credibility in what they do.

This is our problem. It is the crisis of Western man. Whether we like it or not we are inevitably tied to the fate of Western man who has invaded our lands and among whom we now dwell. When he falls we believe we shall still survive. But we know it will be at a terrible cost.

The present position of the United States government is that it holds our lands and communities as its wards. When this doctrine is traced to its origin it lands comfortably within the Doctrine of Discovery and the United States claims its rights over us not by right of conquest but by right of having succeeded to the rights of Great Britain to extinguish our titles to lands. We are completely helpless to ever maintain our lands, our communities and cultures so long as the major reason that they are protected is to enable the United States to one day extinguish them as its legal right against the other Christian nations.

We have been placed beyond the remedies of the Constitution of the United States because the Doctrine of Discovery has never been disclaimed either by the governments of the Christian nations of the world or by the leaders of the Christian churches of the world. And more especially by the leaders of the Christian churches of this country. No effort has been made by Christians to undo the wrongs that were done, albeit mistakenly, and which are perpetuated because Christians refuse to measure their own understanding of the world by the facts of the world in which we all live.

A disclaimer of the traditional Christian understanding of history would carry with it the demand by the peoples of the West that all institutions honestly attempt to appraise the present situation in its true historical light. The American experience would not then appear inevitable. The novelty of the establishment of a democracy would be understood in its own light. The mythology of American history would be seen as merely mythology. The Custers, Chivingtons and Calleys would be seen for what they were. We could all come to the necessity of facing ourselves for what we are. We would no longer have a God busily endorsing and applauding the things that we are doing. We would have to be on God's side in our dealings with other peoples instead of being so sure that God is automatically on our side.

If nothing is certain, then Congress would have no excuse for not dealing justly with us, for industrial and technological progress would not have divine sanction over us. At present the Black Mesa on the Navajo-Hopi reservation in Arizona is being destroyed because it has been said that it is inevitable that more people will need more electrical power and burning the coal deposits of those reservations for power is the cheapest way to get the power needed. The project is justified as the inevitable result of American progress. But is this kind of progress ultimately inevitable or have we been trained to believe it is?

We watch as species after species of wildlife is destroyed by man. We always considered the birds and animals as brothers, joint creatures of one creation. But you have told us that this is not so. You have maintained that God gave man dominion over the animals in the Garden of Eden. You have justified the destruction of God's creation and his creatures as the inevitable consequences of Christian history. You do not yet raise your voices in protest at this destruction because it is intimately tied in with your command to subdue the earth.

The poverty we presently endure, the confiscation of our lands, the destruction of animals we once enjoyed, the obliteration of our valleys and rivers, the exploitation of our holy places as tourist traps, all of these things might have occurred anyway. We might even have done these things eventually, although according to our beliefs this would have been the gravest of sins. But we would never have deliberately done these things as a religious command and when our myths no longer served our purposes we would have found new myths, new songs and ceremonies, new revelations, to incorporate into our understanding of ourselves so that we would not be blindly led to destruction because we could not afford to face the truth of our own situation.

It may be that we cannot change the past but we can certainly begin to try to understand it. We have only to stand today for the things that are right and which we know are right. If promises have been made, those promises must be kept. If mistakes are made they must be corrected. If the lands of aboriginal peoples were wrongly taken by a Christian mandate then what remains of those lands must not be continually taken once the mistake is known.

It remains to you as honest men to ponder what your predecessors have created and what, by your silence, you now endorse. If your understanding of history cannot account for the experiences of mankind then your duty to mankind is clear. You must announce the errors that have led men astray from themselves and lead the search for that understanding or that religious interpretation that can bring them to understand themselves, their fellow men, and the creation in which they live.

Political institutions are viable under most circumstances. But they operate according to their understanding of the world in which they exist. In every era of man's existence religions have acted to give to political institutions the justification, incentive, and heart to exist. If we have political institutions that do not serve us today it is because our religious institutions have not called those governments and the peoples who run them to a greater vision of humanity. Justice has become merely justification of man's condition and not a call for the integrity resulting from credibility or the expansion of man's vision of himself.

Christianity once had a message of the dignity of man. And this is my final question to you. At what point can we as peoples of the creation look to Christianity to demand from the political structures of the world our dignity as human beings? At what point can we become men and not mere appendages of the Christian Doctrine of Discovery?

(1972)

9

IT IS A GOOD DAY TO DIE

The editors of *Katallagete* have placed a very difficult topic before us, especially those of us who have suffered severe dislocations in our outlook in the last several years. Vocation in the old sense was a happy way of justifying working for a corporation while maintaining membership in the better Christian denominations and chastizing those who neither belonged to a denomination nor worked for a corporation. I first became aware of the concept of vocation when I asked our college chaplain at Iowa State if we could study Albert Schweitzer's *The Quest of the Historical Jesus.* He was horrified, as good college chaplains always are, told me not to question my faith, and advised me to find a Christian vocation instead of worrying about expanding my knowledge of Christian origins.

The word *vocation,* consequently, has always had a connotation of the closed mind in my reference system of emotionally-loaded words. Vocation has taken on the unfortunate value of being opposed to personal inquiry and I have always thought of the idea of vocation as something you do when your brain ossifies. A vocation, in the traditional sense, was an occupation based upon the consumption sometime in the distant past of a certain quantity of academic material. If one were very serious about the consistency of this content then one would naturally question the validity of the vocation also. I have not always been dreadfully happy about the world as I have known it and so have not been very eager to base a vocation on the content of knowledge about the world which is now available to us.

I consequently avoided the whole issue of vocation by working as a welder in a machine shop at night while attending a Christian seminary by day for four years. I wanted to discover if they who had preserved the faith to the saints once delivered had any thoughts on the world, which necessarily included vocations, or anything else for that matter.

The assumption that one must make, unfortunately, upon entering seminary is that due to a variety of circumstances, benign or malevolent, one has the inside track in comprehending divine mysteries. The tension, then, between keeping one's mouth shut in order to further explore the presence and knowledge of divinity, and launching a preaching career thereby solving all of the world's problems, increases as the seminary experience broadens. The posture of the seminary as repository of ancient and self-evident truths only increases one's sense of belonging to an elite which has been mysteriously ordained to promulgate the ground rules of the game of life, occasionally calling the fouls, but generally winking at minor transgressions confident that they are being recorded up above anyway.

One of the most heartrending tensions of attempting to learn about the variety of religious experiences and doctrines is finding the proper guideposts in the world by which one can validate his behavior, in order to assure himself of the universal nature of the religious experience. Does doctrine precede and point to experience, or is it the abstraction and crystallization of experience? The difference is startling when one considers it. Doctrines based on experience are virtually useless unless people can discern from their contemporary situation patterns of behavior and answers of another age and place that appear at least compatible. Unfortunately doctrines and creeds involve little more than learned responses to classic situations where sin is not only apparent but gleefully participating. They may be proper and respectable slogans for affluent people to endorse but I have found them to be virtually useless for solving the brutal problems of everyday life. In retrospect, when one is pondering a problem which has been resolved, a conclusion that doctrinal elements might have been present is always a possibility.

Doctrines that precede experience, as ultimate revelation must certainly require, cannot exist without alternative interpretations available for the reflective person. To have followed a rigid doctrinal behavior and then learn of a not-so-doctrinal shortcut or alternative answer is the most destructive acid a doctrine can encounter. And the predictive nature of revealed theological concepts is totally crushing when the church does not act like its definition, and the pastor, priest or minister reveals himself as a fund-raising agent of the establishment and not a prophetic figure of the ages.

Thus seminary, in spite of its avowed goals and tangible struggle with good intentions, provided an incredible variety of food for thought but a glaring lack of solutions or patterns of conceivable action which might be useful in facing a world in which the factors affecting human life shift daily. The premise upon which religion and religious experience appeared to have rested prior to my seminary years—a final and unifying explanation of the meaning of life—was at once too general to be useful and too specific to be meaningful in the novel events of the 1960s and beyond.

Perhaps the best summary I can give of the intellectual content of seminary is that it appears to be more a hopeful bolstering of ancient dogmas and doctrines than a true exploration of man's spiritual problems and yearnings. Seminary projects, and one learns to analyse, problems in sets of questions and answers. Yet in life we dare to live in a condition in which both questions and answers continue to appear and never intersect or relate to each other. The solutions we find to pressing daily problems rarely come into the arena of creedal surety. The answers we find in the heat of battle and the quiet of meditation are answers to questions we did not think we asked.

After four years virtually devoid of revelation and sparse of even elementary information, I emerged into the real world confident that I had, if not the answers, at least the edge in my encounter with the world. The trauma was enlightening. People, it seemed, really didn't think about anything other than their jobs and their projected future which was in a constant state of migratory mortgaging. I passed rapidly into the world of national politics in the American Indian community. The novelty of political action and the solution to specific problems forced me to the conclusion that concepts used in analyses of problems could not be separated from one's knowledge of life itself.

It was only after I had experienced the same problems a number of times, but guised in different clothes each time, that I grew somewhat lazy and began to examine potential patterns of behavior rather than the peculiarities of the events themselves. The ability to predict with certain limits the breadth of the problem, the possible factors involved, and the conceivable leverage points at which problems could be revolved into soluble situations made it seem that at some point a final solution to certain consistent errors of mankind could be devised.

Having entered seminary thinking that religion was real and discovering upon graduation that it had little or nothing to do with life in the manner in which life presented itself, I rather naively entered law school determined to find a constant from which new vistas of humanity could be constructed. The whole tenor of American society has been to advocate a reliance upon the intangible and neutral operations of law to the exclusion of human frailties. Thus where religion could not provide any ultimate values for human life, law could at least provide a resting place and a temporary respite from conflict. Or so I thought.

Anglo-Saxon law and its bastard descendant American common and statutory law are consistent only so long as they remain unexamined. Upon any extensive inquiry into the philosophical or ethical basis for law as we know it, one encounters magic, mystery, and an incomprehensible jungle of conflicting statements about man and society. If theology is abstract with respect to this world and its problems, law is like pasting together pieces of eight different maps and then trying to build a threshing machine from the result.

The hope that law holds out to the uninitiated is that it gives answers to immediate problems and provides a sense of orientation, in the situation man finds himself in, which answers and orientations if not satisfactory, are at least reliable for the foreseeable future. Law appears as a means of ordering our daily universe by clarifying the relationships we enjoy and suffer with others.

Graduation from law school returned the same message as had graduation from seminary. Law was even less related to life than theology. Law was so dependent upon a sense of integrity in the ultimate meaning that to speak of legal matters became, in the last analysis, an effort to discover theological presuppositions of men's action. But the possibility that the law can be manipulated, the dimensions of which had not been vaguely suspected until Richard Nixon and John Mitchell promulgated their concepts of constitutional rights, makes law a demonic force unless welded to a theological conception of man.

What can be said of theological education with respect to salvation can be said manifold in legal education with respect to the concept of property. Both appear to be the primary question and final answer of their respective systems. As absolute values they determine the way that we pose questions, the way that we analyse problems, and the manner in which we determine in our own minds which side we must take in the conflict. Having consumed this absolute during his first year in law school, the student is then forced to reconsider the implications of his knowledge by refuting his definitions for two years by learning the various fields of law which all refuse to relate to property and form a coherent whole.

Of the two types of education, legal education is by far the most crippling to one's mind. In the real world, rights emerge as a limitation on man's experience and not as guides to intelligent activity. The sudden and forced knowledge that *might* really does make *right* in the world as we experience it creates in many sensitive young lawyers a burning desire to advance the cause of justice. That justice is, in the last analysis, a temporary balancing of relative powers to create a more equal confrontation of unequal forces, is a bitter realization.

The incompleteness and fantasy of religion as we know it today drives one to believe in the efficacy of law as man's best hope for meaningful existence. (Witness the comparative numbers of people entering law schools and seminaries.) Law requires no supernatural stamp of approval for its existence, no esoteric revelation for those who would tread its bidden path. Yet law is hollow and without satisfaction when divorced from the moral and ethical sensitivities one must acknowledge exist. A legal victory devoid of moral or ethical satisfaction, although absolutely correct on legal grounds, would be the ultimate disaster. The relationship between law and religion, then, is a complementary one with each ultimately pointing at the other as the binding thesis of its existence.

In identifying this relationship, however, I absolutely and positively do not mean to relate it to the traditional Christian word game of the relationship between law and gospel. In the Western world we have committed ourselves to an explanation of phenomena as basically evolutionary, that is to say, that phenomena grade themselves in time and project an increasingly better or more sophisticated pattern. From this evolution we necessarily place value judgments at certain points thus enabling ourselves to define the *progress* of the evolutionary process at any given chronological moment. In a substantial portion of traditional Christian efforts to relate law and gospel, law is considered as the evolutionary basis of preparation of gospel. Aside of the obvious twisting of the concept of law to include dietary and cultural requirements of the Hebraic Law, the relating of law to gospel implies that gospel is always in a position to act as judge on the operations and conclusions of law.

I would vigorously deny that the relationship between the law or laws of a society and its religion or the religious sentiments and experiences of a society consists of a judgmental position by either on the other. A totally consistent religious sensitivity sails by law and legal theory as if it did not exist. Law can be totally administered from any set of premises providing that those administering it maintain its purpose clearly in their minds. The integrity of one relates to the integrity of the other in that both are experiential fields including both individuals and social groups. An inconsistency experienced in any field of human affairs reflects as detrimentally on all other facets of the totality of the experience as does the apparent breakdown between law and religion.

In accepting the Western evolutionary scheme of interpretation we have traditionally been forced to conclude that customs are a precursor of law in that they regulate behavior without being formally codified. Evolutionary interpretation would maintain that as society becomes more abstract and the need for information on customs is seen, laws become formal instruments promulgated abroad so that they cannot be manipulated to the benefit of those in power.

I would advocate an examination of the customs of a society as the basic requirement of understanding both law and gospel. At that point when customs have been adequately examined, one can lay customs aside and enter the twin fields of law and religion (or gospel in a Christian context) and identify them as components of a constantly shifting value scheme of both individuals and societies. Decision-making using one criteria precludes use of the same situation used the same way by the other. One can be intimately aware of the implications involved in deliberately choosing to characterize a situation as having more similarity to one field than to the other. But to categorize one's choice as necessarily determined by the superiority of gospel or moral demands is to mesmerize oneself.

Perhaps the clearest examples of these situations come today in the protests against the war, the experiences we have suffered in the belated Civil Rights movement, and the question of amnesty. In characterizing one's behavior as a response to a higher moral requirement one should be damn sure that one's opponents understand and agree to the ground rules. The Milwaukee protesters burned the draft board files and claimed that it was a symbolic protest against the war. The District Attorney filed charges against them for breaking and entering. The symbolism was pleasing but did not communicate the moral issue the protestors thought they were raising.

A society appears to me to balance its sense of identity and integrity by altering the allegiances it pays to laws and customs at any particular period of its existence. In transferring its emotional identity toward law it requires further elaboration of its religious explanations in a theoretical or creedal sense. To place the concept of vocation in this mixture as a term descriptive of choice, deliberate or unconscious, would appear to be the greatest peril to mental health and psychological identity of both individuals and societies.

Preparing a statement on vocations, then, necessarily involves determining at what point a person can find the interpretation of the world that provides him with a sense of personal identity and integrity. That is not to say that integrity is always a rigorous exercise of emotions or mentality or that a person can always act with consistency. One need only know that he is violating his own sense of identity and be able to evaluate his actions against his beliefs, abstract and tangible. Here I am not advocating an ethics of relative values. Right and wrong are generally a fairly clear choice, given the situation we confront. Occasionally deliberately choosing to violate one's own sense of being confirms in large measure that one is sane. The traditional picture of Jesus as a man who never acted against his own nature is rather bland and does not fit our experiences as we know them. As an exposition of the gospel it is senseless.

Preparing a conclusion, therefore, as to the meaning of vocation, is to allow the desperate balancing act of a sense of justice (however conceived), an experience, not an eternal surety, or identity, and a continual confrontation of the tough practical problems of the immediate situation emerge. The traumatic possibility that flying saucers exist, that mankind has experienced many diverse and tragic social movements that had apparent religious sanctifications but collapsed, and that once starting to redefine the world one can only find a temporary respite from the task of discovering oneself, may compose the phenomena we once abstracted as the basis for outlining a theory of vocations.

In recent years I have reluctantly come to the conclusion that nothing is really without a sense of purpose. In some obscure manner there appears to be a plan of overwhelming dimensions operating to bring us to certain plateaus of personal and social identity. I am not at all sure that this barely-detected plan is benevolent or that it carries any negative or positive values as we are accustomed to projecting. I am only convinced that on occasions it can be said to be beneficially revealed as constructive. At other times it appears that our own vision greatly surpassed what was actually possible or at least what was finally realized.

My present activity, for one could not say either occupation or vocation (the tedious nature of routine is studiously avoided at all costs), is simply existing as a member of a partially-defined community. The community is an Indian tribal situation which fluctuates between memories of an exotic past and a precarious future defined in derogation of that past. I find so many similarities to other groups in the present Indian situation that I am tempted to say that I exist as a rural person partially consumed by future shock and badly crippled by too much education. Being a member of this community involves a certain tension between a willingness to share its happiness and grief and the personal demand to be its severest critic and most disloyal member, for I can even yet see the clouds of turmoil forming on the horizon.

American Indian people are presently faced with almost certain extinction of their land base and legal rights, and this is bad. But it is, strangely enough, not evil. That Indian people might have not sufficient strength to survive this projected loss would necessarily require a judgment that my own community is not fit to survive. If the realization should come to that, I would somehow have to share our created evil.

The problem is never to surrender to either possibility, success or failure, but to accept the fact the somehow peoples come and go and it is their experience of themselves in retrospect that is ultimately important.

In the Indian community there has always been the acknowledgement that living cannot be postponed. Particularly among the Sioux Indians, anything that has an identity calls men and societies to it. "It is a good day to die," Crazy Horse used to call as he rode out into battle. People accepted his challenge and followed him because he called into question their highest memories of themselves. If there is a sense, then, in which a person can have a vocation, it is to ride into one's community with a challenge to its presuppositions, presuppositions which one cherishes and from which one's identity is received.

If vocation is to exist in today's world it must certainly involve a heady willingness to struggle for both long and short term goals and at times simply for the joy of getting one's nose bloodied while blackening the other guy's eye. I would conclude that vocation has nothing to do with jobs, divine callings, political platforms, or wisdom and knowledge of the world. It is the solitary acknowledgement that the question of man's life and identity is to let the bastards know you've been there and that it is always a good day to die. We are therefore able to live.

(1972)

10

ESCAPING FROM BANKRUPTCY

The Future of the Theological Task

Jean-Francois Revel's book *Without Marx or Jesus* had remarkably little impact in American theological circles when one considers the scope of his vision. In describing the necessary next step for achieving both stability and sanity in the world, Revel suggested that five basic areas of concern be simultaneously reformed. Among the areas which he saw needing reform was a critique of culture encompassing morality, religion, accepted beliefs, customs, philosophy, literature and art. Revel was describing a process of systematic and prolonged examination of human values, but it is curious that he did not suggest a leverage point from which such a critique should begin.

Considering the ultimate meaning of culture as an expression of meaning by varieties of the human species—which definition avoids tautology because of depth of understanding only—one would think that either religious understanding or metaphysics would be the proper arena in which to examine planetary culture that may be emerging. Gary Snyder, in *Earth House Hold,* remarked that "we are now experiencing a surfacing (in a specifically 'American' incarnation) of the Great Subculture which goes back as far perhaps as the late Paleolithic." If Snyder's intuition is correct then a lot of what have seemed to be disruptive and unnecessary incidents in recent years are manifestations of this emergence; in both intellectual and emotional terms the problems of the human species are approaching an intersection in which religion and metaphysics are not simply possible but are an absolute necessity.

Religious people in the twentieth century have shied away from any discussion of metaphysics because it has seemed to them to be unnecessarily abstract and rigid, the pushing together of inhuman conceptions of the world or the endless bickering over basic premises by people unacquainted with the real problems of daily existence. Yet there is a lot to be said for considering metaphysics as a practical field of endeavor, distinct from theology, one would suppose, primarily because it does not rely upon the sacred scriptures of any tradition for its data. But it would seem to be possible today to use metaphysics and religion, or theology, in complimentary senses in that they are efforts by groups of human beings to coordinate their knowledge and experience of the world. In America we have been eminently practical in this task and one could say that the tremendous development of law in the American tradition has served us better than either religion or metaphysics because it has provided the practical boundary for behavior that Americans have sought.

If law incorporates a sense of what the world is about, then a brief survey of social changes and important decisions of the Supreme Court on abortion, the draft, integration, the death penalty, and busing, indicates the scope of change that we are experiencing. It would seem possible, therefore, to raise the question of meaning for our society by taking traditional theology and metaphysics and examine the laws and decisions of previous generations as an expression of the old theological and metaphysical understandings of the world, and by understanding the nature of recent changes in the law we can determine the extent to which the world has changed. Or, we can examine theories that are edging forward to confront us and attempt to determine what shifts in theological and metaphysical understanding are required of us.

Beginning an analysis of this kind can use almost any decision as a starting line and move swiftly to encompass related ideas forming a coherent understanding of the present state of society. But it is on the frontier that we must look for fundamental change, and two developments of recent years seem to be of different quality than others. In 1964 Charles Reich, later of *The Greening of America* fame, published an article in the *Yale Law Journal* entitled "The New Property." In this article Reich argued, and rather persuasively, that social services provided by governmental units to citizens are largely replacing other forms of wealth which had been dominating our conception of law, particularly the concept of property which had marked the boundaries between individuals and the state. Reviewing the many forms in which governmental actions had arisen to affect the lives of people, Reich pointed out that social security, aid to dependent children, occupational licenses, franchises, contracts, subsidies and the use of public resources had become such major sources of economic security and personal identity as to make other forms of wealth and income production rather miniscule.

Reich saw the important development, once this shift had been recognized, as the emergence of a new conception of society as the "public interest state" in which all segments of society are tied together by their relationship to the state and the variety of services that it offers. Certainly one has a difficult time hearing about the condition of New York City without acknowledging the basic validity of Reich's understanding of this shift in emphasis in our world. Services and incomes are so intimately intertwined in the New York City situation that movement in any direction toward a solution seems to provoke an indispensable segment of the city's population, thus rendering any final solution inoperative.

It would seem to be impossible for American society to back away from the present state of government involvement in the lives of individual citizens because the whole economic structure might collapse, revealing that we dwell in a benign feudalism in which a few giant corporations and banks have literal control over our lives. So the façade is continued and in forcing the situation to conform to false conditions and premises, we only hasten through uncontrolled inflation the final unveiling. But there seems to be little doubt that even in a financial catastrophe the pattern has been set so that people will expect the governmental structure to provide them certain fundamentals of human existence regardless of how benign or malevolent that provision may have to be to certain groups or individuals.

The other major development in recent years is Christopher Stone's famous essay on ecology, published in 1972 in the *Southern California Law Review* entitled "Should Trees Have Standing?" This article, according to Stone's confession to Garret Hardin, was put together as a means of testing the scope of the interaction of law and the development of social awareness, and was designed to raise the question of whether it was not time to extend the protection of law to natural objects in the same manner, by analogy to human characteristics, that minority groups, women and corporations had received the right to equal legal status as components of social reality. Stone's essay is brilliant because it understands law as the extension of metaphysical, and by relation religious, views of the world as they are manifested in legal concepts. As such, it is a qualitative degree above the usual claptrap published in law reviews which engages in simply pushing barren conceptions back and forth across the page.

Stone's essay caught the attention of the Supreme Court and both Douglas and Blackman took immediate notice of Stone's contention that the world had changed mightily in both a practical and a philosophical sense since the rules of standing had been outlined. Even better, the majority of the court in the *Sierra Club vs. Morton* case hinted rather broadly that if the question had been reframed and approached directly they would have been happy to expand upon the whole idea that natural objects might have some aspect of irreducible rights in the United States Courts. This hint was more than a casual acknowledgment of the growing importance of the ecological movement as a political force for it indicated that the people on the Supreme Court were more fully aware than even most Americans that isolating the human species from the remainder of the planet was a foolish and shortsighted tack.

It seems tragic that the leadership in two important areas, the relationship of human beings to social institutions and the relationship of human beings to the natural world, should have to be taken in the field of law, which does not ordinarily understand the intangible aspects of the human spirit. Yet the fact remains that from the practical side of human affairs the decisions of the courts give us a pretty good indication of how we view society or how we will come to view society in the near future if only because we will be forced to behave in a manner as if we believed it.

As we begin a journey from the legal arena to theology and metaphysics we traverse again the statement of Gary Snyder that the ancient understanding of the world is once again emerging in our time. So we are able to understand emotionally and structurally that American society is undergoing a profound critique because the nature of things, personal and institutional, is under tremendous practical and short-term pressure to produce results which would have naturally come if the old view of the world had not been subjected to incredible changes in both quality and quantity of life. Whether we like it or not, human beings are revising their understanding of themselves. This change is affecting the manner in which they view both the natural world and the institutions which allow them to live in that world.

Theology and metaphysics enter the picture at this point because they deal with reality as experienced by human beings. The social and conceptional changes described above are changes that have happened not because people had ideas that seemed more reasonable than ideas previously held, but because it became necessary in order to survive and bring order out of impending chaos to take that next step. That Stone and Reich have identified the probable structure of certain parts of present reality does not detract from the immediacy of it nor does it mean that these developments are simply another temporary adjustment in the way men think about the world in which they live. If any comparison is possible it is the comparison of humans today with the first group of humans, whoever they were, who came to awareness of themselves as a species with unique capabilities and the means of transcending the world in which they found themselves. We stand today at the same dawn of creation as original humans did, except that we stand in a cluttered landscape which is littered with intellectual, emotional, and physical debris largely of our own making.

We do not, for the most part, have the feeling of original sin today. It is worthy of note that the rapid breakdown of some of our institutions, primarily the family and small community, are less breakdowns, according to Gary Snyder, than transitions from one form of existence to another. That the younger generation can take sexual freedom so casually and political responsibilities so seriously, and sometimes so fearfully, may be an indication of which forms of human expression are really important. For it is the relationship to multi-human institutions, beliefs, and practices that are causing the difficulties, not the relationships of individual people—although the existence of institutions as an isolating dimension of our present existence, if unnoticed, may make it seem the opposite.

The difficulty with social and individual change originating in fields other than religion and metaphysics, or first manifesting themselves in ecology, law, and social welfare programs, is that the ethics of the situation remains on a crude level. People must initially follow the late Speaker Sam Rayburn's ethical dictates to his fellow House members: "Go along to get along." The dominating theme which we have heard in Watergate, in the C.I.A. investigations, and in revelations of corporate misbehavior is that "I was just doing my job." This theme, this excuse, permeates American society today and is the next logical step in the development of a contemporary ethics which makes human beings parts of a larger machine rather than an adjustable organism. So society arrives at a crossroads in which, unless it has the careful and total critique of which Revel speaks, we are liable to conclude the existence of the human species in the manner in which Karel Capek and Aldous Huxley have predicted, mindless cogs in a universe machine.

For that reason Revel entitled his book *Without Marx or Jesus* to indicate that the task of humans today is to transcend political, cultural and religious backgrounds and arrive at a planetary conception and understanding of the human species in its direct and intimate relationship with the rest of the universe. This vision is very difficult for Christians to accept for it places the Christian tradition in the peculiar position of having to defend and understand its faith for the first time in two thousand years. And when one considers the very intimate relationship between Christian thought-forms, concepts, and understandings of the world it is not at all certain that the Christian religion, or any other religion for that matter, can survive in the world of the future.

It may be time for the human species to achieve a type of maturity which would allow it to relate to other life forms outside our immediate cosmic neighborhood. We must recognize that as these possibilities now emerge it is simply not enough to extend our old beliefs and understandings of the world in an infinite line of logic hoping that the initial grasp of reality was sufficiently universal to survive the buffeting of new experiences coming at us in a Toffler-described increasing curve of future shock. The old theological claim that Christ is Lord of the whole universe, making the encounter of humans with human-like creatures of another solar system entail missionary activities to them on the basis of our understanding of the Christian religion, will simply not work. The rejection of Western values and the Christian religion in Asia and more recently by North American Indians should be sufficient warning that the Christian understanding of religious reality may not be sufficiently universal to be described as the ultimate religion.

There is no way, of course, to determine ahead of time what shape the future will take or if any religion will be capable of confronting the emerging society which will come to dominate our planet. So while we face a sense of discouragement, the central task of having the "courage to be" in the face of adversity must sustain whatever action or reaction we make in the future to new experiences. But we must be absolutely certain that we understand the nature of the world in which we live. We experience change; and there can be no denial that we have such experiences. What is not so clear—and this is the area in which theology and metaphysics are the only disciplines capable of undertaking the task of bringing order out of chaos—is whether we in fact understand the meaning which we ascribe to our experiences. As Ian Barbour has pointed out in his writings, it is not possible to mis-experience, but it is possible to mis-interpret experiences.

It goes without saying, therefore, that the world is making rapid yet sporadic changes as it gropes its way through time. History, in spite of Tillich's great series of analyses of it, does not favor anyone, it simply happens, and we place a label on it after the fact. It is virtually useless to continue to shift favorite Biblical sayings back and forth in an effort to discern from the most obscure texts a new way of understanding the experiences of minority groups, the place of women in societies, the freedom from political or economic oppression, or the value and sacredness of the secular city. Such exercises are but the fruitless rearrangements of one set of concepts to fit increasingly serious and novel situations.

Again, however, we must return to the field of ethics within religion and metaphysics and consider exactly what we are describing when we refer to this field. Ethics seems to encompass aspects of existence which do not easily fit into other categories of explanation. And if we oppose the current theological expressions with current practical expressions the subject of the theological task of our generation becomes clear. We must find a new paradigm within which ethics can be articulated. The brotherhood of human beings which characterized the Christian understanding may have been adequate in a world in which we had to deal with ordinary experiences. We simply projected from our best values and understandings outwards towards our neighbors and treated them as we would like to have been treated. It worked as long as we did not have to face simultaneous change of large masses of people and institutions. When these masses grew so large as to allow differences to be recognized—minority groups, sexual distinctions, age differences—then it became an oppressive ethic because we never attached any personality to that neighbor. We never knew if the neighbor was a he or a she, a black, an Indian, an Asian or a Chicano, or if that neighbor was young, old, our age, or the generation just ahead or behind us.

Today we are faced with those distinctions and part of Charles Reich's hidden agenda in outlining the "public interest society" is that society is composed of distinct groups which have certain indefinable and irreducible claims on society and its members. And then when we add Christopher Stone's admonition that the neighbor includes rocks, trees, animals, and landscapes which require a certain posture from the human species, the old ethical framework which told us how to respond to experiences burst completely.

Those people who are worried about the future of the theological task have reason to worry if all they intend to do is to reshuffle old verses and doctrines to the exclusion of any relationship of those verses and doctrines to the world in which people live and have experiences. But when one considers the many startling and unexpected changes that the human species is encountering and when the vacuum of ethical analysis is understood, then the task of both theology and metaphysics seems to be the most exciting task which any generation has faced. We seem to stand once again at the dawn of creation, comprehending the variety of the world and wondering what our role and relationship is. If we are content simply to name it in order to gain ascendency over it, we will have unwittingly created the most original sin of placing our fate and our future in our heads instead of incorporating it in our hearts and becoming a living expression of what creation must certainly mean to itself.

The articulation of the issues of natural objects achieving a legal status and the recognition of the "public interest state" came from the legal profession primarily because, in a certain sense, there had been sufficient movement and change within that profession to open wide gaps in the data between old concepts and new experiences. Thus it is those people in the coal fields, on the reservations, in the ghettos, and in the communes who have experienced both isolation and community with sufficient intensity to recognize a gap between experience and interpretation of experience, who will produce the new theologies and metaphysics that will allow society and the human species to regain its vision and understanding and take up once again the task of affirming the value of human existence. It will not come from the professional theologians and philosophers who strut about rearranging old concepts in a frantic effort to deny that the universe and its life forms are undergoing constant, profound, and accelerating change.

There should be no bankruptcy in theology and metaphysics today. We are just looking for change in the wrong places. We have come to expect new words to indicate progress and health, whereas it is in the lives of people that the newness exists and it abounds to our delight if we only recognize it.

(1976)

11

ON LIBERATION

Liberation theology assumes that the common experience of oppression is sufficient to create the desire for a new coalition of dissident minorities. Adherents of this movement indiscriminately classify all minorities—racial, ethnic, and sexual—in a single category of people seeking liberation. Such classification is an easy way to eliminate specific complaints of specific groups and a clever way to turn aside efforts of dissenting groups to get their particular goals fulfilled. For instead of listening to their complaints, observers—and particularly liberal observers who pose as sympathetic fellow-travelers—can tie up the conversation endlessly by eliciting questions, framed within the liberation ideology, that require standard and nonsensical answers. Liberation theology, then, was an absolute necessity if the establishment was going to continue to control the minds of minorities. If a person of a minority group had not invented it, the liberal establishment most certainly would have created it.

The immediate response to such an accusation is one of horrified refusal to believe that there could be any racial or sexual minority that does not consider itself to be under oppression. This is followed by the perennial suggestion that if dissident minorities "got organized" instead of remaining separate they would be able to get things done. Those who reject that concept of oppression merely prove that they are so completely the victims of oppression that they do not even recognize it. The circular logic closes neatly in upon them, making them victims indeed. Liberation theology is simply the latest gimmick to keep minority groups circling the wagons with the vain hope that they can eliminate the oppression that surrounds them. It does not seek to destroy the roots of oppression, but merely to change the manner in which oppression manifests itself. No winner, no matter how sincere, willingly surrenders his power over others. He may devise clever ways to appear to share such power, but he always keeps a couple of aces up his sleeve in case things get out of control.

If there were any serious concern about liberation we would see thousands of people simply walk away from the vast economic, political, and intellectual machine we call Western civilization and refuse to be enticed to participate in it any longer. Liberation is not a difficult task when one no longer finds value in a set of institutions or beliefs. We are liberated from the burden of Santa Claus and the moral demand to be "good" when, as maturing adolescents, we reject the concept of Santa Claus. Thereafter we have no sense of guilt in late November that we have not behaved properly during the year, and no fear that a lump of coal rather than a gift will await us Christmas morning. In the same manner, we are freed and liberated once we realize the insanity and fantasy of the present manner of interpreting our experiences in the world. Liberation, in its most fundamental sense, requires a rejection of everything we have been taught and its replacement by only those things we have experienced as having values.

But this replacement only begins the task of liberation. For the history of Western thinking in the past eight centuries has been one of replacement of ideas within a framework that has remained basically unchanged for nearly two millenia. Challenging this framework of interpretation means a rearrangement of our manner of perceiving the world, and it involves a reexamination of the body of human knowledge and its structural reconstruction into a new format. Such a task appears to be far from the struggles of the present. It seems abstract and meaningless in the face of contemporary suffering. And it suggests that people can be made to change their oppressive activity by intellectual reorientation alone.

All these questions arise, however, because of the fundamental orientation of Western peoples toward the world. We assume that we know the structure of reality and must only make certain minor adjustments in the machinery that operates it in order to bring our institutions into line. Immediate suffering is thus placed in juxtaposition with abstract metaphysical conceptions of the world and, because we can see immediate suffering, we feel impelled to change conditions quickly to relieve tensions, never coming to understand how the basic attitude toward life and its derivative attitudes toward minority groups continues to dominate the goals and activities that appear designed to create reforms.

Numerous examples can be cited to show that our efforts to bring justice into the world have been short-circuited by the passage of events, and that those efforts are unsuccessful because we have failed to consider the basic framework within which we pose questions, analyze alternatives, and suggest solutions. Consider the examples from our immediate past. In the early sixties college application forms included a blank line on which all prospective students were required to indicate their race. Such information was used to discriminate against those of a minority background, and so reformers demanded that the question be dropped. By the time all colleges had been forced to eliminate questions concerning the race of applicants, the Civil Rights Movement had so sensitized those involved in higher education that scholarships were made available in great numbers to people of minority races. There was no way, however, to allocate such scholarships because college officials could no longer determine the racial background of students on the basis of their applications for admission.

Much of the impetus for low-cost housing in the cities was based upon the premise that in the twentieth century people should not have to live in hovels but that adequate housing should be constructed for them. Yet in the course of tearing down slums and building new housing projects, low-income housing areas were eliminated. The construction cost of the new projects made it necessary to charge higher rentals. Former residents of the low-income areas could not afford to live in the new housing, so they moved to other parts of the city and created exactly the same conditions that had originally provoked the demand for low-rent housing.

Government schools had a very difficult time teaching American Indian children the English language. (One reason was the assumption of teachers that all languages had Latin roots, and their inability to adapt the programs when they discovered that Indian languages were not so derived.) Hence programs in bilingual teaching methods were authorized that would use the native language to teach the children English, an underhanded way of eliminating the native language. Between the time that bilingual programs were conceived and the time that they were finally funded, other programs that concentrated on adequate housing had an unexpected effect on the educational process. Hundreds of new houses were built in agency towns, and Indians moved from remote areas of the different reservations into those towns where they could get good housing. Since they were primarily younger couples with young children, the housing development meant that most Indian children were now growing up in the agency communities and were learning English as a first language. Thus, the bilingual programs, which began as a means of teaching English as a second language, became the method designed to preserve the native vernacular by teaching it as a second language to students who had grown up speaking English.

Example after example could be cited, each testifying to the devastating effect of a general attitude toward the world that underlies the Western approach to human knowledge. The basis of this attitude is the assumption that the world operates in certain predetermined ways, that it operates continuously under certain natural laws, and that the nature of every species is homogeneous, with few real deviations. One can trace this attitude back into the Western past. Religious concepts, which have since been transformed into scientific and political beliefs, remain objects of belief as securely as if they had never been severed from their theological moorings.

Let us trace a few examples. Originally the continuity of the world was conceived as a demonstration of the divine plan and God, conceived as a lawgiver in the moral sense, became a law-giver in the scientific sense also. Scientific data was classified in certain ways that in the eyes of Western peoples became a part of the structure of nature. Phenomena that did not fit into the structure that had been created were said to "violate" the laws of nature and hence to be untrue in the religious sense and unimportant in the scientific sense. When evolution replaced the concept of creation in the book of Genesis, it became an inviolable law in the eyes of Western people in much the same way that the literal interpretation of the biblical story had been accepted by Western people in former centuries.

The world was originally conceived in terms of the Near East as the center of reality. As awareness extended to other peoples, this world gradually expanded until by the Middle Ages it encompassed those regions that were in commercial contact with Western Europe. The discovery of the Western hemisphere created a certain degree of trauma, for suddenly there was an awareness of lands and peoples of which Western Europeans had no previous knowledge. The only way that these people could be accounted for was by reference to the Scriptures. So it was hypothesized that the aboriginal peoples in North and South America must have been the Ten Lost Tribes of Israel who had crossed into the New World over a land bridge somewhere in northern Asia. The basic assumption of this theory was the creation of the human species as a single act, performed by the Christian God, with its subsequent history one of populating the planet.

The rise of social science, and the downgrading of theological answers to what were considered scientific questions concerning the nature and history of human societies, meant that social science had to provide answers to questions formulated within the theological context. With virtually no reconsideration of the basic question of the creation (or origination in scientific terms) of our species as the product of a single act, anthropologists promptly adopted the old theological explanation of the peopling of the Western Hemisphere, developing the Bering Strait theory of migration to account for the phenomenon. Whether secular or sacred, the classification of American natives as a derivative, inferior group of Asian-European peoples, albeit far removed from those roots by the postulation of many millenia of wandering, became a status from which American Indians have been unable to escape.

The emphasis on objective knowledge by Western peoples has meant the development of an attitude that sees reality as basically physical, the knowledge thereof basically mental or verbal, and the elimination of any middle ground between extremes. Thus religion has become a matter of the proper exposition of doctrines, and non-Western religions have been judged on their development of a systematic moral and ethical code rather than the manner in which they conducted themselves. When a religion is conceived as a code of verbal importance rather than a way of life, loopholes in the code become more important than the code itself since, by eliminating or escaping the direct violation of the code by a redefinition of the code or a relaxation of its intended effect, one can maintain two types of behavior, easily discerned in a practical way, as if they were identical and consistent with a particular picture of reality.

In recent decades Western science had made an important discovery, important at least for Western peoples who had formerly confused themselves with their own belief system. Western science was premised upon the proposition that God had made the world according to certain laws. These laws were capable of discovery by human reason, and the task of science was to discover as many of these laws as possible. So human knowledge was misconceived as the only description of physical reality, a tendency Alfred North Whitehead called the principle of "misplaced concreteness." With the articulation of theories of indeterminancy in modern physics, this naive attitude toward human knowledge radically shifted and became an acknowledgement that what we had formerly called nature was simply our knowledge of nature based upon the types of questions we had decided to use to organize the measurements we were making of the physical world.

The shift in emphasis meant that all knowledge became a relative knowledge, valid only for the types of questions we were capable of formulating. Depending upon the types of information sought, we could measure and observe certain patterns of phenomena, but these patterns existed in our heads rather than in nature itself. Knowledge thus became a matter of cultural preference rather than an indication of the ultimate structure of reality. Presumably if one culture asked a certain type of question while another asked another type of question, the two different answers could form two valid perspectives on the world. Whether these two perspectives could be reconciled in one theory of knowledge depended upon the broader pattern of interpretation that thinkers brought into play with respect to the data. When this new factor of inter-pretation is applied specifically to different cultures and traditions, we can see that what have been called primitive superstitions have the potential of being regarded as sophisticated insights into the nature of things, at least on an equal basis with Western knowledge. The tradi-tional manner in which Western peoples think is now only one of the possible ways of describing a natural process. It may not, in fact, even be as accurate, insofar as it can relate specific facts without perverting them, as non-Western ways of correlating knowledge.

This uncertainty is liberating in a much more fundamental way than any other development in the history of Western civilization. It means that religious, political, economic, and historical analyses of human activities that have been derived from the Western tradition do not have an absolute claim upon us. We are free to seek a new synthesis that draws information from every culture, and every period of human his-tory has as a boundary only the requirement that it make more sense of more data than any other synthesis. Even the initial premises of such a synthesis can be different from what we have previously used to begin our formulation of a picture of reality.

When we apply this new freedom to some of the examples cited above, we see that the proper question we should have asked with respect to housing did not concern housing at all, but covered the more general question of the nature of a community. We discover that the col-lege applications and the bilingual programs should have been tran-scended by questions concerning the nature of knowledge, how it is transmitted, and how it can be expanded, rather than how specific pre-determined courses of action can be implemented. Once we reject the absolute nature of Western conceptions of problems, we are able to see different types of questions inherent in our immediate problem areas. The immediacy we feel when observing conditions under which people live should enable us to raise new issues that contain within themselves new ways of conceiving solutions.

An old Indian saying captures the radical difference between Indians and Western peoples quite adequately. The white man, the Indians maintain, has ideas; Indians have visions. Ideas have a single dimension and require a chain of connected ideas to make sense. The connections that are made between ideas can lead to great insights on the nature of things, or they can lead to the inexorable logic of Catch-22 in which the logic inevitably leads to the polar opposite of the original proposition. The vision, on the other hand, presents a whole picture of experience and has a central meaning that stands on its own feet as an indepen-dent revelation. It is said that Albert Einstein could not conceive of his problems in physics in conceptual terms but instead had visions of a whole event. He then spent his time attempting to translate elements of that event that could be separated into mathematical and verbal descriptions that could be communicated to others. It is this difference, the change from inductive and deductive logic to transformation of perceived realities, that becomes the liberating factor, not additional information or continual replacement of data and concepts within the traditional framework of interpretation.

Let us return, then, to our discussion of the manner in which racial minorities have been perceived by the white community, particularly by the liberal establishment, in the past decade and a half. Minority groups, conceived to be different from the white majority, are perceived to be lacking some critical element of humanity that, once received, would bring them to some form of equality with the white majority. The trick has been in identifying that missing element, and each new articulation of goals is immediately attributed to every minority group and appears to answer the question that has been posed by the sincere but unreflective liberal community.

Liberation is simply the manner in which this missing element is presently conceived by people interested in reform. It will become another social movement fad and eventually fade away to be replaced with yet another instant analysis of the situation. Until fundamental questions regarding the assumptions that form the basis for Western civilization are raised and new articulations of reality are discovered, the impulse to grab quickly and apparently easy answers will continue. Social conditions will continue to be described in a cause-and-effect logic that has dominated Western thinking for its entire intellectual lifetime. Programs will be designed that fail to account for the change in conditions that occurs continually in human societies. Ideas will continue to dominate our concerns and visions will not come.

If we are then to talk seriously about the necessity of liberation, we are talking about the destruction of the whole complex of Western theories of knowledge and the construction of a new and more comprehensive synthesis of human knowledge and experience. This is no easy task and it cannot be accomplished by people who are encompassed within the traditional Western logic and the resulting analyses such logic provides. If we change the very way that Western peoples think, the way they collect data, which data they gather, and how they arrange that information, then we are speaking truly of liberation. For it is the manner in which people conceive reality that motivates them to behave in certain ways, that provides them with a system of values, and that enables them to justify their activities. A new picture of reality, a reality conceived as a vision and not as a series of related or connected ideas, can accomplish over a longer period of time many changes we have been unable to effect while conceiving solutions as short-term remedies.

More important for our discussion is the recognition that all parts of human experience are related and the proposed solution to any particular problem overlooks the changes that will occur in related activities because of their relationship. Fundamental changes initiated by a new picture of reality will create a transformation, and will avoid the traditional replacement of words with new words. In summary we now challenge the basic assumptions of Western man. To wit:

1) that time is uniform and continuous;
2) that our species originated from a single source;
3) that our descriptions of nature are absolute knowledge;
4) that the world can be divided into subjective and objective;
5) that our understanding of our species is homogeneous;
6) that ultimate reality, including divinity, is homogeneous;
7) that by projection of present conditions we can understand human history, planetary history, or the universe;
8) that inductive and deductive reasoning are the primary tools for gaining knowledge.

As we create a new set of propositions that transcend these theses we will achieve liberation in a fundamental sense and the synthesis that emerges will be a theology. But it will transform present feelings of sympathy to shared experiences, it will transform tolerance to understanding, and it will transform appreciation of separate cultural traditions into a new universal cultural expression. And everyone will become liberated.

(1977)

12

VISION AND COMMUNITY

In the last decade liberation theology has moved considerably beyond its original Christian moorings to become an important perspective in addressing the problems of human societies. Even as social, economic, and political institutions tighten their grip on the lives of people and military adventurism runs rampant, there is an identifiable current of spiritual energy flowing through the events and attitudes of our times. Ecological concerns, peace protests, the movement back to small communities, shamanism, interreligious dialogues, and the widespread perception of the common humanity of our diverse peoples are but elements of an emerging vision of wholeness that promises to deliver us from the particularities of history and to present us with a truly planetary view of our common destiny.

In discussing the impact of liberation theology on the American Indian community, it is necessary to see the four segments of this community in its contemporary expression. There are, unfortunately, a good many American Indians who have accepted, without criticism, the premises of materialistic capitalism and who, in spite of the best efforts of the elders and traditional leaders, insist upon salvation through intercourse with transnational corporations and commodities markets. Although they do not constitute a majority in any Indian tribe, these people are favored by the federal government and their demands are accepted as the valid yearnings of the American Indian community for economic freedom. Their basic activity, the exploitation of the reservation's natural and human resources as a means of generating capital for projects, is anathema to the majority of Indians, and consequently every project they undertake is bitterly and sometimes violently opposed by the majority of the people. Unless and until these Indians forsake the enticements of materialistic capitalism, the horn-of-plenty of the consumer society, ultimate American Indian liberation will be a long time coming.

American Indians have been converted, devoted, and practicing Christians for many generations. A good estimate of the number of Indian Christians is difficult to make because of the great and persistent fluidity of the Indian population. Indians living in the urban areas may not attend church regularly or participate in the various outreach programs established by the major Christian denominations. But most certainly these people return to their old reservation churches for the important holidays and look upon themselves as members of century-old missions and parishes. These Indians are more directly related to a fundamental kind of liberation theology. For most of this century Indian churches and chapels have been classified as missions because they have not had sufficient income to be self-supporting in the same manner as prosperous non-Indian parishes. Mission, however, connotes a status in which the immediate human environment is hostile to the church or overwhelmingly lethargic. Indian missions are theologically sound; they represent generations of faithful church attendance; and it galls Indian Christians considerably to be seen as unchurched and needing conversion simply because they lack large parish budgets.

In the last decade Indian clergy and dedicated and active laypeople have made great strides in overcoming this image which has been unfairly thrust upon them by bookkeeping church bureaucrats. New programs for clergy recruitment and retention have been initiated and the Native American Theological Association, although now financially depleted, has worked to create additional opportunities for Indians in Christian seminaries. Charles Cook Theological School—once a Bible-based coloring-book program of enhancement for the native religious leaders who were presumed to be serving at the convenience of the white missionary—has expanded its programs and added sophisticated theological content to its activities. It now serves as a focal point for intellectual adventures of Native Americans wishing to reach beyond the traditional confines of the institutional church programs and engage in dialogue with other people dealing with pressing social, political, and religious issues.

Liberation, for this group of American Indians, is a desperate effort to gain sufficient footholds within the institutional church so that (1) Indian program budgets will not be destroyed in the annual reshuffling that the major Protestant denominations seem to enjoy, and (2) the heritage of American Indians in the spiritual realm will be respected and understood by non-Indian Christians. For these people, freedom and liberation must be seen based in respect. They have no plans for moving outside the institutional ecclesiastical framework and don't seem to understand that liberation from the clutches of non-Indian ecclesiastical bureaucrats inevitably requires them to withdraw from the major denominations and create a Native American Christian church in which both administrative policies and theological content reflect the Indian traditions and experiences.

An equally devoted group of American Indians practice the old ways, and their numbers are probably roughly similar to those of the committed Indian Christians. The twentieth century has seen a massive erosion of traditional tribal religions because of substantial outmigration from the reservation communities and the extensive importation of the electronic media in the form of telephones, radios, televisions, and videocassette recorders. With outmigration, kinship responsibilities have declined precipitously as missing relatives make it necessary for people to substitute other relatives in roles and functions which they would not otherwise undertake. The electronic entertainment media have become surrogate parents and grandparents and consequently it has become increasingly difficult to pass down the oral traditions of the tribe to the proper people and in the properly respectful context.

In many ways the practice of traditional religion today is somewhat akin to the practice of Christianity, being available to meet life crises and to provide the colorful context for social events, but not dominating the day-to-day life of the people in the communities. In the summertime today many reservations are in a state of constant flux as competing medicine men sponsor their own Sun Dances or Sweat Lodges or Sings. Concern for the continuing well-being of the community or tribe is thus expressed in a situation in which the participants withdraw from the community rather than represent it, thus individualizing a religious tradition that had its most powerful influence in its ability to synthesize diverse feelings, beliefs, and practices.

This segment of the Indian community is showing amazing strength in some obscure places in the United States and is attracting the younger people. The chief characteristic of this strength is the voluntary withdrawal from tribal politics, educational programs, and secular activities and the effort to live on a subsistence basis away from the confusion and disorder that mark the modern agency settlements. Rigorous traditionalism, therefore, is a threat not simply to organized Christian efforts to extend the influence of reservation churches but to the programmatic schemes of the materialistic capitalist Indians who see the reservation primarily as a resource to be exploited. Unfortunately many of the people who have been adopting this mode of life have already been through years of alcoholism, unemployment, and sometimes crime of various kinds. There is a real question, therefore, whether the old traditionalism has a message for young people embarked on the road of personal and professional dissolution or whether it can serve only as a spiritual rescue mission for people who have no other place to turn.

The last identifiable group of Indians, considerably smaller in number than any of the groups already discussed, are those people who have experienced traditional tribal religion to some degree, who have significant knowledge of and experiences with the white people's world, and who now insist that they have been commissioned to bring the tribal religions to the aid and assistance of the non-Indian. As a rule these people live and work far from their own reservations where they would be severely chastised by people for commercialization of tribal rituals. They form a reasonably close network of people who travel the conference and psychological workshop circuit performing for whoever is willing and able to pay the sometimes exorbitant entrance fees.

This group is very interesting. Some of the practitioners are unquestionably fraudulent and their message can be found in any of the popular books on Indian religion such as *Black Elk Speaks* or *Book of the Hopi*. To a white populace yearning for some kind of religious experience it is enough that they speak kindly and administer a message of universal fellowship during a friendly ceremonial occasion. Few people have any extensive knowledge of the ways of any tribal religion and so the ceremonies used by these practitioners, which would be instantly discredited within the reservation context, are taken as real expressions of religious piety by their followers. But it cannot be denied that on many occasions what these people have done has helped the people they have served. There is sufficient evidence that some kind of religious energy is present in these modernized versions of tribal ritual so that the movement cannot be discredited on the basis of its commercialism alone.

It is in the objective vision possessed by this last group of Indians that the importance of the American Indian contribution to liberation theology can be found. Obviously the materialistic capitalists possess only the idea of accumulating wealth and power, and their view—for it can hardly be called a vision—of reality is hardly an improvement on the speculations of English political and economic thinkers of the eighteenth century. Indian Christians also lack a unifying vision; basically they attempt to fit themselves into a two-thousand-year-old paradigm of salvation which has little relevance to the longstanding tribal traditions. The purist reservation traditions are bound in the same way, using the old images and visions as a framework within which present realities can be judged. While there is considerably more power and familiarity in these old visions, nevertheless there is very little in them that addresses the modern social and physical context in which people live. And so we are left with the vision of the new Indian missionaries/entrepreneurs, partly by default, partly by the emphasis on outreach.

The new vision is not without its faults and, like other things of the Spirit, is hardly predictable. But an examination of its positive aspects is necessary before its negative attributes can be considered. First, within this context the vision is one of a unified and *experiencing* humanity. We must emphasize the element of experience because the philosophical message of the Indians who participate in the workshop network is as much a demand for new ceremonial and ritual participation as it is an explanation of the basis for the experiences. So the justification for sharing some of the tribal ceremonies and philosophies is that these beliefs and practices have a universal applicability and the practitioners have a divine commission to share them.

The positive second dimension is the emphasis placed upon the living nature of the universe. This belief is solidly tribal in origin but has been given an added value because it is now being connected to the beliefs of other traditions and to the findings of modern science. In this respect the modern shamanism teaches its adherents to develop once again an understanding of the animals and to cultivate relationships with them. Primarily this is now accomplished by a variation of Jungian active imagination, but within the Indian context. People who would otherwise have a reverence for birds and other animals, except for their lack of familiarity with the natural world, come to see that in the most profound sense humankind cannot live alone. Not only do humans need a companion and community but they also need the fellowship, help, and sense of community of all living things. Surprisingly this idea is strikingly powerful when it is experienced in ceremonies and made concrete in people's lives.

The third point of positive stature in the Indian missionary thrust is a corollary of the second point but must be stressed in this context because it carries with it a call to action that makes it a unique experience in itself. Companionship, in the religious sense, is stressed by these outgoing religious representatives so that people following their directions find themselves dealing with higher and/or different spiritual personalities in both a healing and personal-vocational sense. In the old traditional way of handling these experiences there was an alliance between the Vision Quest participants and higher spiritual personalities, but this kind of alliance was generally restricted to those who had successfully endured the ordeal and for whom the spirits had shown pity. The experiences of people today are not nearly as powerful as they were in the old days, but they are more precisely tuned to the needs of average persons. It helps them deal with the many minor personal vocational and ethical choices which, taken together, make up the consistency of human social life. It is almost as if the spiritual energies inherent in the American Indian tribal universe were deliberately expanding, losing some of the potency they enjoyed in the restricted traditional context, but in turn providing spiritual guidance for an increasingly numerous group of people.

In contrast to these positive aspects of the modern effort to extend the influence and practice of traditional tribal religions into the non-Indian world, there are a number of negative things that can be identified and which, unless they are corrected, can abort this kind of spiritual expansion and reduce it to simply another American fad, a fate which too many spiritual and artistic energies suffer in our society. Most important in this respect is that these experiences, while helpful to most people attending the workshops and conferences, are not held in or responsible to any identifiable community. A network is not a community—it is simply an elongated set of connections held together by common interests or experiences. A network can easily become a set of highly charged spiritual dominoes unless it finds a center, becomes sedentary and indigenous, and begins to exert a constant influence on a group of people whose lives and actions are thereby changed for the better. Here we need not so much institutionalization as we need to find a means of stabilizing religious experiences within a definite geographical context so that as people accumulate spiritual insights and powers, they can have a community in which these powers can be manifested. Community is essential because visions are meant for communities, not for individuals although it is the special individual who, on behalf of the community, undertakes to receive divine instructions for the community.

The second danger is that as people gain in spiritual understanding they run the danger of misusing what they have received in the constant effort to spread the word of the realities they have experienced. Many of the Indian practitioners who tread the workshop network today are very close to falling into this trap. Surveying the progress and accomplishments of the ten most popular and respected of the Indians who work the non-Indian social networks will show that there is virtually no individual spiritual progress. The feats which they are able to accomplish are basically those gifts which first enabled them to gain a measure of respect and a following in the non-Indian world. Thus while there is progress in bringing the substance of tribal religions experiences to non-Indians, the workshops, Sun Dances, and Sweat Lodges are becoming something akin to the Christian Mass. These presentations on the non-Indian circuit are not only repetitious but lack potential to probe spiritual realities at any increasing depth of experience or understanding.

The traditional religious revelation of the tribes was very people-specific. That is to say, tribes held their religious secrets very firmly to themselves because the nature of the original revelation required the people to follow certain paths, to act in certain ways, and to fulfill a specific covenant with higher powers. Unlike Jews and Christians, who have interpreted their religious mission in terms of absolute divine commissions to oppose other religious traditions, regardless of value or content, the tribal-specific revelations did not spawn religious intolerance. Rather the Indians rigorously followed the universal admonition to remove the mote from their own eyes before they arrogated to themselves the power to correct their neighbors' practices and beliefs. There is not one single instance of wars or conflicts between or among American Indian tribes, or between Indians and non-Indians, which had as its basis the differences in religious practices or beliefs.

Given this tradition, there is a real concern among the reservation traditionals of the impact and meaning of spreading the tribal teachings to anyone who has a spiritual or emotional need. The belief has always been that the Great Spirit and/or the higher spirits are also watching others and they will provide the proper religious insights and knowledge to others. Therefore it behooves Indians to obey the teachings of their own traditions and hold them close. If they were meant for other people, the other people would have them. Such thinking has prevented most tribes from engaging in religious imperialism, and the humility underlying this attitude is admirable. But what happens today when individuals of the various tribes spend their time on the lecture-workshop-conference circuit indiscriminately instructing non-Indians and non-tribal members in a variety of beliefs, some giving simple homilies and others offering deep and profound truths? Will not this kind of behavior, which in traditional terms is utmost sacrilege, ultimately call down the wrath of the spirits on the tribe? These concerns are real and pressing for many American Indians and there is no easy or certain answer to them.

The present situation of American Indians speaks directly to the context in which liberation theology is being done. It is not difficult to trace the paths which liberation theology must inevitably tread, and consequently an intersection between other people and American Indians can easily be discerned sometime in the future. Liberation theology first and foremost seeks to help human beings overthrow or deflect the tremendous oppression that is visited upon us by our own institutions which, in the name of a variety of false deities, have taken control of our lives and emotions. For the first two groups of American Indians there is no question that liberation theology has an immediate and profound message. The sabbath is made for human beings; human beings are not made for the sabbath: and so it is with all of our institutions. To the degree that oppression exists because of ill-informed or ill-intentioned use of human social, religious, and economic structures, to that degree people must act to take control of their lives. Institutions must be responsible to people and people must take responsibility to eliminate institutions and replace them with the free-flowing and spontaneous positive energy of love that flows from deep within themselves.

As liberation theology energizes and inspires people to become what they are intended to be, the task will be shifting from the need to escape from oppressive institutions and situations to the responsibility to free oneself from oppressive doctrines and beliefs and the corresponding practices which keep them in the forefront of our spiritual and emotional lives. Eventually liberation theology must engage in a massive critique of itself and its historico-theological context and inheritance. Here, as the issues become sharper and more profound, liberation theology will encounter traditional American Indian religions and their practitioners, first the modern Indian missionaries of the workshop network and then at last the few remaining traditionals on the reservations. Liberation theology must not only confront these representatives of American Indian religion but it must have a message for them which transcends their experiences and practice *and* makes sense of the Indian tradition in a more universal and comprehensive manner.

At this point of interaction liberation theology must dig deep into the Judeo-Christian tradition and bring forward whatever insights into the nature of reality it may have to present to the traditional Indians. It is not difficult to see that the cupboard is exceedingly bare at this level and that liberation theology must, perhaps inevitably, depart from its historico-theological moorings and deal with important philosophical questions. Is the world dead or alive? And what does that mean for the daily lives of people? What is the place and status of the human being in a world filled with sentient and powerful spirits? Is the world a fallen world from the beginning of time or does it simply have a set of historical difficulties which have been nearly impossible to resolve? What are the purpose, task, and meaning of human existence? The questions and issues which divide traditional American Indian religions from the world religions are many and profound and not capable of resolution through reference to a pre-existing set of doctrines and dogmas.

The basic philosophical difference between the American tribal religions and the world religions, Christianity being the world religion most likely to come into direct contact with the tribal religions, is the difference between time and space, between times and places, between a remembered history and a sacred location. At this point Christianity, and by extension liberation theology, is in mortal danger. History is a highly selective interpretation of the events of our lives loosely strung in sequence to prove the validity of the argument. That is to say, by arranging certain kinds of facts in a certain sequence, it is not difficult to prove to the disbeliever that certain spiritual truths and realities exist. But in performing this arrangement of human memories and experiences, a good deal has to be omitted and a great many facts have to be given a specific twist in order to fit the pattern. We hear from the Christians that God works and is working in history. But this history does not reflect humanity's complete and comprehensive experiences. This history is valid only if the listener surrenders his or her critical sense of inquiry and accepts the many premises that history, any particular history, requires for validation.

The tribal religions, however, bound as they are to specific places and particular ceremonies, do not need to rely upon the compiled arguments of history. It is only necessary that people experience the reality of the sacred. The attraction of the Indian missionaries on the lecture circuit is that they do provide new kinds of experiences, and in the world today people crave their own experiences and judge the truth of a proposition by the manner in which it helps them understand themselves. Consequently in the conflict or competition between Christianity and the other world religions and the tribal religions, a competition that is approaching on the horizon, there is no question which tradition is capable of speaking meaningfully to the diversity of peoples. A Sweat Lodge, a Vision Quest, or a Sing performed in a sacred place with the proper medicine man provides so much more to its practitioners than a well-performed Mass, a well-turned sermon argument, or a well-organized retreat. Christian rituals simply have no experiential powers.

Ultimately religions ask and answer the question of the real meaning and purpose of human life. The fatal flaw in the world religions is their propensity to try to provide answers to these questions knowing full well that both questions and answers must come from honest and open participation in the world. The Apostle Paul, filled with the Spirit and zealous to pass on his received theological truths, found no audience in Athens because no one was asking questions. Consequently his answers, already pre-formed in his mind and pushing for expression, had no relevance to his situation. Tribal religions do not claim to have answers to the larger questions of human life. But they do know various ways of asking the questions and this is their great strength and why they will ultimately have great influence in people's lives.

American Indians should wish liberation theology well in its endeavors. There is no question that humanity needs liberation from the many ills that plague it. But even the sacralization of the institutions, governments, and economic systems that are represented in our various human societies could not answer the ultimate questions that we must answer in our lives. Sacralization would only provide a benign and comfortable context in which these questions could be asked. It would always be up to the Great Spirit and the higher spirits, to the community of living things and to the humans themselves to derive cooperatively the proper answers. Liberation theology, however, can and must clear out the underbrush which we have carelessly allowed to obscure our vision of the forest, and this task cannot be accomplished too quickly. All living things now stand on the brink of oblivion and extinction. Mass destruction cannot be allowed to be the answer to all of our other questions, or, for that matter, to foreclose the possibility of asking the proper questions.

An old Crow chief, asked about the difference between the Indian way of life and that of the whites, responded that for the Indian there were visions, for the whites there were only ideas. Visions, in the Indian context, require action and this action manifests itself in the community, enabling the people to go forward in confidence and obedience. The vision is complete, it is comprehensive, it includes and covers everything, and there is no mistaking its applicability. Ideas, on the other hand, have only a limited relevance. They explain some things but not all things; they are rarely comprehensive and there is great difficulty in finding their proper application. Most important, however, the idea never reaches the complete community—it only reaches those who have the ability to grasp it and it leaves the rest of the community struggling for understanding.

It is difficult to discern, at the present time, whether liberation theology is an idea or a vision. It has the requisite characteristics of praxis and community, and in the struggle for freedom from oppression it even has the experiences. But within its larger theological context it is tied to a narrow and historical understanding of the human experience. When and whether it can transcend this foundation and provide the context in which the ultimate questions can be asked is an exciting and perilous possibility that hangs over us today. Hopefully we can glimpse a vision of community through the praxis that liberation theology asks and demands of us.

(1990)

WORLDVIEWS IN COLLISION

Deloria once identified Immanuel Velikovsky, the pioneer of planetary cata-strophism, as one of the most significant intellectual influences he had encountered. Velikovsky was a Russian-born scholar whose 1950 book *Worlds in Collision* provoked an explosive controversy within the scientific establishment. Arguing that ancient texts and oral traditions contain infor-mation about actual—if seemingly fantastic—events, his best-selling book proposed a new narrative for the planetary past based on historical readings of mythic accounts. Velikovsky published several more popular studies of global cataclysm including *Ages in Chaos* and *Earth in Upheaval,* but he achieved very little acceptance among American scientists until the seven-ties, when NASA space probes began confirming some of his hypotheses about the formation of planets.

Deloria has referred to Velikovsky's ideas in a number of writings, includ-ing two articles written for scholarly journals devoted to Velikovskian stud-ies. His first exploration of Velikovsky's approach appeared in *God Is Red,* where he extends the method of mythic correlation to a consideration of the origin of religions. Religious traditions are not delusional or imaginative curiosities, Deloria argues, but originate in actual historical events that some-times assume catastrophic proportions on a global scale. *God Is Red* is best known for Deloria's useful distinction between chronological/historical and spatial/geographical worldviews, which he constructs as broad generaliza-tions about how Western people and tribal people think. He juxtaposes these generic systems in order to get at the roots of contemporary power relations, and the book as a whole constitutes a formidable critique of colo-nial ideology. It is commonly misread as an exercise in essentialist identity politics, however, perhaps because it seemingly documents a cultural binary corresponding to the political binary that characterizes relations between tribal nations and the federal government. In uncovering the philosophical and cultural basis for colonial conflict through the analysis of worldviews, Deloria's intentions are more ambitious than merely exposing American Christianity's original sins. He is after a unified theory of religion grounded in collective human experiences of specific natural environments.

119

Deloria provides a concise overview of the religious situation, raising many of the issues addressed more fully in *God Is Red,* in the first essay in this section. "Religion and the Modern American Indian" was originally published in the monthly journal *Current History* for an issue on tribal affairs. Highlighting the difference between propositions and experiences as bases for religious commitment, and between salvation history and sacred land as rubrics for religious identity, Deloria surveys contemporary tribal communities to illustrate his points. This technique of comparative analysis accompanied by generalized description reflects Deloria's reformist strategy, pursuing social change through cross-cultural education and persuasion. Admitting the difficulty of predicting future developments in times of rapid change, he concludes that "perhaps the only certainty is that Indians will continue to understand the conflict between Indians and the rest of society at its deepest level as a religious confrontation."

In the next two essays, Deloria identifies some important differences between idealized tribal and Western worldviews. "Native American Spirituality" was the title essay in a thematic issue of *Gamaliel,* a quarterly publication of the Community for Creative Nonviolence, a Catholic pacifist group in Washington, D.C. Contrasting rationality with reflection, Deloria describes the latter as "a way of life, the consistent direction and substance of individual existence, ... a matter of extended consistency in behavior." It is a "special art" that "requires maturity of personality, certainty of identity, and feelings of equality with the other life forms of the world," the difference between knowledge and wisdom. Emphasizing the importance of kinship relations encompassing the land and all other living things, Deloria depicts how respect and reciprocity can produce an interlocking circle of relationships more coherent and durable than linear cause-and-effect reasoning. The spirituality that emerges from such a context is an experience-based set of values and behaviors rather than an assortment of abstract propositions. Deloria expands on this work in "Civilization and Isolation," which appeared as a feature article in *The North American Review,* a humanities journal based at the University of Northern Iowa. Returning to philosopher Alfred North Whitehead's idea of the "fallacy of misplaced concreteness," Deloria here critiques Western intellectual provinciality by contrasting isolation with relatedness. The deconstruction and interpretation characteristic of a scientific worldview can produce an abundance of fragmented knowledge, but only the perception and synthesis practiced out of an experiential worldview can comprehend the fullness of life as "a complex matrix of entities, emotions, revelations, and cooperative enterprises." Tribal oral traditions may very well bear important information about the history of the Americas. Deloria foresees a new era of intellectual maturity as he poses "the fundamental question underlying the scope of human knowledge: Is truth divisible into categories or is it synthetic, incorporating all aspects of experience and understanding?"

The last essay in this section was presented at a consultation on "Creation and Culture" sponsored by the Lutheran World Federation. In "Christianity and Indigenous Religion: Friends or Enemies?" Deloria explicitly addresses differences in religious worldviews by engaging in an extended critique of Christianity. He qualifies his remarks in pointing out that abstract representations of religious traditions are always selective and subjective; discourse is qualitatively distinct from experience. His argument is organized around four key points on which generalized Christian and tribal religious worldviews differ: the nature of the universe, the nature of human experience, the nature of religion, and attitudes toward life. Deloria identifies a number of theological differences in these areas, all of which proceed from the "concept of creation" to which religious communities ascribe. "Tribal peoples do not hold a doctrine of creation intellectually; they may tell their stories of origins but their idea of creation is a feeling of kinship with the world. Christians, on the other hand, have reasonably precise doctrines about creation but seem to have no feeling that they are a part of the world." Our religious narratives of the planetary past may very well determine whether we have a planetary future.

J. T.

13

RELIGION AND THE
MODERN AMERICAN INDIAN

Religion permeates the lives of American Indians today. But its importance to Indian communities is apparently disregarded by people looking for the exotic aspects of Indian existence. Observers of Indian culture have usually looked for certain barbaric traits; when these have not always been present, observers have expressed sharp disappointment at the apparent loss of the valuable beliefs of Indian traditions. This attitude has been puzzling to many Indians because it represents a steadfast refusal on the part of non-Indians to see in changing cultural and technical institutions the eternal values that sustained Indian tribes for many centuries.

People educated in the Western European religious tradition have come to regard religion as a set of propositions to which believers must give at least intellectual assent and to which they will hopefully orient their daily lives. Little emphasis has been placed by Westerners on the nature of religious experience (outside the Pentecostal branch of Christendom); consequently, their ceremonies have long since lost experiential content. With such a past, Westerners have generally dismissed the ceremonials of Indian religion as pagan practices that accomplish little and tend to perpetuate superstitions better forgotten.

The important aspect of Indian tribal religions, however, has been their insistence on developing and maintaining a constant relationship with the spiritual forces that govern the lives of humans. As ceremonies have lost their content, with the changing of life styles, they have been forgotten or abandoned. The recent efforts of Indian activists to reclaim tribal ceremonies have highlighted the dilemma of today's religious Indian. A traditional Indian finds himself still experiencing the generalized presence of spiritual forces; at the same time he finds himself bound by the modern technology of communications and transportation, which speed his world far beyond its original boundaries.

Of modern Indian tribes that maintain a traditional religious life the Pueblos stand out as the most consistent and persistent of the nation's Indian groups in continuing their old ways. Pueblo life still revolves about the ceremonial year, and although most Pueblos are employed in modern jobs that require a thorough knowledge of the white man's world, they cling to the religious ways that have served them for countless generations. The Pueblos block off all roads leading to their towns and villages at ceremonial time. Although they apparently allow nontribal members to observe their festivals, in reality they allow outsiders—both white and Indian—to view only those aspects of the Pueblo religion that can be known by people outside the Pueblo.

The Hopis are one of the most traditional of the old Pueblo people, although the Taos people are also rigorous in their adherence to tribal ways. In recent years, the Hopi stand on non-violence, which goes back many centuries, has attracted white people of similar persuasion. But when the whites have arrived at the Hopi villages, ready to be embraced with open arms, they have often been rebuffed. The Hopis do not believe that because people understand common philosophical propositions they have anything else in common.

The most persistent problem of the Hopi and other Pueblo people is the degree of adaptation that will be allowed inside the villages. Often the conflict is framed in practical terms, such as the question of allowing refrigerators inside the village. Younger people, having attended Bureau of Indian Affairs boarding schools, are accustomed to having cold milk to drink, but a pueblo without refrigerators precludes the preservation of foods and drinks that are dependent upon cold. The conflict is sometimes heated and represents a challenge of no small proportion to traditional Indians. Does one forsake a philosophical and religious tradition in which things "happen" for the sake of bodily comfort?

Tradition is also strong among the Navajo, particularly with respect to healing ceremonials. The Navajo religion is deeply philosophical and ceremonially complex, and the Navajo medicine men still practice the ancient rites of healing for a surprising number of the tribe. The first reaction of the United States Public Health people to the Navajo medicine men was rejection and was based on cultural prejudices rather than on any profound knowledge of the Navajo religion. In recent years, this prejudice has broken down as whites have learned about the Navajo religion and customs; a program to train medicine men now forms an important part of the health program on the reservation. Medicine men

and white doctors often work together successfully to heal Indians who
have complex health problems.

The Apache groups of Arizona and New Mexico also adhere rigorously
to their traditions. Ceremonies are the most serious part of their community life; the Crown Dancers often perform at pow-wows and rodeos, but
they also have a strong religious function within the tribe. The Apache
people have an amazing sense of solidarity; they do not share their
songs, secular or religious, with other Indian groups, because they do not
want the songs profaned by people who would not understand their
meaning to the Apache.

The Iroquois of New York state and Canada also maintain a very
strong sense of tribal solidarity although some of them follow the very
ancient longhouse ceremonies while others follow the Handsome Lake
teachings that originated as a reform movement in the first part of the
nineteenth century. Their ceremonies require both the use of masks and
sacred wampum belts and the recitation of tribal legends and histories.
The Iroquois are troubled by the intrusion of non-Indians in Iroquois
religious practices. For some reason, anthropologists have taken it upon
themselves to criticize the present practitioners of the longhouse as failing to maintain the religion in its primitive purity. Their attitude is probably based on the necessity to maintain scholarly reputations rather than
on an intimate knowledge of Iroquois religious ceremonies.

The tribes of the northern plains have reinstituted their traditional
Sun Dance after many decades of its prohibition by the government. The
Sun Dance involves the piercing of the flesh of the dancers and their fasting and enduring considerable pain. Because of these elements, the Sun
Dance has in recent years attracted all kinds of sensation-seekers who
come to the dance merely to view the unusual. As a result, the seriousness of the ceremony has been overshadowed by the obvious publicity-
generating aspect of brutality. This popularization may eventually result
in the destruction of the religious aspect of the dance; within our lifetimes it may become little more than a tourist attraction.

Christianity has made gigantic inroads into many tribes because of the
nearly sixty years, from the 1880s to the 1940s, when the native religions
were prohibited by the government. During this time, Christian denominations were given a free hand in gathering converts on the reservations;
at one time the churches merely divided up the various reservations
among those groups that desired to proselytize tribal members. Such
allocations are no longer made and today competition among various
missionary societies on reservations is accompanied by peripheral conflict of a religious nature that intrudes into the social, political and economic life of the tribes.

The Five Civilized Tribes of Oklahoma—the Cherokee, Creek, Choctaw, Seminole and Chickasaw—adopted Christianity very early (in comparison to other tribes), and they have a very strong membership in the Baptist and Methodist denominations. Among these tribes the tradition of native leadership is well established, and they have produced outstanding preachers and teachers. In general, the Five Civilized Tribes tend toward fundamentalism in their theology and resemble the rural churches of Appalachia and the Deep South. The Five Civilized Tribes are not wholly Christian, however, and medicine men and women still perform their healings and ceremonies in the traditional communities. Considering the national rate of Indian acculturation, one might suggest that the Five Civilized Tribes have reached a proportion of traditional versus Christian religious beliefs that all other tribes will eventually approximate: eighty percent Christian, and twenty percent traditional.

About five years ago a movement began in Canada to assemble the native Christian ministers and the traditional medicine men to discuss how religious conflict might be avoided between the two distinct religious paths being taken by Indians. This movement came to be called the "ecumenical movement," and, while conferences have been held in various parts of the United States and Canada, the movement seems to have settled in Alberta at Morley in the past several summers. The conference seems to have attracted as many observers as religious leaders, and it is possible that the movement has bogged down because observers demand more and more spectacular speeches and beliefs on the part of the participants.

In some aspects, Indian religions have taken a militant edge; medicine men have been present at some of the dramatic protests of the past several years. Medicine men were present during the occupation of the Bureau of Indian Affairs headquarters in November, 1972, and many Sioux medicine men supported the Wounded Knee protest in 1973. During negotiations to end the Wounded Knee occupation, religious ceremonies were held. The emphasis placed by the protesters on the occupation indicates that it was as much a religious protest as a political event.

NATIVE AMERICAN CHURCH

One of the most attractive pan-Indian religious movements is the Native American Church, which uses the peyote in its ceremonies. The Native American Church incorporates some aspects of Christian belief in its teachings, but its major ceremonies are of pre-Columbian origin, coming from the desert southwest into the plains and Great Lakes area in post-Columbian times. For several decades in this century, the Native

American Church was very controversial, but as the religious attitudes of the government and the major missionary denominations have become more flexible and mature, the conflict has largely subsided.

The books about Don Juan, the Yaqui medicine man, have been very popular among young non-Indians; many of them assume that the religious and philosophical ideas of these books are incorporated in the beliefs and practices of most tribal religions. Indians have tended to shy away from the Don Juan books because the books do not present ideas that are immediately familiar in a tribal context. It is very difficult, after reading the books, to determine the degree to which their ideas relate to any particular tribal religion, but the specific content of the various tribal religions apparently precludes the generalizations made in the Don Juan series. Still, in terms of abstract ideas, the tribal religions may not be in conflict with the books if only the philosophical nature of statements about the world is considered.

Western religions concentrate on the idea of history and what it has revealed to human beings about the nature of God. Both the Christian and Jewish religions are dependent on the recitation of historic events and their interpretation as the means of determining the validity of their beliefs. With the development of the social programs of the past decade, many Indian tribes have begun to write their own history, and, while this history is not cloaked in wholly religious terms like the Christian and Jewish theologies, still some tribes have insisted on including tribal religious legends as an integral part of their tribal histories. One might view this development as necessary for the reformation of tribal society, except that many Indian tribes today are affected by past events that were primarily legal rather than cultural. The placing of several tribes on one reservation, for example, led to their political merger, but in many instances their cultural and linguistic identities have been preserved. A tribal history of the tribes on the reservation, therefore, would not be a history comparable to either the Christian or Jewish traditions.

THE SACRED LANDS

In the southwest, among the eastern Iroquois, and in some areas of the northern plains, the ceremonial life of the Indian tribes has apparently survived efforts to stifle it; it remains a viable alternative as a religious tradition. Of much more importance than ceremonials or specific practices is the fact that the old view of the world that arose from the tribal traditions still survives; this attitude toward life and toward peoples who are outside the tribal fold has very important implications for the contemporary Indian.

Almost every tribal religion was based on land in the sense that the tribe felt that its lands were specifically given to it to use. The proceedings of treaty councils are filled with protests and declarations by Indians to the effect that lands cannot be sold since no human has the power or right to own them. Some of the old chiefs felt that, because generations of their ancestors had been buried on the lands and because the sacred events of their religion had taken place on the lands, they were obligated to maintain the tribal lands against new kinds of exploitation. The famous Nez Percé war began because white settlers invaded the Wallowa Valley in eastern Oregon and because Chief Joseph's father had made the young chief promise never to sell the lands in which his ancestors lay buried.

In the southwest, where there were few treaties because of Mexico's prior claim to the area (a claim recognized by the United States and assumed by the Americans following the Mexican War), the sacredness of lands has been even more important than it was elsewhere on the continent. Especially among the Pueblos, Hopi and Navajo, the lands of the creation and emergence traditions are easily identified and are regarded as places of utmost significance. Much of this land cannot be commercially exploited but is held by the government in large tracts for national parks and forests. Government officials have ruthlessly disregarded the Indians' pleas for the restoration of their most sacred lands, and the constant dispute between Indians and whites centers around this subject.

Many younger Indians feel the moral outrage of the government confiscation of tribal lands, although they do not necessarily understand the implications of a tribal religious attachment to them. The occupation of Wounded Knee, for example, was triggered by a deep ethical outrage on the part of many of the Sioux, but the place itself was not originally sacred to the tribe. Historic events—the original massacre and the succeeding decades of government exploitation of the Oglalas—had made the site one of the most revered places of the Sioux people. One can see in this attitude an evolution of the concept of sacred lands from the original conception of sacred places as sites where religious revelations had taken place to sites of deep historic significance, sanctified by immediate past events.

Another dimension of tribal religions that has carried over into this century is the Indian emphasis on hospitality. The traditional assumption that people are not naturally malevolent and that they intend to deal honestly ran very strong in most tribes. Treaty documents clearly show that, while the United States was busy perpetrating outrageous frauds upon the tribes, Indian spokesmen were clinging to the belief that white people were only trying to help them. The incredible traditional naïveté of tribal leaders in dealing with the government has survived almost intact, in spite of a startling series of betrayals that would severely tax the patience of other groups.

MODERN EMPHASIS

Today, the emphasis in the western states is on the development of energy resources, and western tribes hold massive deposits of coal and own a great deal of water on major rivers. Pressures have built up for rapid, total development of Indian resources, and the federal government, which is supposed to protect Indian resources from unfair exploitation, leads the groups seeking to force the development of tribal assets. While there is a great deal of resistance on the part of young activists against the further ruination of tribal lands, the elected tribal leaders themselves seem unable to understand that the government is not their friend. Too often, they fail to protect tribal assets because they are led astray by government officials who appear to be looking out for their interests. It is a sad commentary on contemporary life that although the foremost enemy of the Indians is their federal trustee, tribal leaders still believe in the Bureau of Indian Affairs.

The awakening of younger Indians to the positive aspects of tribal culture in the last decade has created a significant demand for the restoration of traditional religious ceremonies. Indian religions are now seen as value systems that have been preserved from intrusions by whites. In some instances, this preservation can be demonstrated, particularly by those tribes in the southwest that have already been discussed. In a number of other tribes, the recorded observations made by scholars about the nature and substance of the old religion seem to be very important. The Black Elk books of John Neihardt and Joseph Epes Brown are popular among the Sioux, and Frank Waters' work on the Hopi and Pueblo peoples is widely read. Many ideas currently popular among younger Indians derive from these books rather than from the traditional teachings.

Perhaps the most important future movement is being developed by the Indians of the Joint Strategy and Action Committees of the major Protestant denominations. They are making a significant effort to bring the old teachings to bear on modern problems in a Christian context. Foremost among the leaders of this movement is the Reverend Cecil Corbett, director of the Cook Christian Training School in Tempe, Arizona, who has taken the lead in establishing short courses and seminars at the school to combine traditional Indian beliefs and the modern Christian social gospel.

This combination of philosophies seems to be the best meeting ground for ancient beliefs and modern concepts of social reform.

Perhaps the old antagonisms that revolved around the proselytizing of converts away from the tribal religions will finally be laid to rest as this movement takes hold.

One cannot project the future because of the very high tension in the various activist protests that have included traditional religious activity. The degree of political polarization in the national Indian movement is immense, and traditionalists are seen as primarily activist oriented. This is a complete reversal of their former role, when they represented the most conservative elements in the tribes. Even the most learned observers are puzzled. Perhaps the only certainty is that Indians will continue to understand the conflict between Indians and the rest of society at its deepest level as a religious confrontation.

(1974)

14

NATIVE AMERICAN
SPIRITUALITY

American Indians look backwards in time to the creation of the world and view reality from the perspective of the one species that has the capability to reflect on the meaning of things. This attitude is generally misunderstood by non-Indians who act as if reflection and logical thought were synonymous. But reflection is a special art and requires maturity of personality, certainty of identity, and feelings of equality with the other life forms of the world. It consists, more precisely, of allowing wisdom to approach rather than seeking answers to self-generated questions. Such an attitude, then, stands in a polarized position to the manner in which society today conducts itself. Therein, at least partially, lies the important difference between American Indians and the rest of American society.

One of the difficulties that presently plagues American Indians is the assumption, made by educated non-Indians, that an objective knowledge of something totally describes it. When this assumption is coupled with the presumption that nothing really important has happened until it is reported in the media, or until non-Indians discover it, the gulf between aspirations and reality becomes immense. Misunderstandings abound, and non-Indians, frantic to discover a means of establishing roots in the alien soil of North America, seek out American Indians hoping to discover an easy formula possessed by Indians which will ground them in a sense of permanence and meaning. The present intense interest in Indians, therefore, has little to do with who Indians are, what they believe, or what they can contribute to American society as a whole. Rather it is the product of an intense longing for a sense of reality in experience which the non-Indian world does not provide. When this longing is expressed in cheers for the people at Wounded Knee it is welcome, but misunderstood. For people capture the drama of history as re-enacted at Wounded Knee rather than the essence of Indian complaints, conditions, and alternatives. Messages, if any are passed in activist events, are garbled and incoherent at best.

The essence of the Indian attitude toward peoples, lands, and other life forms is one of kinship relations in which no element of life can go unattached from human society. Thus lands are given special status because they form a motherhood relationship with the peoples who live on them. Too often this dimension is twisted when non-Indians make it a sentimental truism and the Indian philosophy appears shallow and without insight. But the true meaning of the motherhood of the land is that, like a mother, it shapes and teaches our species and, according to the peculiarity of the area, produces certain basic forms of personality and social identity which could not be produced in any other way. White Americans see the basic differences in peoples which are expressed regionally but they too often mistake historical experiences for the influence of lands on people. To find a "southern" identity without understanding the unique characteristics of the southeastern lands is to vest in the memories of our species a shaping ability which does not exist. According to geographical area radical differences occur which are more than historical accidents and which require reflective consideration to understand fully.

With respect to other life forms, this attitude manifests itself in what one could call "kinship" cycles of responsibility that exist between our species and the other species. Hyemeyosts Storm attempts to bring this unique web of responsibilities into play with modern terminology in his book *Seven Arrows,* when he allows non-human characters to participate in the unfolding of the story. This transformation brings out a dimension of life common to Indians but unique and unsuspected by non-Indians. For the responsibility of our species is to perform responsible tasks with respect to each form of life that we encounter, learning from them the basic structure of the universe, and ensuring that they receive in return the respect and dignity accorded them. And this acknowledgement of the dignity of other life forms, which is a simple but profound recognition, underlies all Indian attitudes toward the organic world. Our species is allowed to use them for food but in return we must ensure that their sacrifice becomes a means of fulfillment. Social scientists, observing Indian behavior toward animals and plants, usually describe this activity as "totemistic" or "animistic" implying that Indians intellectually believed the universe to contain uncontrolled and arbitrary powers. But the essence of this behavior is the maintenance of dignity throughout the organic world. The struggle for dignity thus dominates Indian spirituality but the struggle is one of conferring dignity, not seizing or manufacturing it.

Many non-Indians come to understand the bestowing of dignity on others, even on other life forms, but they still fail to see the fundamental distinctions which flow from the Indian attitude of reflection. Perhaps the most basic of these distinctions is the recognition of sexual and age differences. The traditional ethical norm for non-Indians is the admission of the brotherhood of our species and the concomitant responsibility to treat others like we would like to be treated. Equality and unity easily become a homogeneity in this ethic. American Indians view ethical relationships with much more sophistication, allocating duties, privileges and respect according to a unique system of family relationships, older people becoming grandfathers and grandmothers, men and women becoming brothers and sisters, wives and husbands, and even strangers occupying the place of cousins within the network of specific relatives who must show concern for one another. Apart from participation in this network, Indians believe, a person simply does not exist. But within the network attitudes and behaviors must be expressed in particular terms, not in general and often unfulfilled rules of conduct.

Following directly from this ethic is the American Indian understanding of human personality and the meaning of life. If we are required to show respect and create dignity for others around us, then this respect and dignity cannot be simply a surface admission of social status. Dignity can be given even to the unworthy with devastating irony and people within the community can see in the most precise fashion whether or not the individual who is honored in fact deserves such praise. Such lavish but undeserved praise can be more damning than an insult. Individuals strive as best they can to deserve the dignity which the community gives them and it is extremely embarrassing to be praised and honored by one's better while failing to perform according to expectations. Giving dignity therefore encourages individuals to deserve the accolades they receive and the unified attitude of social groups towards the world and towards others is the cultivation of virtues. A person hailed as wise, strives to be wiser, a person acclaimed as brave, seeks to be braver, and a person honored as a parent seeks to become better in that endeavor.

The intense individual concern to deserve the respect and dignity which one's family and society accords one produces a mature attitude of reflection which grows with the passage of years and the accumulation of experiences. Experiences are hardly an individual affair, however, for within each community is the collective memory of past events and the behavior of people within that immediate history is common knowledge. Over decades of community life the leadership emerges as the community recognizes in the continual activities of individuals a sense of consistency, of commitment to the community, and of the course of wise decisions. As people come to deserve the respect and dignity with which they are presented, the community forms around the time-tested people of substance. In most Indian communities in the old days the most respected person was the one who gave freely of physical wealth, who showed a concern for the unfortunate, and who allowed weaker members of the community to rely on him/her. Reflection, then, is a way of life, the consistent direction and substance of individual existence, and not a unique intellectual ability. It is a matter of extended consistency in behavior, not a matter of correct or numerous beliefs.

The circle of these concepts can be seen to be integrated into a basic attitude toward life and its experiences. Rather than leading to a logical conclusion we see a network of attitudes and behaviors which characterize both individuals and societies. Nothing derives from a cause-and-effect chain of circumstances. Everything becomes an aspect of everything else, distinguishable only by the unique situation in which individuals are called upon to respond to new conditions. Without the logical chain of reasoning it is impossible to initiate the "Catch-22" propositions which have been seen in recent times as utterly destructive of human beings and societies. Any effort to "escalate" the intensity of a situation is regarded as madness since intensification of anything must issue into the other aspects of life, not the concentration of energies in one course of action.

It is not difficult, therefore, to see that American Indians and their non-Indian neighbors have failed to communicate with each other. Both systems of thought and behavior are exclusive of the other. Linear reasonings continue indefinitely until they produce conclusions directly opposite to their initial premise. The integrated relationship of attitudes and behaviors which characterizes Indian existence cannot be stretched to admit linear propositions. When either system of thought is confronted with the other, it must begin to adopt the characteristics of the other or reject it out of hand. Thus a great many Indians have shattered the circle of their existence and have become linear and fragmented individuals. And in recent years many non-Indians have begun to bring the linear dimensions of their existence into a circle of relationships. The interaction of these two tendencies cannot be underestimated. When Indians speak of returning to their own culture, they are really speaking of reforming the circle of individual and social existence, a renewal of meaning, not a flight from reality.

*

When we speak, therefore, of Native American spirituality, we do not speak of an abstraction, a set of beliefs, or a genetic propensity to be poetic and stolid. We rather describe an attitude toward the world which derives out of many experiences and which, when seen in a social setting, can be transmitted to others by the proper behavior of the possessors of the tradition. Today in the United States non-Indians demand that Indians become militant in order to achieve political goals. But the very quiescence of the traditional Indians and their seemingly infinite patience with the government is damning indeed when understood in the traditional Indian context. For they are bestowing dignity upon a government and a system of life with the expectation that this government and this way of life will come to a sense of understanding and will begin to act with maturity and dignity towards them. It is a great embarrassment that such expectations are unfulfilled. But in understanding the calm of American Indians, non-Indians should feel great shame at their own behavior, for silence is the greatest critique of all. It is the way that reflective people wait for children to quiet themselves before they continue with the lessons of life.

(1977)

15

CIVILIZATION AND ISOLATION

"Men can be provincial in time, as well as in place," Alfred North Whitehead once remarked. When we apply this insight to the realm of human knowledge, quite frequently we refer to the non-Western peoples and point out that they have failed to keep pace with the technical developments that other peoples, particularly Western peoples, have made. Thus non-Western societies are considered by many social scientists as remnants of stages of human evolutionary growth struggling to reach levels of sophistication that were achieved and surpassed by Europeans many centuries ago. Rarely is the question of provinciality applied directly to Western European peoples, and on those occasions we find that provinciality is applied as a criterion to determine efficiency and sophistication within the worldview of that tradition.

Provinciality, however, is a characteristic of societies and individuals who fail to conduct periodic critiques of their beliefs and who assume, with some degree of smugness, that the knowledge they possess, because it has been their possession for so long, provides the basis for intelligent existence in a world of sudden and unexpected change. Western Europeans have been so much dazzled by their own technology that they have fallen into a provinciality in regard to human knowledge so narrow as to exclude major portions of human experience. Whitehead called this attitude the "fallacy of misplaced concreteness," and he meant by this the exclusionary approach to the physical world coupled with the belief that whatever approach one did use properly excluded things that have no value.

When Native Americans have been forced to confront this attitude on the part of non-Indian neighbors we have generally come off second best. A good many factors must be included in any analysis of our failure to confront and overcome the attitude of superiority which non-Indians have thrust upon us. The most important factor would probably be the efficiency of technology which non-Indians brought with them. Marvelous instruments and tools of iron and other metals blinded us and produced an uncritical assumption that whatever the white man was doing must be based upon some superior insight into the world of nature. We forgot, to our detriment, that the first Europeans we encountered thought they were going to sail over the edge of the world, that succeeding expeditions had fantasies about Fountains of Youth, Cities of Gold, and northwest passages to Cathay.

Native Americans did not realize that Europeans felt a dreadful necessity to classify us within a view of the world already made obsolete by discovery of our continent. While we could not participate in the heated theological discussions concerning our origins—whether we derived from Noah's Ark or were survivors of the Ten Lost Tribes of Israel—we perhaps could have been more insistent on making the non-Indians provide more and better arguments for their version of world history and human knowledge. Any group that frantically dug gold in the west in order to transplant it to the east and bury it cannot be quite right and their insights cannot form the highest achievement of our species.

The world is much more sophisticated today, and groups of widely varying backgrounds can communicate with each other even though they form the minority of particular societies. Thus the modern emergence of Indian peoples and the concentration by them on revival and revitalization of culture should include a persistent emphasis on the validity of their own histories, technologies, and social and political institutions. In some measure Indian groups have already begun this process of defending and justifying cultural insights tribes have preserved over the centuries of contact with Europeans. Unfortunately, much of this activity has been phrased in an anti-white format which does not produce a justification of the Indian tradition but merely points out the inadequacies of the non-Indians. We do not take time to adapt this approach to the problem. One glance at the Western democracies and we discover that the political leaders, when they are not lusting in their hearts after forbidden fruit, are demonstrating that intelligent life probably does not exist on the planet or, in the alternative, are planning ways to extinguish whatever intelligent life might accidentally arise here.

Transcending this childish tactic of accusatory relationship with the non-Indian is not difficult but it involves creating or re-creating a confidence in the Indian traditions. Such a task intially involves a determination of the techniques which Indians used to accumulate, evaluate, and perpetuate their knowledge of the world and to translate this knowledge into Western terms that can speak rationally and intelligently to those people within the Western cultural milieu who are prepared to listen. I will attempt to outline the variances which I see between the Western European traditions and the Indian traditions, primarily the North American peoples, with the hopes that the differences—and there are radical differences to be seen—will be illustrated so clearly as to enable us to embark on a new interpretation of human knowledge which is not provincial in either time or space.

If I were to choose the single attribute that characterizes the Western approach to human knowledge, indeed to almost all human activities, I would unhesitatingly choose "isolation." In scientific and philosophical terms we are perhaps speaking of William of Occam and his famous razor which has cut the throat of more than one effort to synthesize human knowledge. Briefly, we can rephrase this doctrine as the belief that by continual subdivision of any problem we can reach a certain and ultimate knowledge. For most of the last couple centuries the scientific concern with finding the tiniest element of the atom demonstrated the potency of this belief. It also, incidentally, illustrated the basic Western belief in the primacy of matter over spirit. But isolation remains the dominating attitude which Western peoples have adopted toward the world. We see this approach eloquently in our political institutions and the assumption that one human being is interchangeable with another and that the conglomerate of human decisions, counted statistically, produces the proper course of action for a nation to adopt. This belief reduces wisdom to public opinion polls and produces those nasty and distasteful compromises which substitute for intelligent activities in most of the Western democracies.

We find additional confirmation of this belief in isolation in the various religious traditions that are characteristic of Western peoples. Almost always, in the last analyses, we find the solitary individual in the hands of an angry—or at least disgruntled—god. Even those Western peoples who have rejected the traditional religious denominations of their culture have not found another approach to the religious question but have simply adopted the Eastern version of solitude, listening to one hand clapping, and other symbolic gestures, and are now contentedly recycling their own energies endlessly. Even the atheists and humanists ground their justifications in the primacy of the individual rather than the maturity of the species.

One reason for the scientific and philosophical isolation of the elements of experience is the belief, deeply held although rarely practiced, that one cannot trust sense perceptions, human emotions, or the intuitional abilities of the human personality. This article of faith must certainly go as far back as the Greek philosophers and the prophetic movement in Israel, but was not a dominating factor in Western existence until the relatively late period when Descartes, Leibnitz, and Newton demonstrated the efficiency of the mathematical descriptions of the physical world. Since that time Western peoples have increasingly depended upon mathematics for their analyses and insights of nature. This approach has proven spectacular in the physical sciences, particularly physics, and the technology that has been produced as a by-product of physical theory has only served to entrench in Western minds the belief that mathematics is the proper description of reality. So influential is this attitude that in the last century we have seen the development of social sciences which seem to suggest that statistical truth is equivalent to ultimate reality. The social sciences now insist that all human activities can be described as functions of complicated formulas. I have seen this attitude applied to elections in the United States, but I have generally rejected that approach and bet on the people who counted the votes rather than on those statistics which projected who would vote. Mayor Richard Daley of Chicago, now deceased, never failed me in this respect.

As mathematics has been more influential in representing the scientific quest, and as the scope of human knowledge has expanded, the old tendency toward isolation has produced a strange phenomenon in which human knowledge is divided into separate categories variously called disciplines, fields of study, or what have you. As sciences have given rise to subgroupings of knowledge and specialties have been developed, knowledge itself has suffered a fragmentation and the sole guarantee of the validity of knowledge has been in the similarity of techniques employed to accumulate and interpret data. Briefly, even this field of methodology has degenerated as the various disciplines have moved away from each other, so that the sole criterion of truth today seems to lie in the sincerity of the researcher and his or her relative status within the specific field of endeavor. Sincerity is no guarantee of anything except an emotional state and quite often not much of a characterization even of that.

Isolation, in the Eastern context, seems to be the isolation of emotions and personality, but in the Western context can only be understood if seen in the context of the physical universe conceived as a giant machine that operates according to certain immutable laws. Conceiving physical reality as if it were a machine not only squeezes emotions and intuitions out of the data but introduces into the data the belief that the unusual cannot occur. Causality becomes the primary mode of interpreting data and eventually becomes the manner in which people describe a situation, so that even observations of events become incomplete and only the mechanical aspects of the happening are reported.

When this attitude emerges in the field of history its effect is to reduce the intensity of experience and homogenize human activities so that everything can be classified under the same categories of interpretation. History becomes at first a chronology and eventually a trivial commentary that has no criteria by which factors are described or understood. Most contemporary interpretations of world history are simply the imposition of uniformitarian principles on factual data that has been emptied of any human content. Ultimately, history becomes a collection of data of what we would like to believe about the world as dictated by the ideals we hold, rather than even an accurate chronology of what actually happened. We become helpless integers involved in a process over which we have no control and with respect to which we have little understanding.

Perhaps the final consequence of approaching the world with the intent to isolate and thereby achieve dominance over things is the belief that the way we see things is the proper manner of describing them. Thus we approach and reunite with the original contention that we are dealing with the fallacy of misplaced concreteness. But we have not engaged in a reasoning process as much as taken a tour around the intellectual and conceptual universe of the Western European to illustrate the various modes that this basic error can take. A few illustrations may be in order, to demonstrate both the provinciality of the Western attitude and the manner in which Indians and dissatisfied non-Indians can begin to move away from this mooring and expand the horizons of all concerned. The treatment of non-Western peoples, particularly North American Indian peoples, provides a perfect setting in which we can examine the manner of escape.

The Europeans, arriving in North America, discovered a people that had no written language, laws, religions, or customs, yet governed themselves so well that the American constitutional fathers were encouraged by Benjamin Franklin to model themselves after the Iroquois League when they came to devise a constitution. Europeans, looking at Indian societies, decided that these people lived in savagery because they had no written rules and regulations to govern them. Here we find the intense desire to objectify, to render human activities to mechanical form, and to accord respect by discovering similarity and homogeneity. Finding a qualitative difference between Indians and themselves, the Europeans promptly characterized the North American people as a lawless breed devoid of the attributes of civilized society. A great many wrongs were done to Indians because non-Indians believed them to be without laws and therefore unable to make intelligent or just decisions regarding their lives.

All of these beliefs about Indians changed as social science became more influential in Western society and more sophisticated in its observations. In 1926, with the publication of Malinowski's famous book *Crime and Custom in Savage Society,* which demonstrated that customs could be as restrictive and socially integrating as written codes and laws, the perception of people made a radical shift and Indians were considered savages because they were so tightly bound by custom and lacked the freedom of Western democratic peoples. How a whole race could shift in one century from most lawless to most law-bound remained a mystery to the Indians who came into contact with Western intellectual history, but it should have been an indication to non-Indians that all was not well with the Western way of perceiving human activities.

This example illustrates that much of what Western peoples have understood as knowledge is simply a reorientation, within their own framework, of the thesis used to interpret phenomena, and is not a corresponding development in the phenomena itself. Even more, the example indicates that no final statement, and perhaps no reliable statement, can ever be made concerning knowledge of the world. There is always another viewpoint by which interpretations of data can be made and when this situation becomes entrenched in the academic worldview of a culture, inevitably the reality that it describes becomes a verbal or mental reality. When phenomena do not fulfill our expectations, they are disregarded, downgraded, or derided and the opportunity to come to grips with another facet of reality escapes us.

When we turn to the North American Indian worldview we discover an entirely different perspective on the world. Instead of isolating things, Indians encompassed them; togetherness, synthesis, and relatedness characterized their experiences of the universe. The ordinary distinctions between mind and matter, human and other life forms, nature and human beings and even our species and the divinity were not considered valid ways of understanding experience. Life was a complex matrix of entities, emotions, revelations, and cooperative enterprises and any abstraction was considered stupid and dangerous, destructive of spirit and reductionist in the very aspects that made life important. A great many non-Indians have intuited this "togetherness" from observing Indians and reading of the "Indian way," but have failed to understand the remarkable system of relationships which undergirds a seemingly innocent and simple life.

Relatedness is a much better description of the Indian way of looking at the world. Here we are not describing a comparative knowledge in which no absolute value exists. Indeed, all values are absolute because they are experiences and because they deal with specific relationships between specific individuals. A good example of this specificity is the manner in which the Osage Indians fed themselves. In the early spring they would plant their corn along the bottomlands of the Missouri River about the place where St. Louis is today. After they had sown their crop they would depart for the far Rocky Mountains in Colorado and Wyoming to do their summer hunting. The Osage would spend most of the summer in the high mountains hunting deer, buffalo, antelope and other large game animals, and they would dry their meat in the sun, making it suitable for preservation.

In the middle of July they would begin to examine one of the mountain flowers and when this flower began to turn to seed they would know that it was time to begin their journey back to their winter homes. They would pack up their summer's hunting surplus and return to Missouri where their corn would now be ready for the harvest. Such behavior may seem the utmost of simplicity except that to accomplish such a task required that the Osage know the relationships of plants, animals, and lands over a distance of some 1,000 miles and know these complex relationships so well that they could transfer an abstract sense of time, time in the sense of organic growth, from plant to plant over that distance and use the growth of a mountain plant as a gauge or calendar for their corn.

Here we have no general knowledge, no principles valid in all cases, no knowledge that can be tested in the laboratory. We have a knowledge totally unlike Western scientific knowledge and yet an understanding of great profundity. Within this scope of knowledge we have an intuitive understanding of the spiritual nature of life which enables people to act in a purposive and predictive sense. Classifications, in this system of thinking, defy Western categorization; they are not deductive and cannot be reached through any complicated logical path. Yet they exist and serve amazingly well in determining how a specific people will relate to an environment. Thus if we can learn anything from this example the first lesson must be that classifications, as we have been used to them in the Western schemata of knowledge, are useless when we approach a more intimate relationship with the universe.

The hallmark of relatedness or synthesis is experience rather than interpretation. In the synthetic process we first experience the unity of exis-

tence and then, upon reflection and further experience, we begin to separate elements of that experience into useful categories of knowledge in
which similarities and intimacies are the most important criteria. For
that reason most Indian classifications of birds, animals, reptiles, and
other life forms begin with the activities of these creatures and seek to
identify similar purposive behaviors. Simple morphology, as Western
peoples have conceived the organic world, have little part in the Indian
format; when they do, the morphological features that are chosen are
understood as indicating similarity of temperament, not evolutionary
origins. Thus our species, birds, and bears are considered to be the "two-
leggeds," and we behave in many respects as if we were a single species.
A good Indian medicine man can conduct a sophisticated tour of human
and animal personality by describing the traits that convinced Indians
long ago that the "two-leggeds" were a specific group.

The shift from isolating things to relating them involves the recognition of a different form of preserving knowledge. When we isolate and
then interpret phenomena, our basic intent is to derive principles from
which we can predict future behavior, illustrate mechanical operations,
or analyse into further component parts. Our interpretation and
rearrangement of data is most important. In the tradition which relates
everything in specific terms the immediate experience is most critical
and everything is oriented toward a preservation of the exact conditions
under which something happened. Little effort is devoted to rearranging
the elements of the incident or experience, for it was the uniqueness of
that particular experience that first attracted us and made it seem important. Thus the tradition seeks to preserve as accurately as possible everything that took place.

When we look at the traditions of the North American peoples we
discover that they have carried down over the generations many
accounts of phenomena we would consider amazing today. The Ojibway
of western Ontario, for example, relate stories of the water monster who
lived in the lakes and rivers and tipped over the canoes of the unwary
and unlucky. Pictures of this creature are liberally scattered over much
of Ontario and eastern Canada. The Sioux also relate the story of water
monsters and their description correlates to an astounding degree
with the Ojibway tale. Further west the Indians of the Pacific Northwest
have traditions that the lakes of the region were formerly much larger
and contained monsters who stirred the waves unmercifully whenever humans ventured out on the water. A correlation of all accounts, of
petroglyphs and pictographs of the various tribes, and an acknowledgment that this particular set of stories is always intimately tied to specific lakes should be sufficient to inform us that at one time within the

memory of these tribes, a different and perhaps more spectacular form of life inhabited this continent. If we use our imaginations we can see in this tradition the presence of the group that we have always called "dinosaurs."

Now to suggest that human beings have been living in North America since the Mesozoic is radical only when we restrict our interpretation of human knowledge to that already accumulated by Western peoples through the process of isolating elements of experience. The suggestion seems less radical when we remember that the oral traditions do not seek to interpret as much as they attempt to recall and remember precisely the unusual events of the past. The possibility that these stories contain the elements of past experiences is heightened considerably when we view contemporary research on the dinosaurs and discover that the latest and most precise interpretation of this group conceives them as warm-blooded, bearing their young live, and traveling in herds, all characteristics of mammals and not reptiles, and possessing behavior patterns not unlike those which the Indian water monster tales relate.

What are we to do when a tradition which has always been seen by Western peoples as primitive and superstitious now threatens to become an important source in a new and important revolution in paleontology? Are there other important areas of experience that have been preserved by oral traditions that have been neglected or discarded by the scientific mind because of the all-consuming goal of achieving truth by the isolation of elements of experience? Here we have a dilemma of major proportions which strikes the Western mind at precisely the most vulnerable point. Isolation has not produced truth as much as it has produced specialists who studiously avoid synthesis in favor of a continuing subdivision of information into increasingly separated disciplines. We finally arrive at the fundamental question underlying the scope of human knowledge: Is truth divisible into categories or is it synthetic, incorporating all aspects of experience and understanding?

The present situation calls for a sense of maturity between cultures that no other period of human history has required. We must now begin to transcend all other parochial considerations in our understanding and move forward into a new period of synthesis in which all information is brought into a coherent whole. Alfred North Whitehead remarked rather casually in *Science and the Modern World* that "it takes a very unusual mind to undertake the analysis of the obvious." Now the obvious always refers to those things that are so commonly accepted as to be considered beyond serious consideration by scholars. So the task of moving human knowledge forward has generally fallen to the amateur, to those who simply wish to know, and to the humble souls who refuse to surrender an idea to the guardians of human knowledge, the academics; those souls who understand knowledge as the possession of the whole human species and not the plaything of the specialist.

North American peoples have an important role to play in the determination of knowledge in the future. They represent thousands of years of experience in living on this continent and their customs and traditions, the particular and sometimes peculiar ways they have of approaching problems, of living, and of protecting the lands, are not simply the clumsy adjustments of primitives but the seasoned responses of people who synthesized and summarized the best manner of adapting themselves to the world in which they lived. Insofar as their insights can be translated into principles which can reorient Western thinking, scientific and social, and insofar as North American peoples can understand their own traditions and abide by them, to that degree we can produce a more sophisticated, humane, and sensible society on this continent.

So the provinciality of which Whitehead speaks is really the provincial manner in which we today look at the experiences and memories of our ancestors and define the history of our species and planet. World history, Arnold Toynbee once remarked, is a parochial affair comparable to a map of the Mediterranean area being considered a true and accurate map of the world. Human knowledge cannot be provincial, but must enclose the planet and render an accurate account of its nature and growth. We are today on the threshold of a new era in which this task will be accomplished—and it is perhaps the most exciting time of any that our species has experienced. Let us have the emotional and intellectual maturity to bring it to pass.

(1978)

16

CHRISTIANITY AND INDIGENOUS RELIGION

Friends or Enemies?

Let me start by saying that any discussion of popular or of private religion is necessarily a gathering together of many strands of thoughts and emotions and choosing from many traditions a few things that appear to be common themes and interests. In fact, many traditional Indian people would find such a gathering together of material quite humorous. This is not the way they would talk about religion—as if we had to pretend that religious experience is a cafeteria and we could pick and choose a reasonable religion and then devote ourselves to it. So we are doing a certain amount of sinning against all traditions when we consider them from afar.

I will only say that when I looked at the set of topics sent by Dr. David Burke, I immediately wanted to pick the topic: "Indigenous Religions and Christianity: Friends or Foes?" This topic itself illustrates one of the chief failings of Christianity, namely that it traditionally sees other religions as foes rather than simply as different. It sees other traditions as inferior rather than as having their own integrity. The question is, should such differences really matter, unless, of course, those of one tradition act imperialistically and try to infringe on the integrity of another tradition? These are not things we should have to worry about if we are all following the best teachings of our ancestors and societies. That Christianity takes special pain to ask whether we are friends or foes, to me, betrays the fact that Christianity is indeed an imperialistic religion and so polarizes religious communication in a hostile manner.

Let me say further that my great-grandfather was an Indian medicine man, my grandfather was a converted Christian and Episcopal priest/

missionary, my father is a retired priest and missionary. So I was brought up in the Christian faith but with a strong family recognition or admission that the old Sioux ways had a real validity in and of themselves. I attended a Lutheran seminary and received a degree in theology. Yet, I have in my lifetime concluded that Christianity is the chief evil ever to have been loosed on the planet. I am probably one of that generation who is not satisfied with what is here but who cannot return to anything that was past, so must move forward not knowing a whole lot about anything. With this background, I operate from the position of now wishing to see what is probably the nature of the world—and of religious reality— that tribal people once knew, some of which they still preserve today, and what responsibility one has to this view of life. In trying to find a satisfactory answer to the questions that arise in this context I have come to the conclusion that the tribal religions have a great deal of insight and can be very helpful to people today.

I have organized my presentation according to a four part exposition. In part one I want to discuss *the nature of the universe* as it is understood in tribal religions and by this topic I mean both the physical universe and whatever experiences, sensations, and reflections are productive of intelligent commentary on the universe we experience. In part two we will take up *the nature of human experience.* How is it that we experience life and what does it mean? In part three we should look at *the nature of religion.* How do we view religion itself? Are we able to push it away, to abstract it, and to learn something from our view of it? Finally, in part four, our concern will be with the *attitudes toward life* that are produced, encouraged, or generated by these two different traditions. Discussing creation and even having a doctrine of the creation and/or creator makes no sense if it is simply a way of explaining something. We need to understand creation in a manner that will help us act correctly on our beliefs.

THE NATURE OF THE UNIVERSE

We can outline the various beliefs of tribal religions but we would find ourselves hopelessly involved in a list of specifics that would only cause us intellectual disagreements. And we would find that many beliefs previously held by tribal peoples have been radically changed since contact with Western civilization so that the clear differences that once existed are not as clear as they once were. Additionally we would find that through the constant contact between tribal peoples and Western Europeans, tribal peoples have had to emphasize certain aspects of their traditions in order to communicate. So there are recent twists and turns in

the tribal traditions that make it impossible for us to present a general theme with any degree of confidence.

Nevertheless even on this broad and modern canvas there are startling differences between the native religious traditions and Christianity. The most profound, in my opinion, is in the evaluation of the nature of the universe. Tribal peoples always find it to be a good universe. There may be, and often are, evil spirits in it, but on the whole it is a pleasant place, it is a real place, and it is a place that demands our involvement, appreciation and respect. The universe has many secrets which are revealed in the ceremonies and it has many duties and responsibilities for us. We are mutual workers with all other forms of life in making certain that the universe works out its own plan of development or unfolding and so everything in the universe has a role and a status as a cooperative creature.

Christianity proclaims a good creation, at least as Yahweh finishes his work on the sixth day, but within a very short time the universe has crashed into evil because of the disobedience of one of the minor, and not too intelligent, species. Nature becomes evil and hostile toward our species and consequently we are in conflict with every other form of life. We come to believe that we are above all other forms of life. We come to believe that our salvation redeems the other life forms simply because we are more important than they are. And we look for the destruction of this world and the creation of another world where, presumably, *we will not be allowed* to screw things up so readily. Because the universe is evil and must eventually be destroyed, we have no real responsibility to it. We are pilgrims here and what we do may have some eternal significance in another arena but much of what we do has no significance at all in the larger cosmic scheme of things.

Another way of drawing this contrast between tribal religions and Christianity would be to say that for tribal peoples, nature is not evil, but it is not neutral either. It is an active force that demands our participation, and tries to ensure that this participation will be of a positive nature. Christianity sees nature as evil and, occasionally for a freethinker or Christian of a scientific bent, neutral; it just goes along evolving species and wiping them out with no moral content in its process. When we grasp the point that if there is going to be an intelligible process it must also be moral, we really stand with the tribal peoples. If we attempt to inject sufficient morality to overcome evil or, at best, neutrality, we stand with the Christians. Therefore the initial appraisal of the content of the universe, whether it is a good universe or a bad one, is critically important for whatever will follow in our thinking and behavior.

The next important thing about the universe is whether or not it is alive. Tribal peoples almost unanimously declare that it is a living thing. The universe is a fabric, a symphony, a tapestry; everything is connected to everything else and everything is alive and responsible to its relationships in every way. The human being is not the crowning glory of creation and certainly not its master. We are but a small, but nevertheless vital, part of the universe and at least part of our task is to serve as a focus for some of the things that must be done for the universe really to prosper and fulfill itself. Because everything is alive and because we have responsibilities to all living things, we cannot force the rest of nature to do what we want. Indeed, we must respectfully approach the rest of nature and seek its permission to initiate a course of action. When we do this in a humble and respectful way, we find that other parts of the universe take joy in cooperating with us in the production of something new and important. Natural entities become our friends and we are able to do marvelous things together.

The Christian response to this question is disappointing at best, usually tragically wrong, and at worst catastrophic for the other forms of life as well as the universe itself. My best guess is that the Christian universe is dead, except for man, and that anyone who believes otherwise and tries to communicate with the other entities of nature is not simply heretical but an idolater. The Christian God is not only jealous, but seems to resent deeply any interspecies communication at all. This God further has created the birds, animals, reptiles, and other forms totally dumb and if not dumb, at least lacking sufficient intelligence to gain God's respect or the human's respect and kind treatment. This God is content to damn every other form of life in order to punish human beings and ruthlessly curses all species because of anger toward a snake and two humans and an apple.

The living universe, in the tribal setting, has its heartbeat, its means of communication, in the drum. The drum is the pulse of life that exists in every creature and needs nothing more than a constant rhythm to keep itself attuned properly. Songs become the means of passing information and powers from one species to another in the living universe and it is possible that many times and in many ways the creatures who compose the universe have given each other powers and information that has helped to create a more enjoyable experience of life for everyone concerned. It is difficult to discover what Christianity believes the heartbeat of the universe really is. Sometimes it appears to be prayer, other times it is preaching and, to hear Christians sing, it is rarely song or rhythm. The best that could be said is that Christians appreciate the logical construc-

the tribal traditions that make it impossible for us to present a general theme with any degree of confidence.

Nevertheless even on this broad and modern canvas there are startling differences between the native religious traditions and Christianity. The most profound, in my opinion, is in the evaluation of the nature of the universe. Tribal peoples always find it to be a good universe. There may be, and often are, evil spirits in it, but on the whole it is a pleasant place, it is a real place, and it is a place that demands our involvement, appreciation and respect. The universe has many secrets which are revealed in the ceremonies and it has many duties and responsibilities for us. We are mutual workers with all other forms of life in making certain that the universe works out its own plan of development or unfolding and so everything in the universe has a role and a status as a cooperative creature.

Christianity proclaims a good creation, at least as Yahweh finishes his work on the sixth day, but within a very short time the universe has crashed into evil because of the disobedience of one of the minor, and not too intelligent, species. Nature becomes evil and hostile toward our species and consequently we are in conflict with every other form of life. We come to believe that we are above all other forms of life. We come to believe that our salvation redeems the other life forms simply because we are more important than they are. And we look for the destruction of this world and the creation of another world where, presumably, *we will not be allowed* to screw things up so readily. Because the universe is evil and must eventually be destroyed, we have no real responsibility to it. We are pilgrims here and what we do may have some eternal significance in another arena but much of what we do has no significance at all in the larger cosmic scheme of things.

Another way of drawing this contrast between tribal religions and Christianity would be to say that for tribal peoples, nature is not evil, but it is not neutral either. It is an active force that demands our participation, and tries to ensure that this participation will be of a positive nature. Christianity sees nature as evil and, occasionally for a freethinker or Christian of a scientific bent, neutral; it just goes along evolving species and wiping them out with no moral content in its process. When we grasp the point that if there is going to be an intelligible process it must also be moral, we really stand with the tribal peoples. If we attempt to inject sufficient morality to overcome evil or, at best, neutrality, we stand with the Christians. Therefore the initial appraisal of the content of the universe, whether it is a good universe or a bad one, is critically important for whatever will follow in our thinking and behavior.

tion of the universe. Immense and intense rationality seems to be the only resonant fact of the Christian world.

We next confront the question of the history of the universe. The Christian sees a single creation set in motion and then punctuated by periodic destructions wrought by divine anger. The final day of judgment will presumably end the universe and a new universe will be created where things will be considerably better. This scenario raises the question of why the deity could not have simply created a workable universe in the first place since the logic is that God has the power to do so, eventually, in the latter days. The universe is indistinguishable from religious history in Christianity and we sometimes get the feeling that even the material world has no firm reality in it. The material world itself suffers immensely from humanity's moral shortcomings and the inevitable end of human history also means the destruction, in fact the needless destruction, of all other forms of life which have had no voice in the errors of humans and who generally have studiously avoided humans insofar as they are able.

The tribal perspective generally sees the universe as a cyclic pattern of creation and destruction. People call these cycles "worlds" and remember past worlds and how they came to destruction and predict future worlds and tell how they will come to destruction. For each world there is a moral law and ceremonies are given to the people that they may live properly in each world. Worlds do eventually go bad. I suspect they simply wear out their possibilities and need renewal. There are, after all, only so many different things that can be done respectfully and conclusively in the world in which we live. Familiarity, I suppose, ultimately does breed contempt; at least it breeds disrespect. When the individual worlds come to an end, the suffering is distributed on an impartial basis. The faithful few who have tried to fulfill the moral law of the universe, and many of the animals, and those miscellaneous few who happen to be in the right place at the right time, survive and are given instructions, ceremonies and prophecies as the next world begins.

The tribal explanation of cosmic history bears a much closer correspondence to scientific, geological interpretations of strata than does the Christian single-world explanation. Within most of the tribal traditions there is even an explanation of the demise of species, including prophecies on the actual disappearance of the tribe itself. The meaning of history is not that we are saved from it but that we participate in it. Thus our own demise is not a real catastrophe but a fulfillment of the larger cosmic meaning. Every other species finds meaning in this larger scheme of things and that is why other species are willing to feed and clothe us. We,

of reference. The individual is expected to stand alone in all his or her endeavors. Even in the Garden of Eden the humans are segregated from the rest of creation; they are unable to commune with the other forms of life, with the possible exception of the snake, and are expected to perform whatever moral duties are assigned to them as individuals. While the Christian tradition has many times expressed its sense of community, its ability to illustrate its sense of community has many times been lacking. Particularly in the modern world, community is represented by conglomerate.

Whatever knowledge humans achieve or experience in the Christian world seems to be derived from their own innate sense of reason and logic. During the Middle Ages there were two sources of truth, reason and revelation, with reason apparently serving as an empirical verification of revealed truth. Human experience—and knowledge—is built upon a technique of deriving generally applicable propositions from a series of similar events or experiences and there is a lack of specifics in every Western intellectual proposition. These general propositions enable Western and Christian people to manipulate the world without fully understanding—or accepting responsibility for—the implications of human actions.

The Christian tradition de-emphasized the family. While it uses images such as the family of God, or children of God, it is not difficult to see that its images bespeak the nuclear family in a two-generational setting. There is no admission of the importance of grandparents or peripheral relatives. In neglecting all of the possible human relationships, Christians unnecessarily limit their understanding of the deity since this assumes that God can function only in a limited number of ways. The Indian conception of the deity as a grandfather or grandmother opens up considerably more flexibility and descriptive terminology which can be used to be more explicit about human-divine experiences.

The emphasis on the individual's relationship with God to the exclusion of his or her responsibilities to others creates an immoral society. As long as individuals are "right" with God, so the idea goes, they can do whatever they want with respect to other humans or creatures. In this frame of reference there is no empirical verification of the "rightness" of this relationship. Recently we have had Christians praying for the death of equally sincere and devout Christians because of political disagreements. God is often an abstract weapon for many Christians rather than a deity with whom one has a family relationship.

Human experience within the Christian context is always an adversarial situation. Whether it is the devil, others as pagans, the animals or even members of one's own community, the responsibility for most individuals is to oppose or avoid others since involvement with them could contaminate the soul and hamper its chances of justification and salvation. The Christian teaching is to love others as one loves oneself. This requirement suggests that the individual is completely at peace with himself or herself, although this situation cannot possibly occur since the individual is part of nature and yet alienated from it. Therefore individuals only love in the neighbor those positive characteristics they see mirrored in their own self-understanding. The characteristics that distinguish one individual or people from another are threatening to Christians and consequently it is very likely that they will be inclined to employ force to extinguish them. The history of Christianity is replete with examples of its hatred of innocent cultural patterns and values which it does not understand and cannot tolerate.

The Western institutional hierarchy of Christianity imposes limitations on some individuals and bestows immense powers on others in a wholly whimsical manner. People fall on either side of the line of distribution of power for a variety of reasons, not all of them proper or even rational. To become a spiritual leader within the Christian context one needs only to be born within a family of sufficient wealth to enable an individual to complete a course of study. No actual spiritual content or experience or power is required. Because the certification of institutional power becomes a matter of fact in our lives, manifestations of the spirit become exceedingly dangerous to society. An individual alleging or demonstrating a direct and powerful relationship to God becomes suspect and must be kept away from institutional life. Thus even the founder of the Christian religion had too much religious power for the institutions of his world and had to be executed.

Within the tribal context there is a demand that the individual receive qualification and certification from the divine itself. People are just as skeptical and demand just as many tests of power and spiritual insights as would any other society when individuals make these claims. But it is expected that God will contact and use human individuals so there is no great social need to discredit or destroy a spiritual individual. The proof in that person's spirituality is not to be found in certification by a human institution but in an evident ability to display and follow divine teachings and powers. If that person cannot produce, he or she is irrelevant; in the Christian context it does not matter that the person is irrelevant if the proper credentials can be presented.

Human experiences as an epistemological product have much different interpretations in each context. The tribal peoples see what we experience in the world as real; they also believe that what we see in dreams

and visions is real, and they know that what we do in ceremonies and rituals is real. There is no aspect of life that is not real and that is not taken seriously. This tendency to credit reality to a wide variety of experience means that a different kind of logic is operating. There are no mistakes in the tribal world; there is always purpose. We may not understand the reason for any particular thing that happens to us, but we have the responsibility to remain alert and reflective and learn what larger patterns we are part of.

The Christian view is exceedingly strange. This world is not believed to be the real world but somehow it is an imitation of reality, often a pale imitation. Yet when Christians have unusual or spiritual experiences, it is believed that they have been deluded or have hallucinated or otherwise lost their mental capacities. Since the physical world is not ultimately real, within Christian society science attempts to describe what the nature of the physical world *really is.* Because this picture changes so drastically with each new formulation of the scientific worldview, the religious understanding of experience also changes. Dreams and visions are fine for the patriarchs of the Bible and even ascension and transfiguration are proper objects of belief during the founding days of Christianity, but they are no longer credible interpretations of experience because our scientific perspective says that they are physically impossible, and therefore really impossible. So the Christian is ultimately a materialist and allows his culture to determine the shape of his religion.

Human experience is in some way dependent upon the manner in which we understand creation. On the whole tribal religions take the individual and community experiences and repeat them as the anecdotes which give an adequate recapitulation of the initial experience. But new stories and interpretations can be added without subtracting or discrediting the old knowledge. The cumulative burden of tribal society may be the endless recitation of tribal experience which in some important ceremonies may take several weeks to recount. Within the Christian context there seems to be a continual effort to summarize experience and express it in precise and logical form. Therefore previous formulations are always being outmoded and the nature of religious knowledge changes considerably with each revision. The Indians seek wholeness in their knowledge and experience by remembering the specific incidents which tell them something about reality. The Christians achieve wholeness by formulating a summary which discusses within broad guidelines the most important aspects of some parts of experience. For Indians everything seems to be real, for Christians, nothing seems to be real, at least nothing that we can rely upon in this world.

THE NATURE OF RELIGION

We now come to the nature of religion. The majority of tribal religions, as far as I can tell, look at religion as a healing and balancing process, whereas I understand the Christian tradition as a commemorative, historical, institutional phenomenon. Within the tribal context, the healing and the balancing of human lives and experiences are religious functions. Healings are a cooperative enterprise between people, animals, and spirits or powers. The healing can be mental as well as physical, clearing up emotional problems and resolving physical illnesses. When one looks at the ceremonies of the different tribes, there is always a healing aspect but for the tribes whose traditions go very far back into the past, particularly the tribes which have lived in certain areas or on certain lands as long as anyone can remember, with migrations being a distant echo, there is an additional balancing function to religion.

The balancing function of religion seems to suggest that we are dealing with extremely strong cosmic powers and that these powers rely upon humans to perform certain kinds of ceremonies which minister to specific environments. The Iroquois, Hopis, Pueblos, Creeks, and perhaps even Cherokees and Choctaws, incorporate a ceremonial year with their other religious functions. Human life must move in a cosmic rhythm with the rest of nature and this trip must be acted out in basic ceremonial form. The Pueblos, for example, spend forty days in the kivas during the winter to assist the sun in regaining strength so that he can make his accustomed rounds during the summer and ensure the growth and maturation of all living things. There we have more than an agricultural religion which looks to fruitful harvests and celebrates dying and rising vegetation gods. Rather we see religion as a cooperative enterprise and perhaps even humankind as a specific expression of cosmic personality and intelligence.

The idea of balancing precludes absolutes of both good and evil. It does not, however, seek a golden mean between two poles of moral expression. Rather the balancing that must be done is that of ensuring that every living thing finds and continues on the path of individual growth and expression. Everything must become what it is intended to be. Yet we do not know the outcome of anything that we undertake. Therefore we need balancing to ensure that we are devoting the proper respect and energy to our own integrity and the integrity of the social groups with whom we are related. The mandala symbols of sand painting, the motions of the sacred pipe, the concern with directions and colors, and special circles and medicine wheels all seek wholeness and completion. If something becomes complete, it realizes its own self and contributes to the enjoyment of the universe, and above all, to the understanding of the universe.

The Christian notion of religion seems to be commemorative in the sense that its ritual repeats and reenacts the sacred story of its founder's life. Over the centuries these stories have been fitted into an annual chronology which suggests a bit of the old dying and rising God but places this motif within the historical lifetime of one man. The Eucharist reconsecrates followers in the death and subsequent resurrection of the savior, and baptism is the initiatory ritual that segregates the committed followers from all secular people. Preaching appears to be used in sacramental fashion by Protestants, while Catholics, Orthodox and some denominations of Protestantism have additional sacraments depending upon the particular theology of the denomination.

Tribal religions and Christian churches do share one fact of contemporary religious life in that both groups seem to have allowed some of their most important rituals to lapse or languish from lack of use. Of the seven rites of the Sioux, for example, only two, the Lamenting for a Vision and the Sun Dance, are performed regularly. I do not count the sweat lodge in this category since it is always practiced in conjunction with the other rites. But some of the condolence rites have been largely abandoned. Confirmation may be of some importance in a few Christian churches but Holy Unction, the Churching of Women, and some of the other ceremonies which were once practiced rigorously are hardly used at all today. Within the Indian tribal tradition the falling away of ceremonies is a sign that this world is approaching its end. Christians seem to take their cues from their cultural context and consequently there is no good explanation for the loss of some ceremonial obligations other than that they are regarded as old-fashioned or inappropriate.

Religion in almost every cultural context has a doctrinal context which determines the accuracy of both the expression of the faith and the performance of the ceremonies. Christianity has traditionally made creeds, doctrines and dogmas its major concern. Thus it is an intellectual religion that depends as much upon the allegiance or concurrence of its followers to prescribed formulations of theology as it does upon actual religious experience. It is believed by most Christians, and particularly by most Protestants, that the proper recitation of holy formulas is as important, if not more important, than following the precepts of the religion. This situation testifies to the extreme intellectualism of Christianity and also gives evidence of some embarrassing historical moments. The Nicene Creed, for example, owes its formulas describing the substance of God less to divine revelation and more to the political problems of the Roman Empire since one of the emperors settled on the formula and enforced it with police state brutality in order to prevent civil unrest.

Indian tribal religions have a comparable experience in the matter of doctrine but this rigidity seems to be more directed at the procedures and steps of the ceremonies and rituals rather than the recitation of beliefs. Thus the sweat lodge must be constructed in a certain way. Sand paintings must incorporate the proper colors and geometric shapes. Objects of reverence used in ceremonies must be of particular quality and origin. This precision is focused on the nature of the ceremony and is really subject to human interpretation and dissension in the same way that Christians can argue about sprinkling or full immersion in baptism. One could compare the two by saying that Indians demand precision in ceremonies, the Christians in the expression of intellectually correct beliefs.

The control mechanism in tribal religions is social shame. Everyone belongs to one family or another and in many tribes the clan system places additional responsibilities on family members. A person is presumed to represent his or her family and clan so that no individual act stands alone; it always involves other people. This extension of personal acts and personal responsibility to a larger social entity makes shame a perfect means of social control. An individual's relatives must make certain that evil deeds are punished or that compensation is made to the injured parties. The fact that an individual can shame a whole family makes social behavior of the individual person important and therefore the rules which regulate tribal society are those which ensure that large family groups will be able to resolve their problems amicably.

In a sense, because shame does not attach as a permanent mark on an individual, but rather exists as a temporary condition that is identified with a specific act or action, tribal religions are freed from the overwhelming sense of guilt which is the hallmark of the larger world religions, particularly Christianity. The difference is important here. Guilt is a condition described by an external law and suggests a form of retribution or vengeance as a way of erasing its effect. I do not personally understand how either guilt or shame can be considered transferable to succeeding generations but of the two, it would seem to me that shame can be the more persuasive of the two. A family can become a shameful unit for a community for several generations depending upon the enormity of the social infraction or injury. It is strange, therefore, that Christianity does not deal with shame but with guilt, and guilt of cosmic proportions which includes all living creatures in its application. The central doctrine of Christianity suggests that the human being is guilty of a cosmic sin simply by virtue of being human, and with the universal application of the idea, since it is rarely connected to any immediate experience of the individual, it loses all its impact. Baptism alleges to remove the cosmic guilt and thereafter the person is judged on the basis of individual deeds. But baptism seems to have little effect on the actions of the individual and it is impossible to determine, from observation of external actions, whether or not the person has been baptized. Therefore while the shame of the tribal religions can be verified empirically very easily, the guilt of Christianity has no useful empirical guidelines that can be applied. To respond that the condition of the world testifies to the presence of sinful guilt is simply to return to the original difference in discerning whether the universe is good or not.

Finally, there is a distinct difference in the idea of revelation between the two traditions. Presumably God authored the books of the Bible, whether by inspiring their writing or actually dictating the phraseology. With the closing of the canon there has been no public message or revelation from the deity for nearly two thousand years. The Catholics once made a point of describing papal encyclicals as a direct revelation but it is my impression that this notion was a popular interpretation rather than a direct claim to instant revelation. At any rate, papal messages today are seen as a modern interpretation or restatement of traditional faith and practice rather than a direct communication with the deity.

In tribal religions there is always an open expectation that revelations will and can be received. Much of this expectation is a result of the ceremonies which produce visions or dreams that provide information and predictions about the future. When the universe is conceived as one in which interspecies communication becomes possible, and is probable given the proper set of circumstances, revelation is a major part of religious practice. Within the tribal setting, however, revelation is not regarded as an unusual situation and so it does not suggest the correction of doctrine or the promulgation of any new belief, or the adjustment of the existing understanding and experience of cosmic reality. It at best clarifies the meaning of life and religious experience for individuals who have undertaken to open themselves to receive whatever messages are intended for them which deal with social responsibilities they must assume, powers of healing and prophecy they must demonstrate, or vocations they must follow.

The nature of tribal religion is not radically different from the cosmic processes which we can observe and which affect our ordinary lives. There is no great gulf between what we see and do and what our religious nature demands of us. There is a noticeable lack of institutional authority; everything exists in the ceremonies and powers which are a part of human experience. In Christianity, on the other hand, there is little reliance on natural law or processes. Individuals are judged and guided by a law which has little to do with the human situation.

Christians are encouraged to become perfect in distinction to the tribal admonition to become complete. Hence Christians, even the best examples, spend their energies in *imitatio Christi* surrendering the responsibility to become what they are and attempting to emulate a semi-divine figure who set impossible non-human standards of behavior and conduct. Natural rhythms and processes are indeed regarded as evil things to be overcome in Christianity so that religion is truly not a thing of this world. Revelation in Christianity is a technical adjustment of sacred formulas, not an encouragement to seek an expanded horizon of goals and life purposes.

Finally, the Christian religion places such a heavy burden of cosmic guilt upon the solitary individual that persons would soon become mad by contemplating the consequences of their actions and attempting to make amends. Indeed, the Christian God seems to be a divine book-keeper whose time is entirely spent marking in a cosmic book all the little errors and miscalculations of followers. Tribal religion, on the other hand, seeks to adjust shameful conditions brought about by human misconduct, adjust the balance of social reality by compensation and forgiveness and move the individual on in his growth processes without burdening that person with sins which are impossible to resolve apart from having the divinity assume and bear the full responsibility.

ATTITUDES TOWARD LIFE

Tribal peoples, on the whole, have a very tolerant attitude for other religious traditions, for other peoples, and for the rest of creation. This attitude is based upon a recognition of our own limitations and an acceptance that many things cannot be explained under any conditions that satisfy us. There is a great mystery to the world and our most hopeful sign is that we can come to understand the environment in which we live and the creatures that live with us. Here the tribal concept of revelation is very helpful. A sacred experience always has a specific content and a direct focus to it. There are no general applications of religious experience and it is best not to generalize or universalize the content or structure of a single experience or even to suggest similarities that might have a wide application. Every situation has the potential for being new and for revealing something that we had not previously known about the world.

Communication with animals, birds, and spirits shows human beings that we are far from being the superior species and that in every species there are specific limitations which enable them to become part of the fabric of life—but no more. Receiving instructions and information from other species makes humans respect and appreciate them and it also encourages people to show great regard for the unusual activities since they also may give us further insight into the nature of the world. Additionally, because the experiences are always specific to the person, they are understood as personal and therefore form a part of the personal essence of the individual. It is the privilege, but not the responsibility, of religious personalities to reveal as much or as little of their own religious knowledge as is appropriate for the situation. Since they do not know what others may know, there is a great range of flexibility in personal attitudes and behavior that pervades tribal life.

Christianity, on the other hand, purports to know the solitary truth about the universe before which all other faiths and beliefs are false and the work of the forces of evil. In an adversarial religion there can be no compromise with any element of experience outside the purview of the institutional setting. Consequently, there is little room for negotiation and tolerance. Truth is not personal, it is universal, it does not depend upon experience. It is already given with the preaching of the word. If others do not follow and agree with what a Christian believes and teaches, they are simply wrong and must be corrected. Any religion that claims sole possession of the truth can tolerate no other alternatives or comparisons. But the claim of sole possession of the truth places a responsibility on the possessor always to interpret the truth correctly. Consequently Christianity has always been a schizophrenic religion that has experienced numerous struggles within itself to define the truth in a satisfactory manner. Inner conflict rather than outer enemies has been the order of the day, and under the logical presuppositions of Christianity there can never be anything except conflict with everything outside and opposition to every possible interpretation within.

The responsibility to truth forms the major part of any attitude toward life. Tribal religions see life as a reality here and now and, consequently, their responsibilities are with respect to all forms of life around them. Christians traditionally have seen this creation as evil, a deterrent to the good life in heaven, and their responsibility has always been to another world to come, not to the world in which we live. The Christian environment is always a ruined and destroyed, a totally exploited, environment. Even under the most optimistic Christian interpretations of their duty, when Christians begin to realize the City of God on earth, they ruthlessly destroy their environment in order to make it more like their conception of heaven. That is the dreadful possibility that we face in electing a zealous Christian to political office. Such a person may well feel morally and religiously compelled to blow up the planet on the supposition that God wanted history ended. Albert Schweitzer's portrait of Jesus suggests this very atmosphere of megalomania.

The last aspect of attitude that we should discuss is the notion of discussion itself. Christians seem blissfully content to talk about their faith but they are woefully deficient in acting on it. We always hear about it, but we rarely see it. In ethics there is an idea that if good people happen to commit a moral act and they are not professing and confessing Christians, they are "secret" Christians; that is, they are unconsciously following Christian ethics. Otherwise, this concept assumes, how else could they do ethical things, not knowing Christianity? The problem is, and every Christian ethicist will admit this fact, that the ethical actions of Christians and non-Christians are indistinguishable. So, being a Christian does not mean that one is perhaps more capable of doing good, or that one can even be identified as doing good because one is a Christian. The only way to tell who Christians are, is to have them *tell* you. They cannot show it in a meaningful distinguishable way.

Tribal holy people are, on the other hand, easily identifiable. They stand out in a crowd, they have a holy presence that attracts people, their power is evident; there is simply something about them. Indians who follow the traditional ways are also easily distinguishable. They have placid, confident faces; they have a gentle humility, they are not boisterous and loud, they do not project the attitude that they have something to prove. Traditional Indians have social graces which are qualitatively above people in industrial society. They do not tell you about traditional religion; you have to ask them about it. They do not claim to know the truth; but they will tell you of their experiences.

All of the differences which I have recited and discussed are ultimately derivative from the concept of creation that is held by tribal peoples and Christian peoples. Tribal peoples do not hold a doctrine of creation intellectually; they may tell their stories of origins but their idea of creation is a feeling of kinship with the world. Christians, on the other hand, have reasonably precise doctrines about creation but seem to have no feeling that they are a part of the world. The alienation of Genesis is a constant theme after two millenia and shows no signs of abating. Unless they have been wronged terribly, Indians do not hold grudges, at least with respect to other people's beliefs. Even with the great pressures that Christians brought to bear on tribal religions in the past century, which acts should infuriate people, I have rarely heard any criticism of Christianity among traditional people who look for good in everything. On the other hand at least a third of the Christian missionaries and representatives I have ever met have been convinced that Indians dwell in darkness and that their religion and culture should be suppressed as quickly as possible.

Today, of course, following the receptivity of American culture, Indian religion is a matter of interest to many non-Indians, so the pressure on tribal religions has eased. But this movement does not demonstrate a willingness of Christians mutually to search for a larger truth; it represents the secularization of American society and the search for emotional novelty. About all that can be said in conclusion to the representatives of Christianity is: Stop talking, and let's see what you can *do*.

(1987)

HABITS OF THE STATE

Sociologist Robert Bellah has been an influential observer of religion in American culture for more than three decades. His early writings on civil religion helped convince many scholars of the importance of the religious dimensions of public life, while his widely read *Habits of the Heart* has brought his critical insights on "individualism and commitment" to an even broader audience. Deloria shares Bellah's concerns about the impact of secularism on a collective American consciousness, the crisis of meaning in a post-traditional world, and the importance of morality for a sense of national purpose. He has diverged from Bellah's self-conscious emphasis on the dominant (white, middle-class) culture, however, instead critiquing American society from the vantage point of minority religious communities. Acutely aware of the stifling political power that a dominant majority wields, Deloria has analyzed civil religion and secularism in relationship to the practice of religious freedom in a pluralistic society. "Habits" are routine mannerisms, patterned behaviors, normative customs, unexamined assumptions; the free expression of a minority religion is often less dependent on the disposition of its practitioners' hearts than on the character of the political state within which it finds itself. Deloria has explored the practical dilemmas of minority existence in a number of writings. The essays in this section address the sociopolitical dimensions of religious diversity in the modern nation-state.

The first two essays originated as public lectures at conferences where Bellah was also a featured speaker. "Completing the Theological Circle: Civil Religion in America" was a keynote address at an annual convention of the Religious Education Association and was later published in its journal *Religious Education*. Deloria suggests that Bellah and other mainstream scholars have misinterpreted "the metaphysics of American existence" by theorizing civil religion from inside the confines of Christendom. Reversing the analytical perspective, Deloria examines the situation from the standpoint of America's religious outsiders and concludes that the United States government and the political process constitute nothing more than a "late-blooming Christian denomination," albeit one that is ecumenical in scope. Civil religion is not the product of the American historical experience; rather,

"America" makes sense only in the context of the Christian worldview, even if this relationship has not always been made theologically explicit. Deloria continued his engagement with Bellah's work more than a decade later in "American Indians and the Moral Community," which was presented at the third in a series of consultations on law and theology sponsored by the Presbyterian Church, then published in the denominational journal *Church and Society*. Law and theology commonly facilitate the impersonal "world of systems" represented in the nation-state, whereas the tribal "life-world" is organized by narrative traditions; stories preserve and personalize "the particularity of the world." Though he is critical of Bellah's assessment of religious individualism in an institutionalized society, Deloria finds the notion of the moral community useful in revisioning the future.

Examining an important test case, Deloria documents a significant failure of the American moral community in "A Simple Question of Humanity: The Moral Dimensions of the Reburial Issue," which was the lead article for an issue of the Native American Rights Fund's *NARF Legal Review*. He excavates some disturbing inconsistencies in public life by showing how tribal people have been singled out for exploitation by secular science, denied protection for their dead despite profound and abiding religious sensibilities regarding the disposition of human remains. The American Indian Religious Freedom Act of 1978 has proven to be ineffective at ending these abuses. Reading the reburial crisis as a referendum on American character, Deloria suggests that continuing debate over the issue reflects the dominant culture's unresolved doubt regarding the basic humanity of tribal people, a manifestation of both racial discrimination and religious persecution.

In the next two essays, Deloria assesses the current status of religious freedom in the wake of two disastrous Supreme Court rulings. "Sacred Lands and Religious Freedom" was written for the Association on American Indian Affairs, a member of the Religious Freedom Coalition organized in response to the 1988 *Lyng* decision. Subjecting tribal religious traditions to legal criteria derived from the Western religious heritage, the Court ruled that devastating infringements on the religious freedom of minority faiths are an unfortunate inconvenience, a requisite sacrifice for life in a modern democracy. Deloria counters this reasoning by proposing a functional typology of sacred sites, using examples from biblical and American history to demonstrate the broad applicability of such an approach to the stewardship of public lands. Deloria condemns Christian complicity in the persecution of tribal religions in "Worshiping the Golden Calf: Freedom of Religion in Scalia's America," which appeared in *New World Outlook,* a publication of the United Methodist Church, as part of a thematic issue on the Columbus Quincentenary. The tone of this essay reflects the mood of many tribal and religious leaders after the 1990 *Smith* decision; shock, anger, fear, and determination led to intensified efforts at comprehensive legislative relief. Pointing out the irony of a legal ruling that protects immigrant idolatry while proscribing indigenous sacrament, Deloria recalls Bellah's warning about the rise of a secularized citizenry. "The ultimate goal of religious people today," Deloria argues, "must be to establish, in belief and behavior, a clear difference between religion and secularism."

Deloria provides a synthetic overview of the religious situation in the last essay in this section. "Secularism, Civil Religion, and the Religious Freedom of American Indians" was the lead article for a thematic issue of the *American Indian Culture and Research Journal.* Reflecting on the impotence of the American Indian Religious Freedom Act and the folly of the *Lyng* and *Smith* rulings, Deloria asks whether these events reflect anti-Indian or anti-religious sentiment. He surveys the history of secularization and fragmentation in American religious life and finds this process has produced a virulent strain of civil religion that acknowledges "no higher value than the state." Tribal communities encounter American civil religion when they interact with federal agencies, where secular bureaucrats administer public resources in accordance with the values of capitalism and science. "Traditional religions are under attack not because they are Indian," Deloria concludes, "but because they are fundamentally religious," which is an example of "the secular attack on any group that advocates and practices devotion to a value higher than the state." Since these essays were written, Congress has passed several important pieces of religious freedom legislation, though dissenting religious communities continue to struggle with principalities and powers in the midst of Western cultural decline.

J. T.

17

COMPLETING THE THEOLOGICAL CIRCLE

Civil Religion in America

In his response to his commentators in *The Religious Situation,* Robert Bellah writes that "what I mean by civil religion is a set of religious beliefs, symbols, and rituals growing out of the American historical experience interpreted in the dimension of transcendence." It is, perhaps, as close and precise a definition as we can expect but when it is placed in tandem with C. Eric Lincoln's remark in his essay, "Civil Religion and the American Presidency," published in the preconvention issue of *Religious Education,* that "[p]residential politics is clearly the arena in which the implicit religion of the people is made explicit," we have the necessary context in which to ask the ultimate question which people seem unwilling or unable to ask. Is not the United States government and its informal political processes the latest denominational expression of the Christian religion? Does not the American understanding of social and world reality really derive from and depend upon the Christian theological and metaphysical understanding of the world to such a degree that America would not make sense aside from this context?

The assumption which Bellah, as far as I can tell, and his critics and admirers, fail to examine is whether when they discuss "civil religion" as a phenomenon they have not avoided an examination of the metaphysics of American existence. That is to say, the civil religion and its doctrines did not really spring out of "the American historical experience interpreted in the dimension of transcendence" at all. Rather the Christian interpretation of the meaning of the universe and its peculiar emphasis on the reality of history over and against geography structured the understanding of the Western European immigrants to North

America so that they understood their experiences in the context of the Christian religion.

The various slogans and doctrines which Bellah and others find in the present phenomenon of civil religion were not ideas that randomly occurred to people over the course of four centuries but were an integral part of their outlook as they arrived on these shores. To the degree that these beliefs vary from traditional theological doctrines of the Christian faith, we can determine the impact of the North American continent and the values and beliefs of its original inhabitants on the conglomerate of beliefs and values that made up the Christian intellectual universe prior to its encounter with the New World.

Thus believing that the New England coast was a New Israel, a promised land, that the American people had a "Manifest Destiny" to control and settle, exploit and eventually destroy the interior of the continent, and that God was always on the side of the American people are all objective manifestations of the fundamental Christian belief that the world was intended for a certain group of people who followed the commands of Genesis to populate and subdue. The continuing myth perpetrated by American thinkers that the Europeans landed on an empty continent is merely a subconscious wish to put aside the immorality of reality in favor of a subjective doctrine that justifies the continued existence of American social and political existence.

American history can be neatly divided into two phases, pre-Revolution and post-Revolution. In the pre-Revolutionary period we find the articulation of a variety of Old Testament doctrines which serve to provide a secular context within which a growing concern for unity is manifested. How else were the scattered little colonies of immigrants to find a common basis for existence and mutual support except by believing that they shared part of a greater and transcendent purpose? The great variety of religious communities and their conflicting views of specific theological doctrines of the church, baptism, the role of the ministry, and the identification of true believers had to reach a common expression at some point and what Bellah and others find as the evolution of "civil religion" is the coming together of a new Christian metaphysic which is not dependent upon creeds nearly as much as it is dependent upon the acting out of a common purpose.

This common purpose is spelled out in the American State Papers and in the classic state documents such as the Declaration of Independence and the Constitution, which are really credal statements of the new overarching Christian denomination known as the United States of America. The true measure for understanding this phenomenon is not to distinguish from among the variety of the existing Christian denominations a new "civil religion," for all of these institutions exist and relate to each other and justify their existence within the framework of the Christian understanding of the universe. Rather the proper method of checking out the civil religion thesis is from the standpoint of a group which has never shared that understanding of the universe and which has always rejected it emotionally and intellectually. That group is the American Indian communities.

American Indians are the most closely regulated group in this country and the field of federal Indian law is probably the most complicated subject field in the world transcending corporate law, international law, domestic relations and other exotic topics. But the basis of this law and what holds it together as an identifiable body of knowledge and concern is the Doctrine of Discovery which provides a justification for holding Indian lands in a tenuous state unvested as property for over four hundred years and the corresponding legal doctrine concerning the status of Indian tribes which holds that they are simultaneously "wards" of the United States government and yet "domestic, dependent nations" with a certain measure of international prestige.

From the very beginning there has been a conflict between the newly arriving settlers and the aboriginal inhabitants and the conflict was largely caused by the ideological propositions held by the immigrants, not by the attitudes of the people already living here. At Jamestown in 1609, Powhatan addressed John Smith as follows:

> Why will you take by force what you may have quietly by love? Why will you destroy us who supply you with food? What can you get by war? We can hide our provisions and run into the woods; then you will starve for wronging your friends. Why are you jealous of us?

But Smith, writing later about the early days of Jamestown, said of that same feeding:

> . . . and shortly after it *pleased God* (in our extremity) to move the Indians to bring us Corne, ere it was halfe ripe, to refresh us, when we rather expected that they would destroy us . . .

Smith's remark illustrates the fantasy drama which clouded the minds and feelings of the whites in their relations with Indians. For him it was not the peaceful, friendly and loving outlook of the Indians that had made the corn available but the actions of God who "moved" the Indians to provide food. American history is replete with examples such as this one where the white man has understood his experiences not in the context of encountering a people religiously and metaphysically distinct from himself but as an objective manifestation of the workings of divine purpose in the universe. For a contemporary example of this attitude one need only cite Denis Brogan's mention of a "neglected point," the only genuine examples of religious persecution in modern American history were the treatment of the politically as well as sexually heretical Mormons and the political persecution of the Protestant churches in the Confederacy and in some of the border states, during and after "the War of the Rebellion." Apparently Brogan does not count the Wounded Knee massacre where hundreds of Indians who were followers of the Ghost Dance religion were slaughtered.

Religious persecution and simply persecution justified by reference to religious principles are virtually indistinguishable in American history. John Underhill, second in command at the Mystic, Connecticut, massacre of the Pequots, justified the action as follows:

> In may be demanded, Why should you be so furious? . . . Should not Christians have more mercy and compassion? But I would refer you to David's war. When a people is grown to such a height of blood, and sin against God and man, and all confederates in the action, then he hath no respect to persons, but harrows them, and saws them, and puts them to the sword, and the most terriblest death that may be. Sometimes the Scripture declareth women and children must perish with their parents. Sometimes the case alters; but we will not dispute it now. We had sufficient light from the word of God for our proceedings.

Thus it has been that from either the religious or the political side of events, justification of actions has been based upon the doctrines inherent in the Christian view of the world.

Fanatic acceptance of this conception of the reality of the world from 1607 to 1775 enabled the signers of the Declaration of Independence to charge the King of England with the purpose "to bring on the inhabitants of our frontiers, the merciless Indian savages, whose known rule of warfare is an undistinguished destruction of all ages, sexes, and conditions," in defiance of the fact that the undistinguished destruction of peoples was the standard rule of warfare practiced by the whites against Indians. We may try and delude ourselves but does anyone really doubt that it was the Christian God, no matter how described, who appears in the Declaration of Independence? That God, Jehovah, revealed that the universe was essentially a courtroom over which he presided, and it was the technical legal language which had structured and defined that Christian universe with concepts such as atonement, redemption, saviour, repentence, judgment, messiah, sin, and guilt. When we understand this aspect of Christian theology and then view the many articles of indictment that form the Declaration of Independence, there can be no question *which* God the Americans are asking to judge their case.

The first real crisis in the confrontation of Indians and the United States government which involved a determination of the internal integrity of the American political system occurred in the Cherokee cases in 1831 and 1832 when the Supreme Court was asked to decide whether or not the treaties of the Cherokees with the United States took paramount importance over the state laws passed by the Georgia legislature. The Supreme Court denied the Cherokees a political status which the treaties clearly implied they possessed and a line of reasoning used by one of the judges involved in the decision is instructive. In denying any ultimate political status to the Cherokee Nation, Justice Johnson remarked that

> their condition is something like that of the Israelites, when inhabiting the deserts. Though without land that they can call theirs in the sense of property, their right of personal self-government has never been taken from them; and such form of government may exist though the land occupied be in fact that of another. The right to expel them may exist in that other, but the alternative of departing and retaining the right of self-government may exist in them.

The important thing to note in Justice Johnson's parallel is that the images have shifted significantly since the colonial days. No longer is it the whites who are Old Testament figures. They have, through their revolution, become the heavenly city of the New Testament. It is the Indians who will now occupy the place and status of Old Testament figures who are searching for the light, waiting for the final revelation. And these concepts are not taken out of the context of the Christian denominations but rather are the theories upon which Supreme Court decisions, statutes and federal programs for Indians are justified.

It is not difficult, thereafter, to trace out the impact of Christian ideologies which are used to justify, and in some cases become the models for, United States policy in the field of Indian Affairs. Thus Andrew Jackson, in his second Annual Message, described the progress in removing the Five Civilized Tribes from their homelands in the South, achieved through a violation of their longstanding treaties, as follows:

It will separate the Indians from immediate contact with settlements of whites; free them from the power of the States; enable them to pursue happiness in their own way and under their own rude institutions; will retard the progress of decay, which is lessening their numbers, and perhaps cause them gradually, under the protection of the Government and through the influence of good counsels, to cast off their savage habits and become an interesting, civilized, and Christian community.

The record is not all bad. Just as Christian attitudes inspired and justified exploitation of the Indians, they also provided a needed cushion which at times prevented the military extinction of the tribes. Commissioner Taylor, a member of the Indian Peace Commission, remarked in 1868:

> . . . Assuming that the government has a right and that it is its duty to solve the Indian question definitely and decisively, it becomes necessary that it determine at once the best and speediest method of its solution, and then, armed with right, to act in the interest of both races.
>
> If might makes right, we are the strong and they the weak; and we would do no wrong to proceed by the cheapest and nearest route to the desired end, and could, therefore, justify ourselves in ignoring the natural as well as the conventional rights of the Indians, if they stand in the way, and, as their lawful masters, assign them their status and their tasks, or put them out of their own way and ours by extermination with the sword, starvation, or by any other method.
>
> If, however, they have rights as well as we, then clearly it is our duty as well as sound policy to so solve the question of their future relations to us and each other, as to secure their rights and promote their highest interest, in the simplest, easiest, and most economical way possible.
>
> But to assume they have no rights is to deny the fundamental principles of Christianity, as well as to contradict the whole theory upon which the government has uniformly acted towards them; we are therefore bound to respect their rights, and, if possible, make our interests harmonize with them.

Taylor's insistence that Christianity demanded a recognition of the political rights of Indians carried the day and made possible the last significant series of Indian treaties, those signed with the tribes of the western plains in 1867–1868 which define the legal rights and status of such tribes as the Crow, the Sioux, the Cheyenne and Arapaho, the Shoshone, the Ute, and the Navajo, and which treaties are now the subject of controversy growing out of the Wounded Knee occupation.

*

What we are considering when we identify the United States government as a late-blooming Christian denomination is the consistency with which that institution has relied upon the doctrines inherent in the Christian worldview when called upon to deal with a people who do not share that view of the world. For it is in the spontaneous reversion to doctrines for justification for actions that characterizes the status of an institution, not whether it has adopted external forms of ceremony and ritual which parallel other institutions which originate out of the same worldview.

After the tribes had settled upon the reservations and the Indian wars had largely stopped, two major considerations had to be made concerning the settlement of the large expanses of the western plains. The gigantic land holdings of the Indians had to be reduced to appease the thousands of settlers who were being brought west by the railroads, and the railroads had to have an unrestricted right to build transportation facilities through the West so that they could bring settlers to populate the area. The tribes fought back against both of these developments and they lost both battles.

The Osage tribe protested against the United States government giving the Missouri, Kansas, and Texas Railroad Company a right of way through its reservation. The controversy landed in the Supreme Court and that court justified the congressional action in these words:

> Though the law as stated with reference to the power of the government to determine the right of occupancy of the Indians to their lands has always been recognized, it is to be presumed, as stated by this court in the *Buttz* case, that in its exercise the United States will be governed by such considerations of justice as will control a Christian people in their treatment of an ignorant and dependent race . . .

In other words, the criterion for deciding the legal rights of the Osage was not the legal documents which detailed the rights and responsibilities of the United States and the Osage tribe, but a higher criterion which took precedent, "such considerations of justice as will control a Christian people in their treatment of an ignorant and dependent race . . ."

Allotting the reservations and declaring the remainder of the tribal land estate "surplus" and therefore capable of being sold to the United States for settlement by immigrants brought west by the railroads, became a goal of the government and the various Christian denominations. Mr. Perkins, Representative from Kansas, warmly endorsed the Dawes Severalty Act on the floor of the House of Representatives proclaiming:

This bill is in keeping with the sentiment of the country, as it is, in my judgment, responsive to the best interests of the Indians, the best interests of the whites, and the best interests of the country generally. It has the warm indorsement and approval of the Secretary of the Interior, of the Commissioner of Indian Affairs, and of all those who have given attention to the subject of the education, the Christianization, and the development of the Indian race.

The Dawes Act passed Congress and Bishop Hare of the Episcopal Church remarked upon its passage, "Time will show whether the world or the Church will be more alert to take advantage of the occasion." Again the great drama of Christian history interpreted events of the real world and blinded the whites to the actual situation which they were creating.

The developments that followed are familiar and not necessary to repeat. Children hustled off to boarding schools, tribal languages banned in schools unless they were used to teach the Bible, and Indian religious ceremonies banned. As late as 1921 it was the policy of the United States government to prohibit the performance of Indian religious ceremonies. The Office of Indian Affairs Circular No. 1665, dated April 26, 1921, reads as follows:

The sun-dance, and all other similar dances and so-called religious cere-monies are considered "Indian Offences" under existing regulations, and corrective penalties are provided. I regard such restriction as applicable to any dance which involves . . . the reckless giving away of property . . . fre-quent or prolonged periods of celebration . . . in fact any disorderly or plainly excessive performance that promotes superstitious cruelty, licen-tiousness, idleness, danger to health, and shiftless indifference to family welfare.

Two years later on February 14, 1923, the Commissioner of Indian Affairs supplemented this directive, noting:

That the Indian dances be limited to one in each month in the daylight hours of one day in the midweek, and at one center in each district: the months of March and April, June, July, and August being excepted.

That none take part in the dances or be present who are under 50 years of age.

That a careful propaganda be undertaken to educate public opinion against the dance.

As the institutions of the federal government have eroded in recent years, religious freedom has increased for Indians and to the degree that secular humanism has dominated the ideology of the federal government, in that degree Indians have been able to practice their tribal religions. But what do we do when in a recent Wounded Knee trial involving the Sioux holy man Leonard Crow Dog, who wished to swear his oath upon the Sacred Pipe, a prospective juror blurts out, "My God, he doesn't believe in our Lord Jesus Christ!" And Leonard is convicted of criminal charges for his presence at Wounded Knee although all Indian testimony indicates that he was asked to come to Wounded Knee to perform religious ceremonies for the people who were there?

The bumper stickers telling us to "Kill a Commie for Christ" are not to be taken lightly. Nor is the perennial slogan of the right-wing Christian denominations, "Christianity or Communism" to be dismissed as simply overblown patriotism. In the minds of a substantial number of Americans, when a crisis of major proportions rises on their horizons, there is no real difference between the Christian religion and the United States of America and its political institutions. To distinguish this worldview from the institutional churches and discover a "civil religion" that is parallel to denominations but not one of them seems to me to be a false distinction which is possible only because the people who want to make this distinction exist and derive their tools of analysis from within the Christian religion and culture. It is like an Indian making a careful distinction between the various bands and warrior societies of his tribe. From the outside there is really no difference in a practical sense and it is the world of practicality, not the world of ideas, in which we live.

(1976)

18

AMERICAN INDIANS AND THE MORAL COMMUNITY

Habits of the Heart, although it deals primarily with the changing behavior patterns of mainstream Anglo-America, speaks to the conditions of American Indians because it interprets these patterns in terms of three vivid images: the moral community, the therapist, and the manager. When Indians think of the old days we often tend to dwell on the moral community that once was and, like other Americans, we look to the therapist and the manager to return us to former glories. In relying on the expertise of others we unknowingly forfeit our opportunity to revitalize and restore the moral community because we forget that morality is a function of our social being and not a gift bestowed upon us by professionals. And too often we tend to identify morality with those customs and traditions that we have maintained, and we charge white society and the federal government with stealing or destroying what we have lost or abandoned. It is difficult for us to admit that, while our societies must change, our moralities must remain constant, and that our task as responsible community members is to find the format or the institution that will allow us to live in the moral community.

Dr. Bellah has suggested that law and theology are part of the life-world, that they originate in that world, are useful to it, and are supposed to function to protect and preserve it. It is when the world of systems clashes with the life-world that we most need law and theology, but when we attempt to use them we find that they are also vulnerable to the overtures and intrusions of the world of systems. Indeed, more often than not, law and theology have been the instruments of oppression for American Indians and have served the colonial representatives of the world of systems well. It is difficult, therefore, to conceive of law and theology originating in the moral community unless we return to the original condition of the tribes where, as Dr. Bellah pointed out, stories encompass and replace both of these disciplines.

In many respects Indian societies are distinguishable from most other groups by the fact that law and technology have remained within the narrative format and have not been brought together or forced apart through systematic thinking, logical analysis, or the search for general, universal principles. It is still possible in many tribal settings to find within a specific story the basis for law, the revelation of religious reality, and the practical technology for economic subsistence. Keith Basso's recounting of the testimony of the old Apache man about water eloquently illustrates that point. Only when law and theology are severed and isolated do they become demonic, without human controls or guidance, and capable of the most monstrous injuries.

We can trace the breakdown of much of the old morality of the people in the fact that we must, for the most part, operate in a world that does not recognize or respect our language. From the very beginning of Indian-white relations it has been the goal of the non-Indians to force Indians to use the English language and abandon the use of their own tribal tongues. Indians were declared to be illiterate unless they were conversant in English; yet it has been admitted by every linguist who has seriously studied the tribal languages that they convey deeper and more precise meanings than does English. So one of our fundamental problems in dealing with the modern world is not simply that it does not speak our language, but that it forces us to use a language that conveys very little of what we want to say.

Language loss cannot be laid solely at the doorstep of the non-Indian, however, because we find the greatest language loss occurring today, not in the remote past. It is perfectly possible to raise children in a bilingual setting if people possess the discipline to do so. Today we see little effort by Indian elders to continue our languages. Children are placed in front of the TV set at an early impressionable age and this entertainment medium instructs them in the latest English slang long before they are taught the proper ways of behavior in their own language. While we have tried to continue our stories, we have forsaken and abandoned the proper language in which they make sense and have impact. This kind of erosion of the moral community cannot be allowed to continue without the most dire consequences.

Stories, whether told in English or the tribal language, have a certain responsibility, and that is to preserve the particularity of the world. The oral tradition has little use for broad, sweeping generalizations that seek to explain human experience. Rather it tells what happened to these particular people at this specific place. The vast collection of stories contained in a people's tradition personalize the world and keep it from being overwhelmed by the world of systems. Here again, the tribal world differs significantly from the world described in *Habits of the Heart*. The Western tradition of law, theology, philosophy, and science seeks general propositions, a body of knowledge which, if applied, can help humans control their physical surroundings and individual and social lives. Few general propositions exist within the Indian view of things. *All things are alive* and *all things are related* might be the only general propositions with which all Indians would agree. But even these ideas are derived not from gathering diverse information into a set of principles but from experiences gained while living in the world.

The world of systems creates the need for objectivity, impartiality, and fairness. It seeks uniformity and homogeneity in everything, since a system cannot work efficiently unless its parts mesh precisely. In the Western tradition we see objectivity not only in science and technology but in social and religious beliefs as well. Christian ideas about "the Fatherhood of God," "the brotherhood of man," "the community of true believers," and even "the sinners in the hands of an angry God" all suggest a homogeneity we do not find in everyday human life and that even the New Testament, in its parable of the prodigal son, refutes. Western democracies also suggest a uniformity of citizens with, presumably, no one above the law and with the equal protection of laws for all citizens.

Strangely, Christian theology and Western political thought highlight the ideas of contract and covenant when dealing with the mass of citizens and believers, but they fail miserably in their effort to create "peoplehood." Instead a hierarchical gradation seems to evolve and people come to occupy positions within this hierarchy based upon material considerations and accomplishments. The good news of *Habits of the Heart* is that behavior is changing and that people are not uncritically accepting all the general principles and beliefs that have made the systems of modern society so formidable. But the rise in critical appraisal, at least for the present time, seems to lead first into isolated individualism before it begins to seek affirmation of the individual as part of a larger and more human group.

Indian tribes begin their social/political existence in our society in much better shape. Almost all tribal names mean "the people" or "the first people" and both contract and covenant are kept within the specific context of the group. The idea that the contract or covenant could be expanded outward to include all of humanity is absurd to most Indians. They merely point to the existence of other groups and affirm that these groups also have a particularity to which they must be faithful. Black Elk's great vision saw the world consisting of many hoops, many life-worlds—and it did not suggest that one hoop had the power, potential, or mission to absorb or devour other hoops.

The foundation of the idea of being a "people," at least for American Indians, is found in the family and clan structures. The family/clan is not simply a nuclear, biological minimum as it is in non-Indian thought. Rather it includes all possible relationships by blood and law, all important, lasting friendships, and all the special covenants established with plants, animals, and other forms of life through unique personal experiences. The family is exceedingly comprehensive even though it does not deal with all the possible relationships and experiences. Groupings of families, however, can extend their responsibilities and personal knowledge outward so that the tribe, as a whole, has specific relationships with every being it may encounter.

Recognizing that over the passage of time it would be difficult to maintain the same intensity of feeling, many tribes drew a line at the first-cousin boundary and then, instead of allowing the family to dissipate, made what non-Indians call second cousin a brother or sister again. Most tribes had a special ritual, the making of relatives, so that when a place in the family was vacant, outsiders could be invited to become a part of the variety of roles during his or her lifetime: son/daughter, parent, husband/wife, grandfather/grandmother, uncle/aunt, cousin. It was expected that each of these relationships demanded a different kind of response and carried a special set of responsibilities. In order to protect the basic biological family, the nuclear family of the Anglo world, Indians moved the teaching and disciplinary functions from parents to uncles and aunts and allocated, according to the blood relationship of the parent, duties of criticism and praise, thus leaving the basic parent/child relationship one of unconditional love.

The clan structure began to evolve as the tribal populations grew and the tribes came to occupy a large territory. Each individual born into a tribe was also born into a clan, and a complex set of relationships between clans was organized so that social relations could be managed with a large population. One could travel from one part of a tribe's territory to another and one would find some family belonging to one's clan. That family had a duty, strong as a blood tie, to welcome the stranger and care for him or her as their own. Clans functioned on the national level as intervening structures that made government and concerted community efforts possible. An objective examination of the clan system might suggest to the critic that tribes were generating their own world of systems, but the fact is that clans only enhanced the life-world and never reduced it to a mechanical process.

The family/clan form of organization was the chief repository of tribal history, laws, theology, and morals. Indians did not conceive of the family as consisting of those members then living but looked backwards several generations and forward to the generations to come. When I was reading texts of treaty negotiations I often came across speeches by Indians. Many times the chief would demand that the government pledge to feed and protect his people for seven generations. At first, following orthodox beliefs about the primitive nature of Indian time-keeping, I thought this phrase meant that the Indians were concerned about having federal services and protection for a long time and that this phrase represented the only way they could say it. However the phrase was too commonly used not to mean something specific in the Indian context. It is difficult to know exactly what was meant by seven generations; however, by relating that phrase to other knowledge about the Indian way of life it is not hard to understand what they were concerned about. Basic to the understanding of the human being is the belief that a good person is blessed with a long and fruitful life. A good family could anticipate that a child born into it would know and remember his great-grandparents. If that person lived a good life, she would live to see her great-grandchildren. Each person, we might say, is the fourth generation and looks back to three generations and forward to three. When the old chiefs spoke of the seventh generation they were basically saying that they wanted their great-grandsons, whom they hoped one day to see, to have the same rights and privileges as they themselves did. So instead of being a vague term for time, seven generations has a reality and precision within the family context as specific as any written contract ever drawn.

During our 1986 conference at Charles Cook Theological School, a ninety-year-old Navajo medicine man spoke. He recounted some of his early spiritual experiences, told some of the events of his life, and spoke of the larger universe, its many forms of life, and our responsibility for them and to them. He touched only briefly on the belief that a long life was a blessing. Yes, he said, it was a blessing because, if you had a long life, you would finally come to know the meaning of prayer. The family, ultimately, provides the context within which individuals are blessed but only as they have fulfilled their daily obligations to the world and people around them.

The family differs quite substantially from Western forms of religion and social organization in another way. In the Western milieu we continually hear of the rights and privileges, the benefits and comforts produced by belonging to a nation or a church. Christians immediately receive forgiveness of sins and eternal life upon conversion and even if they fall away (as some of them do with alarming regularity), repentance is always available; it is to be presumed that upon a deathbed confession all mistakes are wiped away and the individual is sent to his or her reward. The political/social contract of Western civilization is based upon the premise that the individual, corporate or human, cedes a measure of personal sovereignty which had been acquired at birth from nature and that the state, delighted to acquire this power through individual acquiescence, vests the individual with certain inalienable rights and privileges: A good citizen performs minimal duties for the state and receives maximal benefits.

The tribal family knows very little about rights. Its basis is responsibility and duty. It presumes that if every possible role is understood and that if every person fulfills his or her duties as best they can, society will function. It is therefore absurd in the traditional context to suggest that the individual has certain rights *against* the tribe, or that privileges might be given to one group and not another. Nor are duties standardized as are citizenship requirements within the secular Western political context. A person's role and responsibilities change with age as the person grows and occupies different places within the family and tribe. Ultimately decisions are made by the oldest and wisest people in the tribe because it is they who have fulfilled their responsibilities and who have the knowledge and experience to make important decisions. Indians consider it sheer folly to count the speculations of an eighteen-year-old equal with the deliberations of an eighty-year-old and merely to count the number of bodies present and how they feel about something.

Tribal societies tell us to give so that eventually we can receive. Non-Indian societies seem to be telling us to go out and get so that eventually, if you wish, you can give. But in most cases a lifetime of getting does not incline the person to an old age of giving. With a world system of rights, we are always in an adversarial position with respect to society and other people. With a life-world of duties, we are always assisting other people and becoming the recipient of their spontaneous giving.

Robert Bellah has noted that when land and labor become a part of the market, that development—the reduction of living things to measurability—laid the groundwork for the inevitability of imposing large systems on many human activities. There is no question, looking at Indian history, that most of the problems between Indians and non-Indians have revolved about the non-Indian demand that Indians accept this proposition and the equally firm refusal of Indians to give it credence. The problem has hardly been solved. All government efforts toward Indians are directed toward resource development and wage employability. There is no question that the story of the industrial revolution has been the reduction of time and space (or places) to commercial commodity status. In order to keep our time commercial, without exhausting the individual, we have to allow "re-creational" time and, unfortunately, we have simply ruined most places and are now wanting to exploit outer space. It does not look like we will be able or willing to reverse this trend. Indeed, James Watt, former Secretary of the Interior, told a congressional panel that he believed it was our Christian duty to finish off the job before the Lord came.

The two figures who play the most prominent roles in present socioeconomic and political activities, according to *Habits of the Heart,* are the therapist and the manager. The manager organizes and manipulates the external world, its physical, intellectual, and human resources, while the therapist seeks to organize and adjust the internal life, the relationships which taken together make us human and enable us to feel satisfactions in what we do. These figures make it *possible* for us to live in the complex modern world. But they also make it *necessary* for us to do so and there is the contradiction.

Every society, even the simplest Indian tribes, differentiated skills and leadership roles within the community. One need only look at the complex warrior and hunting societies in most tribes to see the beginnings of a professional class, even though these societies did not develop their professionalism as an income-producing class. It seems, however, that until recently professionalism had a real function in the community in that it represented a minimal idea of community substance and morality. We like to portray this morality in lovable figures such as "Doc" on *Gunsmoke* and the tough but kindhearted detective who seeks justice in addition to solving the crime. In a sense the community was able to perpetuate itself by rallying around these professional figures because they were also holistic personalities who always went beyond the confines of the profession to show a dash of humanity and understanding. Certainly the requirement for admission to a warrior society was the willingness to sacrifice over and above their duties as family members.

The therapist and the manager are characters quite different from any personalities society has seen before. They are indeed not a personality at all but a function performed quite seriously by a group of individuals devoted to making institutions and individuals function properly. They are mechanics of the most fundamental kind and, given an entire healthy organism or institution, they would *still* make adjustments since, ultimately, change consumes their whole being and they could not function unless they were active in some way. But each figure, whether Bellah et al realize it or not, is playing out the remaining cards in its hand. The external world has now reached the degree of complexity that almost any change aggravates existing conditions; there are no more solutions, only more complex ways of creating chaos. We can only look forward to groups of managers competing with each other for control of institutions with a resulting breakdown and abandonment of social and economic structures.

Therapists are also finding their future clouding rapidly. They originally inherited the badge of authority once worn by the priest and the medicine man, and they simply substituted science for religion and offered a variety of techniques, based on experiential evidence, for resolving human emotional crises. But human emotions are a very difficult bundle to carry successfully. In the last decade the floodgates of experience have been opened and a wide variety of ancient beliefs and modern superstitions has replaced not only established religion but establishment science as well. Shamanic cults, reincarnation beliefs, tarot cards, astrology charts, channeling spirits, and countless Eastern techniques designed to hasten and encourage personal, individual salvation have greatly eroded the life-world and are threatening to spill over into the world of systems. The so-called New Age literature which can range from familiar spiritualism to alien abduction scenarios has erased the old boundaries and made religion a matter of personal intellectual choice tempered by personal experience. That is to say, today a person can choose a set of beliefs and also find a practitioner to teach techniques for gaining an experiential affirmation of the doctrines. Modern society may retain a bit of civility simply because we are unable to manifest all of our choices within a short period of time.

Habits of the Heart suggests that religious individualism has sufficient staying power to maintain itself as the dominant paradigm for some time to come. This individualism, however, acts and reacts to one of two images of God: a wholly other and a higher self. Bellah feels that the mainline churches have attempted to avoid this dichotomy but his arguments and evidence seem greatly confused. If the mainline churches have attempted to build a sense of community it is not readily evident, and more often than not they have spent their time dipping their toes into a variety of social and political problems without offering any answers or even, in the most controversial areas, appearing to be testing the water at all. Religious individualism, like political and economic individualism, seems destined to fluctuate between two radically different views of the world with neither radical pole capable of winning its way to provide direction and substance.

The Indian tribal traditions represented a curious but powerful blend of theological polarity. Most ceremonies revolving about the calendar year and involving plants and animals were communal in nature while many ceremonies dealt primarily with individual and family needs. Individual experiences were believed to be motivated by concern for the community, and communal activities were designed to establish a sphere of sacredness which helped to develop individuals capable of enduring sweat lodges and vision quests on behalf of the community. Individual and group experiences were believed to be complementary halves of a sacred whole and, as experiences, were told and retold as stories and became part of the continuing oral tradition. The Western Apache material of Basso, cited approvingly by Bellah, illustrates the nature of Indian stories. They are an integrated mixture of religious knowledge, human experience, and secular or practical information.

The dilemma of the non-Indian in confronting and deciding upon an image of God occurs because at some point in the distant past these stories were reduced to one dimension. Christianity has traditionally emphasized the workings of time, divine and secular, to the exclusion of space or, in the Indian context, sacred places. Reduction of the story to a historical format forces all actors in the story to be conceived in an abstract manner; it is the interpretation given the story that is important and not the whole story in itself. Black Elk once related the story of the Sioux and the reception of the sacred pipe to John Neihardt, his biographer. The story involved certain events of a supernatural and so, when he was finished, Black Elk told Neihardt that he had faithfully transmitted the story but whether it happened that way or not, he did not know. "But," he said, "if you think about it, you will know that it is true." It is difficult to see how religious individualism can evolve into or assist in creating a corresponding sense of community, particularly when the chief actors in bringing both meaning and order, the therapist and the manager, depend for their skill and expertise on the isolation of individual bits of knowledge and experience and the clever arrangement of these building blocks into an intelligible pattern.

The moral community, according to Bellah et al, is now only a community of memory. As individuals continue to make their own choices, assisted by the therapist and the manager, this memory erodes with increasing rapidity. Presumably the life-world is regenerated by the substance of the stories it takes seriously. If we view the moral community in the light of the seven generations as described in American Indian tradition, stories must be passed along as part of the family heritage in the same manner as physical goods. Most Christians declare that this transmission occurs primarily within their faith and that the Gospel represents the highest achievement in the transmission of stories, of the Good News. Here we have major difficulties: Indians do not quarrel over the manner in which the story is transmitted, its basic outlines, or its intended meaning, but the history of recent Christianity demonstrates that the interpretation of the story creates immense and continuing dissension among Christians. At many points in history people have been willing to kill each other to determine *which* version of the story is correct.

It is necessary to raise the question, therefore, whether or not the Christian community is a moral community or merely a community seeking to be moral. That is to say, does the Christian community have an integrity of its own or does it represent a group of people seeking integrity as a goal? Raising these kinds of questions is difficult because many Christians, in their eagerness to defend their tradition, defend the definitions that have come down (the dead faith of the living, as it were), and then they are forced to backtrack when the evidence is examined. The argument then moves away from community either to the apologetic stance that things would have been worse had Christianity not come along or to the arrogant claim that all are sinners but only Christians are trying to do things about it. Regardless of the manner in which the discussion moves, Christians often claim too much and yet claim it in an exceedingly apologetic manner. One suspects that most of them really don't believe what they are saying but they have agreed to support the doctrines anyway.

Since our seminars are designed to deal with the relationship of law and theology and how their commonly shared understanding of the world can contribute to the solution of problems, it may be well to examine law and theology in the light of the analysis of *Habits of the Heart*. Both law and theology posit the existence of the moral community. Law overstates its case by pretending that it seeks justice, when in fact it attempts to secure the solution of a limited problem that has been reduced to legal terminology. But theology does no better. It pretends that everyone understands the basis of the moral community and that it speaks from inside that community, entrance having been gained by the free choice of the individual in accepting a certain kind of religious explanation and story.

In point of fact, law represents the manager in the *Habits* equation. Not only do most lawyers spend their time adjusting and manipulating large institutional arrangements, they even advertise their wares today, taking them completely out of the community context and placing them in the status of little *deus ex machina* assistants. People are told that only by allowing the lawyer to take charge can they hope to resolve any of their problems. The theologian, on the other hand, can easily be subsumed under the general category of the therapist. Theologians are but a very small part of the field of therapy because they are still tied to specific traditions and have great difficulty moving away from accepted doctrines to confront some of the more pressing problems of modern society. The increase in faith-healing, speaking in tongues, and other experiential activities within the churches provides some benchmarks of the manner in which theologians are making practical efforts to provide therapy.

Beneath everything we find the traditional split between mind and matter that has characterized the West for many centuries. And unfortunately stories, no matter how well told in the West, seem to be regarded as creatures of the spirit but not of the physical world. Western fascination with symbolism and communication preempts the possibility of confrontation with the hard facts of human life, and dealing with the natural world still becomes a matter of economic consideration. It is doubtful, at this late date in human history, whether we could create or rescue enough stories to turn the tide of events. The "Good News" in almost every religious tradition is in fact the "Old News." Apart from some earth-shaking event in which we all participated and in which we saw the deliberate hand of God, it is doubtful that we can find a story within which we can gain our souls and purpose.

Indian tribal societies do offer an opportunity for revival and experimentation. For the most part, while they are under severe pressure to change, they make changes slowly, so that a good bit of the old substance of the life-world remains within the people. There is a problem here that Robert Bellah has correctly identified: the tendency, by both Indians and non-Indians, to romanticize the tribal traditions and make it seem that they had more power and insight than they were really capable of producing. The great power of the tribal religious tradition was its ability to provide religious experiences of great intensity for individuals—the very thing being sought by many non-Indians today. Even at the communal level with the annual cycle of ceremonies, tribal religions had a great power. And when dealing between groups, tribal religions had great flexibility in preventing religious and ideological wars.

Tribal religions depended upon a reasonably closed society in order to function. Living within the modern world, Indians are subject to the temptations and pressures created by the consumer society. If we visualize tribal society as a circle, which is the custom of traditional practitioners, then this circle is being pierced by many lines, networks, other activities that compete daily to make parts of the circle a part of the line. Life in a modern tribal society becomes a matter of balancing an activity that is an integral part of community life with an activity from the outside that is highly entertaining or rewarding but does not have an anchor in community life. Unfortunately, distractions are proving insurmountable for many Indians. The result is the production of individuals with a fierce pride in being Indian but with no consistent pattern of community events in which this pride can take concrete form.

All theologies and all systems of jurisprudence need to get back to a more realistic view of the individual. We never find an individual as a solitary being, but we nevertheless base all of our political, economic, and theological analysis on the proposition that such an individual exists. In fact, we always find real individuals with accompanying kin, non-kin friends and acquaintances, and a personal history, all of which have great influence on the moral and ethical choices. By dropping the pretense that choices and moral responsibilities are the primary province of the individual, we can change the focus of attention back to the moral community once again.

The great power of *Habits of the Heart* and its importance for today is that it gives us a reasonable analysis of community as it is being experienced by individuals. Using anecdotal material to illustrate operative principles, *Habits* tells us how we really act and not what we allege to believe. We can close the gap between mind and matter if we very carefully examine how we act and derive from that what we really believe. It will not be a pretty picture, but it will enable us to make the proper corrections in our behavior so that we can begin to rebuild community and enhance the realities that life-worlds give us. Ultimately the goals should be to allow the life-worlds to intrude into the world of systems and to make certain that institutions serve human beings, thereby eliminating the real possibility that institutions will completely dehumanize us. In Indian terms it is a matter of making lines into circles again.

(1988)

19

A SIMPLE QUESTION
OF HUMANITY

The Moral Dimensions of the Reburial Issue

ARE AMERICAN INDIANS HUMAN BEINGS?

One of the most volatile and controversial issues in America today concerns the retention of the human remains and burial offerings of American Indians by museums, federal agencies and curio shops. The scope of this practice is enormous: The best estimate is that the remains and/or burial offerings of some two million Indians are now in the possession of museums, state historical societies, universities, National Park Service offices and warehouses, and curio shops. These remains are, for the most part, classified as "resources" rather than as human remains. They are used for unspecified "scientific" experiments or simply displayed as part of entertainment or educational programs. Widespread opposition to American Indian efforts to reclaim ancestral remains persists among some anthropologists, archeologists, state historical society personnel, National Park Service officials, and anti-Indian groups such as the Society for American Archeology. Although there have been some successes by American Indians, the battle has just been joined and the overall outcome is still very much in doubt.

American Indians, led by the Native American Rights Fund, the National Congress of American Indians, tribal representatives, and an increasing number of supportive state and federal legislators, are beginning to make a significant impact on this moral crisis, yet a great deal more needs to be done. In May 1989, Nebraska lawmakers enacted precedent-setting legislation which requires state-sponsored museums

187

to return tribally identifiable skeletal remains and associated burial offerings to Indian tribes for reburial. Stanford University, the University of Minnesota, Seattle University and the University of Nebraska have been the first major institutions to step forward on behalf of American Indians, agreeing to return human remains for proper reburial. Recently the Smithsonian Institution, long a major center of opposition to Indian requests for return of human remains, reversed a long-standing, entrenched policy and agreed to return tribally identifiable human remains and associated funerary offerings to requesting tribes. The Smithsonian Institution adopted a modified policy in which access to information regarding the possession of human remains and burial offerings by the institution will be made available to tribes and interested Indian individuals and returns will be initiated. Although the Smithsonian action falls far short of most Indian expectations, it is a welcomed step in the process of educating American society about the issue. But such major museums as the Field Museum in Chicago and the American Museum of Natural History in New York remain outside the growing mainstream of progressive institutions, as their policies remain unchanged.

The most virulent opponent of American Indians at this point is the National Park Service which continues to stubbornly insist that human remains, particularly those of deceased American Indians, are "resources," as defined by the Antiquities Act of 1906 and the Archeological Resources Protection Act of 1979. Purporting to define the scope and intent of this legislation, the Park Service routinely engages in a practice of opposing Indian efforts at the state level when restoration and reburial are the subject of legislative action, and insists that these remains are under the federal control of the Park Service. This posture of the Park Service is in direct defiance of the American Indian Religious Freedom Act of 1978, a congressional directive which charged all federal agencies with the responsibility of avoiding the infringement of the practice of religious freedoms by American Indian tribes.

Exactly what is the controversy? Are American Indians being unreasonable about this matter or is there a real interest at stake here? The lines of the argument are easily drawn. American Indians insist that ancestral remains deserve the respect which the dead of every human society have always been accorded. Some anthropologists, museum directors and National Park Service officials insist that while the dead of other races merit respect, American Indian remains are more properly described as "resources" which belong in display cases, exhibits and scientific labs.

If this issue had been recently discovered and exploited by American

Indians there might be some cause for suspicion and complaint by the other side. The fact is that Indians have been in a desperate struggle to affirm their humanity ever since Columbus visited these shores. Yet, in spite of all their efforts to achieve respect, on the whole Indians have been and continue to be denied the status of human beings. Some years ago Golden Books published a little children's reader featuring various animals with their offspring and an Indian mother and her child; professional sports teams continue to use derogatory and racist images of Indians; and federal agencies seem to work overtime in finding ways to inhibit and prohibit Indian religious and cultural activities. While all these problems are symptomatic of the status of American Indians as a quasi-human species, it is the issue of reburial of human remains that enables us to focus precisely on the issue of humanity. The story goes far back and is worth mentioning.

In 1550, at the request of King Charles of Spain, a council of fourteen prominent Spanish scholars, representing the collective scientific and theological establishment of Spanish society, was convened at Valladolid to hear a debate on the establishment of conditions under which a "just" war could be waged against the Indians. The debaters were Juan de Sepulveda, a secular humanist scholar and leading European authority on Aristotle, and Bartolome de Las Casas, a Dominican scholar, the former Bishop of Chiapas, and an outspoken defender of the rights of the natives of the New World.

Sepulveda had never visited the New World, knew nothing about the inhabitants of it, and probably had not even seen some of the Indians who were living in Spain at that time. His argument, much like the arguments raised by anthropologists and museum directors today, relied upon abstract doctrines of science and politics which sought to maintain that the human species was naturally divided into two kinds of men: (1) the civilized man who was believed to have intelligence, sentiments, emotions, beliefs and values and (2) the brute or barbarian who lacked these essential qualities and who, by his very nature, would find it difficult, if not impossible to acquire them. Civilized men, it was vigorously argued, were naturally masters and brute men were by their very nature slaves.

Las Casas argued on the basis of cultural relativism, showing that in some respects American Indians were superior to some of the ancient societies which the Spanish admired, and that in other instances, they had admirable customs and beliefs comparable in their rationality and sincerity to anything Europe had to offer. Las Casas had vast experience in the western hemisphere; he had been an aggressive opponent of the encomienda system of slavery as it had been practiced by the second generation of Spanish invaders of the New World, and had even denied the last rites to the Spanish landholders who practiced brutality against the natives.

For obvious reasons the debate did not reach a clear conclusion. The members of the council of fourteen apparently wrote some opinions on the debate but shared them only with each other. Las Casas prepared some well written, extensively documented tracts proving by then acceptable scholarship that Indians were the equal of every other human society in many respects. His major work on this subject, the *Apologia, still* has not been published, indicating that its evidence and arguments were too powerful to be refuted and would cause great spiritual discomfort to succeeding generations of Spanish churchmen and intellectuals. Sepulveda's arguments were very popular because they justified wholesale enslavement of the native population and appropriation of their property.

In the course of the last five centuries, other racial groups have been subjected to the same kind of discussions. During the first half of the last century Americans seriously debated whether or not blacks were sufficiently human to have equal rights within the American constitutional system. Immense tracts by legal scholars and theologians sought to justify slavery on the same grounds Aristotelian scholars had originally used against American Indians. It was seriously maintained in the Supreme Court of the United States that black slaves were comparable to cattle, had no independent will of their own, and could not make decisions, and consequently were "freight" instead of human beings (Boyce v. Anderson, 1829). It took a bloody civil war and three constitutional amendments to admit the humanity of blacks and a century later a prolonged Civil Rights movement to begin to open American society to them.

Both the genocide of American Indians and the enslavement of blacks were justified by appeals to Christianity and civilization. The so-called "just war" against the Indians was waged because the Indians did not immediately submit to the dictates of the Gospel when it was read to them in Latin prior to Spanish attacks on their villages. Massacres of Indian villages in New England were justified by citations from the Old Testament; the Sand Creek massacre was led by an ordained Methodist minister. Black slavery was felt to be justified because the slaves were being exposed to Christian slaveholders and would be baptized and converted during the course of their lives in slavery. Earlier in this century in the South a group of blacks was used in an experiment with syphilis with the justification that science could learn a great deal by using human subjects.

With the appearance of Asians in the United States, it became a commonly accepted doctrine that Chinese and Japanese workers had no human sentiments and could do work which no other races could do. These workers were brutally exploited as draft animals when the transcontinental railroads were being built. Then sporadic massacres against them occurred in the western states. Japanese immigrants were denied basic human rights and the rights of land ownership. When they were forced to grow vegetables under high power transmission lines, they were accused of thereby planning to sabotage American industry. During the Second World War the Japanese were rounded up and interned in concentration camps. We still do not know the number of Japanese prisoners killed or brutalized by American guards in these camps. We do know that while Congress has authorized payments to the survivors of these camps, it has been reluctant to appropriate funds to make the payments. And of course we have the constant reminder of the treatment of Mexican farm workers in the newspapers every day. As late as the 1920s there were articles in leading American magazines citing scientific "experts" to the effect that Mexicans were built closer to the ground than other people, and were therefore intended by nature to serve as migrant farm workers.

American treatment of racial minorities has differed from Nazi Germany's treatment of the Jews primarily because it has taken place over a longer period of time and has not been as systemic as the Nazi program. Science and religion, however, have always been available as apologists for the majority who wished to dehumanize minorities for commercial and political purposes. But *none* of the groups mentioned has become the exclusive province (and property) of scholars to the extent that the bones of their dead can be disinterred with impunity to be displayed in museum cases or used in speculative scientific experiments. *None* of the other racial groups has been forced to prove their humanity by using the published works of their opponents. And *none* of the other groups has been systematically exploited by federal agencies charged by federal law to protect them.

When we look at present conditions and then look back at the debates at Valladolid, we find an uncomfortable sense of sameness. We scoff at the Spanish of the sixteenth century. Could people have seriously debated the humanity of a racial group? Wasn't Spanish behavior ludicrous because, while the scholars were earnestly debating the humanity of the Indians, other Spanish people were in the New World doing their best through rape, concubinage and occasional marriage to merge their civilized genes with the eggs of acknowledged brutes and barbarians? It is equally ludicrous today to have one group of scientists and museum directors in the nation's capitol telling congressional committees that the human remains of Indians must be kept in the Smithsonian and other institutions, and at the same time to have lines of theologians, anthropologists and psychologists waiting to be admitted to an Indian sweat lodge so they can experience Indian spirituality—the spirits of the sweat lodge, of course, often being the spirits of the dead.

Now consider the present situation that American Indians face. Museums, state historical societies and the National Park Service are waging a furious battle to prevent Indians from reclaiming their dead. They argue that retention of the human remains of American Indians is essential to the progress of science and is of great benefit in educating the American people about Indians. The human remains of American Indians are, to this way of thinking, an important national resource over which they alone must have custody. They do not and will not admit the proposition that Indians have any sentiment at all towards their dead. And if such a belief is true, the attitude is that it really doesn't matter and that the secular claims of a small group of scientists and National Park Service museum directors should have precedence over the religious beliefs and practices of American Indians.

The schizophrenia here is painfully and embarrassingly clear. How can people hold these contradictory views? Either Indian religions are a real tradition to be experienced and protected and from which it is possible to learn, or they are not. If they are valuable, there should be no question that they should be protected in the fullest capacity of the law as rapidly as possible, without any debate whatsoever. If Indian religions are not valuable, the scholars and theologians and the general public should stop the traffic in Indian artifacts, cease visiting reservations for research and spiritual enlightenment, and return all of these worthless things lying around museums and art galleries to the simple people who do, in their primitive ignorance, cherish these things.

HOW VALUABLE ARE INDIAN HUMAN REMAINS FOR SCIENCE?

When Indian tribes approach museums and other institutions to seek return of human remains, they are often told that it is necessary to keep the Indian human remains because of their great value to science. Allegedly profound and sophisticated experiments are being conducted with these remains which promise great things for all of humanity. But what are these profound studies? In spite of the repeated attempts by American Indians to get a bibliography of the studies being done by these so-called scientists, scholars have yet to produce any significant materials which would justify their claims. Scientific arguments should therefore not be given credence unless and until a clear and concise statement is made explaining the urgency and hysteria behind the scientific opposition to the reburial of Indian human remains. At the present time the arguments used by museum directors and scientists appear to be merely a crude appeal to the authority status of science and little else.

Assuming, for the moment, that American Indian human remains are critical to scientific knowledge, no explanation has been given regarding the peculiar characteristics which make Indian remains more valuable than the remains of other races. What could possibly be learned exclusively from Indian bones which could not also be learned from the bones of other races? The answers that Indians generally receive to this question are superficial and unsatisfactory. Diet? The annual reports of the Commissioner of Indian Affairs, particularly the reports of the Indian agents, can provide much more accurate information on the diets of these people in historical times. For periods of time earlier than modern recorded history, it is a matter of such tenuous speculation that scientific tests would not reveal much of anything. It is a fact, recorded in the agents' reports, that many Indians starved to death on the reservations when Congress failed to appropriate funds for rations which were due Indians. To conduct tests to see whether or not Indians starved is superfluous and would be comparable to testing the bones of holocaust victims to see if they had died of malnutrition.

Some representatives of science claim that the prevalence of disease can be recorded using human remains in specific tests. But most of the diseases afflicting Indians in historical times are well recorded in government reports; discovering diseases of earlier Indians would produce information only mildly interesting and, in any case, speculative in the extreme. It is also suggested that by testing bones and other materials it is possible to demonstrate that American Indians actually came from Asia. But why should this proposition need to be supported by tests? It is absolute doctrine for most scientists in spite of the massive evidence in the oral traditions of the tribes that they had their origin elsewhere. In any case, tests on human remains cannot tell which way the footprints were heading and it may well be that Asia was populated from the western hemisphere, but no present test could confirm or deny that proposition.

Let us suppose for the moment that a great deal of information about disease can be elicited from human remains. Why use Indian remains when there are so many other, easily identified remains that would yield an incredible body of important and vitally needed information? In the nineteenth century the southern coastal cities were periodically ravaged by epidemics of typhoid fever and cholera. What actually caused these epidemics? Did they strike only the slaves, the free whites, or the slave-owning families? We have records and graveyards available. We can run precise tests on the remains of people who died of these diseases and those who survived them. Why isn't the Smithsonian Institution digging up the family graveyards of the first families of Savannah, Charleston, and New Orleans, perhaps even Mobile, in an effort to obtain this data?

It is a known fact that human beings in America are growing in average size and stature of skeletal structure. Soldiers who served in the American Revolution were a bit smaller than those who were engaged in military service in the Civil War. The First and Second World Wars also saw a rise in the average size of the men in the military. What caused this increase in size? Was it the benefits of democracy, since most of these wars were waged to establish and protect democracy? Was it the rations or the military training? Did the size and capability of the weapons influence the growth of body size? These questions are important because we intend to continue waging wars and we should be at work now doing everything we can to produce future armies that are bigger and better than what we have historically fielded in our wars.

During the First World War, America was hit with a devastating form of influenza. Perhaps more deaths were suffered from this flu than from military service. We have never had a satisfactory explanation of what this sickness was. In subsequent decades the nation has been periodically visited by serious kinds of flu; during Gerald Ford's presidency "Swine Flu" became as serious as the current AIDS epidemic. We should exhume the remains of the people who died of this flu and those who survived in pre-determined test groups so that we can identify the origin and potency of this disease. During the Second World War a substantial number of men could not pass their physical examination for admission into the Armed Forces. Some scientists have attributed this high rate of rejection to the bad diet of the Depression years. But is this answer satisfactory? Could not other factors be involved here? The cemeteries of every American town and city and the military cemeteries overseas could give us better answers than we have now.

The point of the scientific argument reaches the deceased of every racial, ethnic and economic group in America if it is taken seriously. The answers we can get from Indian remains will always be highly speculative because we don't know very much about these people. Where we already have good data on human remains we can ask increasingly sophisticated questions and receive more precise data. We need to know why we have such good athletes, why we can produce more Nobel Prize winners than anyone else, why we have so many self-made millionaires.

Exhumation and testing of their remains would yield invaluable information that would increase the gross national product significantly. We really *owe* it to humanity to provide answers to these questions and we should start excavating the remains of specific individuals immediately.

HOW LONG SHOULD HUMAN REMAINS BE AVAILABLE TO SCIENCE?

Although some of the human remains of American Indians now in museums and state historical societies are relatively recent, most of the remains have been held by these institutions for many years, some remains for more than a century. What can possibly justify this practice? Are there so many different kinds of tests now available to science that human remains must be held for more than a century? Or must institutions keep these remains so that each generation of scholars can perform the same tests on these bones? The justification, of course, is that valuable information is being obtained but, as we have seen, this information is not easily located and is not readily available to people who would like to see it.

Recently a group of scientists from the University of Arizona exhumed the remains of the men who were allegedly murdered and eaten by Alfred Packer, the West's most notorious cannibal. In spite of the sophisticated tests that were conducted on these remains and in spite of the fact that a good deal was known about the circumstances under which these people were believed to have been killed, the only significant information that was obtained was that one of the men might have resisted Packer's advances, a conclusion hardly worth the expense of exhumation and tests. What is more important in this respect is that the human remains were not kept by the University of Arizona for use in training its students nor were they put on display. The bones were in fact given a proper reburial.

Much the same disposition is made of other human remains that become the subject of scientific inquiry. Remains found in the desert which suggest foul play receive a variety of tests and then are properly interred. Even remains that are essential to the prosecution of accused murderers are eventually buried even though the appeals of the convicted murderer take as much as a decade to be decided by the higher courts. If there was any justification on a scientific basis for the retention and use of human remains, why aren't scientists making their voices heard in these various instances? The behavior of scientists voids their arguments from the very beginning.

IS THERE A FREEDOM OF RELIGION
QUESTION PRESENT HERE?

American Indians are now citizens of the United States and therefore presumably granted constitutionally protected rights which we know as "freedoms"—press, speech, assembly, due process, exercise of religious preference and so forth. Indians became citizens in 1924 in a short but concise federal statute that few people understood or took seriously. It was not until the 1950s that western states allowed Indians to vote since theretofore they classified Indians as persons in guardianship or *non compos mentis* because of the federal trust imposed on reservation lands. Since it was the practice to regard Indians as being outside the scope of constitutional protections during most of American history, the conveyance of citizenship has meant very little in terms of Indian rights.

In 1978, in order to redress some practices that were badly out of balance, Congress adopted the American Indian Religious Freedom Act and thereby admonished federal agencies to avoid any conflicts with the practice of Indian traditional religions. In the years since the Act was adopted there has been a very significant increase in litigation over Indian religious practices. Courts have generally ruled against the tribes by adopting a balancing test whereby private economic interests and federal agency administrative procedures are found to have superior rights to the practice of tribal religions. About all the Act accomplished was to encourage federal and state agencies to adopt more restrictive formal rules to inhibit the practice of Indian religions.

The Act, when seen in the context of religious freedom in prisons, appears in its true light. Prison cases have generally suggested that Indian religious practices must represent the core or central belief of the religion. If a ceremony is not regarded as essential to the religion itself, it has generally been disapproved. This standard, if applied impartially to all religions represented by the prison population, would prohibit anything except baptism and circumcision, the two absolutely essential rituals in Christianity and Judaism, respectively. Gone would be the services, hymn sings, and dietary restrictions which would be understood as peripheral cultural practices designed to keep the flocks together.

Today when the question of reburial of human remains is raised by Indians, there is a demand that Indians prove that their burial practices are central to their religious beliefs and practices. Presumably, burial ceremonies must be central to Indian beliefs to be acceptable to secular science and interested historical groups. That Indians would be required to prove this basic fact of human existence suggests that Sepulveda's arguments of the non-human nature of Indians are still taken seriously. Can any scholar or museum director honestly argue that Indians do not have the same or similar feelings toward their dead as other people? On what possible basis could this argument be sustained? Every society of which we have knowledge has dealt gently with its deceased and it is incredible to have people seriously arguing that Indians hold no feelings for their dead.

On what basis has this distinction been made? Presumably, Indians have approached death in a somewhat different manner than some other human societies and this difference is supposed to indicate a less than human reverence on the part of American Indians. What does the evidence actually show? Most tribes had extensive ceremonies of condolence designed to deal specifically with the experience of death. Warriors, when they knew they were about to die, sang "death songs" which bravely summarized their lives and declared that death had no ultimate power over human personality. Relatives of the deceased often went to extravagant lengths to show their mourning, gashing their arms and legs with knives, cutting their hair, painting their faces black, killing beloved dogs and horses of the deceased, and burying personal property of the deceased with the body.

In many tribes the family of the deceased spent a year in mourning and did not appear as active participants in community affairs until the time of mourning had passed. The Plains tribes had a special ceremony called the "Keeping of the Soul." In this ceremony a small piece of hair from the deceased relative was put into a medicine bundle along with intimate things that were often specifically associated with the dead person. This bundle was kept in a special place in the home and was treated as a regular member of the family for a designated period of mourning. Some families kept these bundles as long as they needed to have the presence of the departed near them. Finally, in a special ceremony, the soul was released and the bundle carefully buried.

All of these customs testify to the very deep and religious feelings of Indians regarding the dead. Non-Indian behavior, on the other hand, is often impersonal, callous, and lacking in any significant depth of religious belief. It is characterized chiefly by a studious avoidance of the subject of death. A person is "sleeping," has "passed away," or, in military intelligence terms, has been "terminated." Insurance salesmen sell billions of dollars of life insurance "in case something happens" with the implication that, barring some accident, we are all immortal. Most non-Indians are buried in leakproof caskets although we all know the body decays and turns to dust. Even Christians generally believe that the soul receives a new body at Judgment Day, but concurrent with this belief is the faith that the original body will somehow be made new again, a wholly unwarranted materialistic belief. Even today the burial service for sailors relates how the sea will one day be forced to give up its dead. So the physical aspect of death is avoided and concern for the body often outweighs the concern for the soul.

Non-Indians are further encouraged to forget the dead as soon as they can manage it. The family is expected to withhold any show of emotion during the burial service and prayers at the grave. When they do show a sign of grief, a bevy of priests, ministers, and friends rushes over to console them and remind them not to show grief in public. The task of the non-Indian in the death situation is to pretend that death has not happened, that nothing essentially is wrong. Words of comfort are more often logical analyses of how the bereaved can continue without the missing family member—you can always have more children, you can remarry, you can't expect Grandpa to live forever, and most important, they say everyone died instantaneously—all rational propositions to make death seem logical if not eminently reasonable.

As between American Indians and non-Indians, there is no doubt that Indians view death as one of the two fundamental experiences of human life, and their religious traditions and customs have some elaborate rituals to deal with death. Non-Indians, on the other hand, do not seem to take death seriously; their religious response is to deny death, both its effect and its occurrence, and they are determined to pick up their lives following a death as if nothing fundamental had happened. Judging in these terms the non-Indian should have an exceedingly difficult time proving that death is a part of the religious tradition in which he or she stands. There is no question, then, that Indian burials are within the scope of constitutional protections, regardless of when or where they may have been made.

SHOULD BURIAL OFFERINGS BE INCLUDED WITHIN THE RELIGIOUS FREEDOM PROTECTIONS?

An exceedingly strange argument has recently been raised concerning the burial offerings that have been excavated along with the human remains in Indian graves. While admitting that some human remains should be returned to the tribes and communities from which they were taken, some museums and historical societies have insisted that any offerings that were found must remain with the museum or historical society if and when the human remains are returned. It is not exactly certain how this demand is justified, but apparently at the bottom of the argument is the idea that Indians were simply throwing away burial offerings or the personal property of the deceased when they placed these things in the grave with the body.

Not only is there not a shred of evidence to support this argument but merely raising the question denies the humanity of Indians once again. Funerary objects of a very personal and religious nature have always been placed with bodies when buried. The motive for placing anything with a body can be exceedingly varied; it can range from deep religious convictions to the personal desire to place the individual's most prized personal belongings with him or her. Different tribes have different customs; while some tribes would burn personal effects, others would distribute them to friends and relatives or place them with the body. The fact that one tribe might destroy personal effects does not mean that all personal effects found with bodies should be the subject of confiscation. One might as well draw distinctions between the way various Christian denominations treat burials, as use tribal customs to justify confiscation of personal goods and burial offerings.

The comparable situation in the non-Indian world would be the inclusion of rosaries, confirmation prayer books, Congressional Medals of Honor, musical instruments, spurs and chaps, good luck charms, and wedding rings with the bodies of non-Indians. Does anyone seriously support the right of a museum or historical society to dig up graves and take possessions of these things for its own enrichment? All burial offerings and personal goods of non-Indians are protected by law. Non-Indians are not required to cite scholarly articles which suggest that the deepest religious beliefs of Catholics hold that the spirit of the dead will need the beads and prayer books in the afterlife, that the buried war hero will need his medals for a parade in Valhalla, or that the dead rodeo rider will need his equipment to compete in that heavenly roundup. Yet museums and state historical societies argue that Indians must justify the protection of burial offerings with some scholarly evidence as to the utility of the object in the afterworld.

Museum people, in part, dismiss as superstitious the Indian belief that the soul actually uses burial offerings in the next life. But if the belief is held—as it is by some tribes—then the burial offerings should be protected under the religious freedom provisions, not classified as superstition. How do we *know* that this belief is not true? Some years ago on the Rosebud Reservation in South Dakota my father conducted a funeral for an aged Indian man. His extensive family passed by the grave and reverently placed different kinds of food on the grave. The white priest who had assisted with the funeral service began to object violently to this practice and started to take the food off the grave. "When do you think the soul of this man will come up and eat this food?" he angrily asked the family. One of the sons pointed at a grave of a white man, recently buried and now covered with wreaths of flowers and said, "About the time your friend comes up to smell the flowers."

The objection to this comparison might be that we all know that the dead don't smell flowers or eat food, but that bit of common sense is not shared by everyone. We actually don't know if the dead eat or smell things; a certain percentage of people prefer to believe that they don't. But if Indians do believe that souls partake of food offerings or prefer to have their personal belongings buried with them, that is all the more reason why the Indian graves should be protected. They mean something; they are a part of a living religious belief system.

WHY ARE ONLY INDIANS REQUIRED
TO PRESENT EVIDENCE OF THEIR BELIEFS?

The protections of the Constitution are supposed to treat all religions as equals, the protecting principles applicable to every religion on an impartial basis. But such is not the case when it comes to American Indian religions. Indians must defend their faith against an array of museum directors, anthropologists and archeologists, National Park Service personnel, and state historians—people representing not only their own personal and professional interests, but representing secular science as well. Legislators at the state and federal level quite frequently give great weight to the arguments of the secular scientists and balance their opinions against the testimony of Indian religious leaders and practitioners.

What body of evidence would lead any legislator to think this way? How can any scholar, no matter how well educated, possibly know more about the religious beliefs, feelings and practices than a practitioner of a religion? The most frequent answer to this question, usually delivered with a sneer of contempt, is that the scholar has objectively studied the Indian religion and therefore sees things which members of the tribe miss. But it is a well-known fact, confessed by every scholar writing on tribal religions, that all the information on religion comes from "informants"—that is, people who are willing to talk about certain aspects of their religion. The scholar is not the objective scientist which he or she is made out to be. Rather, the scholar picks up that bit of information which Indians wish to share. There are vast bodies of knowledge concerning tribal religions about which scholars know very little or nothing. *Every* scholarly writing on tribal religions is *woefully* incomplete.

How would other religions protect themselves if subjected to the same attack and criticism by scholars and scientists? How can devout Jews prove, to the secular mind, that religious circumcision has any religious significance at all? Aren't non-Jews also circumcised as a matter of health? Then why call circumcision religious?

Do Christians actually believe that the bread and wine they consume at Mass are the body and blood of Jesus? A simple scientific lab test could dispel this superstition. Why do Moslems avoid pork? Pork products are an important part of the American economy. Every other religion, if forced to defend their beliefs and practices in the manner required of American Indians, probably would not come out as well as most tribes do. Yet, while scholars and secular humanists are not given status as ultimate authorities over these other religions, they are given superior status when the question is one of defining an Indian tribal religion.

So where is the constitutional protection of American Indian religious freedom? Why is the burden of proof placed on Indians to defend their beliefs and practices when it is not placed on the other religions to defend themselves? The answer can only be that in the eyes of a great many people American Indians are not quite human and therefore their religious experiences and sentiments are not to be taken seriously.

THE PRESENT SITUATION

There is absolutely no justification for treating the graves, human remains, and burial offerings and personal property of American Indians differently than those of any other group. Whatever claims can be made by representatives of scientific institutions, museums or historical societies of the need for these things, the same claims, with considerably better justification, can be made against the graves, human remains, and burial offerings and personal property of other groups and of every other religious tradition. The religious significance of death and the corresponding rituals, ceremonies and practices dealing with the experience of death are universal phenomena of human societies. Reverence and respect for the dead are such universal themes that the great Greek play *Antigone* suggests that duty towards the dead, the guarantee of a decent burial, is a higher moral value than even the state itself. To adopt the pretense that American Indians do not fall within the mainstream of human traditions regarding the experience of death is to place Indians permanently outside the purview of the human situation.

If scientists and museum directors are exceedingly anxious to continue their studies on human remains, they should now step forward and volunteer the graves and bodies of their relatives for use in laboratories. Courageous scientists have often infected themselves with disease in order to learn the origin and cure of such afflictions. The dedication to science should start at home. The people who demand that American Indians surrender the bodies of their ancestors for scientific use should minimally make provisions so that their own bodies can be delivered to institutions and museums upon their demise so that science and education can flourish.

The archaic perspective in the two federal laws, the Antiquities Act of 1906 and the Archeological Resources Protection Act of 1979, should be removed. That can easily be done by making some amendments to these acts which would clearly identify human remains as such, and preserve the remains and the burial offerings for immediate, proper reburial. Hearings should be held on these acts to determine the extent to which these acts encourage the exploitation of Indian gravesites and the expropriation of Indian remains and burials offerings. Congress should clearly state that the American Indian Religious Freedom Act does and necessarily must take precedence over any existing sections of federal law which purport to give to federal agencies the authority to intrude upon Indian burials. Whatever the final deliberations of congressional committees regarding the amendments to existing federal law to protect Indian graves, the responsibility lies with Congress to speak in unmistakably clear terms regarding the cessation of exploitation of American Indian dead.

(1989)

20

SACRED LANDS AND RELIGIOUS FREEDOM

Since time immemorial, Indian tribal Holy Men have gone into the high places, lakes, and isolated sanctuaries to pray, receive guidance from the Spirits, and train younger people in the ceremonies that constitute the spiritual life of the tribal community. In these ceremonies, medicine men represented the whole web of cosmic life in the continuing search for balance and harmony, and through various rituals in which birds, animals, and plants were participants, harmony of life was achieved and maintained.

When the tribes were forcibly removed from their aboriginal homelands and forced to live on restricted smaller reservations, many of the ceremonies were prohibited by the Bureau of Indian Affairs and the people were forced to adopt various subterfuges so that ceremonial life could continue. Some tribes conducted their most important ceremonies on national holidays and Christian feast days, explaining to curious whites that they were simply honoring George Washington and celebrating Christmas and Easter. Since many shrines and Holy Places were isolated and rural parts of the continent were not being exploited or settled, it was not difficult for small parties of people to go into the mountains or to remote lakes and buttes and conduct ceremonies without interference from non-Indians. Most Indians did not see any conflict between their old beliefs and the new religions of the white man and consequently a surprising number of people participated in these ancient rituals while maintaining membership in a Christian denomination.

During this century, the expanding national population and the introduction of corporate farming and more extensive mining and timber industry activities reduced the isolation of rural America. Development

pressures on public and reservation lands made it increasingly more difficult for traditional religious people to conduct their ceremonies and rituals. Since many of the sacred sites were on public lands, traditional
religious leaders were often able to work out informal arrangements with
federal agencies to allow them access to these places for religious purposes. But as personnel changed in state and federal agencies, a new generation of bureaucrats, fearful of setting precedents, began to restrict
Indian access to sacred sites by establishing increasingly narrow rules
and regulations for managing public lands.

In 1978, in an effort to clarify the status of traditional religious practices and practitioners, Congress passed a Joint Resolution entitled the
American Indian Religious Freedom Act which declared that it was
the policy of Congress to protect and preserve the inherent right of
American Indians to believe, express, and practice their traditional religions. The resolution identified the problem as one of a "lack of knowledge or the insensitive and inflexible enforcement of federal policies and
regulations." Section 2 of the resolution directed the President to have
the various federal departments evaluate their policies and procedures
and report back to Congress on the results of this investigation and any
recommendations for legislative action.

Most people assumed that the resolution marked a clarification of federal attitudes toward traditional religions and it began to be cited in litigation involving the construction of dams, roads, and the management
of federal lands. Almost unanimously, however, the federal courts ruled
that the resolution contained nothing in it that would protect or preserve
the right of Indians to practice their religion and conduct ceremonies at
sacred sites on public lands. Some courts even hinted darkly that any
recognition of the tribal practices would be tantamount to establishing a
state religion, an interpretation which, upon analysis, was a dreadful
misreading of American history and the Constitution and may have been
an effort to inflame anti-Indian feelings.

In 1988 the Supreme Court decided the *Lyng v. Northwest Indian Cemetery Protective Association* case which involved access to sacred sites high
up in the Chimney Rock area of the Six Rivers National Forest in northern California. The Forest Service proposed to build a six-mile paved logging road that would have opened up the high country to commercial
logging, destroying the isolation of the ceremonial sites of three tribes
and introducing new processes of environmental degradation. The lower
federal courts prohibited construction of the road on the grounds that it
would have made religious ceremonial use of the area impossible. Before
the Supreme Court could hear the appeal, Congress passed the California

Wilderness Act making the question almost moot. The Supreme Court nevertheless insisted on deciding the religious issues and ruled that the Free Exercise clause did not prevent the government from using its property in any way it saw fit.

Most troubling about the Supreme Court's decision was its insistence on analyzing tribal religions within the same conceptual framework as Western organized religions. Justice O'Connor observed that "A broad range of government activities—from social welfare programs to foreign aid to conservation projects—will always be considered essential to the spiritual well-being of some citizens, often on the basis of sincerely held religious beliefs. Others will find the very same activity deeply offensive, and perhaps incompatible with their own search for spiritual fulfillment and with the tenets of their religion." Thus, ceremonies and rituals performed for some thousands of years were treated as if they were personal fads or matters of modern emotional, personal preference based upon the erroneous assumption that belief and behavior can be separated. Justice Brennan's dissent vigorously attacked this line of reasoning but failed to gather support within the court. Most observers of the Supreme Court were simply confounded at the majority's conclusion which suggested that destroying a religion did not unduly burden it and that no constitutional protections were available to the Indians.

When informed of the meaning of this decision, most people have shown great sympathy for the traditional religious people. At the same time, they have had great difficulty understanding why it is so important that ceremonies be held, that they be conducted only at certain locations, and that they be held under conditions of extreme secrecy and privacy. These problems in understanding highlight the great gulf that exists between traditional Western thinking about religion and the Indian perspective. It is the difference between individual conscience and commitment (Western) and communal tradition (Indian) and these views can only be reconciled by examining them in a much broader historical and geographical context.

Justice Brennan attempted to make this difference clear when he observed that "Although few tribal members actually made medicine at the most powerful sites, the entire tribe's welfare hinges on the success of individual practitioners." More than that, however, the "World Renewal" ceremonies conducted by the tribes were done on behalf of the earth and all forms of life. To characterize the ceremonies as if they were a matter of personal emotional or even communal aesthetic preferences, as was done by Justice O'Connor, is to miss the point entirely. In effect, the court declares that Indians cannot pray for the planet or for other people and other forms of life in the manner required by their religion.

Two contradictory responses seem to describe non-Indian attitudes toward traditional tribal religions. Some people want the medicine men and women to share their religious beliefs in the same manner that priests, rabbis, and ministers expound publicly the tenets of their denominations. Other people feel that Indian ceremonials are remnants of primitive life and should be abandoned. Neither perspective understands that Indian tribes are communities in fundamental ways that other American communities and organizations are not. Tribal communities are wholly defined by family relationships whereas non-Indian communities are defined primarily by residence or by agreement with sets of intellectual beliefs. Ceremonial and ritual knowledge is possessed by everyone in the Indian community although only a few people may actually be chosen to perform these acts. Authorization to perform ceremonies comes from higher spiritual powers and not by certification by an institution or even by any formal organization.

The Indian community passes knowledge along over the generations as a common heritage that is enriched by the experiences of both individuals and groups of people in the ceremonies. Both the ceremony and the people's interpretation of it change as new insights are gained. By contrast the non-Indian communities establish educational institutions which examine, clarify and sometimes radically change knowledge to fit their needs. Knowledge is the possession of an exclusive group of people—the scholars and the professionals who deeply believe that the rank and file of their communities are not intelligent enough to understand the esoteric truths of their society. Basic truths about the world are not expected to change regardless of the experiences of any generation and "leading authorities" are granted infallibility based on their professional status alone.

A belief in the sacredness of lands in the non-Indian context may become a preferred belief of an individual or group of non-Indian individuals based on their experiences or an intensive study of pre-selected evidence. But this belief becomes the subject of intense criticism and does not, except under unusual circumstances, become an operative principle in the life and behavior of the non-Indian group. The same belief, when seen in an Indian context, is an integral part of the experiences of the people, past, present, and future. The idea does not become a bone of contention among the people for even if someone does not have experience or belief in the sacredness of lands, he or she accords tradition the respect that it deserves. Indians who have never visited certain sacred sites nevertheless know of these places from the general community knowledge and they feel them to be an essential part of their being.

Justice Brennan, in countering the near-demagogic statement by

Justice O'Connor, that recognition of the sacredness of certain sites would allow traditional Indian religions to define the use of all public lands, suggested that the burden of proof be placed on traditional people to demonstrate why some sites are central to their practice and other sites, while invoking a sense of reverence, are not as important. This requirement is not unreasonable but it requires a willingness on the part of non-Indians and the courts to entertain different ideas which until the present have not been part of their experience or understanding. The subject is considerably more complex than most people expect.

If we were to subject the topic of the sacredness of lands to a Western rational analysis, fully recognizing that such an analysis is merely for our convenience in discussion and does not represent the nature of reality, we would probably find four major categories of description. Some of these categories certainly are overlapping in the sense that different individuals and groups have already sorted out their own beliefs so that they would not accept the classification of certain sites in the categories in which Indians would place them. Nevertheless, it is the principle of respect for the sacred that is important.

The first and most familiar kind of sacred lands are those places to which we attribute a sacredness because the location is a site where within our own history, regardless of group, something of great importance took place. Unfortunately, many of these places are related to instances of human violence. Gettysburg National Cemetery is a good example of this kind of sacred land. Abraham Lincoln properly noted that we cannot hallow the battlefield at Gettysburg because others, the men who fought there, had already consecrated it by giving "that last full measure of devotion." We generally hold these places sacred because there men did what we might one day be required to do—give our lives in a cause we hold dear. Wounded Knee, South Dakota, is such a place for many Indians. The Lincoln Memorial in Washington, D.C., might be an example of a location with a non-violent background.

Every society needs these kinds of sacred places. They help to instill a sense of social cohesion in the people and remind them of the passage of the generations that have brought them to the present. A society that cannot remember its past and honor it is in peril of losing its soul. Indians, because of our considerably longer tenure on this continent, have many more of these kinds of sacred places than do non-Indians. Many different kinds of ceremonies can be and have been held at these locations and there is both exclusivity and inclusiveness depending upon the occasion and the ceremony. In this classification the site is all-important, but it is sanctified each time ceremonies are held and prayers offered.

A second classification of sacred lands has a deeper, more profound sense of the sacred. It can be illustrated in Old Testament stories which have become the foundation of three world religions. After the death of Moses, Joshua led the Hebrews across the River Jordan into the Holy Land. On approaching the river with the Ark of the Covenant, the waters of the Jordan "rose up" or parted and the people, led by the Ark, crossed over on "dry ground," which is to say they crossed without difficulty. After crossing, Joshua selected one man from each of the Twelve Tribes and told him to find a large stone. The twelve stones were then placed together in a monument to mark the spot where the people had camped after having crossed the river successfully. When asked about this strange behavior, Joshua replied, "that this may be a sign among you, that when your children ask their fathers in time to come, saying, `What mean ye by these stones?' Then you shall answer them: That the waters of Jordan were cut off before the Ark of the Covenant of the Lord; when it passed over Jordan" (Joshua 4:6–7).

In comparing this sacred site with Gettysburg, we must understand a fundamental difference. Gettysburg is made sacred by the actions of men. It can be described as exquisitely dear to us, but it is not a location where we have perceived that something specifically religious has happened. In the crossing of the River Jordan, the sacred appeared in the lives of human beings, in an otherwise secular situation. No matter how we might attempt to explain this event in later historical, political, or economic terms, the essence of the event is that the sacred has become a part of our experience.

Some of the sites that traditional religious leaders visit are of a similar nature. Thus, Buffalo Gap is at the southeastern edge of the Black Hills of South Dakota and marks the location where the buffalo emerged each spring to begin the ceremonial year of the Plains Indians. It may indeed be the starting point of the Great Race which determined the primacy between the two-leggeds and four-leggeds at the beginning of the world. Several mountains in New Mexico and Arizona mark places where the Pueblo, Hopi, and Navajo peoples completed their migrations, were told to settle, or where they first established their spiritual relationships with bear, deer, eagle and other forms of life who participate in the ceremonials. As we extend the circle geographically, we must include the Apache, Ute, Comanche, Kiowa and other tribes. East of the Mississippi, even though many places have been nearly obliterated, people still have knowledge of these sacred sites.

In the religious world of most tribes, birds, animals, and plants compose the "other peoples" of creation and, depending on the ceremony, various of these peoples participate in human activities. If Jews and

Christians see the action of a single deity at sacred places and in churches and synagogues, traditional Indian people see considerably more activity as the whole of creation becomes active participants in ceremonial life. Since the relationship with the "other peoples" is so fundamental to the human community, most traditional practitioners are very reluctant to articulate the specific elements of either the ceremony or the locations. And since some ceremonies involve the continued good health and prosperity of the "other peoples," discussing the nature of the ceremony would violate the integrity of these relationships. Thus when traditional people explain that these ceremonies are being held for "all our relatives," that explanation should be sufficient. It is these ceremonies in particular that are now to be denied protection under the Supreme Court rulings.

It is not likely that non-Indians have had many of these kinds of experiences, particularly since most churches and synagogues have special rituals which are designed to de-naturalize the buildings so that their services can be held there. Non-Indians have simply not been on this continent very long; their families have moved constantly about so that any kind of relationship that might have been possible for people has been forfeited. Additionally, non-Indians have engaged in senseless killings of wildlife and utter destruction of plant life and it is unlikely that they would have understood any effort by other forms of life to communicate. But it is also a fact of human experience that some non-Indians who have lived in rural areas of relative isolation and whose families have lived continuously in certain locations, tell stories about birds and animals not unlike the traditions of many tribes.

The third kind of sacred lands are places of overwhelming Holiness where Higher Powers, on their own initiative, have revealed themselves to human beings. Again we can use an Old Testament narrative to illustrate this kind of location. Prior to his trip to Egypt, Moses spent his time herding his father-in-law's sheep on or near Mount Horeb. One day he took the flock to the far side of the mountain and to his amazement saw a bush burning with fire but not being consumed by it. Approaching this spot with the usual curiosity of a person accustomed to the outdoor life, Moses was startled when the Lord spoke to him from the bush, warning, "Draw not hither; put off thy shoes from thy feet, for *the place where on thou standest is holy ground*" (Exodus 3:5, emphasis added).

This tradition tells us that there are, on this earth, some places of inherent sacredness, sites that are holy in and of themselves. Human societies come and go on this earth and any prolonged occupation of a geographical region will produce shrines and sacred sites discerned by the occupying people. One need only look at the shrines of present-day

Europe and read the archaeology of the site to understand that long before Catholic or Protestant churches were built in certain places, many other religions had established their shrines and temples on that spot. These Holy Places are locations where human beings have always gone to communicate and be with higher spiritual powers. This phenomenon is worldwide and all religions find that these places regenerate people and fill them with spiritual powers. In the western hemisphere these places, with some few exceptions, are known only by American Indians. Bear Butte, Blue Lake, and the High Places of the *Lyng* case are all well known locations which are sacred in and of themselves.

Among the duties which must be performed at these Holy Places are ceremonies which the people have been commanded to perform in order that the earth itself and all its forms of life might survive. Some evidence of this sacred dimension, and of other sacred places, has come through in the testimony of traditional people at various times in this century when they have explained to non-Indians, in and out of court, that they must perform certain kinds of ceremonies at certain times and places in order that the sun may continue to shine, the earth prosper, and the stars remain in the heavens.

Skeptical non-Indians, and representatives of other religions seeking to discredit tribal religions, have sometimes deliberately violated some of these Holy Places with no ill effects. They have thereupon come to believe that they have demonstrated the false nature of Indian beliefs. These violations reveal a strange non-Indian belief in a form of mechanical magic that is touchingly adolescent, a belief that an impious act would or could trigger an immediate response from the higher spiritual powers. Surely these impious acts suggest the concept of a deity who spends time recording their minor transgressions as some Protestant sects have envisioned God. It would be impossible for the thoughtless acts of one species to have a drastic effect on the earth. The *cumulative* effect of continuous secularity, however, poses an entirely different kind of danger and prophecies tell us of the impious people who would come here, defy the Creator, and bring about the massive destruction of the planet. Many traditional people believe that we are now quite near that time.

Of all the traditional ceremonies extant and actively practiced at the time of contact with non-Indians, ceremonies derived from or related to these Holy Places have the highest retention rate because of their planetary importance. Ironically, traditional people have been forced to hold these ceremonies under various forms of subterfuge and have been abused and imprisoned for doing them. Yet the ceremonies have very little to do with individual or tribal prosperity. Their underlying theme is one of gratitude expressed by human beings on behalf of all forms of life and they complete the largest possible cycle of life, ultimately representing the cosmos, in its specific realizations, becoming thankfully aware of itself.

Having used Old Testament examples to show the objective pre-sense of the holy, we can draw additional conclusions about the nature of these Holy Places from the story of the Exodus. Moses did not make that particular location of the burning bush an object of worship for his people although there was every reason to suppose that he could have done so. Rather they obeyed and acted on the revelation which he received there. In the absence of further information, we must conclude that this location was so holy that he could not reveal its secret to other people. If he had been told to perform ceremonies at that location during specific days or times of the year, world history would have been entirely different. In that case, the particular message received at these locations becomes a definitive divine command which people must then follow. We have many tribal migration stories that involve this particular kind of divine command and sacred sites which originate in the same revelation. For traditional Indian religious leaders who have been told to perform ceremonies as spiritual guardians of this continent, there is no question of obedience.

The second and third categories of sacred lands result from revelations of the holy at certain locations. The ceremonies that belong to these sacred sites involve a process of continuous revelation and provide the people with the necessary information to enable them to maintain a balance in their relationships with the earth and other forms of life. Because there are higher spiritual powers who are in communication with human beings, there has to be a fourth category of sacred lands. Human beings must always be ready to receive new revelations at new locations. If this possibility did not exist, all deities and spirits would be dead. Consequently, we always look forward to the revelation of new sacred places and new ceremonies. Unfortunately, some federal courts have irrationally and arbitrarily circumscribed this universal aspect of religion by insisting that traditional religious practitioners restrict their identification of sacred locations to those places that were historically visited by Indians, implying that at least for the federal courts, God is dead.

In denying the possibility of the continuing revelation of the sacred in our lives, federal courts, scholars, and state and federal agencies refuse to accord credibility to the testimony of religious leaders, demand evidence that a ceremony or location has *always* been central to the belief and practices of the tribe, and impose exceedingly rigorous standards on Indians who appear before them. This practice does exactly what the Supreme Court avows is not to be done—it allows the courts to rule on the substance of religious belief and practice. In other words, courts will protect a religion if it shows every symptom of being dead but will severely restrict it if it appears to be alive.

Today a major crisis exists in Indian country because of the *Lyng* decision. As the dissent noted, there is no real protection for the practice of traditional religions within the framework of American constitutional or statutory law. Courts usually automatically dismiss Indian petitions without evidentiary hearings and at the same time insist that traditional people identify the "central belief" of the tribal religion. Presumably this demand is benign and made with the hope that by showing centrality for the site or ceremony, courts will be able to uphold some form of constitutional protection on some future occasion.

As human beings we live in time and space and receive most of our signals about proper behavior primarily from each other. Under these circumstances, both the individual and the group *must* have some kind of sanctity if we are to have a social order at all. By recognizing the sacredness of lands in the many aspects we have described, we place ourselves in a realistic context in which the individual and the group can cultivate and enhance the experience of the sacred. Recognizing the sacredness of lands on which previous generations have lived and died is the foundation of all other sentiments. Instead of denying this aspect of our lives, we should be setting aside additional places which have transcendent meaning.

Sacred sites which higher powers have chosen for manifestation enable us to focus our concerns on the specific form of our lives. These places remind us of our unique relationship with spiritual forces and call us to fulfill our religious vocations. These kinds of experiences have shown us something of the nature of the universe by an affirmative manifestation of themselves and this knowledge illuminates everything else that we know.

The struggle by American Indians to protect their sacred sites and to have access to them for traditional ceremonies is a movement in which all peoples should become involved. The federal agencies charged with managing public lands who argue that to give recognition to any form of traditional tribal religion is to establish that religion have raised a false issue. No other religion in this country speaks to the issue of the human relationship with the rest of the universe in this manner. The alternative use of land proposed by the Forest Service, the Bureau of Land Management, and the National Park Service is the rapid exploitation of natural resources by a few favored private clients—a wholly secular and destructive use of the lands.

The truly ironic aspect of modern land use is that during the past three decades, Congress has passed many laws which purport to protect certain kinds of lands and resources from the very developers who now seek to exclude Indian religious people from using public lands. The Wild and Scenic Rivers Act, the Wilderness Act, the National Environmental Protection Act, the Clean Air Act, the National Historic Preservation Act, and several other statutes all take definite steps to protect and preserve the environment in a manner more reminiscent of traditional Native American religion than that of uncontrolled capitalism or the domination of land expounded by the world religions. No real progress can be made in environmental law unless some of the insights into the sacredness of land derived from traditional tribal religions become basic attitudes of the larger society.

At present, legal remedies for Indian religious practitioners are limited to those procedures provided by various environmental and historic preservation laws which, in some circumstances, may provide an indirect means for protection of sites. The only existing law directly addressing this issue, the American Indian Religious Freedom Act of 1978, is simply a policy statement with "no teeth." While it has led to some administrative regulations and policies providing for limited additional opportunities for input, it provides no legal cause of action to aggrieved practitioners.

Examples of sacred sites currently threatened are (1) the Medicine Wheel in Wyoming, where the Forest Service proposed (and is now reconsidering after protest) construction of a parking lot and observation platform at the site of the ancient Wheel which is sacred to many tribes in Montana, Wyoming, Oklahoma and South Dakota; (2) Badger Two Medicine in Montana, where oil drilling is proposed in a pristine area sacred to the Blackfeet and other tribes; and (3) Mt. Graham in Arizona where telescopes are proposed which would not only destroy an Apache sacred site but also cause the extinction of an endangered species of squirrel.

As a result, the Religious Freedom Coalition (Association on American Indian Affairs, Native American Rights Fund, and National Congress of American Indians), as well as tribes and other Indian organizations, are seeking legislation which will provide for a legal cause of action when sacred sites may be impacted by governmental action. Proposed legislation would also provide for more extensive notice to and consultation with tribes and affected parties in such circumstances. The legislation would ensure that the principle of religious freedom (rightfully urged upon the rest of the world by the United States) truly incorporates and applies to the unique needs of Indian religions.

(1991)

21

WORSHIPING
THE GOLDEN CALF

Freedom of Religion in Scalia's America

Recently, the Supreme Court wrought a marvelous revolution in constitutional rights that will affect religious individuals and communities far into the next century. In *Employment Division v. Smith* (1990), the court decided that two men, active participants in the ceremonies of the Native American Church, which uses peyote in its rituals, were not eligible for unemployment compensation if they had been discharged from their jobs as individuals using a prohibited drug. The governor of Oregon has since signed a law that allows the defense of "sacramental use" for anyone caught in a similar situation in the future. But the impact of the reasoning of the law has caught a New York and a Seattle church in the web of municipal ordinances and stripped away their immunity from harassment by local government.

It is no secret that recent appointments to the Supreme Court, and the appointment now pending, have been made with the primary purpose of rolling back all human rights decisions made by the Court in the past three decades. Instead of nominating outstanding judges and acknowledged experts on constitutional law, the tendency has been to find nominees who have done so little in the way of scholarship and decision-writing that no objections can be made to their elevation to the Court. The result has been the rapid ascent of second-rate minds and third-rate writers to the highest tribunal of the land. Not only has the reasoning of recent decisions been appalling (for example, the recent step backward into the Middle Ages in the ruling permitting forced confessions) but also the substance of judicial reasoning has created a bizarre direction for future efforts to bring sanity and balance to America's religious sensitivity.

The majority churches all have a bevy of lobbyists in our nation's capital. The collective wisdom of these people suggests that the best solution to the problem raised by the *Smith* decision is to seek an amendment to existing law that would allow the major Protestant denominations to escape the logic and application of *Smith* and force the Indian religions to bear the consequences of the case (or to conform their ceremonies and rituals to acts and substances that are approved by the government). Such a change in the law, of course, would then raise the question of whether or not Congress has established certain kinds of religion and prohibited certain others. Such a move would itself be unconstitutional. Unfortunately for the religious American, the intellectual landscape is so devoid of leadership that the challenge thrown down by the Supreme Court has not been understood, much less confronted.

People read but they rarely understand, so it is not unexpected that the full meaning of Justice Antonin Scalia's decision has escaped notice. In a seemingly casual but ultimately important sentence early in the decision, Scalia writes: "It would doubtless be unconstitutional, for example, to ban the casting of 'statues that are to be used for worship purposes,' or to prohibit bowing down before a golden calf." Only those Americans who have an acquaintance with the Old Testament would know that worshiping the golden calf was anathema to Moses (and also sat uncomfortably with Joshua) and that it has been symbolic of both secularism and pagan superstition for the better part of 3500 years. That it would now be the primary form of religious activity protected by the United States Constitution seems ludicrous—but ironically just—considering the inroads made by secularism in this century.

Considering he is an avowed Roman Catholic, the Scalia contention is amazing. But even more stunning is the absence of any sense of outrage from American Christians. Instead, they are wallowing in the subtleties of sexual behavior—the mainline Protestant denominations debating it and many right-wing evangelicals and television preachers engaging in it. So we have the strange situation of a society thought to be morally informed by Christianity and Judaism being able to protect constitutionally only one religious form—and that one a practice prohibited by both Christianity and Judaism!

The Indians, of course, come as an afterthought. Their religions are considered exotic, primitive, and precisely the kind of spirituality that many Christians wish they could find in their own rituals. Indeed, annually we are treated to many conferences in which American Indians are asked to speak about spirituality. We see Episcopal bishops garbed in outlandish purple vestments, with war bonnets on their heads, trying to hold a communion service that is partially Christian and partially powwow. We see hundreds of Christian clergy coming to the reservations like Nicodemus at night, trying to get into sweat lodges and sun dances so they can have some kind of religious experience. It is all too sad.

After the *Smith* decision, a coalition of American Indians was formed to seek remedial legislation that would once and for all protect the various forms of traditional tribal worship. These forms include the use of peyote in ceremonies as a sacramental substance; the use of eagle and other bird feathers and animal parts in healing ceremonies and medicine bundles; access to sacred places that are presently "administered" by federal agencies; access by Indian prisoners to traditional ceremonies in penitentiaries; reburial of Indian human skeletal remains from museums and curio shops; and repatriation of sacred objects from these same museums and collections.

The Association on American Indian Affairs and the Native American Rights Fund are raising both money and issues in an effort to get redress from Congress on the religious freedom issue. A new omnibus religious freedom act for American Indians is now ready to be introduced in Congress, which has plenary powers in the field of Indian Affairs according to an earlier Supreme Court ruling. Ranged against Indian religious freedom are mining and grazing interests; a large coalition of federal agencies that seek to administer federal lands free from any interference or public scrutiny; and the general ignorance and lethargy of the American public, which seems to be fascinated with holding "Desert Storm" parades and to remain uncritical of anything the government does.

Some time ago, Robert Bellah warned us about the rise and possible triumph of secular religion. Pious intellectuals debated the fine points as church bodies turned to other issues, since they were, for the most part, comfortable with government and, in some instances, receiving federal grants to operate social programs. Scalia's opinion demonstrates that not only has civil religion *overcome* traditional religious expressions, it is now in danger of being *superseded* by very ancient forms of idol worship—a fitting legacy of the Reagan years.

The challenge to religious people is overwhelming. First, the moral and intellectual leadership of the various church bodies must be replaced if it can't move on from its adolescent fascination with sexual mores. Second, if there is going to be any acknowledgment of the existence of higher spiritual powers, the religious community must once again stand against secular values and advocate and articulate the beliefs and values of the religious life. Third, divergent or even competing religious traditions must be protected in their entirety. (Reactionary Supreme Court Justices who seek to suppress tribal and other religions must reach far into the religious freedom clauses to prohibit religious

behavior. The result is oppression for *all* religious expressions.) The ultimate goal of religious people today must be to establish, in belief and
behavior, a clear difference between religion and secularism.

I mourn for any Americans who don't care to protect their own religious traditions and are content with worshiping the golden calf, as rec-
ommended by the Supreme Court. Help American Indians secure
federal legislation that will enable us to continue ceremonies and practices that are thousands of years old. We still believe in higher powers
and communicate with them in ceremonies and prayers. *Just in case* we
are right, it would be a prudent thing to help us.

(1991)

22

SECULARISM, CIVIL RELIGION, AND THE RELIGIOUS FREEDOM OF AMERICAN INDIANS

In 1978, Congress passed the American Indian Religious Freedom Act. At that time, most American Indians believed that the status of their right to practice their traditional religions was protected by that special legislation, even though in floor debate congressman Morris Udall had specifically stated that no major laws were being changed and no disruption of the existing state of affairs would take place. In the decade-and-a-half since then, Indian litigants have cited the Act as an indication on the part of Congress that it was federal policy, to be followed by all federal agencies, that the particular needs of traditional religious practitioners would be accommodated.

In 1988, the Supreme Court turned aside the Indians of northern California, refusing to prohibit the building of a minor logging road that would ruin the high country where they held vision quests and gathered medicines (*Lyng v. Northwest Indian Cemetery Assn.*, 485 U.S. 439 [1988]). In the spring of 1990, the Supreme Court ruled that the state of Oregon did not have to present a compelling interest in order to pass legislation that would have the effect of virtually eliminating a religion, in this instance the use of peyote for religious ritual purposes (*Employment Div., Dept. of Human Resources of Oregon v. Smith*, 494 U.S. 872 [1990]). The consternation that has arisen among American Indians since these decisions is genuine, and many people feel betrayed by both the Congress and the Supreme Court.

The Supreme Court is decidedly anti-Indian. That much is clear. The turning point probably was *Rosebud Sioux Tribe v. Kneip*, 430 U.S. 584 (1977), which returned a devastating 9–0 against the tribe. Since then, through *Montana v. U.S.,* 450 U.S. 544 (1981), and *Sioux Nation v. U.S.,* 448 U.S. 371 (1980), it has seemed as if the Supreme Court simply weaves an argument out of thin air to deprive tribes of long-standing rights. But there is a basic question underlying the *Smith* decision that many people have not yet asked themselves: Was the case lost because it was an Indian case or because it was a religious case? Setting aside the Indian question for the moment, let us consider the religious issue.

THE HISTORICAL BACKGROUND OF FREE EXERCISE

Medieval Europe achieved an intellectual synthesis in which faith and reason were regarded as equally valid paths to truth. The true faith was revealed in the Bible and the teachings of the church, but it was believed possible to arrive at a similar set of propositions by reasoning from the natural laws revealed in the design of creation. With the translation of Aristotelian philosophy in the 1200s, reason was given a comprehensive framework within which all aspects of knowledge and experience could be related. Faith thereafter acted as a conscience and control device to reign in the exuberant adventures of reason. Western science, endorsed by religion—providing it discovered the laws established by the Creator —was free to experiment and investigate to its heart's content.

Martin Luther applied reason to the theological realm, posted his *Ninety-five Theses,* and shattered the homogeneity of Christendom by maintaining that the individual could achieve salvation by faith alone, without the intercession of the church. Thereafter, among the Protestant wing of Christianity, a process of dissent and fragmentation began, as small groups chose minor aspects of the Christian revelation around which to build their version of the true faith. Reason in the natural sciences reached the conclusion, with the philosophy and psychology of René Descartes, that the world consisted of mind and matter, mind being a province in which the church still had a voice, and matter being the indissoluble atoms of the physical world.

By the time Europeans began to look seriously at the New World as a place for settlement, religious conflicts had ravaged the European continent, countries were forced to choose between the Catholic and Protestant versions of Christianity, and a significant segment of European intellectuals had become secular, if not agnostic, thinkers. Expanding technology gave secular science the edge in demonstrating to the civilized world the truth of its method and results. Hence, while religious movements contained considerably more heat than light, the process of secularization was well under way by the time the Pilgrims arrived at Plymouth Rock.

A substantial number of colonizing groups arriving on the Atlantic seaboard were driven there because of religious persecutions in their homelands. Some, such as the people in Massachusetts, promptly established theocracies equally as brutal as the situations they had fled in their original homelands. It is a historical fact that during colonial times, Catholics and Quakers were executed in Massachusetts for preaching their versions of Christianity. Other groups, such as the people in Rhode Island and Pennsylvania, saw religious conflict as disruptive of the civil order and forbade persecution of individuals because of their religious beliefs.

During the writing of the Constitution, it became apparent that some provisions had to be inserted in the nation's basic organic, political document ensuring certain freedoms that had been badly abused by the King of England and by various colonial legislatures. Thus, we had the adoption of the Bill of Rights, which contained two clauses dealing with religion: (1) the prohibition of the establishment of a state religion and (2) the guarantee of free exercise of religion. Ideologically, even these clauses contained the possibility of misunderstanding, since religion itself had been carelessly defined. Jefferson saw religion as a matter of belief and felt that the state could not interfere with the manner in which people chose to view the world. Madison went further and connected religious belief with religious acts, to advocate a much larger sphere in which the guarantee and prohibitions would be operable.

American society was predominantly Protestant/secular in its early years, with few Catholics and no Asian religions; the religions of the Indians, like their other customs and beliefs, were totally outside the realm of constitutional concerns. Christianity shattered on the American shore. Ethnic immigrants reconstituted their own versions of the national churches of their home countries, but American society was subjected to periodic "revivals," surges of religious energy that left in their wake new denominations with less sophisticated and more practical theologies. The rigor and personal discipline required by Lutheranism and Calvinism became translated into the quick, emotional experience of "salvation" on the American frontier. This process of fragmentation has been a major characteristic of American Christianity ever since.

Real controversy over religious freedom did not take place until American society had to deal with the Mormon movement in the 1860s. One tenet of the Mormon faith, taken directly from the pages of the Old Testament, with certain American innovations, was polygamy, and the Mormons practiced it with some vigor and notoriety. Beginning in 1862 and continuing until the Tucker Edmund Act of 1887, Congress attempted to prohibit the practice of polygamy in spite of the constitutional prohibition of this effort, justifying its attempts on the basis that Utah was a territory ruled by Congress and therefore not entitled to Bill of Rights protection until it had become a state. In *Reynolds v. U. S.,* 98 U.S. 145 (1879), the Supreme Court adopted the Jeffersonian interpretation of religion, ruling, in effect, that Mormons were free to believe in polygamy but not free to practice it.

Other than the Mormon controversy, little was done in the religious realm until the Second World War. Congress prohibited the use of federal funds in support of sectarian schools on Indian reservations, but the Supreme Court, in *Quick Bear v. Leupp,* 210 U.S. 50 (1908), found that churches could use tribal funds for their schools, since Catholic Indians needed to have religious freedom. During the First World War, some cases arose but were as easily characterized as free speech cases as instances of oppression of religious practice. With the surge of patriotism in the Second World War came the flag salute cases, in which the Supreme Court first said it was permissible to require Seventh Day Adventist children to salute the flag and then reversed itself and ruled otherwise.

In the interim period between the adoption of the Bill of Rights and the advent of the Second World War, a process of rapid secularization took place. During colonial days, churches dealt with most of the social problems that government handles today. Charity for the poor was a church function, as were education, hospital care, and even some aspects of penitentiary administration. With the great fragmentation of Christendom in America, it was impossible that any one denomination could resolve society-wide problems, although the Roman Catholics, from start to finish, insisted on having their own school system. Nevertheless, over the decades, churches withdrew from active involvement in domestic problems and confined their activities to gathering new members and issuing pious pronouncements endorsing the actions of government.

Only since the end of the Second World War has there been a significant amount of litigation involving either free exercise or the establishment of religion. In general, the free exercise cases have involved overly zealous members of recognized Protestant churches whose allegiance to the articles of faith, in practice, have created conflicts with civil law. Establishment cases have dealt primarily with efforts to provide financial support to Catholic school systems or with the presence of Christian symbolism in displays of public celebration, particularly on what were once religious holidays. Supreme Court justices have tiptoed with extreme caution through the thickets of the free exercise clause, hoping not to arouse a religious constituency. Thus, numerous "tests" have been devised by the Court to provide guidance for lower courts in handling religious free exercise cases. Until *Smith,* the test most frequently used originated in *Sherbert v. Verner*, 374 U.S. 398 (1963), which involved a three-step process for determining when the state could constitutionally impinge on religious activities, the most important step being a demonstration that the state had a compelling interest in controlling specific kinds of behavior.

With *Smith*, the *Sherbert* test was discarded. In its place was substituted the strange and nonhistoric proposition that the right of free exercise of religion had to be linked to some other freedom guaranteed in the Bill of Rights: Free exercise could not stand alone. It is important to note that the Court did not say anything about Indians, although it had the opportunity to do so with the Indian position fully briefed and the presence of a federal regulation specifically exempting the Native American Church from the enforcement of drug laws because of its religious ritual use of the cactus.

AMERICAN INDIAN RELIGIOUS FREEDOM

Government treatment of traditional Indian religions has been inconsistent, fluctuating with the perceptions of Congress and the Bureau of Indian Affairs. Early treaties sought only to obtain the permission of the tribes for missionaries to visit them; later treaties gave some denominations grants of land in exchange for providing educational or health services. During the Grant administration, churches were allowed to appoint Indian agents for most reservations, and suppression of tribal religions was seen as a positive step in preparing Indians for American citizenship. This program failed dismally when many of the church-appointed agents proved incompetent and others embezzled tribal and government funds during their tenure as representatives of civilization. In the 1890s, an Indian agent named "Pussyfoot" Johnson prowled the Oklahoma Indian settlements, attempting to quash the use of peyote, while in Washington, D.C., the Commissioner of Indian Affairs denied that such activity was taking place.

At the close of the First World War, hearings were held to consider a prohibition against the use of peyote, but social scientists, defending this practice as cultural, turned back the efforts of major missionary churches to ban use of the substance. With the New Deal, religious freedom for traditional religious activities was encouraged; and since 1934, more and more Indians have felt free to bring suppressed ceremonies into the open. Throughout this period, Indians traveled to off-reservation sites to conduct ceremonies in sacred places, as they had for thousands of years. Congress even provided legislative authority for the people of Taos Pueblo to use the sacred Blue Lake area, which had been confiscated and placed in a national forest preserve. There was not much conflict between federal agencies and Indians until the 1960s, when it became apparent that tribes wanted to reclaim certain sacred areas from the government.

Taos Pueblo, in pursuing its land claim in the Indian Claims Commission, informed the government that it did not want financial compensation for its Blue Lake area—it wanted the land returned. By severing this region from its claim and seeking congressional legislation, Taos was able to get Blue Lake restored. That law was quickly followed by the return of a portion of Mount Adams to the Yakima for religious purposes. Fearful that these precedents would enable Indians to reclaim more lands, the Forest Service and the National Park Service tightened up the regulations allowing the traditional Indians to perform ceremonies at sacred places.

During the seventies, tensions increased. New conservation and ecological laws meant the writing of new administrative regulations, and with each effort by the federal government to protect and administer its lands, traditional Indian practitioners were increasingly restricted in their ability to conduct ceremonial activities. Sporadic conflict over eagle feathers and other animal parts needed for ceremonial costumes and medicine bags meant further oppression. As an illustration of the inconsistencies of the situation, an Indian could have eagle feathers only for religious ceremonial purposes, while senators and congressmen could have eagle feather war bonnets for decorative purposes.

In 1978, Congress adopted the American Indian Religious Freedom Act, which directed federal agencies to survey their rules and regulations and try to accommodate the practice of Indian religions. Congressman Morris Udall assured the House of Representatives that the resolution had no practical effect; later, when this resolution was cited by Indians in court, judges and justices quoted Udall and turned them aside. The resolution was, therefore, simply a cosmetic attempt to speak to an extremely complicated subject without any knowledge of the subject at all. Litigation based on this resolution increased substantially after its passage, and courts attempted to find a test by which they could determine the probable validity of the Indian claims. But determining a central belief or practice for religions that regarded the physical world as a living entity proved almost impossible.

RELIGIOUS FREEDOM TODAY

A major phenomenon of this century has been the erosion of the power and influence of organized religion in American society. The trend has been one of secularization, in which churches, in order to receive the blessings of the government, have increasingly characterized their religious activities as basically secular in nature. Secular science, which routed religion in the courtroom in the 1925 *Scopes* trial in Tennessee, has gradually become entrenched as the final authority on the natural world, so that during the 1980s, when fundamentalist churches sought to include "creation science" in state curricula, the churches were turned away. The religious message increasingly has become one of simple belief, and religious hucksters now imply that the purpose of Christianity is to enable people to make money and live affluent lives. Only with the rise of the abortion question has organized religion made a move toward involvement in secular affairs, and on this question there is no united religious front.

As secularization has progressed, there has been a strange melding of political and religious beliefs, which has been characterized by Robert Bellah as the new "civil religion." In medieval Europe, after the crowning of Charlemagne by the Pope, political power was believed to be validated by the church. Civil religion—a blending of theological concepts, a generalized religion that endorses and affirms the state—moves society back toward that condition. But whereas the Pope could energize Europe by calling for a Crusade, today the churches wait for the president to announce state policy so they can endorse it. The beliefs of the civil religion blend vaguely with mythical American history, so that America somehow gets a Judeo-Christian heritage sanctified by the blood of its pioneers and enthusiastic about current military adventures. The recent orgy of parades after the Persian Gulf bombing was an example of the fervor of civil religion.

Indian tribes encounter civil religion when dealing with the various federal agencies charged with administering public land and federal projects. Here the bureaucrats act in a priestly role, presiding over their forests, national monuments, and irrigation projects with the care and paranoia that formerly characterized village priests and New England ministers. But their perspective is wholly secular, determined in large part by the spate of environmental legislation passed over the last three decades. In the National Environmental Protection Act, the Wild Rivers Act, the Wilderness Act, the Clean Air Act, and many other recent federal statutes, we find an articulation of the relationship between humans and nature as defined and understood by inadequately educated federal employees.

Although the hard sciences—physics, chemistry, et al—define modern scientific methodology, the social sciences, which purport to deal with human beings, follow the general perspectives of the scientific community, which understands birds, plants, animals, and all living things, including human beings, as merely phenomena that can be subjected to scientific inquiry. No other values are recognized or admissible. It is hardly a surprise, then, to understand that one of the issues of real conflict is that of the treatment of human skeletal remains. American Indians are the chief victims of the perceived scientific need to investigate; and since the founding of the United States, it has been the practice of scientists, whether their theories are well founded or not, to use Indian human remains for scientific work, teaching materials, and public displays.

The attitude of the federal agencies toward Indian remains, an attitude supported and applauded by museum directors and archaeologists, has been that they were resources, comparable in most respects to timber, oil, and water, belonging to the federal agency on whose land they were found. The Native American Rights Fund, led by Walter Echo-Hawk, challenged this conception and, in a series of negotiations, secured restoration of many human remains and saw enacted several state and federal statutes placing Indian human remains on a near-equal standing with non-Indian skeletons. Make no mistake about the power of secularity in this struggle, however, since the attitude of federal employees and social scientists was that there is no evidence that we have any relationship to the departed, once bodily functions cease. Consequently, in their view, any belief *or experience* relating to the dead or to spirits of the dead was wholly superstition. Civil religion thus denies the possibility or importance of the afterlife and limits human responsibilities to tangible things that we can touch.

A further aspect of civil religion is that the practice of religion must be within the boundaries of municipal law and civil order. Thus, state police powers are believed to be the final arbiter of values in human society. Beliefs and practices must conform to city ordinances, state laws, and federal regulations; and insofar as they conflict, they must surrender themselves to civil authority. In *Lyng,* the Forest Service was determined to build a road, apparently merely in the interests of symmetry, since the evidence revealed no practical or economic reason for construction, and the practice of Indian religions had to step back.

The power of civil religion and the inability of organized religion to articulate a set of values superior to those of the state combine to define the present situation in the following manner: Religious behavior must be justified on secular grounds in order to be protected. The possible examples of this proposition are frightening. A rock concert promoter could get permission to use a natural amphitheater, but a traditional Indian could not get permission to use the same location if he wished to perform a ceremony. A person could wear long hair as a symbol of freedom of speech but could not do the same thing if his motive were religious belief. A municipality can display a manger scene at Christmas only if it is interpreted as a generally accepted cultural tradition and not if it is for the purpose of religious devotion. That explains, perhaps, the inclusion of Rudolph, the Ninja Turtles, and some Disney characters in Christmas displays.

Since *Smith,* lower courts have discarded the old balancing test and are now placing churches under municipal ordinances, denying requests for dietary exemptions, authorizing autopsies when they are against the practices of religious groups, and generally allowing civil laws, particularly criminal laws, to be the definitive statement of what is acceptable religious behavior. The chief victims of *Smith* are mainline churches and their members, insofar as those members take their religious duties seriously.

THE QUEST FOR RELIGIOUS EXPERIENCE

The psychological subconscious of American society and its constituent members is a tempestuous sewer. Americans crave some form of religious experience, and they are unable to obtain it from any of the old, mainline Christian denominations. This condition became obvious in the sixties, when people began to take drugs to help them deal with the pressures of modern society. Two responses were forthcoming. The right-wing fundamentalists diluted their message even more, making Christianity a talk show phenomenon and asking only for uncritical obedience to a set of slogans articulated by reactionary politicians and huckster preachers. Fundamentalist Christianity, which loves the unborn and hates the living, has become a powerful political force in this country primarily because it has aligned itself with reactionary economic oligarchies and parroted their concerns about the status quo. The evidence is there to see: Ronald Reagan, a divorced man whose second wife was pregnant when he married her and who neglected his children, overwhelmingly was preferred by the electorate to Jimmy Carter, a Baptist who believed that beliefs should result in behavior.

Mainline Protestant churches, such as the Episcopalians, Presbyterians, Lutherans, Disciples of Christ, and United Church of Christ, responded to the public's desire for religious experience by transforming Christian doctrines into permissive declarations that endorsed secular values. Whatever problem seemed to be bothering the unchurched, these denominations found a way to endorse the most blatant secular version of the problem. In their attempt to be relevant to modern society, they became its greatest expositors. It is now impossible to find any sinful behavior that would not be endorsed or advocated by these churches. In the Middle Ages, there were seven deadly sins and a whole host of minor or venial sins. In the past three decades, the fundamentalist Christians have taken one of the deadly sins—GREED—and made it the primary Christian virtue. The mainline churches then promptly made the multitude of venial sins respectable.

The response of serious Americans has been to look elsewhere. Asian religions—including various aspects of martial arts—old European religions such as witchcraft and devil worship, astrology, reincarnation, and a bewildering variety of self-help techniques have offered a religious experience buffet to a hungry American society. A sizable number of people have come to American Indians, seeking to join tribal religious practices or take from the tribal traditions those things they find most attractive. Thus the proliferation of "medicine wheels" and "pipe carriers" in the non-Indian population has become astronomical. Even the simplest kind of religious experience in an Indian setting or with an Indian theme is held as a cherished memory by non-Indians.

Traditional people in every tribe have made astounding progress in reviving the old ceremonies. Dances and ceremonies that had not been held for generations are now common once again in the isolated parts of the reservations. Traditional religion and customs are widely believed to be the real solution to many of the pressing social problems plaguing Indian communities today. Within a decade, it will be necessary to be a traditional religious leader to be elected to office in many tribes. If the rest of American society is not solving its basic quest for religious experience, Indians are doing so.

Most people miss the critical distinction between New Age "religious" life and tribal ceremonies. American society, particularly its organized religions and its political institutions, is built on the idea of the solitary individual as the foundation of everything else. A gathering of individuals becomes a congregation, a corporation, a legislature, or a club. In a mass society, rules must apply equally to everyone, since everyone is regarded as interchangeable, and that is the ideology underlying our institutions today. New Age movements, lacking an institutional base, are not hierarchical organizations designed for manipulation of the masses but are networks of people—strings of people who are linked together by similar philosophies, experiences, or desires.

Indian tribes violate this basic reality of mass society in that they are communities, as are the major Christian groups that have run afoul of the free exercise clauses—primarily Amish and Jehovah's Witnesses (held together by rigid discipline but easily identifiable). It is impossible for the institutions of mass society to reach within the tribal community and manipulate individuals, since the community is held together by blood and common sets of experiences. Hence, Indian tribes will always be askew in comparison with everything else in America, and particularly with political institutions.

Traditional religions are under attack not because they are Indian but because they are fundamentally religious and are perhaps the only consistent religious groups in American society over the long term. If kidnapping children for boarding schools, prohibiting religious ceremonies, destroying the family through allotments, and bestowing American citizenship did not destroy the basic community of Indian people, what could possibly do so? The attack today on traditional religion is the secular attack on any group that advocates and practices devotion to a value higher than the state. That is why the balancing test has been discarded and laws and ordinances are allowed primacy over religious obligations. Under the auspices of civil religion, there can be no higher value than the state. Communism was the civil religion of the Soviet Union, and it failed; chauvinistic patriotism is the civil religion of the United States right now, and it will soon break into bickering pressure groups and oppression and suppression of all dissenting views. But the quest for religious experience by human beings cannot be suppressed permanently. Consequently, we will find a solution, although we might thereby create an exceedingly unpleasant condition.

The movement to secure religious freedom in all its aspects by the Indian coalition is now getting under way. It should receive support from all serious American citizens who wish to preserve the right to have their own philosophy and their own religious experiences. This act will be the first step in rolling back the intrusions by the institutions of mass society that have changed our lives into a gray uniformity of acts and opinions. Indians can always retreat to the isolated places on the reservations, so the impact of the *Smith* decision really affects only those Indians who wish to practice their religion outside the reservations. But unless this group is protected within the constitutional framework, what chance have other groups, even Christian groups, of following their consciences or religious dictates? For the first time in American history, then, Indians have a common cause with other Americans.

(1992)

OLD WAYS
IN A NEW WORLD

Tribal origin accounts commonly trace ancient migrations across strange lands and through successive worlds, primordial journeys that culminate in the formation of a people. Oral traditions, preserved in the multiform medium of language, speak to the ubiquity of displacement in human history and to the consolation that comes with finally achieving a homeland. America has seemed a new world to generations of immigrants—some refugees, some captives, a multitude of opportunists—all of whom brought old ways with them as they struggled to survive a severe relocation. Drastic transformations of the Americas, part of a global metamorphosis in recent centuries, have shown this impression of newness to be a self-fulfilling ideology. Yet few of these now-dominant traditions seem capable of ensuring the survival of the human species, much less allowing tribal peoples to continue their pilgrimages through space and time. Preserving the integrity of tribal communities, positioning their accumulated knowledge of this land to help safeguard the fate of the planet, has been a pivotal concern for Deloria throughout his professional life. Applying indigenous wisdom to contemporary problems is a recurring theme in his writings, from *Custer Died for Your Sins* to *Red Earth, White Lies*. Tribal traditions are eminently relevant to present and future crises, not quaint artifacts of a bygone era. Old is not necessarily obsolete.

This section begins with Deloria's introduction to the 1979 reprint edition of *Black Elk Speaks*, the acclaimed "Life Story of a Holy Man of the Oglala Sioux" as told by poet John Neihardt. Deconstructionist critics have questioned the authenticity of the narrative, emphasizing Neihardt's editorial presence at the expense of Black Elk's quintessential role in their "conversations and companionship," something more than collaboration. Deloria acknowledges these literary debates but proposes a more synthetic reading of the text, one that recognizes its status as a "religious classic" capable of expressing universal dimensions of the human experience. Noting the book's popularity among the younger generation of tribal people, he perceives "the emergence of a new sacred hoop, a new circle of intense community among Indians far outdistancing the grandeur of former times." Deloria uses insights from Black Elk's narrative to frame the next essay, a poetic reflection on the organic relationship between community and homeland. "The Coming of the People" originally appeared in *The American Land,* an illustrated anthology published by the Smithsonian Institution. Recounting tribal narratives of migration, Deloria suggests why it is "necessary to live as relatives" after settling in "exactly the right place." Abstract theories of creation and history are no match for experiential knowledge of the world; creation *is* history, a "continual search for cosmic rhythms which remind us of our true selves." The American landscape is mapped in the faces of its mature inhabitants.

As he did in these first two pieces, Deloria takes a characteristically optimistic approach to the topic of the third essay in this section. "Out of Chaos" was written for *Parabola,* a publication of the Society for the Study of Myth and Tradition, as part of a thematic issue on exile. Rather than dwell on the obvious injustices surfaced by a political reading of this theme, Deloria explores the religious significance of exilic suffering and alienation. The general pattern of expulsion, transformation, and return he outlines here brings to mind the liminal trauma of the vision quest and other ceremonial rites of passage. Exile should be measured in a people's ability to fulfill their responsibilities to the land, though even the forcible destruction of ceremonial life is not the final word. Anticipating a prophetic intervention, Deloria concludes that we might "expect American Indians to discern, out of the chaos of their shattered lives, . . . a new interpretation of their religious tradition with a universal application. . . . Perhaps out of the confusion of modern Indian society will come a statement about the world that we have come to expect when the exiles return." He extends his investigation of the relationship between peoples and lands in "Reflection and Revelation: Knowing Land, Places and Ourselves." This essay was originally presented at a symposium on "The Spirit of Place" and later published with other symposium papers in *The Power of Place: Sacred Ground in Natural and Human Environments.* Responding to growing interest in tribal environmental knowledge, Deloria points out that tribal wisdom represents the "distilled experiences" of a community. He analyzes the sacredness of land by distinguishing between reflective and revelatory experiences, which are available to all people, but only after prolonged occupation of a specific place. "Civilized life precludes most of the fundamental experiences that our species once had in relating to lands and the natural order." Yet he again ends on a hopeful note, encouraged by the efforts of some to reverse the tide of environmental exploitation.

Deloria assesses the downside of religious adaptation in the next essay. "Is Religion Possible? An Evaluation of Present Efforts to Revive Traditional

Tribal Religions" appeared in *Wicazo Sa Review,* a journal of Native American studies. Pointing to the careless appropriations taking place on the New Age circuit, in the environmental movement, within Christian churches, and even among secular tribal organizations, he concludes that "Indian traditional religious affairs are a complete disaster area." The quiet efforts of some traditional people indicate it may be possible to revive certain ceremonies, though Deloria cautions against the seduction of religious nostalgia. We are left to assemble the surviving fragments of revelation in the hope that they will lead us into the future, which is "all the old ways ever promised they would do." The final piece is Deloria's introduction to *Vision Quest: Men, Women and Sacred Sites of the Sioux Nation,* a book of contemporary portraits by Don Doll, a professional photographer and Jesuit priest. Black Elk's dark vision of generations in struggle is a heavy burden for contemporary Sioux people to bear, but "we take fearful steps in order that our nation move through the difficult times and emerge into a better world." Deloria looks ahead and sees other paths converging with theirs, even as sociopolitical realities work against any static conception of Sioux identity. "But as long as the people live on the land and can point to the places where Sioux history was experienced, there will always be a Sioux people."

J. T.

23

INTRODUCTION TO
BLACK ELK SPEAKS

The twentieth century has produced a world of conflicting visions, intense emotions, and unpredictable events, and the opportunities for grasping the substance of life have faded as the pace of activity has increased. Electronic media shuffle us through a myriad of experiences which would have baffled earlier generations and seem to produce in us a strange isolation from the reality of human history. Our heroes fade into mere personality, are consumed and forgotten, and we avidly seek more avenues to express our humanity. Reflection is the most difficult of all our activities because we are no longer able to establish relative priorities from the multitude of sensations that engulf us. Times such as these seem to illuminate the classic expressions of eternal truths and great wisdom comes to stand out in the crowd of ordinary maxims.

How fortunate it was that in the 1930s as the nation was roaring into a new form of industrialism a Nebraska poet named Neihardt traveled northward to the reservation of the Oglala Sioux in search of materials for his epic work on the history of the West. That their conversations and companionship should produce a religious classic, perhaps the only religious classic of this century, is a testimony indeed to the continuing strength of our species. *Black Elk Speaks* was originally published in 1932, when people still believed that progress and the assembly line were identical and that the Depression was but a temporary interlude in an inevitable march toward the millennium. Its eloquent message was lost in the confusion of the times. It was not rejected, but it was hardly received with the veneration it now enjoys. The reception, in fact, reflected one of those overly romantic but simplistic views which suggests that all religions have some validity if they prevent us from acts of bestiality and even the most primitive expressions of religious truth are an effort to connect with the larger reality of Western civilization.

Black Elk Speaks did not follow other contemporary works into oblivion. Throughout the thirties, forties, and fifties it drew a steady and devoted readership and served as a reliable expression of the substance that undergirded Plains Indian religious beliefs. Outside the Northern Plains, the Sioux tribe, and the western mind-set, there were few people who knew the book or listened to its message. But crises mounted and, as we understood the implications of future shock, the silent spring, and the greening of America, people began to search for a universal expression of the larger, more cosmic truths which industrialism and progress had ignored and overwhelmed. In the 1960s interest began to focus on Indians and some of the spiritual realities they seemed to represent. Regardless of the other literature in the field, the scholarly dissertations with inflections and nuances, *Black Elk Speaks* clearly dominated the literature dealing with Indian religions.

Today the book is familiar reading for millions of people, some of whom have no clear conception of Black Elk's tribe, the Oglala Sioux, and others of whom do not, as a rule, even like Indians. The spiritual framework of the pipe ceremonies and the story of Black Elk's life and vision are well known, and speculations on the nature and substance of Plains Indian religion use the book as the criterion by which other books and interpretive essays are to be judged. If any great religious classic has emerged in this century or on this continent, it must certainly be judged in the company of *Black Elk Speaks* and withstand the criticism which such a comparison would inevitably invite.

The most important aspect of the book, however, is not its effect on the non-Indian populace who wished to learn something of the beliefs of the Plains Indians but upon the contemporary generation of young Indians who have been aggressively searching for roots of their own in the structure of universal reality. To them the book has become a North American bible of all tribes. They look to it for spiritual guidance, for sociological identity, for political insight, and for affirmation of the continuing substance of Indian tribal life, now being badly eroded by the same electronic media which are dissolving other American communities.

Black Elk shared his visions with John Neihardt because he wished to pass along to future generations some of the reality of Oglala life and, one suspects, to share the burden of visions that remained unfulfilled with a compatible spirit. Black Elk might have been greatly surprised at the popularity of the book today. He could not help but be pleased by it. If the old camp circle, the sacred hoop of the Lakota, and the old days have been rudely shattered by the machines of a scientific era, and if they can be no more in the traditional sense, the universality of the images and dreams must testify to the emergence of a new sacred hoop, a new circle of intense community among Indians far outdistancing the grandeur of former times. So important has this book become that one cannot today attend a meeting on Indian religion and hear a series of Indian speakers without recalling the exact parts of the book that lie behind contemporary efforts to inspire and clarify those beliefs that are "truly Indian."

As successful as the book is, the future appears unlimited in contrast with its present achievements. We have not yet seen that generation of theologians who always attend the birth of great religious traditions. The present generation of Indian college students may well be harbingers of this era. Christianity and Buddhism both took half a millennium to adequately express in theological and philosophical frameworks the vision of universal substance which their founders promulgated and lived. Neihardt's *Black Elk Speaks* and *When the Tree Flowered,* and *The Sacred Pipe* by Joseph Epes Brown, the basic works of the Black Elk theological tradition, now bid fair to become the canon or at least the central core of a North American Indian theological canon which will someday challenge the Eastern and Western traditions as a way of looking at the world. Certainly in Black Elk's visions we have a natural relationship to the rest of the cosmos devoid of the trial-court paradigm but incorporating the theme of sacrifice so important to all religions in a consistent and comprehensible way.

Present debates center on the question of Neihardt's literary intrusions into Black Elk's system of beliefs and some scholars have said that the book reflects more of Neihardt than it does of Black Elk. It is, admittedly, difficult to discover if we are talking with Black Elk or John Neihardt, whether the vision is to be interpreted differently, and whether or not the positive emphasis which the book projects is not the optimism of two poets lost in the modern world and transforming drabness into an idealized world. Can it matter? The very nature of great religious teachings is that they encompass everyone who understands them and personalities become indistinguishable from the transcendent truth that is expressed. So let it be with *Black Elk Speaks.* That it speaks to us with simple and compelling language about an aspect of human experience and encourages us to emphasize the best that dwells within us is sufficient. Black Elk and John Neihardt would probably nod affirmatively to that statement and continue their conversation. It is good. It is enough.

(1979)

24

THE COMING OF THE PEOPLE

There was a time, Black Elk told his biographer, John Neihardt, when the people were many but they were not a nation yet. "All were relatives, but sons did not know their fathers, nor fathers their sons, nor brothers their sisters." If there is a beginning, it is the memory of this primordial chaos when people had no relatives in the Indian way and they were not yet truly people. The Sioux were at that time, according to Black Elk, living on a great body of water, probably the Gulf of Mexico, and in the course of events the Holy Men had visions which led the Sioux through long journeys to the sacred island hill—the Black Hills of South Dakota—and they became a people.

Cultural traditions with a scientific bent view creation as an event distant in time in which the cosmic process began its steady and mechanical progression. The mystical traditions of the East speak of a cosmic dance in which manifestations of individuality, albeit ephemeral, produce the plentitude of life which we see around us. The individual then must achieve the realization that all is really one and return to the cosmic unity. Even the fundamentalist traditions which credit God with instantaneous creation and see in the operations of nature a divine intention to produce goodness are intertwined with the progression and inevitability of things. But it is not so with the American Indians.

These ideas are all too abstract and general. They tell us nothing about the world and less about ourselves. Speculations must not replace experiences. The Crow chief Arapooish, talking with Robert Campbell of the Rocky Mountain Fur Company at one of the last rendezvous, described his land: "The Crow country is a good country. The Great Spirit put it exactly in the right place; while you are in it you fare well; whenever you are out of it, whichever way you travel, you fare worse . . ." And he went on to tell about its marvels: The Crow country is exactly in the right place. It has snowy mountains and sunny plains, all kinds of climate and good things for every season. When the summer heats scorch the prairies, you can draw up under the mountains, where the air is sweet and cool, the grasses fresh, and the bright streams come tumbling out of the snowbanks. There you can hunt the elk, the deer, and the antelope, when their skins are fit for dressing; there you will find plenty of white bear and mountain sheep.

In the autumn, when your horses are fat and strong from the mountain pastures, you can go into the plains and hunt the buffalo, or trap beaver on the streams. And when winter comes on, you can take shelter in the woody bottoms along the rivers; there you will find buffalo meat for yourselves, and cottonwood bark for your horses; or you may winter in Wind River Valley where there is salt weed in abundance.

Yes, Arapooish concluded, the Crow country is exactly in the right place, and a flood of pleasant memories filled him to confirm his belief.

Our species, for ever so long, has believed that we are strangers in the world and many people have looked to the heavens for a sign that some time, in some place, they would no longer be strangers in the land. And so long as people felt incomplete and sought to find a home they were not really created. The Indians also had this feeling but they had one great virtue which many of the other peoples lacked—they were able to listen to the Earth. And so when they came here they waited for instructions, believing that they would be guided to the right place.

The oldest of the people, the Hopi, came in several migrations and brought with them the knowledge of former worlds, times, and places. Survivors of primordial catastrophes, they had endured the cold of outer space when the Earth's axis refused to turn. Tested in the trauma of a world gone mad with power, they returned to the simple task of finding relatives in order that they might live in harmony with the rhythms of the land. Four migrations around the continent they made, each time seeking to establish their roots and center their universe. The most ancient monuments of the land testify to their travels and, blocked by the massive walls of ice in the north, they finally came to the high mesa of the Southwest where the giant canyon of light informed them of its antiquity. Not far from the center of the Earth, an area that has existed in geological stability for millions of years, they planted their villages.

Other peoples, then spiritual adolescents in comparison with the Hopi clans, arrived later, also seeking to find the right place and also listening for instructions. The Iroquois and Sioux say they arrived from the direction where the sun rises; the Three Fires—the Chippewa, Ottawa, and Potawatomi—traveled from the mouth of the St. Lawrence to the Great Lakes. The Okanagon moved eastward on a chain of islands and, looking back at the submerging lands they were leaving, steadfast in their determination to find the right place, arrived at the mouth of the Columbia River and moved up its hospitable waters to the mountains where many rivulets had agreed to come together to form the mighty river.

Were some peoples already here? The Klamath, living in comfort in the Cascades, watched the Okanagon arrive, burned red from the ordeal at sea, and were bemused at the newcomers living in tents while they busied themselves in their stone houses. Other peoples, coming into their own lands, found ruins and wondered where the former inhabitants had gone, why they had not found peace in their place, and whether this place was indeed special. The Yakimas, discovering relics of a former people, preferred to continue a nomadic life, uncertain at the fate of any group that would dare to effect a permanent settlement. They always hurried through these remnant dwellings on the Columbia for fear that the fate of the ancient ones might become their own.

So over the centuries the people found their places and, like the Crow, they all knew their country was in exactly the right place. No land seemed formidable when it was designed for a particular people. The Hopi, living on the high desert mesa, received special ceremonies to enable them to plant and harvest. The Iroquois, in the eastern forests, learned quickly that they were related to all beings in their country. The Three Sisters—corn, beans, and squash—showed them how to live, and the mutual spirituality of the Sisters kept their lands fertile and hospitable. The peoples of the Plains learned from the cottonwood how to make tipis, and the tree became their sacred relative participating in the annual sun dance. It was not simply a task of living in their country as human beings. It was necessary to live as relatives.

How does one find relatives among the peoples of creation? The human being, the old ones relate, is a strange creature. The eagle's eye is stronger. The bear's arm is stronger. The swallow is able to fly. The fish is a better swimmer. The deer is much quicker. The panther can leap farther. The wasp has greater poison. The hawk is a better hunter. The snake is more in tune with the Earth. The dog is friendlier. So the human being must learn from these other peoples. Watch, listen, and learn.

The peoples seem to be the same—but they are not. The Great Spirit teaches the birds to make nests—yet each bird makes a different kind of nest. The Great Spirit teaches animals to hunt—yet each hunts in a different way. The Great Spirit teaches each people to care for its young—yet each people has a different manner of instruction. The Great Spirit provides the outline of how to live; each people contributes the content of life by becoming themselves.

Simple observation was often not sufficient to teach the lessons of life.

The peoples were all related and, like relatives, they had to give and share. The humans could contribute very little, but a way was found for them to do so. One day, a long time ago, a great race was held. The race course extended from the Black Hills clear across Wyoming to the Big Horns, far south, and then farther north. It was a serious race, for the two-leggeds—human beings and birds—were racing the four-leggeds to determine which should feed the others. It was the most serious covenant ever established. The winners would feed upon the losers from that day forth. Only when the winners returned to the earth and their bones became the soil and they brought forth food would the losers feed upon them.

The two-leggeds were no match for the four-leggeds. All of the peoples joined in. Sometimes the winds aided the four-leggeds and prevented the wings from flying. Other times the day would be very hot and the four-leggeds would slow down while the two-leggeds caught up. The race was even and it lasted many, many days. But as the days passed and each member of the two groups took their turns running, the magpie devised a scheme: Instead of flying, she sat on the buffalo's horn, catching a ride and preserving her strength. The racers neared the finish line and the four-leggeds, seeing the buffalo chief in the lead and no two-leggeds in sight, began to cheer and shout, shaking the Earth with their noise. As they neared the finish line the magpie flew from the buffalo's horn and crossed the finish line ahead of him, saving the day for the two-leggeds and demonstrating that while physical strength is important, it must be used intelligently.

The cycle of life was established. While the two-leggeds were to feed on the four-leggeds, they were not to fear death for it provided the means of completing the bargain. The bodies of the two-leggeds, after their spirits had departed, provided the soil in which the plants grew to feed the four-leggeds. Neither group ever feared the other for they were relatives and knew that while they might receive, they were also expected to give.

There were, of course, people who could not listen to the instructions of the land. And there were people who forgot the teachings that they had been given. There are many ways that people can be taught. In the Cascades the people began fighting with each other and there was no harmony. The trouble became so bad that the greatest chief of all, known by the whites as ancient Mount Multnomah, exploded, killing the disobedient people and destroying the country which had been so fruitful. When the smoke cleared and the survivors gathered around, all that was left of the great chief was a much smaller mountain and the three wives who sat in mourning over the lost innocence of former days. The white men now call this ruin the Three Sisters and tell us that it is the remnant of a mighty volcano which exploded in a very remote geological era. But the Indians know better. Mountains are people too, and when our species brings turmoil and disharmony to the creation, eventually all the other peoples are injured also.

In various parts of Turtle Island this bitter lesson had to be learned. On the Great Plains the people began quarreling. Some said that greed began to dominate human relationships and people no longer cared for their relatives. Others said that selfishness and the determination to exclude other peoples from the bounty that was the High Plains caused the trouble. Either of these faults would have violated the personality of the Plains and angered its spirit. On the Plains one must be wild and free with no artificial boundaries and no gathering of things to oneself. When the lands became soaked with blood from the quarreling of the humans, the Spirit of the Plains decided to punish the people.

Calling upon his relatives, the Sky and Winds, the Spirit of the Plains let forth a loud bellowing noise, and dark clouds gathered. The land shook, darkness filled the skies, and fires burst forth from the bowels of the Earth. Violent thunderstorms swept the Plains clean of people, and heavy smoke and dust filled the air, making it impossible to see. For a long time it was as if Sky and Earth had merged together to prevent people from living on the Plains. When the air finally cleared and it was possible to see once again, in the midst of the fertile grasslands were places barren of vegetation, eternally scarred and discolored, and devoid of any ability to produce life. Only small patches of the massive Plains were in this desolated condition, and life returned to most of the area very shortly. But generations of people passing near these lands—which came to be called "badlands"—saw and remembered what had happened here.

Southern California is among the most ancient parts of Turtle Island and certainly one of the most fruitful. But inland a short distance lies Death Valley, a tremendous sink much below sea level, and inhospitable to nearly every form of life. It was not always a cursed land. Not so many years ago, at least within the memory of some of the tribes, it was a happy, fruitful land. So fruitful in fact that its riches stirred feelings of greed among the people who lived there, and each wanted the valley exclusively for themselves. The medicine men warned the people to stop fighting with each other but to no avail. The buzzard came as a special messenger of the spirits and warned that the land could not stand senseless killing and might punish the people. No one listened.

Finally, the mountain sheep who used the valley in the summers made a special visit to the warring tribes and demanded they make peace before the land and spirits rebelled. Still the people refused to listen. Their pride injured by the intrusion of their relatives into their raiding activities, they defied both spirits and relatives and rejected the overtures of the mountain sheep. So the spirits of the place became very angry. They blew the tops off the mountains and poured hot lava on the warriors who refused to live peaceably. The Earth became spongy like jelly and shook continually, causing the warring people to flee hither and yon. Still their pride caused them to refuse to make peace.

Great cracks in the Earth appeared, and finally the spirits split open a mountain range and poured ocean water into the valley, creating a vast inland sea. The people scrambled to the heights of the mountains along the lakeshore but the angry spirits pursued them there. The great inland sea dried up, leaving salt flats in its place. As the people sought refuge in the mountains each range was twisted and split into many fragments; with the demise of each range of mountains the valley sank lower and lower. Finally, satisfied that they had punished the people for their transgressions, the spirits caused torrential rains to pour down upon the valley and remove many traces of human habitation which had survived the catastrophe. Only the debris of nature was left to testify to the awful punishments that had been inflicted.

All over the continent, whenever the people lost their humility and began to mistreat their relatives, the land rebelled and rebuked them. The unusual features of the land testify to the events in the experiences of many peoples. So creation, if we insist that it must include the configuration of landscapes, is also history. The water marks on Steptoe Butte in eastern Washington remind us of the great flood that destroyed the transgressors of the natural laws. Grand Coulee, farther up the valley of the Columbia, once poured forth a tidal wave of water that flooded the central plain and created immense sandbars which now appear as small hillocks in the plains of eastern Washington. The lava flows of western New Mexico tell us of the rebellion of the land there also. And the yawning mouth of Crater Lake in southern Oregon is an eloquent voice reminding us to have respect for all creatures.

It is exceedingly strange that we do not today understand that creation is really history—the story of how peoples found their relatives and came to know their sacred places. When we get older we begin to see that creation is history because it is the continual search for cosmic rhythms which reminds us of our true selves. Black Elk reflected that "everything the Power of the World does is done in a circle." And he illustrated his insight with the vivid examples that could only come from a person who was in harmony with all of creation and knew their ways: "The Sky is round and I have heard that the Earth is round like a ball and so are all the stars. The Wind, in its greatest power, whirls. Birds make their nests in circles, for theirs is the same religion as ours. The sun comes forth and goes down again in a circle. The moon does the same, and both are round. Even the seasons form a great circle in their changing, and always come back again to where they were. The life of a man is a circle from childhood to childhood and so it is with everything where power moves."

In the unique and cosmic rhythms, special events stand out and are recognized as those special occasions when Earth, peoples, and the Power of the World shared a unique and sometimes chastising experience.

When a people have finally reached their sacred place and come to understand its ways, they begin to take on its characteristics. "We are a part of the nature around us, and the older we get the more we come to look like it," the Sioux medicine man Lame Deer once remarked. "In the end we become part of the landscape with a face like the Badlands." In the same way, one can move around the continent and discover in the faces of the people almost a mirror of the lands on which they live. Photographers, perhaps unaware of the nature of Indian life and thinking that creation is a distant event, still continue to take pictures of older Indians without realizing that their photographs are capturing the essence of creation itself.

There are, of course, many other stories about the continent, and each tribe preserves its special knowledge and memories about the sacred mountains, rivers, lakes, and valleys. Almost every tribe can point out those features of the landscape which mark the boundaries of their lands and tell how the people first knew that this was their country and that it was in exactly the right place. The more knowledge one has, the more significant do the various traditions seem, for the conglomerate taken together testifies to the uniqueness of the continent.

The white man, when viewed in this context, appears as a perennial adolescent. He is continually moving about, and his restless nature cannot seem to find peace. Yet he does not listen to the land and so cannot find a place for himself. He has few relatives and seems to believe that the domestic animals that have always relied upon him constitute his only link with the other peoples of the universe. Yet he does not treat these animals as friends but only as objects to be exploited. While he has destroyed many holy places of the Indians, he does not seem to be able to content himself with his own holy places . . . for his most holy places are cemeteries where his forefathers lie under granite slabs, row upon row upon row, strangers lying with strangers.

Insightful whites have intuited aspects of creation. Carl Jung remarked that the dreams of American patients generally held a special messianic figure cast in the form of an Indian. Franz Boas demonstrated that by the third generation of immigrants, the people had changed facially and were beginning to look like the Indians who preceded them.

D.H. Lawrence noted that while the Indian would never again possess the continent, he would always haunt it and it would always find affirmation in his spirit. John Collier saw in the Indian folkways the solution to many of the pressing problems of modern industrialization. And song writers have long noted that natural features have a personality of their own. It is not for naught that we romanticize "Ol' Man River." The process of creation continues and will do so until everyone has a special place to live and relatives to enjoy.

It has always been this way. John Neihardt spent a great deal of time discussing the Indian tradition with Black Elk, the Sioux Holy Man. One day, after Black Elk told Neihardt about how the Sioux had received the sacred pipe which is present at almost all the tribe's ceremonial occasions, Black Elk remained silent for several minutes. Finally he turned to Neihardt and said: "This they tell, and whether it happened so or not I do not know; *but if you think about it, you can see that it is true!*" And so it is with the Indian understanding of the land and the coming of the people.

(1979)

25

OUT OF CHAOS

When we talk about exile today we are more than likely to have a political situation in mind; but the original use of the word is considerably more enlightening. The roots of the idea of exile are most prominently displayed in a religious or mythic context. Moses and Oedipus immediately come to mind—as well as a host of other historical and mythological figures—all experiencing exile or suffering the sense of alienation which such a status entails. The religious aspect of exile, in contrast to its political meaning, involves many intangible factors which help us change and enhance our knowledge of the world.

The mythic and traditional idea of exile entails the expulsion of the chosen one from his comfortable and often exalted position in society. He is then thrust into a barren place where he has to abandon his former knowledge of this world. He learns humility and faith, comprehends the transcendent nature of ultimate reality, and is initiated into the mysteries and secrets of the other, higher world. Then the exile returns to his society armed with his superior knowledge, and creates fundamental and lasting reforms, so that society marks its distinctive identity from the time he received his exilic commission.

Considering all the modern racial and ethnic groups to whom the idea of exile might be applied, none appears more deserving or representative of this status than North American Indians. In the half-millennium since the discovery of the western hemisphere, almost all Indian tribes have been forcibly removed from their ancestral homelands and subjected to cultural and religious indignities comparable in many ways to the manner in which the old culture heroes were stripped of their beliefs and presuppositions. At least this view is the popular explanation of the condition of Indians in modern American society. But there is considerably more to the story.

We immediately remember the removal of Indians from the Ohio valley and deep South as the most prominent historical instance of Indian exile. The bitter picture of thousands of Cherokees, Creeks, and Choctaws, their heads bowed in sorrow, walking west in the driving rain of a cold winter is deeply etched on our consciousness. Federal policy to clear the country east of the Mississippi of Indians was carried out with almost scientific precision, even gathering small bands of Winnebagos in Wisconsin and moving them a few hundred miles to Nebraska. Removal was understood as a sensible solution to the Indian problem until the 1890s; plans were even suggested to gather all the tribes in western Oklahoma, ring the area with forts, and maintain a massive concentration camp until such time as the Indians had either acculturated or vanished.

When we look at a map of the United States, however, we find that there were tribes that escaped this fate. Beyond the Mississippi-Missouri border, tribes were generally settled on reservations within their aboriginal homelands; and if we note that many groups are still living within their original occupancy areas, we might argue that exile is not an appropriate description of the condition of western Indians. But we would be mistaking the possession of the title to lands for the right to live on them freely, and substituting our own political concepts for the rich feeling toward lands that has always characterized Indian society.

Within the Western context we are always inclined to see land as a commodity and think first of its ownership; in contrast, the traditional Indian understanding of land focuses on its use, and the duties people assume when they come to occupy it. When an Indian thinks about traditional lands he always talks about what the people did there, the animals who lived there and how the people related to them, the seasons of the year and how people responded to their changes, the manner in which the tribe acquired possession of the area, and the ceremonial functions it was required to perform to remain worthy of living there.

The idea of lands, therefore, tells us the difference between Indian and non-Indian views so we can determine whether or not an exile has occurred. Whites acquire land through purchase and sale, and land is a quantifiable, measurable entity; their primary responsibility as landowners is simply to prevent a loss of value; hence any responsibility the landowner may have is only to himself. Indian tribes acquire land as a gift from higher powers, and in turn they assume certain ceremonial duties which must be performed as long as they live on and use the land. Removing an Indian tribe from its aboriginal territory, therefore, results in the destruction of ceremonial life and much of the cultural structure which has made ceremony and ritual significant. So the western tribes, although not completely removed from their lands in a geographical sense, experienced exile in much the same way as did their brothers from the east. Restrictions in the manner in which people use lands are as much a deprivation of land as actual loss of title.

Indian exile, because of its impact on ceremonial responsibilities, includes a religious dimension which modern political exile lacks. If we understand ceremony and ritual, performed as a condition of living in certain places, as the critical element which distinguishes each Indian group, then the cultural life of the people, its continuance or destruction, is the important fact in considering whether an exile has occurred. So while the Sioux, Apache, Blackfeet, and Crow, for example, all live within their original lands, persistent efforts to change their culture and exclusion from sacred places has produced a profound sense of exile.

A good example of this intangible, cultural/religious exile can be seen in the struggle of Taos Pueblo during this century to regain the Blue Lake area. Deprived of exclusive use of the lake, located near the Pueblo and central to its ceremonial life, when a national forest was established at the turn of the century, the Pueblo was given a "use permit" that only enabled it to visit the lake and conduct ceremonies but did not give it exclusive use. When the Pueblo filed its claims in the Indian Claims Commission, it carefully segregated the claim for the Blue Lake area and asked for restoration of the land to the Pueblo instead of a financial payment for its loss. After an intensive struggle in Congress the Pueblo finally succeeded in getting a bill passed in which the United States recognized in the Pueblo the title to the lake area.

It might appear to the casual observer that title was the primary concern of the Pueblo during this argument and that the Pueblo was only acting in the same manner as any other landowner faced with similar circumstances. Such was not the case. Rather, from the Pueblo point of view, its religious responsibilities to the lake and surrounding lands were paramount and could only be carried out in their totality by the complete exclusion of all other activities from the area.

Obligations demanded by the lands upon which people lived were part of their understanding of the world; indeed, their view of life was grounded in the knowledge of these responsibilities. Tribal ritual life was intimately related to the seasons of the year. Other species shared the land and also responded to the annual rhythms of nature. Thus the people perceived that a social contract existed between men and the other animals. The human ceremonial life confirmed the existence of this equality and gave it sustenance. One could, perhaps, list the tribes according to the complexity of their ceremonial year and project their approximate longevity. We need not distinguish sedentary agricultural tribes from migratory hunting and fishing tribes. Indians had an intimate and precise knowledge of the habits and personality of both plant and animal life and therefore successful relationships with fish and game were no less indicative of the responsibility to land than were successful agricultural activities.

Migratory tribes suffered a considerably greater exile than did agricultural tribes when the Indians were restricted to the reservations. Some of the most important ceremonies needed to be conducted at certain sacred places at specific times of the year. While tribes could hold ceremonies at the proper time, they could not always hold these rituals at the proper place. Sometimes the sacred materials essential to the ceremony could only be obtained at these sacred places and so different materials had to be substituted. These conditions changed ceremonial life considerably, introducing a process of erosion which has since eaten away the substance of rituals and responsibilities. One might even say that the ceremonial year of the migratory tribes was highly dependent upon sacred places whereas the sacred calendar of sedentary tribes had long since become dominant over special places for enactment. On this basis, perhaps, we can determine both the longevity of a tribe and the degree of trauma which confinement produced.

Not only did their geographic confinement work to destroy the sacred calendars of tribes, but the effort to perpetuate a traditional life within the confines of the reservation was vulnerable to overtures by the federal government, seeking to make the people abandon old ways and adopt new practices which were carefully orchestrated by a new sense of time—a measured time which had little to do with cosmic realities. It is debatable which factor was most important in the destruction of tribal ceremonial life: the prohibition of performances of traditional rituals by the government, or the introduction of the white man's system of keeping time. The answer to this question can be found in an analysis of the impact of each factor on individual tribes.

Many of the old people among the Sioux felt that the government prohibition of the ceremony of the "keeping of the soul," an important condolence ceremony which linked generations of the tribe together in a more comprehensive cosmic reality, brought about the real destruction of ceremonial life in that tribe. On the other hand, in the Pacific Northwest the government tried to impose an agricultural system, and the farming calendar conflicted directly with fishing activities, producing the same erosion of ceremonial life. Prohibition of the potlatch was not nearly as important as the government's insistence that the Indians become farmers and the orientation of all programs to achieve that end.

Certainly the combination of these factors must be present in the immediate past of every tribe. We can safely suggest that the new sense of time introduced into Indian life produced a sense of alienation which made Indians strangers in a land that was becoming increasingly strange—as whites changed it to suit themselves—and that the old ceremonies might have provided an emotional bulwark against this alienation, but their prohibition only increased the feeling of exile among the people of the tribe.

Unless time is understood as sacred, experienced in all its fullness, and so dominant a consideration in the life of a people that all other functions are subservient to it, it is impossible to have a complete and meaningful ceremonial life. Rituals lose their efficacy because they are performed within a secular time which does not always make room for them or give them the status they deserve. They soon take on the aspect of mechanical adjustments made to solve problems which occur within that kind of time. Forced adaptation to secular, mathematically measured time has produced a fundamental sense of alienation.

Although the loss of land must be seen as a political and economic disaster of the first magnitude, the real exile of the tribes occurred with the destruction of ceremonial life and the failure or inability of white society to offer a sensible and cohesive alternative to the traditions which Indians remembered. People became disoriented with respect to the world in which they lived. They could not practice their old ways, and the new ways which they were expected to learn were in a constant state of change because they were not a cohesive view of the world but simply adjustments which whites were making to the technology they had invented.

Had whites been able to maintain a sense of stability in their own society, which Indians had been admonished to imitate, the tribes might have been able to observe the integrity of the new way of life and make a successful transition to it. But the only alternative that white society had to offer was a chaotic and extreme individualism, prevented from irrational excesses only by occasional government intervention. The experiences of Indians since the 1880s have been uniform in the sense that they have been confined within the boundaries of white individualism and whenever and wherever they have attempted to recapture the old sense of community, technology and domestic American politics have combined to beat back their efforts.

There is no question that American Indians have been mired in a century-long exile. Almost anything that has happened to Indians in the decades since the establishment of the reservations can and must be seen in this light. Individual incidents are but minor episodes indicating the extent of the pattern that has encompassed tribal life. We find little of the ebb and flow of sentiment and understanding which keeps a community healthy and growing, only apparent movement back and forth between the poles of political independence and dependence. In Indian cultural and religious life we have seen a unilateral shedding of old forms coupled with a paralyzing inability to create new customs and traditions which have a relationship with the past. While Indians have copied many ways of white society, on the whole they have done so badly and sporadically. Tribal governments, for example, do not behave like the old tribal councils, nor, unfortunately, do they perform like modern municipal governments. Their activities suggest some strange hybrid institution which has no knowledge of its constituents or responsibilities.

What, if anything, can Indians do to escape or overcome this condition? Originally, as we have seen, exile had a specific religious direction which suggested that exilic alienation was necessary to prepare an individual for a significant mission. The Old Testament, if we can accept some of its prophetic ideas, saw the exile of the Jews as the means of preparing them to move forward from a parochial, tribal religion and become advocates of a more universal interpretation of the meaning of human social life. Their exile did not produce a new religious understanding so much as it enabled the people to see themselves as representatives of a tradition which had within itself the potential to become an exemplary society, at peace with its neighbors and its environment. We may not be able to apply this model completely to the situation in which American Indians find themselves; but it is certainly important to our discussion of exile to try to do so.

We might, therefore, expect American Indians to discern, out of the chaos of their shattered lives, the same kind of message and mission that inspired the Hebrew prophets. Indians would, in this situation, begin to develop a new interpretation of their religious tradition with a universal application. They would further begin to seek out areas in which they could communicate with sympathetic people in the larger society, and put their own house in order. A process of intense commitment to certain social goals might then emerge in which the traditional values of pre-contact days would be seen as religious principles having a universal application. Most important, Indians would begin to probe deeper into their own past and view their remembered history as a primordial covenant.

It would be important and significant if we could report, in the activities of Indians today, the emergence of such behavior and beliefs. Unfortunately the nature of modern society precludes, or at least substantially inhibits, the development of new religious realities and statements. The vast majority of people, including Indians, believes that the world is primarily a physical thing, and the existence or importance of spiritual realities is given but token acknowledgement. Indians are the popular American minority group and the white majority deeply believes that Indians *already* have the secret mysteries which will produce a wise and happy life. Therefore Indians are plagued with a multitude of well-wishers and spectators hoping to discern, from within the Indian communities in which they visit, some indication of the substance of religious experience. This inundation of pilgrims makes it impossible for Indians to experience the solitude and abandonment which exile requires in order to teach its lessons.

Finally, modern American life is comparable to a large and bountiful Christmas tree. It promises only joy and fun, and never suggests a period of doubt when ultimate realities are experienced and understood. Indians are wandering in this plush fantasy desert in the same way as sensitive non-Indians. It will require considerably more thought and significantly less recreation and entertainment before Indians will be able to discern in their own traditions the substance and energy which lies dormant.

The exile of today is filled with frustration because it is being experienced in the midst of many other intensely competitive factors, all of which require energy and attention and none of which provide any lasting sustenance. It may be that technology has so insulated human society that the religious context of exile is now a thing of the past, incapable of realization in a wholly artificial world. If so, we have lost an important key to unlocking the potential which human social existence suggests. It may be that American Indians contain the last best hope for spiritual renewal in a world dominated by material considerations. The multitude of non-Indians arriving at reservation doors seeking answers would seem to indicate an intuition in many hearts that Indians do give us the last hope for resurrection. Perhaps out of the confusion of modern Indian society will come a statement about the world that we have come to expect when exiles return.

(1985)

26

REFLECTION AND REVELATION
Knowing Land, Places and Ourselves

The increasing interest in land, ecology, the living Earth, and our responsibility toward other forms of life comes none too soon, considering the conditions we find developing on our planet. The end of organic life is now clearly possible, if present trends of exploitation and pollution continue. Therefore it behooves us to find in our history and ourselves some ways to reverse ecological destruction and bring environmental stability to the places in which we live.

When the nearly terminal condition of the planet is discussed, many people say that American Indian religious traditions offer a good understanding of land and life and may provide the larger society with conceptual tools to rescue itself from its own destruction. American Indians have thus become one of the previously neglected peoples to whom others will listen—albeit for the moment—to find the answers they seek. But what exactly is it that non-Indians want from Indians? Here the situation is not clear, and until Indians can get some kind of guidance about what non-Indians seek, we cannot offer much help.

Non-Indian interest seems to focus on the sacredness of land, the perception that Indians understand land much more profoundly than other peoples, and on the possibility of adopting or transferring that kind of relationship to the larger social whole. I believe there is some truth in this perception. However, I also believe that this assertion is being made by people who do not really think deeply about what land and sacredness are, and by people who would be content to receive the simple poetic admonitions and aphorisms that pass as knowledge in the American intellectual cafeteria.

Intellectually, tribal wisdom is not much different from insights a person with some degree of sensitivity and awareness about the world could discover upon serious reflection. But there is a nuance here that bears examination. Tribal wisdom is the distilled experiences of the community, and not the aesthetic conclusions of sensitive individuals or the poetic conclusions of personal preferences. Tribal insights have been subjected to the erosions of time; they have been tested by uncounted generations, and they have been applied in a bewildering variety of settings in which they have proven reliable. That is to say, tribal wisdom is *communal* wisdom; it is part of the tribal definition of what it is to be a human being in a social setting. Therefore, tribal wisdom differs considerably from the slogans and beliefs of the networks of concerned people that pass for communities in the modern world.

Within tribal traditions there is a real apprehension of and appreciation for the sacredness of land, and more specifically, for the sacred nature of places; the two ideas are but different expressions of the underlying relationship of humans with the world around them. It is possible to dissect this knowledge for the purpose of discussion, but the discussion should follow a particular sequence. It should not rely wholly on the goodwill of the listener. We can analyze what constitutes sacredness, but we must also recognize that some of what we say can be understood only by experience. Our task is to live in such a way that the information we receive through analysis becomes—over the passage of time and through grace and good fortune—our experience also.

The sacredness of land is first and foremost an emotional experience. It is that feeling of unity with a place that is complete, whatever specific feelings it may engender in an individual. There are two fundamental categories of emotional responses to sacred places: reflective and revelatory. The vast number of experiences we have with land, and in particular with places, are of a reflective kind. We experience the uniqueness of places and survey the majesty of lands. There we begin to meditate on who we are, what our society is, where we came from, quite possibly where we are going, and what it all means. Lands somehow call forth from us these questions and give us a feeling of being within something larger and more powerful than ourselves. We are able to reflect upon what we know, and in reflection we see a different arrangement, perhaps a different interpretation, of what life can mean. A wise person might be able to discern the intellectual content of these reflective experiences by intense thought, but his or her conclusion would be only a logical proposition and would lack the intensity of the emotion which lands and places evoke. Land has the ability to short-circuit logical processes; it enables us to apprehend underlying unities we did not suspect.

Revelatory experiences are another thing altogether. They tell us things we cannot possibly know in any other way. Moses approaches the burning bush, is told that it is a holy place, learns the name of God, and is given a vocational task to perform on behalf of his community. With this information come directions through which a new future is possible. Encountering a holy place always involves the manifestation of a personal spirit of immense and unmeasured power, a real spirit of place with which our species must have communion thereafter. Holy places exist in all countries and form the sacred configuration of the land. These places speak of the ultimate holiness of creation. They give a meaningful context to the reflective locations.

This distinction between reflective and revelatory places is not intended to downgrade the validity of reflective experiences of lands. It is the ability to reflect that creates the awareness and sensitivity of peoples to the qualitative intensity of revelatory places. But the distinction is necessary because revelatory places are known only through the experience of prolonged occupation of land, and they cannot be set aside because of the aesthetic or emotional appeal of particular places.

The most common experience of Indian tribes today is that of reflective places. One must suspect that common knowledge of lands among Indians always featured a high percentage of reflective places throughout Indian occupation of this continent. Tribal histories, for the most part, are land-centered. That is to say, every feature of a landscape has stories attached to it. If a tribal group is very large or has lived on a particular piece of land for many generations, some natural features will have many stories attached to them. I know some places in the Dakotas about which at least a dozen stories are told. These stories relate both secular events such as tales of hunting and warfare and sacred events such as personal or tribal religious experiences.

Each family within a tribe has its own tradition of stories about tribal ancestral lands. In theory it would be possible to gather from the people of the tribe all the stories that relate to every feature of the landscape. If these stories were then arranged chronologically, the result would be a history of the people somewhat similar to what whites mean by history. But the history would be considered artificial by most Indians because the intensity of the original experience—which was a function of the place and important in explaining the incident or event—would have been abandoned in favor of the chronology.

When non-Indians admire or try to emulate the Indian love of the land, they generally think of the reflective emotions that Indians have about lands and places. Unfortunately, most whites lack the historical perspective of places simply because they have not lived on the land long enough. In addition, few whites preserve stories about the land, and very little is passed down which helps people identify the special aspect of places.

A popular old story makes this point eloquently. A Crow chief, told that the government owned his land, said that they could not own it because the first several feet down consisted of the bones of his ancestors and the dust of the previous generations of Crow people. If the government wanted to claim anything, the chief continued, it would have to begin where the Crow people's contribution ended. This feeling of unity with the land can only come through the prolonged intimacy of living on the land.

Now, there is no question in my mind that a good many non-Indians have some of the same emotional attachment to land that most Indians do. For example, the land has impressed itself upon rural whites in Appalachia, the South, parts of the Great Plains, and other isolated areas, and made indelible changes in the way the people perceive themselves. One could not read *The Grapes of Wrath* or *Raintree County* without encountering such deep feelings. And critical to the recognition of this attachment is the family, the community, as functioning parts of the landscape. It is not too much to argue that without the *group* of people sharing a sense of history on the land, there can be nothing more for the individual than a tourist's aesthetic feeling of beauty, which is but a temporary reflection of the deeper emotion to be gained from the land.

The first dimension of Indian feeling about the land is therefore an admission that we are part and parcel of it physically. However, our physical contribution makes sense only because our memory of land is a memory of ourselves and our deeds and experiences. These memories and experiences are always particular. One thinks of Gettysburg and President Lincoln's magnificent speech recognizing that the sacrifice of so many lives hallowed the ground beyond our power to add or detract. When asked where his lands were, Crazy Horse replied that his lands were where his dead lay buried. He was not thinking of the general contribution of flesh made by generations of Sioux to the Great Plains, but of the immediate past deeds of his generation. These had imprinted on the land new stories and experiences that gave the Sioux a moral title to the lands. Luther Standing Bear once remarked that a people had to be born, reborn, and reborn again on a piece of land before beginning to come to grips with its rhythms. Thus, in addition to the general contribution of long occupation, comes the coincident requirement that people must have freely given of themselves to the land at specific places in order to understand it.

One major difficulty which non-Indians face in trying to make an imprint on the North American continent is the absence of any real or lasting communities. Non-Indian Americans, not the Indians, are the real nomads. White Americans are rarely buried in the places they were born, and most of them migrate freely during their lifetimes, living in as many as a dozen places and having roots in and accepting responsibility for none of these locations. There is, consequently, no continuing community to which they can pass along stories and memories. Without a continuing community one comes from and returns to, land does not become personalized. The only feeling that can be generated is an aesthetic one. Few non-Indians find satisfaction in walking along a riverbank or on a bluff and realizing that their great-great-grandfathers once walked that very spot and had certain experiences. The feeling is one of lack of community and continuity.

When non-Indians live on a specific piece of land for a number of generations, they also begin to come into this reflective kind of relationship. The danger, however, is that non-Indian society as it is presently constituted encourages the abandonment of land and community. Further, it fails to provide a human context within which appreciation for and understanding of land can take place. A good deal of what constitutes present-day love of and appreciation for land is aesthetic, a momentary warm feeling that is invoked by the uniqueness of the place. This warmth does inspire the individual, but it does not sustain communities, and therefore a prolonged relationship with the land is forfeited.

When we discuss revelatory experiences we enter an entirely different realm of discourse. Holy places connected with revelation are exceedingly rare. If we carefully analyze Indian stories about religious experiences, we discover that many things we believed at first to be revelations are in fact reflections of or experiences directed by religious training and supervision. What then are revelatory experiences? Their first characteristic is that the old categories of space and time vanish. New realities take their places and suggest dimensions of life far beyond what we are normally able to discern and understand. Suddenly the everyday world does not exist because it is, in a fundamental sense, a predictable world which we can control. But in revelatory experience we find that we are objects within a place and no longer acting subjects capable of directing events. Some of the medicine men and women describe their feelings as intense dread and foreboding.

This feeling of dread cannot be emphasized too much, because it is this emotion that distinguishes reflection from revelation. A major error made today by people interested in Indian religion, and by Indians who purport to teach traditional ways, is the absence or avoidance of this dimension of the religious experience. The truly great medicine men and women who understood the nature of revelation did everything in their power to avoid the experience. They fully understood that giving up their lives might be required, and that whatever happened, the experience would radically change every measure they used to gauge normal life. Because the experience was so fearful, the great medicine men and women would use the holy places very seldom. They preferred almost any other method to solve their problems, and it was only in times of extreme crisis that they returned to the sources of their own personal vocational revelation for guidance.

Knowledge of the holy places in a tribe's past was a closely guarded secret. Probably only one or two people in any generation actually knew these locations. Knowledge of the holy place was specific to individuals and families, and this produced some strange combinations of information. For example, a family might know a specific holy place but would not know what ceremonies were to be performed there. A medicine man or woman, in a time of tribal crisis, might be told during a ceremony to perform another ceremony at a specific location. He or she might be instructed to obtain directions to the holy place from a secular person. With such specific information spread widely through the tribal community, the tribe could not possibly develop an ecclesiastical hierarchy or priesthood that would dominate the community. Tribes that did have priesthoods were almost always sedentary groups that had long since made their peace with the surrounding lands. In these cases knowledge of the holy places was widespread, but only a few priests knew what ceremonies to use and what occasions necessitated their use.

Indians who know about these things find it extremely difficult to describe what they know. There seems to be an abiding spirit of place that inhibits anyone from trying to explain what has been experienced there. I have visited some of these places, and quite frankly found them terrifying to the casual visitor—and anyone is casual who does not have a specific purpose for coming there. The most prevalent phenomenon is sudden awareness that one is being watched and should not be there. I suggest that a place that has been the site of a revelatory experience always retains something of the intensity of that experience. It is very easy to find oneself disoriented as to direction and time in these places. Consequently Indians have always acted with the utmost respect when they realized they were in such a place.

Another phenomenon attached to holy places is that the more information an individual has about the location, the more likely he or she is to encounter unique emotions and experiences there. Information heightens awareness by providing a context within which experiences can be understood. The intensity of dread is partially defused by a framework to make the experience comprehensible.

We have reports of religious experiences similar to those of American Indians from mystics of other religious and philosophical traditions. Common themes in these traditions are the disappearance or transformation of familiar apprehensions of time and space, and the appearance of a reality undergirding or transcending physical reality. These traditions do not, as a rule, rely on specific locations as does the American Indian tradition. There can be no denying that the European continent has a multitude of sacred places, and it is no accident that, as different religions have come and gone, the same locations appear as sacred and receive adoration, even though the language and religious context continues to change. One can project, then, that sacred places in North America may yet see a series of transformations in which new peoples using new languages rely on them for spiritual sustenance.

Quite frequently the result of a revelatory experience is the creation of a new ceremony, but not all ceremonies arise in this manner. So we cannot say that the creation of a ceremony is one criterion by which we judge whether a place has sufficient holiness to provide new ways of relating to higher spiritual powers. Since the primary content of most revelations within the Indian traditions is the definition of individual vocations that will serve the people in the immediate future, it is exceedingly difficult to classify most locations by a precise description of their primary content. Historically Indians believed that they lived between the physical and spiritual worlds, and consequently there was not much effort to make the kinds of distinctions that non-Indians find useful in understanding topics. Ceremonies were supposed to help keep the people attuned to the rhythms of the spiritual world, and therefore what was important was whether they fulfilled that function.

The most important aspect of sacred places, and in particular the holy places of which we have knowledge, is that they mark the location and circumstances of an event in which the holy became an objective fact of existence. Christians have the same idea in the doctrine of the Incarnation, except that they restrict holiness to the human species. Indians understand that there is holiness in everything, and that human beings are simply a part of the larger whole which must be shaped and informed by the holy. We can see some of the mystery of these things in Black Elk's vision when he meets the Six Grandfathers, and also later when as an old man he stands on Harney Peak and invokes them to help him and take pity on him. The complaint of many traditional Indians against the white man's understanding of things sacred is the tendency to reduce the holy to a subjective category of experience, and to fail to come to grips with the meaning of the objectification of the holy. Indians and New Agers part company at the point where New Agers argue that it is possible to create one's own reality—that belief is an avoidance of sacred experiences, and hence detaches one from real relationship with the land.

If we recognize the two kinds of sacred lands and admit the objectification of the holy as a particular event at a specific place, the question arises as to whether one can have the sacred experience of relationship to land. Is this experience restricted to American Indians, or is it possible for any devout and sincere individual seeking a higher spiritual reality? We can only discuss theoretical possibilities since it would be presumptuous to argue that fundamental experiences are limited to American Indians. But there are certain preconditions that make it unlikely that non-Indians would have these kinds of experiences, and these conditions also make it probable that it will be increasingly difficult for most American Indians to enter into or maintain such relationships with places.

Civilized life precludes most of the fundamental experiences that our species once had in relating to lands and the natural order. Today we rely entirely too much upon the artificial universe that we have created, the world of machines and electricity. In most respects we have been trained to merge our emotions and beliefs so that they mesh with the machines and institutions of the civilized world. Thus many things that were a matter of belief for the old people have become objects of scorn and ridicule for modern people. We have great difficulty in understanding simple things because we have been trained to deal with extremely complicated things, and we respond that way almost instantaneously. The old traditional Indians were in tune with the rhythms of life. They were accustomed to bringing in and relating to a whole picture of the land, the plants, and the animals around them. They responded to things as a part of a larger whole which was a subjective reality to them. We could say the traditional Indian stood in the center of a circle and brought everything together in that circle. Today we stand at the end of a line and work our way along that line, discarding or avoiding everything on either side of us.

In our electronic/electric, mechanical world, we rely on instruments of our own construction to enable us to relate to the rest of the world. The world becomes an object of our actions in an entirely new way, for we are able to overcome certain aspects of the natural world such as time and space that had always stood as barriers to us. But our mechanical instruments cannot help us relate to the rest of life except by reducing it to an object also. Consequently any apprehension of the sacredness of land must be filtered through our mechanical devices, and consequently we attribute to landscape only the aesthetic and not the sacred perspective.

Land, for traditional peoples, includes the other forms of life that share places with us. Thus some places were perceived by Indians as sacred because they were inhabited by certain kinds of birds and animals. The Black Hills, for example, were regarded as a sanctuary for the animals, and human beings were not supposed to dominate the Hills or make their presence an inhibiting factor in the animals' use of the area. We might even say that the sacredness of lands extends to and is apprehended by other forms of life. Without their presence the land would lack an important dimension.

Not only is the presence of other forms of life necessary for the land, it is sometimes the determining factor in identifying sacred locations. There are many stories among the tribes regarding the role of guardianship played by birds and animals in protecting sacred places. Within the last several years we have experienced events in which Indians going to perform vision quests were prevented from entering certain locations by birds, animals, and reptiles who seemingly had intuited that the humans did not have the proper attitude. Such a situation may seem impossible or simply superstition, but there is a high level of predictability in these things. Within the traditional context, certain individuals being blocked was predicted prior to their efforts to enter a sacred location.

We thus move from simple appreciation of land to an apprehension of its sacredness and to the discovery that our analysis must include proper relationship with animals. But if these other forms of life can inhibit or even prohibit human beings from using lands, what is our status within the natural world? Unlike the religions of the Near East which see humanity as the supreme production of creation, traditional religions see our species as existing about halfway up the scale of life, when such a scale is based on relative strength, wisdom, and talents. Each bird, animal, or reptile is thought to possess major potentials which make it what it is. Thus the eagle can fly highest, the hawk see farthest, the owl see deepest, the meadowlark hear keenest, and so forth. Human beings have some talents, but not developed beyond those of any one of the other forms of life. The special human ability is to communicate with other forms of life, learn from them all, and act as a focal point for things they wish to express. In any sacred location, therefore, humans become the instrument by which all of creation is able to interact and express its totality of satisfaction.

The sacred place and the myriad forms of life which inhabit the land require specific forms of communication and interaction. These forms are the particular ceremonies which are performed at the sacred places. It is believed that birds and animals give up their lives and bodies so that human beings can perform the proper ceremonies by which every crea-

ture is blessed. The ceremony is a form of exchange of gifts and responsibilities. As gifts are given and responsibilities accepted, the world as we
know it is able to move forward to completion of its possibilities. When
we understand this demand for taking mature responsibility for the land
and its places, we can understand the ceremonies which require human
mutilations. Unless humans are prepared to offer their own bodies also,
the circle cannot be completed.

The necessity of some form of sacrifice in the ceremony is a major
stumbling block for non-Indians. Christianity teaches that Jesus made
the one supreme sacrifice, and that following the Crucifixion no other
sacrifices are necessary. But the rest of creation is involved in the
Crucifixion only by logical extension and does not participate in the
same way that Indian ceremonies involve it. Many non-Indians, when
told that the relationship with land involves ceremonies and sacrifices,
seem to feel self-conscious. They experience a sense of inadequacy
because they have been trained by Western religions to feel that sacrifice
is necessary because of their sinful nature. Traditional Indians do not see
that sacrifice necessarily involves a sinful nature; rather it is the only
way that humans can match the contribution of other forms of life.
Without a commitment at this level of being, the relationship with the
land remains only aesthetic, because one has remained detached from
participation in the ceremonial event.

Although we rarely experience it, there must be times when non-
human forms of life perform ceremonies without the presence of human
beings. Traditional people granted this possibility, and as a result set
aside certain specific locations where they would refuse to go in order to
let other forms of life conduct their own ceremonial life. This possibility
is the ultimate boundary of human apprehension of the natural world. In
recent years we have seen good faith efforts by Congress and state legislatures to set aside areas of land as "wild rivers" or "wilderness areas."
These lands are to be protected from commercial exploitation and are to
be used by human beings only under rigid rules of behavior. But this
effort does not go far enough. It is a mere balancing of possible human
uses of land; it does not credit the land and non-human forms of life with
an existence in and of themselves.

Tribes accorded each other respect when it came to using the land.
Several tribes might share an area with different motives in mind, one
tribe using the place for hunting and winter camp purposes, another
using it primarily for religious purposes. Thus sacred lands frequently
intersected, the sacred mountains and lakes of one tribe being the
secular lands of another. It was commonly admitted that each tribal people had its own destiny to complete. Consequently, lands that had a

powerful spirit frequently carried with them a form of sanctuary, so that people could come and go without having to deal with secular considerations. The Sioux and Cheyenne, for example, shared Bear Butte in western South Dakota. Each tribe had a different religious story that made the butte significant, and each tribe had tribal-specific ceremonies to perform with respect to that location. The Pipestone Quarry in southwestern Minnesota was shared by a great number of tribes, since it provided the stone for the sacred pipes.

Over a long period of time tribes developed a general knowledge which linked together the most prominent sacred places. Some of these linkages evolved into ceremonial calendar years, instructing people when and where to hold ceremonies. Other combinations described hunting and fishing cycles and migrations. The Great Serpent Mound in Ohio is said to represent a Hopi migration, and some of the Hopi knowledge of the land is said to be comparable to ley line and geomancy knowledge which the early inhabitants of the British Isles and the Chinese possessed. In general, Indians would not radically change the contours or features of the land, and they tried to blend in changes to mark locations with existing features.

It is apparent that the Indian relationship with the land is one brought about by prolonged occupation of certain places. Non-Indians can work toward this condition, but it cannot be brought about by energetic action or sincerity alone. Nor can mere continued occupation create an attitude of respect, since the basic premise—that the universe and each thing in it is alive and has personality—is an attitude of experience and not an intellectual presupposition or logical conclusion. Yet we see in the present best efforts of groups of non-Indians an honest desire to become truly indigenous in the sense of living properly with the land. Thus we cannot help but applaud the interest non-Indians are now demonstrating in the areas of conservation and ecological restoration. The future looks far more hopeful than previously.

(1991)

27

IS RELIGION POSSIBLE?

An Evaluation of Present Efforts to Revive Traditional Tribal Religions

Many Indians are irritated, and justly so, with the wholesale appropriation of American Indian rituals, symbols, and beliefs by the non-Indian public. Several national magazines and newspapers and a myriad of pamphlets, posters, and bumper stickers proclaim the wonders of studying with the likes of Wallace Black Elk, Richard Erdoes, Sun Bear, Lynn Andrews, Edward McGaa, and a host of lesser luminaries in the New Age/Indian medicine man circuit. Even the staid Christian churches are busy trying to revamp their doctrines and programs to fit with the new interest in Indian religious ideas. Ecologists of all stripes including the self-appointed "Deep Ecologists" claim a kinship with traditional Indian beliefs so that one would wonder whether the tribes did not in fact win the Indian wars and expel the hated invaders from their homelands.

A few knotty problems do exist. The Pope at some point must choose between the Indian and Chicano versions of California history and classify Junipero Serra as a psychopath or a saint. Other Christian denominations must explain why, after five hundred years of persecution and neglect, they are now identifying Indian saints and beloved of the faith— people they would never have allowed in their ecclesiastical deliberations when they were alive. And Indians must determine whether adding a pipe and sweat lodge to organizational banquets and annual meetings necessarily blesses the programs and policies of the participating groups.

In short, Indian traditional religious affairs are a complete disaster area.

We must, if possible, dig beneath the rhetoric and poetry of present expressions of religiosity practiced by Indians and their admirers and examine whether or not there is any substance in the popularity of Indian traditions and whether or not something useful and constructive can be derived from present activities. This subject can be examined from almost any perspective but it is useful to sketch out the claims that are being made in the name of Indian religions and ask what impact these claims have on people's lives. The subject has a certain urgency because Congress will consider comprehensive legislation designed to protect traditional Indian religions in this session and it would be good to begin clarifying exactly what we are asking Congress to protect.

A persistent claim made by the Indians who allege to be practicing traditional ceremonies, on behalf of non-Indians and urban Indian clients, is that they have been instructed by their elders in these rituals and have been told by the same elders that they must go forth and proclaim the truth—often before the apocalyptic end of the present world and the initiation of the next world. Some of these claims, made in letters to me, smack more of the *Acts of the Apostles* than any instructions I have ever heard from tribal elders. If we accept these claims as true, we are basically saying that traditional Indian religions have become missionary-minded and now seek converts in a larger intercultural context. This claim is contrary to every known tenet of any tribal tradition but it may be a new revelation given at the end of this world.

Unlike Western religions which sought to convert a selected number of true believers and convince them that a particular interpretation of planetary history was correct, tribal religions were believed to be special communications between spirits and a specific group of people. The admonition given with the teachings and rituals instructed this particular group of people to faithfully perform ceremonies and act responsibly within the land and historical time period in which they existed as a people. Prophecies which gave the people signs of the impending end of each world, in those cases in which worlds were created and destroyed, often accompanied the ceremonies. No demand existed, however, for the people to go into the world and inform or instruct other people in the rituals and beliefs of the tribe. The people were supposed to follow their own teachings and assume that other people would follow their teachings. These instructions were rigorously followed and consequently there was never an instance of a tribe making war on another tribe because of religious differences. Thus the situation of today is a radical departure from everything we have known about traditional religion.

Assuming, however, that some new revelation has been received by these popular preachers, we should examine the nature of the teachings and practices that are now widespread in American society. The extent of the borrowing seems to consist of a body of teachings which are universal propositions having little impact on the way most people behave and appropriation of the sweat lodge, sun dance, and use of the pipe. For these losses we can thank the ever-present Sioux Indians and their intense desire to act as hosts for the wide variety of people who beat their way to the Pine Ridge and Rosebud reservations. We do not, as a rule, see non-Indians and New Age people performing the ceremonies of any tribe except the Northern Plains Sioux and so we can conclude that for the most part other tribes have lived up to their end of the sacred covenant, *or* that the Sioux have received some special revelation that demands they universalize their traditions—perhaps even to save the religious practices of other tribes.

The message which seems to underlie the practice of New Age and popular Indian religion is that everything is related. A subsidiary doctrine is that everything is circular and within this sacred circularity are the four directions which have a certain degree of power when invoked by creating a "medicine wheel"—made popular by Hyemeyohsts Storm's *Seven Arrows*. It does not seem that this idea, relationships with corresponding use of geometrical directions and figures allocating possible sources of sacred energy, is particularly revolutionary or something that needed to be contained within the specific tribal tradition. Indeed, Albert Einstein advocated the same proposition in articulating his theory of relativity and while he did not specifically apply it to plants, animals and people, he did suggest that all measurements and perhaps even all experiences were possible within a specific framework of the physical world that admitted that the universe did not contain isolated entities. So if we feel that traditional religions have been harmed in some specific way by informing people outside the tribe, then traditional religions must not have contained very many truths at all.

Use and abuse of the sweat lodge, sun dance, and pipe are another matter altogether. The sweat lodge is not exclusively Plains tradition and in fact some version of the sweat lodge was prevalent in Scandanavian countries long before they had Christianity. It has become an intertribal, inclusive ritual in which in many places the predominant number of people taking part are non-Indians. Before we get overly exercised about the universality of the sweat lodge we should remember that many tribes use it as purification prior to engaging in other ceremonies which have a deeper significance. If we admit that the minimum benefit and participation of people today in the sweat lodge is simply purification it does not appear that this violation of traditional religion is detrimental.

The exploitation of the sun dance is considerably more serious and needs much critical examination. Sun dances are being held in places far from the probable points of origin of this ceremony by people who stand well outside the Plains and Mountain tribal traditions. But even within the heart of the Plains we find abuses and popularizations that would not have been tolerated a generation ago. Some sun dances being held on Sioux reservations are more akin to county fairs than religious ceremonies. Some people mix Christianity and sun dances and others allow photographs and bevies of non-Indian writers and onlookers which detract from the religious content of the activities. It may be, as ancient prophecies have told us, that we are nearing the time when the ceremonies of this world become useless and we enter a period between worlds when there are no viable ceremonies remaining. Perhaps a clear statement by traditional people as to the seriousness of the ceremony and a disavowal of authorization for people outside the respective tribal traditions to perform this dance is in order.

Use of the pipe is also serious and complicated. Many non-Indians possess pipes for purely secular reasons and pipe making is an income-producing arts and crafts form that is not likely to be brought under control at this point in time. A strange melding of tradition and modern excitment has created a very confused situation with respect to the pipe. In the old days almost everyone had their own pipe and it was smoked as much for social enjoyment and hospitality as for religious purposes. Today we hear that some people are "Pipe Carriers" as if possessing a pipe initiated an individual into some secret brotherhood which stood apart from everything else. Many of the non-Indians using the pipe allege to be commissioned "Pipe Carriers" and then perform a bewildering variety of motions with the pipe, passing them off as special ceremonies which they claim to have been authorized to perform. They therefore get the benefit of having some obscure office within a traditional religion while escaping the necessity of actually having to live a fully committed religious life.

At the level I have seen many Indians and non-Indians use the pipe, I cannot find much real disrespect and exploitation. They light it, say a few prayers, and pass it around the group asking each person to say a prayer or mumble "All my relatives." In some cases this simple set of actions invokes behavior of great respect by the non-Indians, more respect sometimes than they allocate to their own traditions and practices. In a society totally ravaged by greed and individualism one would hope that the pipe would bring a better sense of community and sharing and if any progress is made along these lines we should be grateful for what the pipe is able to accomplish.

When we examine each aspect of non-Indian exploitation of traditional religion we do not find very many bad things happening so why does this situation upset us so much? Our problem really has to do with the manner in which non-Indians receive traditional practices and beliefs and what they do with them. Non-Indians come from traditions that make much of public display of individual virtues. Converts within these traditions have a frightening tendency to become more zealous than the people from whom they have received the message. Thus the Apostle Paul was considerably more aggressive than were the original twelve disciples and in every generation of non-Indians we find religious zealots and bigots who seem intent on forcing their views on everyone else.

Much of the difficulty that Indians have today with the appropriation of Indian rituals and teachings is the superior attitude which non-Indians project once they have made some acquaintance with things Indian. In most cases they have a sneering, self-righteous posture which communicates the message, to Indians and non-Indians alike, that they know all about Indian religion. It is this message, often communicated with arrogant body language, that infuriates many Indians because, seeing the effect of the transmission of ideas and ritual objects, Indians see how their tradition has been perverted. The non-Indian appropriator conveys the message that Indians are indeed a conquered people and that there is nothing that Indians possess, *absolutely nothing*—pipes, dances, land, water, feathers, drums, and even prayers—that non-Indians cannot take whenever and wherever they wish.

Non-Indians, accused of appropriating Indian religious ideas and sacred objects, often respond that religion is for sharing and some of the New Age Indian medicine men excuse their abuses by insisting that they are simply sharing these ideas and objects. Here we have a basic watershed in interpretation that needs to be seen in its real colors. Western religions insist that they have "Good News"—the gospel—that it is for everyone, and that it must be shared. The problem is that the ideas are shared but nothing else. Thus dispossession of Indians from their lands is excused by the argument that non-Indians brought Christianity and therefore the exchange was an even bargain. Indians are therefore put in a position where we must share with others—everything—but they need not share with us.

In the old traditional ways of most tribes, knowledge of the ceremonies, dreams, and the messages received in vision quests were a private affair. People did not need to be converted to anything because the tribal community already had the basic outlines of what universal reality was and meant. Religious knowledge was a strictly private affair. An individual had knowledge because higher powers intended that he or she have this knowledge; it was not for distribution to the masses simply because it was a nice message because this knowledge imposed duties and responsibilities on the individual who was so chosen. Many people avoided going on vision quests or doing ceremonies because they knew all too well that a heavy responsibility to work for their people would be laid upon them in these kinds of activities. Making communications from higher powers known could not relieve the individual or his or her duty to act upon the religious burden on behalf of the tribal community.

When we introduce the non-Indian into this equation it has entirely different results. The practical effect of preaching the Gospel among non-Indians has been to relieve the individual of the duty to live the tenets of his or her belief and simply to authorize that person to pass the message along to others. The difference can be summarized easily: Real traditional Indians practice, they don't preach, all others preach and don't practice. Thus when we see some of our people holding ceremonies for non-Indians instead of remaining with the Indian community and performing ceremonies for their people we can simply conclude that they have become non-Indians as far as their basic loyalties are concerned. So be it.

We should applaud the *Lakota Times* for its series of articles exposing some of the more bizarre practitioners of quasi-religious arts since there is a good deal of nonsense involved in what they do. But we should also remember P.T. Barnum's dictum that one cannot go broke underestimating the taste of the American public. We have to remember that we are dealing with a public that overwhelmingly elected Reagan and Bush even after their basic plan for governing the country was described—by themselves—as voodoo economics. So the more outrageous the message the more credible it is for most Americans. Can anyone take Lynn Andrews' books seriously? Of course. It is standard operating procedure for Indian medicine women to give ancient religious secrets to art collectors from Rodeo Drive in Hollywood—that was written into the structure of the universe from the very beginning.

In the past year I have traveled to about ten Indian reservations in different parts of this country and have taken part in a number of ceremonies on those reservations and at conferences where we gathered together a good number of traditional people for the purpose of soliciting their views on the religious freedom legislation. I have been tremendously impressed with the revival of very old ceremonies in some of these places and the seriousness with which traditional people are dealing with the problem of appropriation of ceremonies. For the most part they have simply withdrawn from the ceremonies that have been appropriated by non-Indians and are doing ceremonies of considerably more importance and significance. I will not mention any specific ceremony or group of traditional people for to do so would simply make them a target of curious non-Indians who are looking to appropriate even more of the traditional ways.

In trying to make sense of the present situation it has occurred to me that the ancient prophecies of profound and universal planetary destruction may well be true—and not far from us. If widespread physical destruction were a certain possibility the survivors would need to have something in common so they could bring together whomever still lived here and formulate a society. Thus it might not be a bad thing that ancient truths are understood by a large number of people who after having survived massive earthquakes and tidal waves might be inclined to believe that Mother Earth is indeed more powerful than human science and technology. The survivors might have a little humility and respect for the natural world.

Everything we see today seems to be an effort to put new wine back into old bottles and that is simply not possible. When the old circles or hoops of life were broken, thousands of years ago for most non-Indians and a century ago for most Indians, the possibility of recapturing that original sense of awe and respect was lost and could not be recovered. We have simply been playing out the logical possibilities of what the fragments of those original hoops made available to people. The remaining ceremonies and traditional practitioners may well serve as focal points around which people can someday rally and renew themselves. We can now pull together what is left and hope that it demonstrates the viability of what was given us long ago and that may be sufficient for our lifetimes.

We do face a situation of considerable absurdity in the religious freedom situation and people should pay careful attention to that issue. In America the tenets of constitutional law allow each person the right to choose their own religion and, practically interpreted, this right means that everyone has the right to conceive the kind of deity they wish to worship in order to enhance their lives. Enhancement in American terms means material wealth and sensual pleasures. Indian religions have been placed within this context by the Supreme Court and two decisions, *Lyng* and *Smith,* have denied traditional people the right to practice their religious ceremonies. These ceremonies were not held for the purpose of obtaining a new car, job or romance but for the enhancement of the earth and for all living creatures. Yet they were classified as if they sought only individual or community material gain.

The real message of these Supreme Court decisions is that the state is supreme and that no one, Indians or anyone else, need bother to pray for the earth and its living things. Presumably these kinds of prayers would interfere with the prayers of others who want to have BMWs and assorted goodies. Unless traditional people are given the freedom to pray and conduct ceremonies on behalf of the earth and its children, we will enter a situation in which no one is watching the store. It does not matter whether or not people believe in the prayers offered by traditional people. What does matter is the belief, now articulated by the state, that we do not have to pay attention to the rest of creation or have a beneficial relationship with it.

We cannot predict how events will fall in the years ahead. It does seem likely that conditions have now developed that will lead to major catastrophic changes. We need to gather around our traditional people even more than ever before. We need to take their messages and insights very seriously and make fundamental changes in the manner in which we live. Where ceremonies are being revived or are coming out into the open once again, we must make certain that they are shown due respect and do not become another workshop topic in the California New Age circuit. We must be confident that in showing respect for our traditions we are acting responsibly. In a real sense we cannot "revive" a religion for that is going backwards. What we can do is respect religious traditions and allow them to take us forward into the future. That is all the old ways ever promised they would do.

(1992)

28

INTRODUCTION
TO *VISION QUEST*

A long time ago, according to Charles Eastman, giant animals and monsters roamed the earth and gave human beings, the two-leggeds, an extremely hard time. The people offered prayers to the higher spirits asking for relief from their burdens and eventually they were rewarded. A giant tent was erected in the sky, near present-day Devil's Lake, and the giant animals were brought into the tent one by one and reduced in size, making them the equals of humans but no longer their oppressors. Thus was the transition from the giant buffalo to the present smaller bison remembered by the Sioux people. The new bison was useful to the two-leggeds and had few of the malevolent traits which had made his predecessor so fearful.

We often like to think of ourselves as being in transition between the crude and savage character of our ancestors and the more refined behavior which we fancy we see in ourselves and our generation. But not every people view the passage of time and the need for change in such positive terms. As Doris Leader Charge says in this book, many people would gladly go back to the old days when everyone helped one another and the great herds of buffalo grazed as far as the eye could see. One of the great strengths of the Sioux people is their steadfast propensity to judge present actions in terms of the larger historical experiences in which they have been involved. Thus at any particular time the spectrum of opinion existing among the people, their perspective and outlook, is multidimensional and expansive even while remaining traditional.

Adherence to tradition means that the fundamental sets of the historic relationships—with the land, with the animals and birds, and with the larger cosmos—become the defining boundaries within which the people find their being. Lame Deer, commenting on the love of the land, suggested that as the Sioux get older their faces begin to reflect the landscape on which they live, the wrinkles of their faces resembling the rolling plains and Badlands of the Dakotas. He might equally well have described the people as aging buffalo or as reflecting the granite of the Black Hills which contain some of the oldest rocks on earth. It is important to note that many of the traditional Sioux regard these ancient relationships as being so powerful as to be capable of dominating and largely determining the course of individual human lives and fortunes.

National and state archives contain thousands of photographs of the Sioux of the last century, and in the traditional coffee-table books on Indians we often see the old chiefs and anonymous women of the Sioux nation staring out at us. Many of these faces have a wonderful calmness in them, few wrinkles unless the people are very old, and a distant look which seems to transcend the troubles of the time. Strangely, these people always seem to be above the turmoil in which they were involved. The occasion may be solemn but it does not generate grimaces of pain nor project frantic countenances or panic. We get the feeling that they live between worlds and can see beyond the moment into worlds of which we have not dared to dream.

The people and faces appearing in this volume often show us the trauma and pain of Indian experience in this century. The calm and confidence engendered by the old ways only occasionally shine through, and on many faces we can see the immense burden of lives that have struggled to integrate two conflicting ways of living. These people have been forced to find their personal identity and value in faithfulness to the past rather than achievements in a society that could not understand their ways. For the Sioux of this century nobility has consisted of surviving and giving to the small group around them a sense of the sweep of historical reality.

The old prophecies serve as boundary lines within which many Sioux try to find themselves. Black Elk's vision of the generations who must walk uphill in darkness is too intensely painful for many people, yet it always sparks the feeling that as our ancestors moved forward into the unknown future, so must we take fearful steps in order that our nation move through the difficult times and emerge into a better world. But, as we all realize, there are many people lost and falling by the wayside, unable to bear the burdens which their generation must carry—and we mourn each passing.

Ahead on the path we are walking we can see a series of paths of other peoples beginning to converge. A century ago the voice of the Indian was a lonely one. In ceding lands to the avaricious white farmers and ranchers, chief after chief expressed concern for the earth and the peoples living on it. What would happen to the buffalo? The eagle? The meadowlark? How would the rivers and the mountains be treated? These questions were too simple and too complex for the white man to answer. The wilderness, the very planet, was to be subdued and made a slave to human desires. Today these questions are still being asked but joining the voice of the Indians are many other people who understand the perils of treating the earth as a disposable object. While we are *on* the earth, we must understand that we are *of* the earth also.

Recognizing the difference between the Sioux of the past and the people of the present, we must ask what of the future? Even as people today work to provide for the coming generations, the boundaries between the Sioux and other people continue to become blurred. A significant percentage of tribal enrollments today are mixed-bloods, and as intermarriage outside the tribe increases, the computers can now project the day when the Indian genetic heritage will have vanished leaving in its place a large population in which it is possible to trace Indian ancestry but only as a remote factor in the creation of families and individuals. This situation is very serious but not without precedence.

Prior to European contact, in the distant past, there were considerably fewer Indian nations. Over the course of time smaller groups splintered off and distinct dialects and then languages came into being. During this process, as Indian nations sought to establish themselves in various regions of the continent, people intermarried with other groups quite frequently. The tribal traditions, not the genetics, held people together. In the last century some of the famous chiefs of tribes were in fact genetically descended from other groups—Spokane Garry, Washakie, Red Eagle and others. The future of the Sioux, then, is a function of maintaining the traditions and adhering to a discipline which calls forth the responsive and responsible individuals to lead the community.

The transitional nature of human communal life is rarely seen as determinative of the value of individual lives. Too often we mourn the passing of the elder generation, believing that they are the authorities in defining how we should live our lives, and not understanding that as we respond to them, we both define reality for the next generation and act as a filter to bring forward the best of the tradition while leaving behind the shortcomings in making it a reality. As we read the comments of the people included in this book, we must remember that their perception of their lives is that of culture-carriers, a responsibility that transcends all other considerations.

Social and economic complexities in modern society preclude the possibility of Indian nations achieving a real sense of nationhood again.

Absent a severe and catastrophic disruption of civilization, the very idea of nationality may be fading away as more of us accept the role of consumer in the industrial society. Counterpoised against this current is the persistent desire of Indians to bolster and maintain a semblance of boundary lines between themselves and the larger mainstream of integrated individuals. It may be that the children and grandchildren of the people appearing in this book will adopt most of the values and behavior patterns of the larger society. But as long as the people live on the land and can point to the places where Sioux history was experienced, there will always be a Sioux people.

(1994)

AFTERWORD

CONTEMPORARY CONFUSION AND THE PROSPECTIVE RELIGIOUS LIFE

American society, most especially American Indian communities, has changed radically during my lifetime. Growing up in a small mixed-blood community of seven hundred on the eastern edge of the Pine Ridge Reservation in South Dakota, I uncritically accepted the idea that the old Dakota religion and Christianity were both "true" and in some mysterious way compatible with each other. There were, to be sure, Christian fundamentalists with their intolerance and the old traditional Indians who kept their practices hidden, but the vast majority of the people in the vicinity more or less assumed that a satisfactory blend had been achieved that guaranteed our happiness.

Although my father was an Episcopal priest with a large number of chapels in a loosely organized Episcopal missionary district known (to Episcopalians) as "Corn Creek," he was far from an orthodox follower of the white man's religion. I always had the feeling that within the large context of "religion" which in a border town meant the Christian milieu, there was a special area in his spiritual life in which the old Dakota beliefs and practices reigned supreme. He knew thirty-three songs; some of them social, some ancient, and several spiritual songs used in a variety of ceremonial contexts. Driving to his chapels to hold Christian services he would open the window of the car and beat the side of the door with his hand for the drum beat and sing song after song.

His grandfather, a Yanktonais medicine man called Saswe, had received a powerful vision that more or less determined the path our family had taken for several generations. His son, my grandfather, had become one of the first converts to Christianity in the 1860s and eventually became an Episcopal priest on the Standing Rock Reservation at Wakpala, a few miles south of the community of Kenel where his uncles and relatives made their home. Philip became prominent in the missionary movement of the 1890–1930 period and when he died his statue was placed in the "Company of Saints" collection of statues in the Washington National Cathedral. So while the family had made an institutional change in religions, the vision of Saswe that compelled my father and grandfather to accept a Christian vocation was the ground of their understanding and belief.

Christianity, for my father, offered comfort in a world that was grim and foreboding for the Sioux people and the settlers in that barren prairie setting. He loved the Christian hymns and saw them as a means of articulating the larger spiritual world to his congregations. He also prayed consistently to the Christian god when seeking guidance for his life. But when it came to serious illness or physical danger, he reverted immediately to the Dakota understanding of the world, assuring me one time in a frightful thunderstorm that the Thunders were Saswe's friends and therefore obligated to treat our family with kindness. He consulted Black Elk on several occasions, knew the various medicine men in several of the reservations, and had many wondrous things to say about an old Yankton medicine man named Red Leaf whose exploits were well known even after nearly a century and a half has passed.

When I went to college I was exposed to a much larger canvas of human experience upon which various societies had left their religious mark. My first reaction was the belief that most of the religious traditions were simply wrong, that a few of them had come close to describing religious reality, but that it would take some intensive study to determine which religious traditions would best assist human beings in succeeding in the world. It was my good fortune to have as a religion and philosophy professor a Christian mystic who was trying to prove the deepest mysteries of the faith. He also had some intense personal problems which emerged again and again in his beliefs, indicating to me that religion and the specific individual path of life were always intertwined.

Over several years and many profound conversations he was able to demonstrate to me that each religious tradition had developed a unique way to confront some problems and that they had something in common if only the search for truth and the elimination of many false paths. But his solution, after many years, became untenable for me. I saw instead religion as simply a means of organizing a society, articulating some reasonably apparent emotional truths, but ultimately becoming a staid part of social establishments that primarily sought to control human behavior and not fulfill human individual potential. It seemed as if those religions that placed strong emphasis on certain concepts failed precisely in the areas in which they claimed expertise. Thus religions of "love" could point to few examples of their efficacy; religions of "salvation" actually saved very few. The more I learned about world religions, the more respect I had for the old Dakota ways.

My philosophy professor had laid out an intellectual quest in which science would provide insights into the physical world and we would follow along, good theologians all, and wait for that point where science and religion would return to their ancient partnership. Thus he led me into Plato, Whitehead, Augustine, and the German mystics, Tillich, Buber, Berdyaev, Otto, and eventually Albert Schweitzer. Wanting to learn more theology before I found a way to make a living, I used the remainder of the G.I. Bill to attend a Lutheran Seminary in Rock Island, Illinois. I became much enthralled with Rudolph Bultmann and his program of "de-mythologizing" theology but, I am afraid, from an entirely different perspective than Bultmann would have wanted. Instead of throwing out cultural/social/political beliefs of the first century and concentrating on the "spiritual" message of the Bible I became convinced that so-called mythology and miraculous events recorded in the scriptures of many religions might indeed be accurate renderings of spiritual experiences, incomprehensible to us today because of our reliance on science and materialism.

Relying on science and philosophy as guides to an uncharted and highly suspect world, I charged into Heisenberg, Bridgman, Jeans, Eddington, Margeaneau and even Teilhard de Chardin. In all of this searching, however, I could not shake the reality of the spiritual experiences of Saswe, my grandfather Philip, and my father, the vivid stories of spiritual encounters that were family heritage and of unquestioned veracity. Finally, after trying my best to accept science as the authority I discovered that much of Western science is simply the folklore of materialistic industrialism and has no basis in evidence. The reverse methodology developed from Bultmann was thus applied to science producing a nearly total collapse of faith in large bodies of knowledge which others took uncritically as descriptions of reality.

My criteria for judging both religion and science then became simplified—could they produce both answers and behavior that could match their creeds? I don't believe they can; I don't think they even come close. My agenda for more than two decades, then, has been to seek a unified understanding of the world we experience whether science or religion will admit anomalies or inconsistencies or not. I thus had emotional and institutional freedom but also assumed the burden of becoming responsible for finding my own way. Thus far it has been a very lonely but immensely fruitful path of intellectual and emotional inquiry.

With my background as a "church-family" I always had some contact with people in the institutional church and I recognized that breaking through both the historical background of religion among Indian people and changing the institutional patterns of their lives was a task that required utmost patience and understanding. I half-heartedly renounced Christianity causing some surprise among old acquaintances from my youth but did not become a "born-again" traditional Indian practitioner because much of the ceremonial practice was simply foreign to who I was. I have steadfastly defended the rights of traditional people to achieve a real freedom of religion and talk with some degree of regularity with religious leaders of various Indian communities. Sometimes I have been asked to attend ceremonies to which I ordinarily would not be admitted and have tried to treat these occasions with the utmost solemnity and sanctity. But I am not bothered when people say that I have no standing among some traditional groups because, indeed, I do not.

In 1968, while attending law school, I suddenly became the compromise candidate for a seat on the Executive Council of the Episcopal Church. The liberals believed they couldn't elect a black to fill an empty seat and the conservatives were content to take a harmless Indian as the token minority. Upon accepting the seat I immediately drew up a document, "More Real Involvement," and mailed nearly 100 letters to native clergy and influential Indian laypeople asking them to write the Presiding Bishop to support a massive review of church missionary programs and to appoint a national committee of Indians to develop policies for the church. In February 1969 the request was funded by the Executive Council and that spring and summer regional meetings were held to gather data on the various missions and elect representatives for the national committee.

The efficiency of the meetings and the speed with which we put together the committee and report frightened some church bureaucrats and as the process was concluding, the Presiding Bishop quickly intervened and appointed an Indian to head the church programs, taking the power of recommendation away from us and in effect trying to make the national committee a rubber-stamp group. After the report was ready for circulation, I resigned from the Executive Council. *Custer Died for Your Sins,* my first book, had a chapter highly critical of Christian missionary work and I knew it would be out in October so that I would become a controversial figure and I didn't want that to injure the committee as it began its work. But I felt I had accomplished everything that was possible on the council.

Once the Episcopal church developed a national Indian "desk," other denominations such as the Presbyterians, Lutherans, and Methodists quickly followed. For the first time in American history Indian Christians were making policies about Indian Christians. My next step was to suggest to some of the newly appointed Indians of other denominations that we propose to establish an American Indian Christian church by merging all missionary efforts of every church into a new church that would be eligible for membership in the National Council of Churches and would make up its own doctrines of ministry, church polity, and organizational structure. Obviously this next step was moving too fast and I quickly became persona non grata with Indian Christians who were content to have a voice in their own denominations. In view of recent church movements to share ministries and sacraments, this possibility remains alive.

In the mid-seventies I met a remarkable black theologian, James Cone, at a meeting of black theologians to which I had kindly been invited. Black Theology had just achieved some kind of public exposure and I was very interested in what they were doing. James and I became immediate friends although I can't think of a thing that we have in common in theological terms. About this time the idea that other cultures, and their religious traditions, were all "Old Testaments" to the Christian New Testament became popular in the groups I was meeting. And liberation theology from South and Central America became popular. All of these strains of thought were exhilarating but caused a tremor in my mind. I believed then, and I believe now, that they were and are putting new wine into a very old skin.

God Is Red came out in 1973 and had put me on a more secular path so that if I had wanted to become a liberation theologian it would have meant shifting most of the epistemology I had developed during the past decade. Working with the Taos people on their Blue Lake legislation had convinced me that religious writing about the Indian traditions had to emphasize land and sacred places. So while I had great sympathy for James and his group, I could do little more than try to be supportive. James did introduce me to a new circle of theological people, however, and as a result I was invited to a conference where I gave a paper, included here as "Completing the Theological Circle: Civil Religion in America," in which I was able to raise the question of church and state in its informal aspect and it prepared me to meet Robert Bellah and learn from him.

Rev. Cecil Corbett, then director of Cook Christian Training School in Tempe, Arizona, and the most influencial Indian in the Presbyterian Church, asked me about this essay and the implications of the line of thought I was developing. After several good conversations we decided to hold conferences on "Law and Theology" to see if people were ready to think through the implications of the idea that law and theology might be identical frameworks separated by their orientation to their audience. I had first come across this notion when I met James Laue of the Community Relations Service in the Department of Justice in the mid 1960s. An expert in intervention, Jim talked to protestors and Klansmen alike in terms of reconciliation when attempting to solve civil rights problems in the South. Cecil and I wondered why much of legal/political language used in confrontations was actually derived from theological discourse.

Over the next five years we had about five very fruitful meetings and were able to attract some outstanding minds. Christopher Stone of the Southern California law school gave an incredibly clear analysis of social/religious concepts as related to law. Paul Lehman, the great ethicist, Robert Bellah, Milner Ball, James Cone and many others attended these conferences and gave profoundly good presentations. But alas, funding sources, as so often happens in America, wanted the conferences to produce curriculum materials and plans for local parish outreach, whereas we wanted to develop a network of independent thinkers who were pursing similar themes. So try as Cecil might, he could not sell the idea that people need a forum in which they can think out loud and compare notes before they embark on programs that might affect people's lives.

The aftermath of the occupation of the Bureau of Indian Affairs and Wounded Knee produced intense interest in tribal religions not only in New Age circles but among Indians themselves. Over the past two decades I have seen amazing conversions revolving about the old religious traditions in Indian country. People who claimed to have been beaten by nuns for speaking their own language suddenly became "traditionals," making outrageous claims that they had been taken as children into secret canyons and caves and trained as spiritual leaders by the last real medicine man or woman of the tribe. The public performances of ceremonials, most notedly sun dances, have taken on the characteristics of rodeos, basketball tournaments and county fairs. A good many non-Indians have discovered Cherokee blood and become "traditional pipe carriers." New Agers routinely use their own version of sweat lodges and pipe ceremonies, almost always claiming to have been trained and then authorized by a medicine man from Pine Ridge.

Now bookstores are filled with confessional volumes by Anglo psychiatrists or freelance writers who claim to have received the distilled wisdom of a tribe merely by hanging out with a few members for a short time. Perhaps most disturbing has been the enforcement of an orthodoxy in which almost anything recited about the past has become "sacred" and therefore not subject to careful examination. A particular point of pressure has been the sporadic sniping of the Roman Catholic writers who subtly develop the posture that everything contained in *Black Elk Speaks* is actually good Jesuit teaching and that very little represents the old Sioux ways of religion. Thus Indian religious activity has become a generalized part of the fragmented Left that moans about air pollution while driving the large sports utility wagons and overcrowding national parks.

Anticipating this trend, and somewhat worried about it, in the fall of

1992 the American Indian Science and Engineering Society worked with me to sponsor a conference on traditional star knowledge. Speakers from nine tribes attended and discussed the tribal constellations and ceremonial activities related to some of the star groups. This conference, held at the Fiske Planetarium at the University of Colorado, sparked interest in looking at the knowledge that tribal people possessed regarding plants and animals and eventually stories about creation and migration. This last conference presented speakers so powerful that most of the audience simply sat stunned with tears running down their faces, aware for the first time of the emotional power of the old traditions. Again, unfortunately, funding sources quickly dried up as AISES discovered that they wanted curriculum and programs to flow immediately from what were essentially recitations of traditional ways that were dependent on the individual storytellers as much as the material presented.

If we were to evaluate these conferences, traditional knowledge and law and theology, in terms of programs produced or books published, they would probably be colossal failures. Our goals, however, were to demonstrate to the audience, speakers and the larger Indian community that tribal ways of looking at the world were part of a viable tradition that made sense, the non-materialistic non-mechanical understanding of the world. Local and regional conferences have since been held where people have been able to gather important data before the older generation disappears. The need in this area for considerably more scholarly work is obvious. In *Red Earth, White Lies,* I gathered some anecdotal materials, stories related by knowledgeable Indians to inquiring whites in the early contact days—thus reasonably untouched by a compulsion to satisfy the listener. These tales were the tribal explanation of the origin of unusual natural features: rivers, lakes, volcanoes, and other geological phenomena.

Juxtaposed against the orthodox scientific interpretation of the origin of these natural features, the Indian accounts stood out as reasonable, although alternative interpretations of the origins. Most of this century Indian traditions have been classified as either childish folktales designed to educate or discipline children or superstitious tales made up by Indians to explain natural processes which they feared and did not understand. I sought to provide a means whereby two additional categories could be opened for Indian traditional stories: historical eyewitness accounts preserved in memory and unusual religious experiences in which traditional Newtonian space-time concepts were possibly violated.

That Indians cringed before the forces of nature always has amused me. Saswe was a friend of the Thunders and a short story can illustrate his familiarity with them. A white man near Wagner once offered a bet to Saswe that he was a fake and that if he stood in a metal wash tub on a hill during the next thunderstorm, holding a crowbar in the air, he would be killed by lightning. The white man would then get Saswe's best horse. So Saswe said that would be fine and that when the Thunders came to him in that storm that he would merely tell them to go find the white man and kill him—wherever he was. The bet was called off.

When I was a small child my father told me that while the Thunders had given our family many responsibilities, they also were our friends and to always welcome thunderstorms. Many an evening I have stood outside and watched vicious thunderstorms rock the sky with nothing but profound admiration. My father was not only fearless in thunderstorms but had an uncanny ability to predict weather so that he was able to drive through storms of immense magnitude without the slightest concern. The wilder the winds and rain or snow, the more he seemed to relish them. In July 1939, a tornado hit our small town, destroying the Chevy garage, wrecking the theatre, and turning my father's church over on its side. Following that storm he toured Ohio speaking and raising funds for a new church and was thereafter a major personality on the national scene in the Episcopal Church.

Growing up in this milieu, it never occurred to me to question the existence or exact nature of God until I went to college and began to question everything. Although I changed the entire field of acceptable data and arguments concerning deities I have never forgotten the stories of spiritual power and revelation that I learned as a youngster. In the decades since I have been privileged to attend ceremonies of other tribes, talk with spiritual leaders, and have learned to look at spiritual things with a more intelligent eye. Thus I have assumed that some basic level of moral and ethical reality must underlie the worldview of every person and have come to believe that Indian people were among the most spiritual people in human history.

I was fortunate to meet Bill Tallbull, a Northern Cheyenne spiritual leader at a time when I was contemplating the division of Indian traditions into the new additional categories mentioned above. We attended several conferences together and Bill always made a point of smoking with me at breaks in meetings or he would sit next to me in restaurants at mealtime. He would draw close to me so others would have a hard time hearing and begin to tell me things that took my thoughts far beyond where my comprehension had been. Bill had an eerie way of providing the next sentence in a thought so that, at least in our conversations, I would be thinking about something and he would abruptly say something that extended the thought to its unexpected conclusion. It was always enlightening if not startling.

In recent years the examination of tribal traditions has taken on a much broader perspective for me—moving me away from the bent of trying to find a paradigm that will attract the mainstream church leadership and motivate them to adopt a consistent approach to the problems of American Indians. Unfortunately, and I do mean this sincerely, the old mainstream churches have moved themselves to the edge of social activity and hardly have any relevancy for our time. After decades of pandering to external influences they find that they have squandered their religious capital and now have to change their programs every three years in order to place themselves within the mainstream of American popular fads.

While I am able to maintain a friendly relationship with a number of old friends in the major Protestant churches, I feel an almost infinite sadness for them. They cling to the old Christian paradigm and work tirelessly to bolster their churches' efforts to maintain some presence in Indian country while the majority of Indians become secularized, return to traditional tribal practices or join fanatical fundamentalist groups. Their devotional life is buried beneath the flood of gimmicks being sent down by church bureaucrats far away who look at the latest sociological technique for controlling people as a mandate from on high.

Today our ideas about God and our concepts about the nature of religion have become so vague and generalized that almost any belief or practice is subject to appropriation by a strange group we hardly know. I continually get letters and telephone calls from well-meaning young whites who insist that they can get as much real religious insight when they try to do Indian ceremonies as do the Indians themselves. Religion thus has become a kind of New Ager magic rather than a way of life and proper performance of the *form* of the ceremony is regarded as equivalent to experiencing the *substance* of the sacred. Many Indian Christians try to mix religious symbols and the trappings of other religions, in my opinion thus bastardizing both religions. Bishops in Sioux headdresses are not Indian or Christian or religious—they are just silly.

In the West we have assumed that religion is an individual matter, primarily because the Bill of Rights purports to guarantee individual conscience, and partially because the Protestant version of Christianity has always been the dominant religious paradigm. But religion as a function of individual activity must certainly go back to the origins of Christianity when converts were made from the urbanized population of the Roman Empire. Whether they were lacking a sense of community or enticed to enjoy the freedom that comes with shedding family responsibilities, the early converts and the Biblical admonitions themselves were destructive of social order, leading to the persecution of Christians and the eventual disintegration of the social fabric of Europe and the Middle East.

Protestantism attacked the ecclesiastical structures of medieval Europe and removed the role of any intercessory roles between the individual and the deity. And Christianity has fragmented here in the New World as thousands of Protestant cults, more recently encouraged by the use of television, have grown up revolving about a charismatic leader and a comforting message.

Tribal religions were almost entirely focused on the group. The individual may have done the sun dance or vision quest but the traditional motivation was always to sacrifice for the benefit of the people. This focus of religion has not been properly explored by any theologian. Western religious thinkers have assumed that a community of saints is formed from the conglomerate of saved and/or repentent sinners who now share similar beliefs and practices. But is it so easy to form a religious community? Does not that community need to have already-established forms of custom, kinship, and self-discipline so that the religious revelation can express itself in familiar patterns? Revelation is most generally not the unveiling of startling news but the furtherance of already-existing behavior refined and reshaped by a more attractive goal and a new perspective on man's historical journey. We have only to study the rise and success of the Nazis to realize how powerful is the religious sense of our species and how easily it can go astray.

Most of my religious writing is oriented toward the revival of traditional forms, be they Indian or Christian, and a call to live up to professed beliefs. This groundwork is necessary to get people to examine what they actually believe and how they must put those beliefs into practice. The most common complaint I have had is from fundamentalist readers who insist that I qualify my analyses by always saying "some" people do this and "some" people do that—in effect reducing the discussion to comfortable platitudes because, as we are all well aware, when we see "some" as a description of improper behavior, we always find a way to be included in the group that is performing properly.

So I mostly look at my first round of religious writings as doing the groundwork in planting new seeds. As a means of helping people sort out the good plants from the bad, and trying to point out new ways of planting and harvesting. This idea came from the Old Testament as part of the prophet's task—not just to prophesy of things to come but to offer, as a part of condemnation, the view of a more profound way of being. Why, in religion, do we do what we do, why do we believe what we believe, and why do our practices seem to fall so far short of what is possible for us?

(1998)

APPENDIX 1

In 1965 the Catholic weekly *America* published an article titled "The Indian in a Cultural Trap" by one Lawrence E. Barry, a Jesuit priest stationed at St. Stephen's Mission on the Wind River Reservation in Wyoming.[1] The magazine's editors admitted that Barry proposed a "somewhat unconventional" analysis of the problems facing tribal communities, but ran the piece anyway. It provoked an intelligent response from at least two readers, whose letters appeared six weeks later, and another disclaimer from the editors, this one more explicit than the first. Barry's article also found its way to the desk of the executive director of the National Congress of American Indians, Vine Deloria, Jr. He immediately penned a clever rebuttal in the form of a parody, turning the tables on Barry while mimicking his argument point-by-point, but *America* refused to publish it. The manuscript circulated among tribal leaders and an abridged version was included in a 1972 anthology of Indian literature. The original essay is published here for the first time, alongside Barry's provocation. The seeds of Deloria's religious critique in *Custer Died for Your Sins* are easy to see in this piece, and the razor-sharp sarcasm of his trademark sense of humor is also present in ample supply.

J. T.

---

1. *America*, April 10, 1965: 482–84.

THE INDIAN IN A CULTURAL TRAP

Lawrence E. Barry

THE MISSIONARY IN A CULTURAL TRAP

Vine Deloria, Jr.

Indian reservations have been chosen—and wisely so—as target areas in the War on Poverty. The good of the country as a whole demands such actions, since these depressed areas can be breeding grounds for crime and disease. But if anyone thinks that all that is needed is economic opportunity, he has a few suprises coming to him. The Indian has attitudes of his own, and any attempt to help Indians had better be preceded by a careful study of the cultural and legal confusion on our reservations. It is these factors, far more than the lack of economic opportunity, that have made reservations depressed areas; and they are still quite capable of frustrating further efforts to help.

Indian culture and ideas are attractive from a distance. Examined more carefully, however, that culture and those ideals are something less than perfect. Indians have a tradition, for example, of sharing with each other. Those of us accustomed to the American culture, where private property is taken for granted, are tempted to look upon Indian sharing as a generosity that many Americans lack. Again, to a country proud of its tradition of indepen-

Missionaries have been chosen—and wisely so—as targets in the War on Ignorance conducted by the Indian people of this country. The good of the country as a whole demands such actions, since these people can be the breeding ground for doctrines of intolerance, arrogance and unwise policies regarding the American Indian. But if anyone thinks that all that is needed is education he has a few surprises coming. The missionary has attitudes of his own, and any attempt to help him understand cultural differences had better be preceded by a careful study of the cultural and theological confusion in church mission programs. It is these factors, far more than lack of education, that have made mission attempts quite depressing and they are still creating frustrations and confusion.

The missionary and his ideas are attractive from a distance. Examined more carefully, however, that missionary and those ideas are something less than perfect. Missionaries have a tradition, for example, of wanting Indian people to want the same things they want. Those of us accustomed to the Indian culture, where the right to be different is taken for granted, are tempted to look upon conformity to the missionaries' ideas as a pleasant means

dence, the Indian dislike for sticking to routine tasks and following orders can look like a noble tradition. Moreover, in the midst of worries and anxieties, a harassed American may think highly of the Indian tradition of enjoying the present and disregarding the future; he may take it to represent a form of high wisdom. It is comforting—but, alas, not correct—to think that wisdom can be had by simply observing and living with the movements of nature rather than through effort, thought and discipline.

of getting along in modern society. Again, in a culture proud of the tradition of remaining silent unless one is asked by one's peers for one's opinion, the ability of the missionary to be an instant expert on all subjects can look like a noble tradition. Moreover, in the midst of a calm and contemplative life, the ability to spend a lifetime in monotonous repetition of the same basic work can be taken to represent a form of high wisdom and security. It is comforting—but, alas, not correct—to think that wisdom can be had simply by obeying theological doctrines and disciplines.

The American culture respects honest work. We frequently speak with pride of the hard-working men who built our country. Indian culture as I have seen it, on the other hand, does not respect work. In a primitive hunting community, the adult male was a hunter-warrior; he was a highly respected as well as rare person. Hunting was a dangerous business. The average life span was low in general, and a man was more susceptible to disease than a woman. The community was made up of a large number of children, a fair number of women, a few men. The whole group depended on these few men for protection and for their main source of food.

The Indian culture respects the honest man. We speak with pride of the fact that we have not broken a single treaty, that we have kept our word, while the United States government has broken over four hundred treaties. Missionary culture, as I have seen it, does not respect the truth. In an acquisitive society, the doctrine is every man for himself and the devil take the hindmost. So the truth is always submerged in favor of the urge to escape the devil. The average parish was built by converting the most souls to the correct sect with all due haste. The community is made up of a large number of children, a fair number of women, and a few men, as the pressures of piling up treasures upon earth rather than heaven is a killing pace. Since the man is chief provider, he dies sooner than the women and children.

Needless to say, the hunter-warriors were above performing any of the routine tasks of the community.

Needless to say, the missionaries are above performing any of the routine tasks of the community. They

They had a dangerous task that only they could perform. When they returned with their kill, they were kings. In the twentieth-century United States; the hunter-warrior is an anachronism, yet the ideals and attitudes of the hunter-warrior persist in what remains of Indian culture. The man who is willing to follow orders and work steadily at routine tasks is not fulfilling the Indian image of what a man should be.

have a dangerous task that only they can perform. As Soren Kierkegaard would have said, or maybe did say, "they must by their doctrines and preaching fool both God and man." If this isn't dangerous, we are at a loss to explain. When they are talking about things they don't know about, they are kings of the hill. In twentieth-century Indian culture the missionary is an anachronism, yet the ideals and attitudes of the missionary persist in what remains of the mission programs of the churches. The man who is ready to remain silent on subjects he doesn't know anything about is not fulfilling the missionary image of what a missionary should be.

The life of a primitive hunter was often one of feasting followed by starving, as the fortunes of the hunt rose and fell. A good kill often meant more food than he and his family could possibly eat. There were few ways to store it, and the nomadic life did not encourage any kind of saving. Little or nothing could be done about the future, anyway, so there was scarcely any point in worrying about it. So it was natural that the hunter should share what he had with others and expect them to share their good luck with him.

The life of a missionary is often one of feasting followed by starving as the fortunes of the mission rise and fall. A religious revival often means more souls than heaven could possibly hold. There are few ways to explain a revival and the missionary life does not require any more than that Indians should be baptised. Little or nothing is done about developing native clergy as Indians couldn't be missionaries anyway, so there is scarcely any point in worrying about it. James Michener's book *Hawaii* makes this point extremely well. So it is natural that all missionaries should baptize as many Indians as possible no matter how many times they had been baptized before.

Sharing then made good sense; now Indian sharing is a source of degradation and frustration. It is more a matter of social pressures than of willing generosity. The

Preaching then made good sense; now mission activities are a source of frustration. It is more a matter of social pressures to listen to missionaries rather than the fact that they

Indian who does not want to be regarded by his fellow Indians as a "white man" must refuse them nothing, so long as he has anything left to share. If he tries to refuse his fellows, and is in earnest, he is not one of them. And if social ostracism is not enough, the lenient reservation law enforcement sometimes leaves room for other measures. If he has worked and saved while others have not, the result will simply be a lesson to him.

have anything to say. The missionary who does not want to be regarded by his fellow missionaries as an "Indian" must continue to preach at them, so long as he thinks of anything to say. If he decides to keep quiet because he doesn't really understand the Indian culture, he is not one of them. And if social ostracism is not enough, the rigorous discipline of his church sometimes leaves room for other measures. If he has preached and expounded while others have not, the result is still not a lesson to him.

The experience of an Arapahoe woman on the Wind River reservation who bought a telephone illustrates how Indian sharing can work. After her husband died, she felt she should have a telephone. It was installed in January 1961, at a cost of $78 for extra poles. Her Indian relatives and neighbors promptly looked upon the telephone as their own. They made long-distance calls—with promises to pay later, which were almost never honored. The poor woman accepted collect calls frequently; she hadn't the heart to refuse them. She would also get requests to deliver messages to people who lived only "a few miles away."

As a first effort to keep her telephone bill manageable, she requested an unlisted number. But her children had to know it, and so it was not long before everyone did. Her next move was to pay the telephone company only for the long-distance calls she herself had made, but the company naturally took a dim view of this. Last summer her bill for two months came to $86.

The experience of a Catholic priest on the Wind River reservation who wrote an article for *America* magazine last month illustrates how expounding on a subject one is unfamiliar with can work. After having been on the Wind River reservation for a whole four years, he is suddenly an "expert" on a culture that has maintained itself for thousands of years. The basic complaint of this priest is that the Indian culture is one of sharing. He also states that every Sunday there is only about $100 in the collection plate and from one-half to one-third of this comes from those who are Arapahoes. In fact, he feels that it will still take quite a while to reduce this percentage to about five percent which is about all the people in the missionary culture give to others.

Since she would pay only for the calls she had made, the phone is now disconnected—and will remain so until the $86, plus $50 to re-establish credit, is paid.

In *Mater et Magistra,* §112, Pope John XXIII defended the right of private property as a universal right, one that safeguards the dignity of the human person and strengthens the stability and tranquillity of family life. The Indian habit of sharing, which from a distance may look like a virtue, is nowadays, in my judgment, a clearly immoral element of Indian culture, because it is a practical denial of the right of private property.

Chief Red Cloud, in one of his more profound statements said, "You must begin anew and put away the wisdom of your fathers. You must lay up food and forget the hungry; when your house is built, your storerooms filled, then look around for a neighbor whom you can take advantage of, and seize all he has." (See *The Long Death* by Ralph Andrist.)

Here on the Wind River Reservation, members of the Arapahoe and Shoshone tribes have been paid what is called a "per capita," based on income derived chiefly from mineral royalties. It is distributed to the members of the tribes by giving an equal share to each enrolled member: man, woman or child. The payments to minors are given to their parents. For the past ten years, payments to the two tribes have amounted to about $3 million annually. This has meant about $40 per head each month for Arapahoes, and $65 per head for Shoshones. These payments are tax-free.

In the American society, missionaries are paid by what is called "Sunday collections" based chiefly on what church members give during the church service. It is distributed to missionaries by giving them what is leftover after the administrative expenses have been paid. The collections are tax-free.

Furthermore, each Indian owns a plot of land, which is also tax-free. He receives a good deal of free medical care from the government. Last year the Arapahoe tribe won a suit against the government for lands taken from them in the last century. Eighty-five percent of this money is

Furthermore, each church mission station owns a plot of ground which is also tax-free. Last year churches raised a considerable amount of money for mission activities, so that they were able to pay their missionaries about half of a living wage.

being paid out in twelve monthly payments, so that payments to the Arapahoes this year amounted to about $124 per head per month.

The reservation is still, however, a depressed area. Efforts are being made to get a government subsidy for starting industry on the reservation. This will help somewhat, but the core of the problem lies in the Indians themselves. Merchants have a hard time collecting from them. They are just as casual in dealing with their parish, as the following facts will show.

St. Stephen's Mission charges the Indian pupils $4 a month as a lunch fee and $5 annually for registration in the grade school ($10 in the high school). Some Indians are so resentful at the Mission's insistence on these fees that they have transferred their children to public schools, even though the lunch fee is higher there.

There are about two thousand Arapahoes on the reservation, over half of them Catholic. St. Stephen's Mission maintains a large church, with two Masses on Sunday, and two fairly large mission stations with one Mass each on Sunday. The Sunday collections for all of these together come to about $100 a Sunday—and from one-half to two-thirds of this comes from those who are not Arapahoes.

A booklet published by the Bureau of Indian Affairs, *The Ten-Year Plan for Progress on the Wind River Reservation 1965–1975,* discusses problems on the reservation.

Churches are still depressing areas, however. Efforts are being made to get a government subsidy for starting schools in every parish. This will help somewhat, but the core of the problem lies in the missionaries themselves. White people have a hard time understanding them. They are just as crafty in dealing with the Indians, as the following facts will show.

Indian tribes charge them nothing for locating their missions on Indian land. Some churches are so resentful that the Indians do not flock to church that they have transferred their mission activities to deepest Africa, even though they are occasionally put on the menu there.

There are about a million missionaries on each reservation, a good deal of them Catholic. Farmington, New Mexico, has, at last count, twenty-six different churches, all trying to convince the handful of Navajos that they alone have the true doctrine.

The various tribes are thinking of publishing a booklet discussing the problems in the mission field. One of the chief problems, certainly, is the number of missionaries em-

One of the chief problems, certainly, is unemployment. The booklet blames the lack of work opportunities on or near the reservation for the stagnation of employable adults. It adds, however, that qualified Indians often miss the limited oportunities that do exist because they lack sufficient initiative to seize opportunities as they arise.

Another problem discussed by the booklet is the rise in the rates of delinquency, venereal disease, school dropouts and drinking among Indian juveniles. The report declares that many parents "appear to have no feeling of responsibility for the conduct of their children."

Another booklet, put out by the Over-all Economic Development Program Committee of the Wind River Reservation, also discusses the problems of the reservation. The high rate of arrests for drunkenness on and near the reservation, according to this publication, indicates a "chronic and high incidence of social disorganization and family breakdowns among reservation families."

Infant mortality on the reservation, the booklet adds, has been dramatically reduced in the past decade, but it is still several times the rate elsewhere. Most infant deaths occurred, however, not in the period of childbirth and hospitalization, but after the mother and baby had returned home. The deaths seem to have been due, the booklet asserts, to "inadequate parental training and acceptance of responsibility" as well as to inadequacies in general living conditions.

ployed in the mission field. The booklet will blame the number of diverse doctrines in or similar to the Christian religion for the busybody activities of the missionaries. It will add, however, that qualified missionaries often miss the unlimited opportunities to understand the Indian culture because they lack the humility to listen and insist on talking all the time.

Another problem discussed by the booklet is the rise in the rates of publications, articles and books by the younger missionaries. The report will declare that many churches "appear to have no feeling of responsibility for the conduct of their missionaries." It will also point out that the high rates of moving missionaries around indicates a "chronic and high incidence of program disorganization and theological breakdowns among the churches."

The Indian's problem with alcohol is notorious. At the twelfth annual session (1963) of the University of Utah School of Alcohol Studies, a special section was devoted to Indian drinking problems. In one seminar, Omer C. Steward, professor of anthropology at the University of Colorado, put the Indian rate of arrests, chiefly for drunkenness, at seven times the national average, eight times that of whites and three times that of Negroes. (In 1960, Indians, who made up five percent of Utah's population, contributed thirty-four percent of those in the state penitentiary, twenty-five percent of those in the boys' reformatory, and fifty percent of those in the girls' reformatory.)

In another seminar, V. W. Warner, of the New Mexico Commission on Alcoholism, stated that in 1962, in the Gallup area, which boasts of being the Indian capital of America, there were 6,400 arrests for excessive drinking. James Officer, of the Bureau of Indian Affairs, added that a substantial percentage of Indian children are in government boarding schools because they had been removed from homes in which one or both parents drank heavily. All these statistics and criticism of the Indian were made, not to demean him, but to demonstrate how desperately he needs help.

The missionary's problem in understanding other cultures is notorious. In the early days in Europe the Franks were given a choice between death and baptism. During the Crusades the Arabian culture was regarded as in league with the devil and it is well known that the library of Alexandria was burned by zealous missionaries since it contained elements of a culture they did not wish to understand.

The Indian's cultural confusion is intensified by legal confusion. He has three legal statuses, which are in part contradictory. He is simultaneously a full citizen of the United States, a ward of the federal govern-

The missionary's cultural confusion is intensified by theological confusion. He has three theological statuses which are in part contradictory. He is simultaneously a full citizen of the secular world, an agent of

ment, and a member of a nation with which the United States has entered into a treaty. The Indian may seem to be getting the benefit of all three. He enjoys privileges on the reservation, where many jobs are reserved for Indians. His status as a ward of the government exempts him from many taxes, saves him administrative costs, protects him from creditors. As a full citizen of our country, he expects to run his affairs without taking orders from agency officials.

free moral responsibility, and a member of a church with which various cultures have come into conflict. The missionary may seem to get the benefit of all three. He enjoys the privileges of the church where many jobs are reserved for missionaries. His status as a free moral agent exempts him from ethical decisions, saves him from responsibility to provide for others, and protects him from the other people in his world. As a full citizen of the secular world he expects to be able to expound on anything his heart desires and be taken very seriously by Indians.

The Indian's legal confusion, however, also brings him serious trouble. He is made to feel he is someone special, who does not have to conform to the standards of modern America but who deserves its material rewards. He is rarely obliged to face up to his failures or shortcomings. No matter what he does, the reservation is a refuge where he can escape from the reality of experience and where agency officials do not have enough authority to be effective teachers.

The missionary's theological confusion, however, also brings him serious trouble. He is made to feel he is something special, who does not have to conform to the standards of the modern world but who deserves its material rewards. He is rarely obliged to face up to his failures or shortcomings. No matter what he does, the church is a refuge where he can escape from the reality of experience and where church officials do not have enough knowledge to be effective teachers.

We who have inherited European culture have often been tempted to remake others after our own image. Since we are trying very hard not to make such a mistake with the Indian, we have been led to conclude that any attempt to get the Indian to adapt to modern America would be a repetition of that mistake. If avoiding the mistakes of the past were enough to guarantee that one can avoid the mistakes of the present, the problem would be sim-

We who have inherited Indian culture have often been tempted to remake others after our own image. Since we are trying very hard not to make such a mistake with the missionary, we have been led to conclude that any attempt to get the missionary to adapt to Indian culture would be a repetition of that mistake. If avoiding the mistakes of the past were enough to guarantee that one can avoid the mistakes of the present, the problem would be

pler; but unfortunately things do not always work out that way.

Some adaptation is a necessity for the Indian. The right to call private property one's own is not the white man's prerogative; it is a universal mandate of the natural law. A man must be able to take pride in his work and feel that he is a profitable member of his society. But no one, not even an Indian, can be a profitable member of American society so long as he insists that it is his privilege to work only when and as he wishes.

The Indian's problems are not a matter of inherited characteristics. Indians are very much like anyone else. They are not the "noble savages" of European and American imaginations. They have no great wisdom that they received by being born Indian. If they are to succeed, they have to be trained and they have to work as much as anyone else—and with training and work they can do as well as anyone else. James Officer, whom we quoted above, has said that eighty percent of those who take advantage of training and relocation opportunities are successful in their move away from the reservation.

There are some Indians on the reservation who would be acceptable in any community. There are

simpler; but unfortunately things do not always work out that way.

Some adaptation is a necessity for the missionary. The right to call private property everyone's is not the red man's prerogative; it is a universal mandate originally advocated by Jesus of Nazareth. A man must be able to take pride in his generosity and feel he is a contributing member of his society. But no one, not even a missionary, can be a profitable member of society so long as he insists that it is his privilege to keep all his possessions for himself and not share them with those who are less fortunate. We do not expect miracles, we would be willing to settle for fifty percent at present. Say if a man has two coats and his neighbor asks for one, and he only gives one, we would be satisfied.

The missionary's problems are not a matter of inherited characteristics. Missionaries are very much like anyone else. They are not "selfish and greedy" of Indian imagination. They have no great wisdom that they receive by being ordained. If they are to succeed, they have to be untrained and they have to learn to relax as much as anyone else. And with patience and understanding they can learn to be human as well as anyone else. One Indian has said that eighty percent of those who are willing to learn and listen while on Indian reservations are successful in learning something about the Indian culture.

There are some missionaries in the church who would be acceptable on any reservation. There are others

others who are above average. Yet the overall picture on the reservation is not a pretty one. For many Indians, the Indian culture is a trap. who are above average. Yet the overall picture of the churches is not a pretty one. For many clergy, the theological doctrines are a trap that keep them from being human.

(1965)

APPENDIX 2

One of Deloria's responsibilities as executive director of the National Congress of American Indians was the publication of a newsletter known as the *NCAI Sentinel.* In early 1965 he mailed his first issue to the few dues-paying members left, thirteen tribes and forty-eight individuals. Bearing the title "Now Is the Time," his lead editorial emphasized the importance of having a vital national organization to represent Indian interests and challenged Indian America to revitalize the NCAI as it entered its third decade of existence. The quarterly newsletter reported on current developments around Indian country and in Washington, and beginning with his third issue (Fall 1965) Deloria included humorous pieces as well by launching what was to become a regular feature titled "From the Archives." Assuming the voice of an overworked NCAI administrator reporting to the tribes on his encounters with bumbling European adventurers after 1492, he fashioned a compelling alternative narrative of discovery. This entry, dated only twelve years after Columbus happened upon the Americas, was the inaugural column in the series and Deloria's first published writing on religion in America.[1]

J. T.

FROM THE ARCHIVES— DECEMBER 2, 1504

The annual NCAI convention ended last week and I had to make a report to the council on the results. Most of it was long-winded anthropology papers on the strangers who have been visiting these shores. We call them savages since they wear funny clothes and don't know a word of Indian language.

---

1. *NCAI Sentinel* 10, no. 3 (Fall 1965).

There were three papers presented on them. The first was entitled "Lost in Space: A Childhood Psychosis of the European Tribes." It pointed out that each stranger who lands here thinks he is the first to see these shores. It seems a psychopathic fear of sailing over the edge of the world stems from probable early experiences of falling out of bed in cold, windy castles. This experience then submerges into the subconscious and comes to the surface in the dread of sailing across the Atlantic. When they discover they have not sailed over the edge of the world an unbearable tension is created, causing them to insist they have found India and that the edge of the world is beyond that.

"Royalty and the Father Image" was the second paper. It seems these people believe God has given their rulers a divine right to govern them. We have tried over and over to explain democracy to them, with no success. Perhaps in their present state of insecurity it is better to leave their system alone. We have had to make certain concessions to them, however. They insist that every girl they marry here be a princess. This gives them a lot of security and they then think they are as good as everyone else. It seemed so little to do to help them attain a good state of mental health that we passed a resolution proclaiming all unmarried girls "princesses." Although we believe all men to be equal, they insist on making differences and so until they mature I guess we will be stuck with this royalty thing.

The final paper dealt with the origin of these people. A number of theses were presented. Some thought that they had come from Noah's ark with the rest of us. The liberals, of course, thought they had evolved from the apes, perhaps those of Gibraltar as they appear to be as stubborn as that rock in their ideas. Others figured they were of the Lost Tribes of Israel. This is a popular theory that comes from an expression of theirs when they see gold: "Golly Moses!" The Lost Tribes theory was rejected, however, as they have apparently had no contact with the Ten Commandments or at least show none of the effects of that civilizing influence. It seems they have endless arguments about God and solve the question through killing each other. We feel this solution only postpones the discussion to another time and place.

I was appointed to a committee to help them develop a vocabulary. We are extremely tired of the "big canoe" that they always point out. They have been coming over here in frigates, galleons, everything but clipper ships but they always talk proudly about their big canoe with us. They should realize that a canoe doesn't have the proper engineering design to cross the Atlantic and that canoes are used primarily on fresh water.

I hope we can civilize them before they hurt themselves.

(1965)

BIBLIOGRAPHY

This comprehensive bibliography of Deloria's published writings is organized in four sections: books; articles, essays, and interviews; forewords, introductions, and afterwords; and other writings. Like the essays collected in this volume, the citations within each section have been arranged chronologically in order to highlight the emergence and development of key themes in Deloria's work over the past three decades. Items not listed here include his contributions to the *NCAI Sentinel* (early 1965 to late 1967), his scholarly book reviews (which Deloria himself does not keep track of), audiotape and videotape recordings of his public presentations that are available at certain libraries, and reprinted versions of his articles and book chapters. While not exhaustive, this bibliography does represent the most comprehensive accounting of Deloria's published writings available in print.

J. T.

BOOKS

Custer Died for Your Sins: An Indian Manifesto. New York, NY: Macmillan, 1969. Reprinted in paperback, New York, NY: Avon, 1970. Reprinted in Spanish as *El General Custer murió por vuestros pecados: un manifiesto indio.* Barcelona, Spain: Barral, 1969. Reprinted in Swedish as *Custer dog för era synder.* Stockholm, Sweden: PAN/Norstedts, 1971. Reprinted in French as *Peau-Rouge.* Paris, France: Edition Spéciale, 1972. Reprinted with a new preface, Norman, OK: University of Oklahoma Press, 1988.

We Talk, You Listen: New Tribes, New Turf. New York, NY: Macmillan, 1970. Reprinted in paperback, New York, NY: Dell, 1972.

The Red Man in the New World Drama: A Politico-Legal Study with a Pageantry of American Indian History by Jennings C. Wise (editor). New York, NY: Macmillan, 1971.

Of Utmost Good Faith (editor). San Francisco, CA: Straight Arrow Books, 1971. Reprinted in paperback, New York, NY: Bantam, 1972.

God Is Red. New York, NY: Grosset and Dunlap, 1973. Reprinted in paperback, New York, NY: Dell, 1973. Reprinted in German as *Gott ist rot.* München, Germany: Goldmann Verlag, 1987. Revised and republished as *God Is Red: A Native View of Religion,* 2nd ed. Golden, CO: North American Press, 1992. Reprinted in paperback, Golden, CO: Fulcrum, 1994.

Behind the Trail of Broken Treaties: An Indian Declaration of Independence. New York, NY: Delacorte, 1974. Reprinted in paperback, New York, NY: Dell, 1974. Reprinted with a new afterword, Austin, TX: University of Texas Press, 1985.

The Indian Affair. New York, NY: Friendship Press, 1974.

Indians of the Pacific Northwest: From the Coming of the White Man to the Present Day. Garden City, NY: Doubleday, 1977.

The Metaphysics of Modern Existence. San Francisco, CA: Harper and Row, 1979.

American Indians, American Justice (with Clifford M. Lytle). Austin, TX: University of Texas Press, 1983.

The Nations Within: The Past and Future of American Indian Sovereignty (with Clifford M. Lytle). New York, NY: Pantheon, 1984.

A Sender of Words: Essays in Memory of John G. Neihardt (editor). Salt Lake City, UT: Howe Brothers, 1984.

The Aggressions of Civilization: Federal Indian Policy Since the 1880s (editor, with Sandra L. Cadwalader). Philadelphia, PA: Temple University Press, 1984.

American Indian Policy in the Twentieth Century (editor). Norman, OK: University of Oklahoma Press, 1985.

Indian Education in America: Eight Essays. Boulder, CO: American Indian Science and Engineering Society, 1991.

Frank Waters: Man and Mystic (editor). Athens, OH: Swallow Press/Ohio University Press, 1993.

Red Earth, White Lies: Native Americans and the Myth of Scientific Fact. New York, NY: Scribner, 1995. Revised and republished in paperback, Golden, CO: Fulcrum Press, 1997.

ARTICLES, ESSAYS, AND INTERVIEWS

"Special Section." *Indian Voices*, May 1965: 18–20.

"Special Section." *Indian Voices*, July 1965: 18–19.

"Custer Died for Your Sins." *Playboy* 16, no. 8 (August 1969): 131–32, 172–75.

"The War Between the Redskins and the Feds." *The New York Times Magazine*, December 7, 1969.

"Implications of the 1968 Civil Rights Act in Tribal Autonomy." In *Indian Voices: The First Convocation of American Indian Scholars*, 85–104. San Francisco, CA: Indian Historian Press, 1970.

"The Urban Scene and the American Indian." In *Indian Voices: The First Convocation of American Indian Scholars*, 333–55. San Francisco, CA: Indian Historian Press, 1970.

"This Country Was a Lot Better Off When the Indians Were Running It." *The New York Times Magazine*, March 8, 1970.

"Indian Affairs." In *Living History of the World, 1971 Year Book*. New York, NY: Stravon Educational Press, 1971.

"Hobby Farm: On the Reservation." In *Defiance #2: A Radical Review*, edited by Dotson Rader, 22–42. New York, NY: Paperback Library, 1971.

"Grandfathers of Our Country." *New York Times*, February 22, 1971: 29.

"The New Exodus." *Civil Rights Digest* 4 (Spring 1971): 38–44.

"'White Society Is Breaking Down Around Us . . . Even Its Myths—Like the Melting Pot—Are Dead': An Interview with American Indian Writer Vine Deloria, Jr." Interview by Peter Collier. *Mademoiselle* 72 (April 1971): 202–4, 269.

"A Violated Covenant." *Event: Issues and Viewpoints for Laymen* 11, no. 6 (June 1971): 5–8.

"The Rise and Fall of the First Indian Movement." *Historian* 33, no. 4 (August 1971): 656–64.

"American Indians Today." *Soroptimist Magazine*, December 1971.

"Indians, American." In *Compton's Encyclopedia and Fact-Index*. Chicago, IL: F. E. Compton Co., 1972.

"An Open Letter to the Heads of the Christian Churches in America." *Forum for Contemporary History*, no. 1 (January 28, 1972): 1-5.

"The Hidden Americans." *Harvard Medical Alumni Bulletin* 46 (January–February 1972).

"The American Indian and His Commitments, Goals, and Programs: A Need to Reconsider." *The Indian Historian* 5, no. 1 (Spring 1972): 5–10.

"The Basis of Indian Law." *American Airlines Magazine*, April 1972.

"Bureau of Indian Affairs: My Brothers' Keeper." *Art in America* 60 (July–August 1972): 110–115.

"It Is a Good Day to Die." *Katallagete* 4, nos. 2–3 (Fall–Winter 1972): 62–65.

"The Cheyenne Experience." *Natural History* 81, no. 9 (November 1972): 96–100.

"For an All-American Platoon." *Journal of the Forum for Contemporary History* 2, no. 1 (December 1972–January 1973): 11–12.

"American Indians: The End of the Fifth Century of Contact." In *1973 Britannica Book of the Year*, 577–79. Chicago, IL: Encyclopedia Britannica, 1973.

"Some Criticisms and a Number of Suggestions." In *Anthropology and the American Indian: Report of a Symposium*, 93–99. San Francisco, CA: Indian Historian Press, 1973.

"The Rise and Fall of Ethnic Studies." In *In Search of a Future for Education: Readings in Foundations*, edited by Stephen C. Margaritis, 153–57. Columbus, OH: Charles E. Merrill, 1973.

"The Indian World Today." *Journal of the American Indian Culture Center* 4, no. 1 (Winter 1973): 3–5.

"Indian Affairs 1973: Hebrews 13:8." *North American Review* 258, no. 4 (Winter 1973): 108–12.

"Old Indian Refrain: Treachery on the Potomac." *New York Times*, February 8, 1973: 43.

"The Question of the 1868 Sioux Treaty . . . A Crucial Element in the Wounded Knee Trials." *Akwesasne Notes* 5 (Spring 1973).

"Strangers on a Continent." *Washington University Magazine*, Spring 1973.

"Wounded Knee." *Los Angeles Times*, April 2, 1973.

"The American Indian Today." *American Red Cross Youth News*, Summer 1973.

"Final Reflections on Wounded Knee." *The Black Politician* 4, no. 1 (Summer 1973).

"Beyond Wounded Knee." Akwesasne Notes 5, no. 4 (Late Summer 1973): 8.

"The Tribe That Was Made to Be Fisherman." *Smithsonian Magazine* 4, no. 6 (September 1973): 86–92.

"The Theological Dimension of the Indian Protest Movement." *The Christian Century* 90, no. 33 (September 19, 1973): 912–14.

"On Being Indian." *Cross Talk* 2, no. 4, part 2 (December 1973–February 1974).

"The New Activism." *Dialogue* 6, no. 2 (1973): 3–12.

"Russell Means: New Indian Hope." *Indian Voice* 3, no. 3 (1973): 5–6.

"Indian Treaties a Hundred Years Later." *Education Journal of the Institute for the Development of Indian Law* 2, no. 4 (1973): 14–17.

"The American Indian Image." In *Encyclopedia of Indians of the Americas, volume 1, Conspectus, Chronology*, edited by Keith Irvine, 39–44. St. Clair Shores, MI: Scholarly Press, 1974.

"From Wounded Knee to Wounded Knee." In *The World of the American Indian*, edited by Jules Billard, 355–83. Washington, DC: National Geographic Society, 1974.

"Non-Violence in American Society." *Katallagete* 5, no. 2 (Winter 1974): 4–7.

"Religion and Revolution Among American Indians." *Worldview* 17, no. 1 (January 1974): 12–15.

"The Next Three Years: A Time for Change." *The Indian Historian* 7, no. 2 (Spring 1974): 25–27, 53.

"Integrity Before Education." *Integrated Education* 7, no. 3 (May–June 1974): 22–28.

"Myth and the Origin of Religion." *Pensée* 4, no. 4 (Fall 1974): 45–50.

"The Most Important Indian." *Race Relations Reporter* 5, no. 21 (November 1974): 26–28.

"Religion and the Modern American Indian." *Current History* 67, no. 400 (December 1974): 250–53.

"1976: The Desperate Need for Understanding." *Cross Talk* 3, no. 4, part 8 (December 1974–February 1975).

"The Significance of the 1868 Treaty." *Medicine Root Magazine* 1, no. 2 (1974): 14–16.

"The Indian Movement: Out of a Wounded Past." *Ramparts* 13 (March 1975): 28–32.

"Federal Policy Still Victimizes and Exploits." *Los Angeles Times*, August 17, 1975: part IV, 5.

"Breaking the Treaty of Ruby Valley." *New Dimensions Magazine*, September 1975.

"God Is Also Red: An Interview with Vine Deloria Jr." Interview by James R. McGraw. *Christianity and Crisis* 35 (September 15, 1975): 198–206.

"Researching American Indian Treaties: Northwest and Southwest." *American Indian Journal* 1 (November 1975): 14–17.

"Why Aren't Indians Celebrating the Bicentennial." *Learning Magazine*, November 14, 1975.

"The North Americans." *The Crisis* 82, no. 10 (December 1975): 385–87.

"The Twentieth Century." In *Red Men and Hat-Wearers: Viewpoints in Indian History*, edited by Daniel Tyler, 155–66. Fort Collins, CO: Colorado State University, 1976.

"We Pledge Allegiance: A Conversation with Vine Deloria, Jr." *Journal of Current Social Issues* 13, no. 1 (Winter 1976): 12–17.

"The Western Shoshones." *American Indian Journal* 2 (January 1976): 16–20.

"Why the U.S. Never Fought the Indians." *The Christian Century* 93 (January 7–14, 1976): 9–12.

"The Place of American Indians in Contemporary Education." *American Indian Journal* 2 (February 1976): 2–9.

"Completing the Theological Circle: Civil Religion in America." *Religious Education* 71, no. 3 (May–June 1976): 278–87.

"Escaping from Bankruptcy: The Future of the Theological Task." *Katallagete* 6, no. 1 (Summer 1976): 5–9.

"A Last Word from the First Americans." *The New York Times Magazine*, July 4, 1976: 80.

"Organizaciones nacionales de indios norteamericanos." *America Indigena* 36, no. 4 (October–December 1976): 775–89.

"The American Indians." *Gallery Magazine*, November 1976.

"From Reservation to Global Society: American Culture, Liberation and the Native American—An Interview with Vine Deloria, Jr." Interview by Michael McKale. *Radical Religion* 2, no. 4 (1976): 49–58.

"Sovereignty." In *The Great Sioux Nation: Sitting in Judgment on America*, edited by Roxanne Dunbar Ortiz, 16–18. New York, NY: American Indian Treaty Council Information Center / Moon Books, 1977.

"The United States Has No Jurisdiction in Sioux Territory." In *The Great Sioux Nation: Sitting in Judgment on America*, edited by Roxanne Dunbar Ortiz, 141–46. New York, NY: American Indian Treaty Council Information Center / Moon Books, 1977.

"Indian Law and the Reach of History." *Journal of Contemporary Law* 4, no. 1 (Winter 1977): 1–13.

"Native American Spirituality." *Gamaliel* 13, no. 1 (Spring 1977): 38–42.

"The Fascination of Heresy." *Katallagete* 6, no. 4 (Spring 1977): 47–50.

"Why Me, Tonto?" *Rocky Mountain Musical Express*, March 1977.

" . . . But What of Human Rights for Indians?" *Los Angeles Times*, July 6, 1977.

"A Native American Perspective on Liberation." *Occasional Bulletin of Missionary Research* 1, no. 3 (July 1977): 15–17.

"The Confusion of History." *Historical Magazine of the Protestant Episcopal Church* 46 (September 1977): 349–53.

"The Lummi Indian Community: The Fishermen of the Pacific Northwest." In *American Indian Economic Development*, edited by Samuel Stanley, 87–158. The Hague, The Netherlands: Mouton Publishers, 1978.

"A Native American Perspective on Liberation Theology." In *Is Liberation Theology for North America? The Response of First World Churches*, edited by Sergio Torres and others, 12–20. New York, NY: Theology in the Americas, 1978.

"The Indian Student Amid American Inconsistencies." In *The Schooling of Native America*, 9–28. Washington, DC: American Association of Colleges for Teacher Education, 1978.

"Legislation and Litigation Concerning American Indians." *Annals of the American Academy of Political and Social Science*, no. 436 (March 1978): 86–96.

"Civilization and Isolation." *North American Review* 263, no. 2 (Summer 1978): 11–14.

"Catastrophism and Planetary History." *Kronos* 3, no. 4 (Summer 1978): 45–51.

"Largest Collection of Indian Items Is Put on Display." *Smithsonian Magazine* 9, no. 5 (August 1978): 59–64.

"Colorado Requiem: On the Ravages of Rootlessness." *Colorado Quote* 1, no. 1 (September 1978): 18–21.

"Kinship with the World." *Journal of Current Social Issues*, 15, no. 3 (Fall 1978): 19–21.

"Sovereignty: Fact or Fiction? A Debate between Congressman Lloyd Meeds and Vine Deloria, Jr." *La Confluencia* 2, no. 2–3 (October 1978).

"A Conversation with Vine Deloria, Jr." Interview by Larry Evers. *Sun Tracks* 8 (1978).

"The Coming of the People." In *The American Land*, edited by Alexis Doster III, Joe Goodwin and Robert C. Post, 50–55. Washington, DC: Smithsonian Exposition Books, 1979.

"Self-Determination and the Concept of Sovereignty." In *Economic Development in American Indian Reservations*, edited by Roxanne Dunbar Ortiz, 22–28. Albuquerque, NM: Native American Studies, University of New Mexico, 1979.

"GCSP: The Demons at Work." *Historical Magazine of the Protestant Episcopal Church* 48, no. 1 (March 1979): 83–92.

"Perceptions and Maturity: Reflections on Feyerabend's Point of View." In *Versuchungen Aufsätze zur Philosophie Paul Feyerabends*. Frankfurt am Main, Germany: Shurkamp Verlag, 1980. Reprinted in *Beyond Reason: Essays on the Philosophy of Paul Feyerabend*, edited by Gonzalo Munévar, 389–401. Dordrecht, The Netherlands: Kluwer Academic Publishers, 1991.

"The American Indian Image in North America." In *The Pretend Indians: Images of Native American in the Movies*, edited by Gretchen M. Bataille and Charles L. P. Silet, 49–54. Ames, IA: Iowa State University Press, 1980.

"Vine Deloria." In *American Dreams: Lost and Found*, 47–51. Interview by Studs Terkel. New York, NY: Pantheon Books, 1980.

"Token Indian, Token Education." *Four Winds* 1 (Winter 1980).

"Our New Research Society: Some Warnings for Social Scientists." *Social Problems* 27, no. 3 (February 1980): 265–71.

"Anthologies: Main Course or Left-Overs?" *Journal of Ethnic Studies* 8, no. 1 (Spring 1980): 111–15.

"Like the Victory Over Custer, the Sioux's Legal Win Can Mean Defeat." *Los Angeles Times*, July 6, 1980.

"The Indians." In *Buffalo Bill and the Wild West*, 45–56. New York, NY: The Brooklyn Museum, 1981.

"Ein Fiebridge Lust." In *Der Wissenschaftler und das Irrationale*, edited by Hans Peter Duerr. Frankfurt am Main, Germany: Syndikat, 1981.

"The Healing Spirit: Seekers of the Fleece." *Four Winds* 2 (Winter/Spring 1981): 53–55.

"Federal Responsibility: A Historical Overview." *Today*, February 13, 1981.

"Native Americans: The American Indian Today." *Annals of the American Academy of Political and Social Science* no. 454 (March 1981): 139–49.

"Identity and Culture." *Daedalus* 110, no. 2 (Spring 1981): 13–27.

"Institutional Racism." *Explorations in Ethnic Studies* 5, no. 1 (January 1982): 40–51.

"Education and Imperialism." *Integrateducation* 19, nos. 1–2 (issues 109–110, January 1982): 58–63.

"Warriors of the Tall Grass: The Men Who Defeated Custer." *Rocky Mountain Magazine* 4, no. 1 (January–February 1982): 33–34.

"The Substantive Social Contract." *Adherent* 9, no. 1 (March 1982).

"Civil Rights and Civic Responsibilities." *Perspectives* 14, no. 2 (Summer 1982): 29–31.

"American Indians: Landmarks on the Trail Ahead." *Social Science Journal* 19, no. 3 (July 1982): 1–8.

"Felix S. Cohen's Handbook of Federal Indian Law." *University of Colorado Law Review* 54, no. 1 (Fall 1982): 121–42.

"Landlord to Welfare Client: The Decline of the Indian in National Consciousness." *Humboldt Journal of Social Relations* 10, no. 1 (Fall–Winter 1982–83): 116–28.

"Circling the Same Old Rock." In *Marxism and Native Americans*, edited by Ward Churchill, 113–36. Boston, MA: South End Press, 1983.

"Management and Community Consensus." *Journal of Tribal Management* 2, no. 1 (1983).

"Land and Resources." In *Minority Report: What Has Happened to Blacks, Hispanics, American Indians, and Other Minorities in the Eighties*, edited by Leslie Dunbar. New York, NY: Pantheon, 1984.

"Neihardt and the Western Landscape." In *A Sender of Words: Essays in Memory of John G. Neihardt*, edited by Vine Deloria, Jr., 85–99. Salt Lake City, UT: Howe Brothers, 1984.

"The Indian Rights Association: An Appraisal." In *The Aggressions of Civilization: Federal Indian Policy Since the 1880s*, edited by Sandra L. Cadwalader and Vine Deloria, Jr., 3–18. Philadelphia, PA: Temple University Press, 1984.

"'Congress in Its Wisdom': The Course of Indian Legislation." In *The Aggressions of Civilization: Federal Indian Policy Since the 1880s*, edited by Sandra L. Cadwalader and Vine Deloria, Jr., 105–30. Philadelphia, PA: Temple University Press, 1984.

"The Popularity of Being Indian: A New Trend in Contemporary American Society." *Centerboard* 2, no. 1 (Spring 1984).

"The Evolution of Federal Indian Policy Making." In *American Indian Policy in the Twentieth Century*, edited by Vine Deloria, Jr., 239–56. Norman, OK: University of Oklahoma Press, 1985.

"The Distinctive Status of Indian Rights." In *The Plains Indians of the Twentieth Century*, edited by Peter Iverson, 237–48. Norman, OK: University of Oklahoma Press, 1985.

"The Traditional Western Answers Offer No Solution To Me." In *Stories of Survival: Conversations with Native North Americans*, edited by Remmelt Hummelen and Kathleen Hummelen, 13–15. New York, NY: Friendship Press, 1985.

"Indians and Other Americans: The Cultural Chasm." *Church and Society* 75, no. 3 (January/February 1985): 10–19.

"Out of Chaos." *Parabola* 10, no. 2 (Spring 1985): 14–22.

"Reflections on the Statute of Liberty." In *Centennial*, edited by Michael Rosenthal. New York, NY: Pindar Press, 1986.

"Minorities and the Social Contract." *Georgia Law Review* 20, no. 4 (Summer 1986): 917–33.

"Indian Studies: The Orphan of Academia." *Wicazo Sa Review* 2, no. 2 (Summer 1986): 1–7.

"American Indian Metaphysics." *Winds of Change* 1, no. 2 (June 1986): 2–3.

"Power and Place Equal Personality." *Winds of Change* 1, no. 4 (December 1986): 4–6.

"Christianity and Indigenous Religion: Friends or Enemies? A Native American Perspective." In *Creation and Culture: The Challenge of Indigenous Spirituality and*

Culture to Western Creation Thought, edited by David G. Burke, 31–43. New York, NY: Lutheran World Ministries, 1987.

"Revision and Reversion." In *The American Indian and the Problem of History,* edited by Calvin Martin, 84–90. New York, NY: Oxford University Press, 1987.

"Beyond the Pale: American Indians and the Constitution." In *A Less than Perfect Union: Alternative Perspectives on the U.S. Constitution,* edited by Jules Lobel, 249–68. New York, NY: Monthly Review Press, 1988.

"Law and Theology III: The Theme." *Church and Society* 79 (September/October 1988): 8–13.

"American Indians and the Moral Community." *Church and Society* 79, no. 1 (September/October 1988): 27–38.

"Government by Default." *Revue Française d'Études Américaines* 13, no. 38 (November 1988): 323–30.

"Reflections on the Black Hills Claim." *Wicazo Sa Review* 4, no. 1 (Spring 1988): 33–38.

"A Clear Statement from Congress Is Needed on Indian Rights." In *Indian Roots of American Democracy,* special edition of *Northeast Indian Quarterly* 4, no. 4 (Winter 1987) and 5, no. 1 (Spring 1988). 57–60.

"A Simple Question of Humanity: The Moral Dimensions of the Reburial Issue." *NARF Legal Review* 14, no. 4 (Fall 1989): 1–12.

"Laws Founded in Justice and Humanity: Reflections on the Content and Character of Federal Indian Law." *Arizona Law Review* 31 (1989): 203–23.

"Vision and Community: A Native-American Voice." In *Yearning to Breathe Free: Liberation Theologies in the United States,* edited by Mar Peter-Raoul, Linda Rennie Forcey and Robert Frederick Hunter, Jr., 71–79. Maryknoll, NY: Orbis Books, 1990.

"Knowing and Understanding: Traditional Education in the Modern World." *Winds of Change* 5, no. 1 (Winter 1990): 12–18.

"Traditional Technology." *Winds of Change* 5, no. 2 (Spring 1990): 12–17.

"Vine Deloria Jr.: 'It's about time to be interested in Indians again.'" Interview by Robert Allen Warrior. *The Progressive* 63 (April 1990): 24–27.

"Transitional Education." *Winds of Change* 5, no. 3 (Summer 1990): 10–15.

"Property and Self-Government as Educational Initiatives." *Winds of Change* 5, no. 4 (Autumn 1990): 26–31.

"Reflection and Revelation: Knowing Land, Places and Ourselves." In *The Power of Place: Sacred Ground in Natural and Human Environments,* edited by James A. Swan, 28–40. Wheaton, IL: Quest Books, 1991.

"Higher Education and Self-Determination." *Winds of Change* 6, no. 1 (Winter 1991): 18–25.

"Federal Policy and the Perennial Question." *American Indian Quarterly* 15, no. 1 (Winter 1991): 19–21.

"The Perpetual Education Report." *Winds of Change* 6, no. 2 (Spring 1991): 12–18.

"The Reservation Conditions." *National Forum (Phi Kappa Phi Journal)* 71, no. 2 (Spring 1991): 10–12.

"Sacred Lands and Religious Freedom." *Association on American Indian Affairs,* May 1991.

"Worshiping the Golden Calf: Freedom of Religion in Scalia's America." *New World Outlook: The Mission Magazine of the United Methodist Church* 52, no. 1 (September–October 1991): 22–24.

"Commentary: Research, Redskins, and Reality." *American Indian Quarterly* 15, no. 4 (Fall 1991): 457–68.

"Trouble in High Places: Erosion of American Indian Rights to Religious Freedom in the United States." In *The State of Native America: Genocide, Colonization, and Resistance,* edited by M. Annette Jaimes, 267–90. Boston, MA: South End Press, 1992.

"The Application of the Constitution to American Indians." In *Exiled in the Land of the Free,* edited by Oren R. Lyons and John C. Mohawk, 281–315. Santa Fe, NM: Clear Light, 1992.

"American Indians." In *Multiculturalism in the United States*, edited by John D. Buenker and Lorman A. Ratner, 31–52. Westport, CT: Greenwood Press, 1992.

"Voces Indios de Norteamerica: Expectativas Frustradas Y Temores Cumplidos." In *De palabra y obra en el nuevo mundo, volume 2: Encuentros interétnicos*, edited by José Jorge Klor de Alva, Miguel León Portilla and Edna Acosta-Belén, 7–31. Madrid, Spain: Siglo Veintiuno Editores, 1992.

"Is Religion Possible? An Evaluation of Present Efforts to Revive Traditional Tribal Religions." *Wicazo Sa Review* 8, no. 1 (Spring 1992): 35–39.

"Spiritual Management: Prospects for Restoration on Tribal Lands." *Restoration and Management Notes* 10, no. 1 (Summer 1992): 48–50.

"Ethnoscience and Indian Realities." *Winds of Change* 7, no. 3 (Summer 1992): 12–18.

"Relativity, Relatedness and Reality." *Winds of Change* 7, no. 4 (Autumn 1992): 34–40.

"Indians, Archaeologists, and the Future." *American Antiquity* 57, no. 4 (1992): 595–98.

"Secularism, Civil Religion, and the Religious Freedom of American Indians." *American Indian Culture and Research Journal* 16, no. 2 (1992): 9–20.

"Comfortable Fictions and the Struggle for Turf." *American Indian Quarterly* 16, no. 3 (Summer 1992): 397–410.

"Frank Waters: Prophet and Explorer." In *Frank Waters: Man and Mystic*, edited by Vine Deloria, Jr., 166–73. Athens, OH: Swallow Press/Ohio University Press, 1993.

"If You Think About It, You Will See That It Is True." *Noetic Sciences Review* no. 27 (Autumn 1993): 62–71.

"Tribal Colleges and Traditional Knowledge." *Tribal College* 5, no. 2 (Autumn 1993): 31–32.

"But It Was All Ad Hoc: Comment on Gulliksen's Paper." *European Review of Native American Studies* 7, no. 1 (1993): 7–8.

"Treaties." In *Native America in the Twentieth Century: An Encyclopedia*, edited by Mary Davis, 646–49. New York, NY: Garland Publishing, 1994.

"Renewal and Revival on the Great Plains." *Forum for Applied Research and Public Policy* 9, no. 4 (Winter 1994): 114–17.

"Indian Public Policy Today." *American Anthropologist* 96, no. 4 (December 1994): 964–66.

"Alcatraz, Activism, and Accommodation." *American Indian Culture and Research Journal* 18, no. 4 (1994): 25–32.

"The Bering Strait and Narrow." *Winds of Change* 10, no. 1 (Winter 1995): 56–59.

"The Subject Nobody Knows." *American Indian Quarterly* 19 (Winter 1995): 143–47.

"The Struggle for Authority." *Journal of the West* 35, no. 3 (July 1995): 3–4.

"Redefining the Path of Indian Education." *The Circle* 16, no. 9 (September 1995): 16.

"Conclusion: Anthros, Indians, and Planetary Reality." In *Indians and Anthropologists: Vine Deloria, Jr., and the Critique of Anthropology*, edited by Thomas Biolsi and Larry J. Zimmerman, 209–21. Tucson, AZ: University of Arizona Press, 1997.

"Vine Deloria, Jr." Interview by Marijo Moore. *Indian Artist* 3, no. 4 (Fall 1997): 73–77.

"Across the Spectrum: Recent Literature on American Indians." *Social Science Journal* 34, no. 4 (1997): 549–55.

"Thinking in Public: A Forum." *American Literary History* 10, no. 1 (1998): 24–25.

"Response to David Brumble." *American Literary History* 10, no. 2 (1998): 347–49.

FOREWORDS, INTRODUCTIONS, AND AFTERWORDS

"Introduction." In *Indians of the Americas* by Edwin R. Embree. New York, NY: Collier Books, 1970.

"Foreword." In *Taxing Those They Found Here: An Examination of the Tax Exempt Status of the American Indian* by Jay Vincent White, v–vi. Washington, DC: Institute for the Development of Indian Law, 1972.

"Foreword." In *One Hundred Million Acres* by Kirke Kickingbird and Karen Ducheneaux, vii–xv. New York, NY: Macmillan, 1973.

"Introduction." In *A Chronological List of Treaties and Agreements Made by Indian Tribes with the United States*. Washington, DC: Institute for the Development of Indian Law, [1973].

"Foreword." In *Voices from Wah'Kon-Tah: Contemporary Poetry of Native Americans*, edited by Robert K. Dodge and Joseph B. McCullough. New York, NY: International Publishers, 1974.

"Foreword." In *The American Indian: Essays from Pacific Historical Review*, edited by Norris Hundley, vii–xi. Santa Barbara, CA: Clio Press, 1974.

"Foreword." In *The Fourth World: An Indian Reality* by George Manuel and Michael Posluns. New York, NY: The Free Press, 1974.

[Introduction.] In *Pardon aux Iroquois* (translation of *Apologies to the Iroquois*) by Edmund Wilson. Paris, France: Union générale d'éditions, 1976.

"Preface." In *In Honor of Justice Douglas: A Symposium on Individual Freedom and the Government*, edited by Robert H. Keller, Jr., xv–xvii. Westport, CT: Greenwood Press, 1979.

"Introduction." In *A Concise Dictionary of Indian Tribes of North America* by Barbara Leitch, 15–20. Algonac, MI: Reference Publications, 1979.

"Introduction." In *Black Elk Speaks: Being the Life Story of a Holy Man of the Oglala Sioux* by John G. Neihardt, xi–xiv. Lincoln, NE: University of Nebraska Press, 1979.

"Foreword: American Fantasy." In *The Pretend Indians: Images of Native American in the Movies*, edited by Gretchen M. Bataille and Charles L. P. Silet, ix–xv. Ames, IA: Iowa State University Press, 1980.

"Foreword." In *Dammed Indians: The Pick-Sloan Plan and the Missouri River Sioux, 1944–1980* by Michael L. Lawson, xi–xvii. Norman, OK: University of Oklahoma Press, 1982.

"Introduction." In *The Vanishing Race and Other Illusions: Photographs of Indians by Edward S. Curtis* by Christopher M. Lyman, 11–13. Washington, DC: Smithsonian Institution Press, 1982.

"Introduction." In *A Song from Sacred Mountain*, edited by Anita Parlow, xi–xii. Pine Ridge, SD: Oglala Lakota Legal Rights Fund, 1983.

"Afterword." In *A Ballad of the West: Seekers of the Fleece* by Bobby Bridger. Austin, TX: Wiyaka Press, 1983.

"Foreword." In *Sparrow Hawk* by Meridel Le Sueur. Stevens Point, WI: Holy Cow! Press, 1987.

"Introduction." In *Taos Pueblo* by Nancy C. Wood, xi–xvii. New York, NY: Alfred F. Knopf, 1989.

"Foreword." In *Exemplar of Liberty: Native America and the Evolution of Democracy* by Donald A. Grinde and Bruce E. Johansen, ix–xi. Los Angeles, CA: American Indian Culture and Research Center, University of California at Los Angeles, 1991.

"Foreword." In *Native American Testimony: A Chronicle of Indian-White Relations from Prophecy to the Present, 1492–1992*, edited by Peter Nabokov, xvii–xix. New York, NY: Viking Press, 1991.

"Foreword." In *Keepers of the Animals: Native American Stories and Wildlife Activities for Children* by Michael J. Caduto and Joseph Bruchac, xi–xii. Golden, CO: Fulcrum, 1991.

"Foreword." In *Alcatraz! Alcatraz! The Indian Occupation of 1969–1971* by Adam Fortunate Eagle, x–xi. Berkeley, CA: Heyday Books, 1992.

"Afterword." In *America in 1492: The World of the Indian Peoples Before the Arrival of Columbus*, edited by Alvin M. Josephy, Jr., 429–43. New York, NY: Alfred A. Knopf, 1992.

"Foreword." In *Brave Are My People: Indian Heroes Not Forgotten* by Frank Waters, xiii–xiv. Santa Fe, NM: Clear Light Publishing, 1993.

"Foreword." In *The Dream Seekers: Native American Visionary Traditions of the Great Plains* by Lee Irwin, vii–x. Norman, OK: University of Oklahoma, 1994.

"Foreword." In *Look to the Mountain: An Ecology of Indigenous Education* by Gregory Cajete, 11–14. Durango, CO: Kivaki Press, 1994.

"Introduction." In *Vision Quest: Men, Women, and Sacred Sites of the Sioux Nation* by Don Doll, 8–9. New York, NY: Crown, 1994.

"Foreword." In *Native Americans: Enduring Cultures and Traditions* by Trudy Griffin-Pierce. New York, NY: MetroBooks, 1996.

"Foreword." In *People of the Seventh Fire: Returning Lifeways of Native America*, edited by Dagmar Thorpe, xi–xiii. Ithaca, NY: Akwe:kon Press, 1996.

OTHER WRITINGS

"A bill to provide for the social and economic development of the human and natural resources of the American Indian people, and for other purposes." Proposed legislation, 1967.

"More Real Involvement: An American Indian Proposal." Report prepared for the Presiding Bishop and Executive Council of the Episcopal Church, New York, NY, 1968.

Indian Education Confronts the Seventies, 5 volumes: *History and Background of Indian Education; Theoretical Considerations in Indian Education; Special Program Considerations; Technical Problems in Indian Education; Future Concerns* (editor). Oglala, SD: American Indian Resource Associates; Tsaile, AZ: Navajo Community College, 1974.

"Federal Treaty Responsibility for Indian Education." In *Indian Education Confronts the Seventies, volume IV: Technical Problems in Indian Education*, edited by Vine Deloria, Jr., 188–227. Oglala, SD: American Indian Resource Associates; Tsaile, AZ: Navajo Community College, 1974.

Proceedings of the Great Peace Commission of 1867–1868 (edited, with Raymond DeMallie). Washington, DC: Institute for the Development of Indian Law, 1975.

"Legislative Analysis of the Federal Role in Indian Education." Report prepared for the Office of Education, Department of Health, Education, and Welfare, Washington, DC, 1975.

A Better Day for Indians. New York, NY: Field Foundation, [1977].

"The Right to Know: A Paper." Report prepared for the White House Pre-conference on Indian Library and Information Services on or Near Reservations, Denver, CO. Washington, DC: Office of Library and Information Services, Department of the Interior, 1978.

"The 80s Return to Tradition." In *Needs of Elementary and Secondary Education in the 1980s: A Compendium of Policy Papers*, 650–58. Report prepared for the Committee on Education and Labor, House of Representatives, 96th Congress, 2nd session, 1980.

"Testimony of Vine Deloria, Jr., before the Senate Select Committee on Indian Affairs on problems relating to American Indian religious freedom." In *American Indian Freedom of Religion Information Packet*. Seattle, WA: Support for Native Sovereignty, 1992.

"Re-Viewing Religion." Twelfth Annual Lecture, Loy H. Witherspoon Lectures in Religious Studies, University of North Carolina at Charlotte, April 10, 1996.

ACKNOWLEDGMENTS

A number of organizations have granted permission to reprint selections from their publications, and their generous cooperation is gratefully acknowledged.

"Missionaries and the Religious Vacuum" reprinted with the permission of Simon & Schuster from *Custer Died for Your Sins: An Indian Manifesto*. Copyright © 1969 by Vine Deloria, Jr.

"The Theological Dimension of the Indian Protest Movement" reprinted with permission from *The Christian Century* 90, no. 33 (September 19, 1973): 912–14.

"Religion and Revolution Among American Indians" reprinted with permission from *Worldview* 17, no. 1 (January 1974): 12–15.

"The Churches and Cultural Change" reprinted with permission from *The Indian Affair*. Copyright © 1974 by Friendship Press.

"GCSP: The Demons at Work" reprinted with permission from the *Historical Magazine of the Protestant Episcopal Church/Anglican and Episcopal History* 48, no. 1 (March 1979): 83–92.

"On Liberation" reprinted with permission from *Occasional Bulletin of Missionary Research* 1, no. 3 (July 1977): 15–17.

"Religion and the Modern American Indian" reprinted with permission from *Current History* 67, no. 400 (December, 1974): 250–53. Copyright © 1974 by Current History, Inc.

"Civilization and Isolation" reprinted with permission from *North American Review* 263, no. 2 (Summer 1978): 11–14.

"Christianity and Indigenous Religion: Friends or Enemies?" reprinted with permission from *Creation and Culture: The Challenge of Indigenous Spirituality and Culture to Western Creation Thought*, edited by David G. Burke, 31–43. New York, NY: Lutheran World Ministries, 1987.

"Completing the Theological Circle: Civil Religion in America" reprinted with permission from *Religious Education* 71, no. 3 (May–June 1976): 278–87.

"American Indians and the Moral Community" reprinted with permission from *Church and Society* 79, no. 1 (September/October 1988): 27–38.

"A Simple Question of Humanity: The Moral Dimensions of the Reburial Issue" reprinted with permission from *NARF Legal Review* 14, no. 4 (Fall 1989): 1–12.

"Sacred Lands and Religious Freedom" reprinted with permission from *Association on American Indian Affairs*, May 1991.

"Worshiping the Golden Calf: Freedom of Religion in Scalia's America" reprinted with permission from *New World Outlook: The Mission Magazine of the United Methodist Church* 52, no. 1 (September–October 1991): 22–24. Copyright © 1991 by New World Outlook.

"Introduction to *Black Elk Speaks*" reprinted with permission from *Black Elk Speaks: Being the Life Story of a Holy Man of the Oglala Sioux* by John G. Neihardt, xi–xiv. Lincoln, NE: University of Nebraska Press, 1979. Copyright © 1979 by the University of Nebraska Press.

"The Coming of the People" reprinted with permission from *The American Land*, edited by Alexis Doster III, Joe Goodwin, and Robert C. Post, 50–55. Washington, DC: Smithsonian Exposition Books, 1979.

"Reflection and Revelation: Knowing Land, Places and Ourselves" reprinted with permission from *The Power of Place: Sacred Ground in Natural and Human Environments*, edited by James A. Swan, 28–40. Wheaton, IL: Quest Books, 1991.

"Is Religion Possible? An Evaluation of Present Efforts to Revive Traditional Tribal Religions" reprinted with permission from *Wicazo Sa Review* 8, no. 1 (Spring 1992): 35–39.

"Introduction to *Vision Quest*" reprinted with permission from *Vision Quest: Men, Women, and Sacred Sites of the Sioux Nation* by Don Doll, 8–9. New York, NY: Crown, 1994.

"From the Archives—December 2, 1504" reprinted with permission from *NCAI Sentinel* 10, no. 3 (Fall 1965).

Lawrence E. Barry, "The Indian in a Cultural Trap" reprinted with permission from *America*, April 10, 1965: 482–84.

INDEX

the tribal traditions that make it impossible for us to present a general theme with any degree of confidence.

Nevertheless even on this broad and modern canvas there are startling differences between the native religious traditions and Christianity. The most profound, in my opinion, is in the evaluation of the nature of the universe. Tribal peoples always find it to be a good universe. There may be, and often are, evil spirits in it, but on the whole it is a pleasant place, it is a real place, and it is a place that demands our involvement, appreciation and respect. The universe has many secrets which are revealed in the ceremonies and it has many duties and responsibilities for us. We are mutual workers with all other forms of life in making certain that the universe works out its own plan of development or unfolding and so everything in the universe has a role and a status as a cooperative creature.

Christianity proclaims a good creation, at least as Yahweh finishes his work on the sixth day, but within a very short time the universe has crashed into evil because of the disobedience of one of the minor, and not too intelligent, species. Nature becomes evil and hostile toward our species and consequently we are in conflict with every other form of life. We come to believe that we are above all other forms of life. We come to believe that our salvation redeems the other life forms simply because we are more important than they are. And we look for the destruction of this world and the creation of another world where, presumably, *we will not be allowed* to screw things up so readily. Because the universe is evil and must eventually be destroyed, we have no real responsibility to it. We are pilgrims here and what we do may have some eternal significance in another arena but much of what we do has no significance at all in the larger cosmic scheme of things.

Another way of drawing this contrast between tribal religions and Christianity would be to say that for tribal peoples, nature is not evil, but it is not neutral either. It is an active force that demands our participation, and tries to ensure that this participation will be of a positive nature. Christianity sees nature as evil and, occasionally for a freethinker or Christian of a scientific bent, neutral; it just goes along evolving species and wiping them out with no moral content in its process. When we grasp the point that if there is going to be an intelligible process it must also be moral, we really stand with the tribal peoples. If we attempt to inject sufficient morality to overcome evil or, at best, neutrality, we stand with the Christians. Therefore the initial appraisal of the content of the universe, whether it is a good universe or a bad one, is critically important for whatever will follow in our thinking and behavior.

The next important thing about the universe is whether or not it is alive. Tribal peoples almost unanimously declare that it is a living thing. The universe is a fabric, a symphony, a tapestry; everything is connected to everything else and everything is alive and responsible to its relationships in every way. The human being is not the crowning glory of creation and certainly not its master. We are but a small, but nevertheless vital, part of the universe and at least part of our task is to serve as a focus for some of the things that must be done for the universe really to prosper and fulfill itself. Because everything is alive and because we have responsibilities to all living things, we cannot force the rest of nature to do what we want. Indeed, we must respectfully approach the rest of nature and seek its permission to initiate a course of action. When we do this in a humble and respectful way, we find that other parts of the universe take joy in cooperating with us in the production of something new and important. Natural entities become our friends and we are able to do marvelous things together.

The Christian response to this question is disappointing at best, usually tragically wrong, and at worst catastrophic for the other forms of life as well as the universe itself. My best guess is that the Christian universe is dead, except for man, and that anyone who believes otherwise and tries to communicate with the other entities of nature is not simply heretical but an idolater. The Christian God is not only jealous, but seems to resent deeply any interspecies communication at all. This God further has created the birds, animals, reptiles, and other forms totally dumb and if not dumb, at least lacking sufficient intelligence to gain God's respect or the human's respect and kind treatment. This God is content to damn every other form of life in order to punish human beings and ruthlessly curses all species because of anger toward a snake and two humans and an apple.

The living universe, in the tribal setting, has its heartbeat, its means of communication, in the drum. The drum is the pulse of life that exists in every creature and needs nothing more than a constant rhythm to keep itself attuned properly. Songs become the means of passing information and powers from one species to another in the living universe and it is possible that many times and in many ways the creatures who compose the universe have given each other powers and information that has helped to create a more enjoyable experience of life for everyone concerned. It is difficult to discover what Christianity believes the heartbeat of the universe really is. Sometimes it appears to be prayer, other times it is preaching and, to hear Christians sing, it is rarely song or rhythm. The best that could be said is that Christians appreciate the logical construction of the universe. Immense and intense rationality seems to be the only resonant fact of the Christian world.

We next confront the question of the history of the universe. The Christian sees a single creation set in motion and then punctuated by periodic destructions wrought by divine anger. The final day of judgment will presumably end the universe and a new universe will be created where things will be considerably better. This scenario raises the question of why the deity could not have simply created a workable universe in the first place since the logic is that God has the power to do so, eventually, in the latter days. The universe is indistinguishable from religious history in Christianity and we sometimes get the feeling that even the material world has no firm reality in it. The material world itself suffers immensely from humanity's moral shortcomings and the inevitable end of human history also means the destruction, in fact the needless destruction, of all other forms of life which have had no voice in the errors of humans and who generally have studiously avoided humans insofar as they are able.

The tribal perspective generally sees the universe as a cyclic pattern of creation and destruction. People call these cycles "worlds" and remember past worlds and how they came to destruction and predict future worlds and tell how they will come to destruction. For each world there is a moral law and ceremonies are given to the people that they may live properly in each world. Worlds do eventually go bad. I suspect they simply wear out their possibilities and need renewal. There are, after all, only so many different things that can be done respectfully and conclusively in the world in which we live. Familiarity, I suppose, ultimately does breed contempt; at least it breeds disrespect. When the individual worlds come to an end, the suffering is distributed on an impartial basis. The faithful few who have tried to fulfill the moral law of the universe, and many of the animals, and those miscellaneous few who happen to be in the right place at the right time, survive and are given instructions, ceremonies and prophecies as the next world begins.

The tribal explanation of cosmic history bears a much closer correspondence to scientific, geological interpretations of strata than does the Christian single-world explanation. Within most of the tribal traditions there is even an explanation of the demise of species, including prophecies on the actual disappearance of the tribe itself. The meaning of history is not that we are saved from it but that we participate in it. Thus our own demise is not a real catastrophe but a fulfillment of the larger cosmic meaning. Every other species finds meaning in this larger scheme of things and that is why other species are willing to feed and clothe us. We, on behalf of the larger living unity, reflect the enjoyment of all in our stories and songs.

On the basis of this sketchy comparison of views of the nature of the universe, I feel the tribal traditions to be much stronger, more comprehensive, of great latitude in morality, and closer to the probable physical scenario that science suggests as a possibility. That is not to say that science must determine religion but that science, as an observational and experimental activity, does give us broad hints as to what has probably taken place before our own individual and social appearance on the planet. The doctrine of creation in this physical, cosmic setting must be taken seriously because we are in fact within this dimension of reality and our beliefs and practices, if they are to guide us, must have some sensible or possible correspondence with what our minds suggest is reasonable.

THE NATURE OF HUMAN EXPERIENCE

Let us now examine the nature of human experience. The significant thing about tribal religions is that we are born into a tribal society which extends far beyond the immediate nuclear family of Western society. Tribal societies are knit together by a large network of relatives, each of whom has a particular duty toward every other relative. The individual is not an isolated entity that must stand alone. We experience everything together as a unity and both grief and sadness are communal experiences; the intensity of human emotions is not borne completely by one or even a few people. Thus the trauma of the growing processes is cushioned by the fact that it can be distributed to a larger number of people.

Within the tribal world also there is a sharing between the various species. This sharing involves information, technical skill, mutual experiences, and a responsibility to the immediate environment. Some relationships are so close that humans can change into other animals and other animals can become human in form. The individual is always a responsible representative of his or her species and each species is considered a family which has certain obligations to other families or peoples. All persons are subject to certain cosmic rhythms and strive to complete their duties within this context. The range of human experience, particularly human learning experience, is therefore very broad and of great significance. If one were to characterize this kind of human experience, it would have to be that religion determines and produces culture.

Christianity seems to have taken exactly the opposite point of view in interpreting human experience. Here the individual is the primary point